CAPITAL AND LABOUR ON THE
KIMBERLEY DIAMOND FIELDS 1871–1890

AFRICAN STUDIES SERIES   54

GENERAL EDITOR
J. M. Lonsdale, *Lecturer in History and Fellow of Trinity College, Cambridge.*

ADVISORY EDITORS
J. D. Y. Peel, *Charles Booth Professor of Sociology, University of Liverpool.*
John Sender, *Faculty of Economics and Fellow of Wolfson College, Cambridge.*

PUBLISHED IN COLLABORATION WITH
THE AFRICAN STUDIES CENTRE, CAMBRIDGE

OTHER BOOKS IN THE SERIES

CAPITAL AND LABOUR ON THE KIMBERLEY DIAMOND FIELDS 1871–1890

ROBERT VICAT TURRELL

INSTITUTE OF COMMONWEALTH STUDIES, LONDON

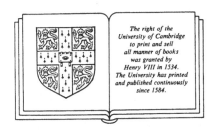

The right of the
University of Cambridge
to print and sell
all manner of books
was granted by
Henry VIII in 1534.
The University has printed
and published continuously
since 1584.

CAMBRIDGE UNIVERSITY PRESS

CAMBRIDGE
LONDON   NEW YORK   NEW ROCHELLE
MELBOURNE   SYDNEY

CAMBRIDGE UNIVERSITY PRESS
Cambridge, New York, Melbourne, Madrid, Cape Town, Singapore, São Paulo

Cambridge University Press
The Edinburgh Building, Cambridge CB2 8RU, UK

Published in the United States of America by Cambridge University Press, New York

www.cambridge.org
Information on this title: www.cambridge.org/9780521333542

First published 1987
This digitally printed version 2008

A catalogue record for this publication is available from the British Library

Library of Congress Cataloguing in Publication data

Turrell, Robert Vicat
Capital and labour on the Kimberley diamond
fields 1871–1890.
(African studies series; 54)
Bibliography.
Includes index.
1. Diamond industry and trade – South Africa –
Kimberley – History. 2. Diamond miners – South Africa –
Kimberley – History. 3. Blacks – Employment – South
Africa – Kimberley – History. 4. Industrial relations –
South Africa – Kimberley – History. 5. Capitalism –
South Africa – Kimberley – History.
I. Title. II. Series.
HD9677.S63K567   1987   331.7′622382′0968711   86-32740

ISBN 978-0-521-33354-2 hardback
ISBN 978-0-521-07179-6 paperback

For Dagmar

Contents

Contents

Plates

Figures

Maps

Tables

Appendix tables

Preface

When I first became interested in Kimberley, some ten years ago, mining history in southern and central Africa was undergoing something of a revolution. Charles van Onselen had just completed his study of black workers in the Southern Rhodesian mines,[1] and Charles Perrings was in the process of finishing his analysis of the proletarianisation of African miners on the early Copperbelt.[2] There were many more to follow. Most of these historical studies, whether based on the mining industry or on the transformation of the African societies from which mineworkers came, were undertaken in Britain. Young scholars found themselves, not unwittingly, as part of what was taking the shape of a broad historical project. Where I was studying, at the School of Oriental and African Studies in London, the issues were given form and direction in a workshop on the social history of industrialization in South Africa. The workshop was inspired by Shula Marks and held at the Centre for International Area Studies. Sessions were loosely structured, often papers were spoken rather than written, and some of those who took part will probably have forgotten that there was ever such a gathering at all. There was, however, a conference in 1980 as a coping-stone to the workshop and two years later a book edited by Shula Marks and Richard Rathbone, *Industrialisation and Social Change in South Africa 1870–1930*, was published.

This workshop was, in many ways, a seminal introduction for a 'raw recruit' from the intellectual hinterland, at that time, of South Africa. 'Resistance', 'consciousness' and 'experience' were the buzz words. Yet, I have written, in relation to compounds – which lay at the heart of the history of early Kimberley – little about workers' consciousness or experience or resistance. I simply could not find enough evidence to support historical knowledge of this nature. Ten years ago any indication of opposition to capitalism from theft to desertion was classed as resistance. There has been a reaction against this avenue into the analysis of workers' consciousness. Human reactions to exploitation are, as Vail and White have pointed out, enormously diverse. 'The moment we go beyond the kinds of organised resistance that are politically or militarily visible', they write, ' . . . we find ourselves in areas where terms like "resistance", "collaboration", "subjective consciousness", "false consciousness", and the like lack the necessary nuance.'[3] I have confined myself to a structural explanation of the part compounds played in the accumulation of diamond-mining capital, and the evaluation of certain indices of social welfare that are open to a measure of objective assessment.

The struggles over the introduction of the compound system determine the shape of the book. These struggles were based on the conditions under which black and white workers were incorporated into the mining industry as wage labourers, the various forms of contract and sub-contract that emerged under partnership, company and joint-stock company ownership in the mines, and the political conditions that enabled or obstructed the concentration and centralisation of capital in Kimberley. There are chapters on dramatic points of conflict: the Black Flag Revolt, the strikes of 1883 and 1884, and the clash between town and mine over illicit diamond buying.

Mining finance receives special attention here in two chapters, due, in no small measure, to the important but, when I first began research, underused Standard Bank Archive in Johannesburg. I was introduced to this archive by Mr James Henry, author of the fine book *The First Hundred Years of the Standard Bank* (Oxford, 1963). In the process of his research into the bank's history, he selected extracts from the General Manager's(s') correspondence with the London Office and had it typed and bound in volumes. It is these volumes to which I refer as the Henry Files; I am grateful to Mr Henry for allowing me to read them at his home in Cape Town. They provide some of the richest economic data on the South African colonies after 1863 and on South Africa in the twentieth century. It was through them that I set about reading the original correspondence and, most importantly, the bank's branch Inspection Reports. Each Standard Bank branch was subjected to annual (or approximately annual) inspections, at which time the security of advances, discounts and other business had to be explained and justified. To this end the branch manager assessed in detail – detail which declined after the turn of the century – the credit-worthiness of every customer, often that of bill endorsers as well, and sometimes provided special statements of the health, wealth or liabilities of larger borrowers. This information was included in the reports, sometimes running to 1,000 folio pages, which the inspector submitted to the head office with his own survey of the financial and other aspects of the branch. These Inspection Reports had never been used by historians before I looked at them in 1979, and I am indebted to Mr Henry for drawing my attention to them, as well as to Roz Dawidovitch, the Standard Bank archivist at the time.

I am also indebted to John Smalberger for making research into the most important official archive used in this book, the Griqualand West Archive in the Cape Archives Depot, a far less daunting task. He left an enormous collection of photocopies – deposited as the Smalberger Papers at the University of Cape Town – culled largely from this archive. From 1871 to 1875, before and during Governor Southey's period of office, the archive is organised by department, and files are named according to their contents.

But thereafter from 1876 to 1880, during the Administrators' periods of office, correspondence was simply collected into files in a continuous sequence unhelpfully called *Records*. Consequently, Smalberger's research into this section of the archive – which he did not publish before he died – has been of great help in identifying files and locating documents.

There is an additional reason for the importance of the Smalberger Papers. He was given access to the De Beers Consolidated Archive in Kimberley, access which was denied to me. Amongst his Papers are well-annotated notes and photocopies of company directors' minutes, which are the most important of apparently limited material in the archive on the period before De Beers Consolidated was formed in 1888. He was, however, interested in labour and extracted information relating to little else.

The Gregory Papers in the Anglo-American Corporation Archive in Johannesburg make up for what is missing. They are the notes put together by a team of researchers for Sir Theodore Gregory's *Ernest Oppenheimer and the Economic Development of Southern Africa* (Cape Town, 1962). The Papers, beginning with the discovery of diamonds, contain over 80 boxes of transcriptions, summaries and photocopies, all well indexed. Strange to relate all the material under the heading of De Beers had been removed. However, Sir Theodore was a methodical man, and he was in the habit of cross-filing and double-duplicating. So, if the information under De Beers related to, say, compounds or amalgamation, it was also filed under the heading of compounds or amalgamation. I am grateful to the archivist, Betty MacFarlane, for her help.

The richest source on mining finance for the pre-1888 period, is the Stow Papers in the McGregor Museum, Kimberley. Frederic Stow was one of the original four Life Governors of De Beers Consolidated. Because he fell out with Rhodes he decided to keep his official and private papers out of the reach of the company. Through the wisdom and foresight of Fiona Barbour they were deposited in the McGregor Museum. I would like to thank her for her hospitality and for allowing me to read the Papers in the congenial atmosphere of her home in the Duggan Cronin Art Gallery, a magnificent residence originally built by J. B. Currey, the Manager of the London and South African Exploration Company, in the 1890s.

The thesis, on which this book is based, was researched between 1977 and 1980 while I was a Postgraduate Governing Body Scholarship holder at the School of Oriental and African Studies, University of London. It was turned into a book between 1984 and 1986 while I was a Postdoctoral Research Fellow, funded by the Economic and Social Research Council, at the Institute of Commonwealth Studies, London. The most important influence on the transformation of thesis into book was, although he bears no responsibility for it, Bill Freund. In 1982 he visited the University of Cape Town where I was teaching African history and set an example, through his lectures and the discussions of his books,[4] of how a materialist

Preface

understanding of African history could be made accessible to students. My major intellectual debt is to Shula Marks who stimulated my interest in Kimberley and supervised my thesis. I am also grateful to her for encouraging my attachment to the Institute, of which she is now the Director, as a Postdoctoral Fellow. The staff of the Institute have made it one of the most pleasant working environments in academic London, and I would particularly like to thank Janet Rogers and David Blake. Charles van Onselen was, although he will not remember it, the only person to take time out to give me a lesson in writing. Gervaise Clarence-Smith, Ted Matsetela, Andrew Porter, Richard Rathbone, Andrew Roberts, Stanley Trapido, Brian Willan and Kevin Shillington corrected articles, polished drafts or shaped my understanding of the problems involved. Most importantly, I am grateful to Dagmar Engels, who enabled me, in more ways than one, to write this book, but who refused to allow me to burn the midnight oil in its preparation.

Abbreviations

AAA	Anglo American Archive
AG	Attorney General
AGM	Annual General Meeting
BBNA	Cape of Good Hope, *Blue Book on Native Affairs*
CAD	Cape Archives Depot
CO	Colonial Office
CPP	Cape Parliamentary Papers
DOK	Kimberley Deeds Office, Cape Archives Depot
DMC	Diamond Mining Company
f	folio
GDM	Gold and Diamond Mining Company Documents, Cape Archives Depot
GH	Government House
GLW	Griqualand West
GM	General Manager
GM/LO	General Manager to London Office correspondence, Standard Bank Archive
HA	House of Assembly
ICS	Institute of Commonwealth Studies
IDB	Illicit Diamond Buying/Buyer
JAH	Journal of African History
KPL	Kimberley Public Library
LC	Legislative Council
LND	Crown Lands and Mines, Cape Archives Depot
MLA	Member of the Legislative Assembly, Cape Colony
MOIB	Insolvent Estates, Cape Archives Depot
MM	McGregor Museum
MMS	Methodist Missionary Society, London
Ms	Manuscript
NA	Native Affairs Department
n.d.	no date
OFS	Orange Free State
PRO	Public Record Office, London
RAL	N. M. Rothschild and Sons Archive, London

Abbreviations

RIDM	*Reports of the Inspector of Diamond Mines*
RIM	*Reports of the Inspector of Machinery/Mining Engineer*
RHL	Rhodes House Library, Oxford
SAL	South African Library, Cape Town
SBA	Standard Bank Archive, Johannesburg
SOAS	School of Oriental and African Studies, London
UCT	University of Cape Town
USPG	United Society for the Propagation of the Gospel, London
Vol	Volume
XL	Correspondence from London, Standard Bank Archive

1

Diamond mining: an overview

In 1867 the first diamonds were discovered in South Africa somewhere in the vicinity of the Orange River and traded in Hopetown in the northern Cape some 600 miles from Cape Town. Over the next two years itinerant traders and hunters bartered for diamonds with Tlhaping, Kora and Griqua who lived in the Vaal River valley north of Dikgatlhong. Most of these diamonds were found on the surface near the river; by 1869 Africans no longer trusted to chance and organised systematic searches for diamonds. Chiefs managed to restrict the access of white prospectors to the 'river diggings' of the Vaal River, at least on the north bank, until the early months of 1870. At this time whites took advantage of conflicting claims to authority between Kora and Tlhaping chiefs over access to the diamond-rich area and the great white diamond rush to the 'river diggings' began. In July 800 whites were congregated at Klipdrift, later renamed Barkly West, and in October 5,000 white diggers were working on the banks of the Vaal River.

By October 1871 African chiefs had lost control of the 'river diggings' and the Vaal/Harts region had been annexed by Britain. Two major factors prompted imperial intervention: the territorial ambitions of the Afrikaner republics, the Orange Free State and the South African Republic, and the Cape Government's own ambitions for control of the region. Recently, Kevin Shillington has disclosed another factor which increased the pressure for British annexation: the machinations of colonial merchant speculators who sought to manipulate rival claims to the area for their own advantage.[1] In this sense the strategic aim of keeping the trade and labour routes into the interior out of republican hands, was overlaid by economic interests in land claims. While this saga of the 'river diggings' and its hinterland is fascinating in itself – the basic outline of how the region was determined to belong to the Griqua and then taken under British 'protection' has been told many times[2] – our concern is only with the 'dry diggings', a day's ride away from the river at what became known as Kimberley. The discovery of diamond mines here provided an added incentive to British annexation of the territory called Griqualand West, which conveniently included both 'dry' and 'river diggings'.

In November 1869 two adjacent farms, on which the Bultfontcin and Dutoitspan diamond mines were later to be developed, were acquired by

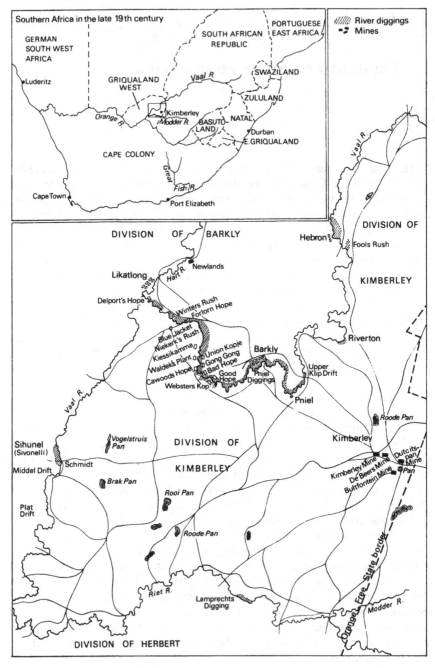

Map 1 Kimberley Division, Griqualand West, showing the river diggings and diamond mines [Based on original surveys, 1882]

merchant speculators from their Afrikaner owners. The one farm, Bultfontein, was bought by the Hopetown Company for £2,000; the other,
Dorstfontein, was leased for ten years by the same company. The Hopetown Company was a three-cornered partnership between the Hopetown
merchants, Lilienfeld Brothers, the 'gentleman', Henry Barlow Webb, and
the Cape Town lapidary, Louis Hond. Lilienfeld Brothers, renowned for
their purchase in March 1869 of the famous 'Star of South Africa', a pure
white 83-carat diamond, were supported by the important eastern Cape
merchant house, Adolph Mosenthal and Company. Mosenthals managed
to interest the Posno family, major Amsterdam jewellers, Ochs Brothers,
leading London diamond brokers, and C. Martin, a London diamond
merchant, in the promotion of a new company in London for speculation in
diamonds and land. In November 1870 the London and South African
Exploration Company was formed with a capital of £20,000. In March 1871,
it bought Dorstfontein farm for £2,600 and in January 1875 the Bultfontein
farm for £11,000. Martin Lilienfeld and Henry Webb of the Hopetown
Company became major shareholders in what turned out to be the most
profitable company ever formed to make money out of Kimberley diamonds.[3]

In April and July 1871 two more mines, De Beers and Kimberley, were
found on a neighbouring farm called Vooruitzicht owned by Johannes de
Beer. The Hopetown Company was beaten to the purchase of this farm by a
syndicate of Port Elizabeth merchants, who bought the farm in October
1871 for £6,000. The syndicate was led by Alfred Ebden, MLA and partner
in Dunell, Ebden and Company, and included John Patterson, MLA and
leader of the eastern Cape separatist movement. In 1873 John Merriman,
MLA, and George Manuel, MLA, bought a one-sixteenth share in the
syndicate at the rate of £50,000 for the whole farm; in 1875 it was bought by
the government of the Griqualand West for £100,000.[4] The Vooruitzicht
farm was a richer property than that of the neighbouring London Company
estate.

After Griqualand West was annexed by Britain it was run by three
temporary Commissioners. Prior to this Olaf Truter, a *landdrost* (magistrate), administered the diamond fields as a whole on behalf of the
Orange Free State. Republican rule was appreciated by white diggers;
many resented British annexation. The Colonial Office hoped to pass
Griqualand West on to the Cape Colony, but found that the definition
of the boundary between the land of the Griqua and the Orange Free
State was the critical stumbling block to Cape annexation. Consequently, in January 1873 Griqualand West became a Crown Colony
with a Lieutenant-Governor, and executive and legislative councils. In
late 1875 the Colony's Governor was sacked and replaced by an Administrator. In October 1880, after years of negotiation, Griqualand West
was annexed by the Cape Colony and run by a system of Civil Commissioners.

Diamond mining: an overview

DIAMONDS

Before the fifteenth century diamonds were relatively insignificant in the galaxy of precious stones. Pearls were the most precious, but rubies, emeralds, opals and sapphires all ranked above diamonds. At this time a diamond's distinguishing feature was its hardness, whereas the rare qualities looked for in precious stones were perfect colour and proportion. But this changed when it was discovered how to cut facets on the face of a diamond. In 1456 a European lapidary, Louis de Berquem, perfected scientific faceting and, in doing so, he turned diamonds into perfect reflectors of light, unleashing the interior beauty of the stone. By the nineteenth century diamonds were well established as the most precious of all gem stones.[5]

The market value of a diamond depended on its weight, its form and its colour. Large stones were rare before diamonds were discovered in the Cape. Indeed, so rare were large stones from Brazil, the world's largest producer in the mid nineteenth century, that slaves who found stones weighing 17 carats[6] and over were rewarded with their freedom. At Kimberley stones of this weight were a common occurrence. More large stones were found there in the two decades, 1870–90, than in Brazil in 170 years or in India in 1,000 years.[7]

Large diamonds were vastly more valuable than the run of the mine one-carat stone. The price of diamonds increased exponentially with their weight and stones over 100 carats were sold for whatever a prince or potentate could be made to pay. Many stones were literally priceless and found their way into the Crown Jewels of European and Asian monarchies.

A huge diamond lost between a half and three quarters of its weight in cutting. The Koh-i-nur from Golconda in India was 793 carats in the rough but was cut into a gem stone weighing 186 carats. This was often the fate of stones the size of a man's fist, but the finished diamond was still large enough to be unusual. If the rough stone, pure crystallised carbon, had a regular octahedron or rhombic-dodecahedron shape, less weight was lost in the manufacture of the finished diamond. Such a shape was ideal for the brilliant cut which was the most common form of gem stone.[8]

Although weight and form were important, it was the transparency and flawlessness of a diamond which fundamentally defined its market value. In the early days on the Kimberley diamond fields the majority of stones were slightly yellow in colour. So abundant were they that all off-coloured stones that came on to the market were designated Cape diamonds. This destroyed the reputation of all Cape diamonds and to overcome this association in the market, many Kimberley diamonds were sold as Brazilian.[9]

The colour-less and water-clear quality, prized in the best of Indian and Brazilian diamonds, was relatively rare in the Kimberley mines. But the Cape production, four times the annual production of Brazil by 1873, more than compensated in quantity for this lack of quality. Still, there were enough stones with the treasured blue-white quality to make rich men of yeoman farmers and shop-keepers from the port towns. The 160-carat Porter Rhodes diamond found in Kimberley Mine was absolutely perfect. It was classified as a stone of the first water, while going down the scale, stones tinged with colour, but otherwise flawless, were classed as second water and stones with obvious colour defects brought up the rear and were termed third water. But colour did not destroy a gem entirely. Coloured diamonds of perfect transparency were highly valued. They were called fancy stones and included red, blue and green diamonds. Such a basic description of diamonds, which were classified into over 200 varieties, gives some indication of the complexity of the diamond dealer's trade.[10]

THE KIMBERLEY MINES

The four diamond mines at Kimberley bore no resemblance to deposits in Brazil or India. Consequently, an entirely new method of mining was developed at Kimberley. It had little in common with precious or base metal mining and was a far riskier undertaking. To begin with the richness of a gold or copper mine could be assayed from a sample of ore, but this procedure was impossible in the Kimberley mines. There was no reliable method of predicting the future results of mining. Diamonds were not evenly distributed in the blue ground, the true diamond-bearing *breccia*, which was found after about 60 feet of yellow ground had been excavated in all the mines. And the diamond yield varied with depth and position in the blue ground. This simple geological fact made it extremely difficult to assess the extent of diamond theft, which became a running sore for the mine-owners, and still is.

Nonetheless, there was an imperfect measure of the yield of the diamond-bearing soil. It could be quantified on the basis of the past results of mining. The yield was calculated from the number of carats found in a load of soil, the standard industry measure, of 16 cubic feet of broken blue.[11] For example, in 1883 the average yield of Kimberley mine was 1.2 carats, while it was only .9 carats in De Beers Mine. On the basis of geological quantity these were the two richer mines of the four at Kimberley. In contrast, the yield of the other two mines, Dutoitspan and Bultfontein, was .25 and .33 carats respectively. Once underground mining was undertaken the measure became even more inaccurate as so much shale, or dead ground, was excavated with the blue. Still, mineowners had little else to go by and, imperfect though it was, men came to know the rich from the poor claims.[12]

The abundant yield of Kimberley Mine made it the richest mine in the world, but it did not produce the finest diamonds. That honour went to the Dutoitspan mine, poor in geological quantity but compensated with quality. Bultfontein diamonds had nothing special to recommend them as they were mainly small and spotted, whereas De Beers diamonds were remarkable for their size. And, although Kimberley Mine had a rich yield, it produced 90

5

per cent of the industry's *boart*, the diamonds used for industrial purposes.[13]

Kimberley Mine was ten acres in size and originally divided into 470 claims.[14] In the early days claims closest to the sides of the mine were excavated with the greatest energy as hauling was easier from the edges of the mine. It took on the shape of a dough-nut with blocks of ground standing in the centre. It was only in the later 1870s that the centre ground was taken down and the mine turned into a basin. But digging was not all productive in this rich yielding pit. There were poor layers of ground scattered throughout the claims and there was one section, the West End, that was poor throughout.[15]

The wealth that was dug out of Kimberley Mine in the early days attracted most diggers and left the other mines undeveloped. In the early days of De Beers, gullies were sunk in enchanted spots between the poor expanses of ground in the West and East Ends. In the 1880s Baxter's and Schwab's Gullies in the north, the ambiguously named Poor Man's Gully in the centre, and Australian Gully in the south remained the richest sections of the mine. Its rate of development was far slower than that of Kimberley Mine. In 1874 only 48 per cent of the pit was worked but even then only on an irregular basis. In 1881 only 34 per cent of the mine had been dug into the blue ground, while of the remainder only 40 per cent were worked at all. Thereafter, under a regime of company production the pit was rapidly developed.[16]

The poor mines, Dutoitspan and Bultfontein, were two miles away in the direction of the Orange Free State border. Until the late 1870s they were only intermittently worked. Before then Dutoitspan was used as a camp latrine and Bultfontein became known as the 'poor man's diggings'. Both were larger than the rich mines, the former being 31 acres and the latter 22 acres in size. Even when they came back into favour their development was slow. In Dutoitspan, as in De Beers, certain gullies named after pioneers – Solz's, Fry's, Odendaal's, Robinson's, Young's – spearheaded progress in the mine. But in 1880 even the most advanced gullies were only an average of 80 feet deep, barely a quarter of the depth of Kimberley Mine. A similar state of affairs existed in Bultfontein, although once company production began in the 1880s the 'poor man's diggings' became a regular paying prospect and it was developed faster than Dutoitspan.[17]

THE REEF

The containing walls of the open-cast diamond mines were called the reef, unlike in gold mining on the Rand where the term refers to the gold-bearing ore. The reef, composed of yellow, pink and predominantly black shales, extended 300 and more feet down into the mines until it hard rock or *melaphyre*. Whereas the hard rock stood firm, the reef did not and began to break up soon after it was exposed to the atmosphere by the removal of the blue ground.

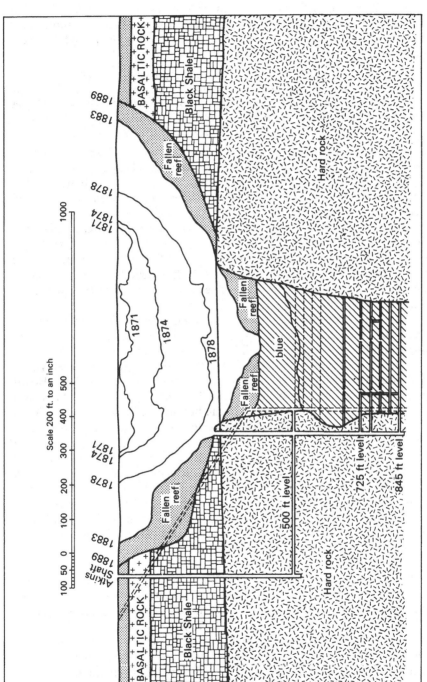

Fig. 1 Section through Kimberley Mine, 1889. (Source: CCP, RIDM, 1890)

The collapse of reef on to the claims below was an ever present threat to diggers. A heavy fall could retard production for anything from three to six months while the debris was cleared off the claims. When a big fall of reef occurred it was a spectacular sight:

> Along the towering face at various points little bits of rock broke away, increasing rapidly in number and quantity during the next hour or so. The gaps between the solid ground and the doomed section increased visibly as one watched, and the gigantic body rolled over, crashed, and like an enormous tidal wave swept everything away in its path.[18]

Usually the reef gave ample warning that it would collapse. Great cracks appeared on the top of the reef and they were carefully measured so that diggers could estimate when it was due to fall. But there were other occasions when huge chunks of it came away without warning and buried workers in the claims.

Kimberley Mine faced reef problems first because it was excavated earlier and faster than the other mines. It was only after 1878 that reef falls emerged as a threatening issue in De Beers Mine. The poor mines were spared this problem largely through their lack of development until 1885 in Dutoitspan and 1887 in Bultfontein. The only true solution to the threat was underground mining.

Before the institution of underground mining in the rich mines between 1883 and 1886, reef extraction made production expensive and often unprofitable. The Kimberley Mining Board, set up in 1874 to administer common aspects of mining and financed by a general rate on mineowners, organised the extraction of reef in Kimberley Mine. At times the Board employed a reef contractor, but normally claimholders cleared their own reef and charged it to the Board. In the first five years of Kimberley Mine production one load of reef was extracted to every seven loads of blue ground. Then, the reef problem rapidly worsened and by 1883 nearly five loads of reef were extracted to every load of blue ground. The Board had tried to stop the reef collapsing by cutting it back in terraces, but the idea was implemented too late. When reef collapsed on to claims, owners were unable to pay the Mining Board rate. In 1883 the situation of non-payment became so acute that the Board went bankrupt with liabilities of £360,000 against assets of only £60,000. Between 1871 and 1882 eleven million loads of reef were removed from Kimberley Mine at a cost of £2 million.[19]

The claimowners of De Beers Mine learnt from the harrowing experience of Kimberley Mine. Between 1878 and 1882 the De Beers Mining Board cut the reef back in terraces. It gave the claimowners a crucial breathing space but it was only a temporary measure. In 1885 an avalanche of reef fell into the mine from the East End. Then the worthless, yellow ground in the West End collapsed on to the blue ground and production was halted for six months. The mineowners were forced to begin the development of underground mining.[20]

THE FIVE PHASES OF COMPETITIVE DIAMOND PRODUCTION

Between 1845 and 1870, when Brazil was the largest producer of diamonds, her average output was 200,000 carats a year.[21] The diamond production of the Cape outstripped that of Brazil fairly quickly. In 1872, barely three years after the first diamond rush, over a million carats were mined and by 1888 production had climbed close to four million carats (see Table 1).

The rapid growth in output was determined by the application of steam-power to the production process and a substantial increase in the productivity of labour. While steam machinery made mining at depth possible, it did little to lighten the load of the mineworker in the pit. Diamond mining was a labour-intensive industry in which the basic tasks of drilling, picking and loading were made more strenuous as powerful steam-driven machinery was able to extract greater quantities of reef and process more and more blue ground. Output also grew significantly around 1880 when the three relatively unworked mines, De Beers, Dutoitspan and Bultfontein, became paying propositions. In addition, underground mining enabled round-the-clock production in contrast to the thirteen hour day in summer and nine hour day in winter in the open-cast mine. But it also led to a greater intensity of labour, as for the first time mineworkers were paid piece- rather than time-wages.

Growth in labour productivity was absent in the first two phases of diamond digging. In the first phase (1871–73) the yellow and blue ground was loaded into buckets, hauled out of the mines by windlasses and dry-sorted on diggers' encampments. Over 1,600 production units operated in Kimberley Mine while the other mines remained largely unworked. This phase ended with the productive capacity of the mine sapped by the accumulation of water in the claims and the initial collapse of the reef. In the second phase (1874–77) a novel system of haulage based on aerial tramways was developed. It allowed the centre of the mine to be worked, while the richly regarded reef claims suffered under an accumulation of water and debris. The blue ground had to be loosened by powder or dynamite, hauled out of the pit by horse-driven whims or small steam engines, and left to decompose on depositing floors for varying lengths of time. From 1875 diamonds, instead of being dry-sorted by hand, were extracted from the blue in large rotary washing machines. In this phase there was a steady differentiation between claimholders with steam machinery and those with less progressive horse-driven appliances.

Out of this process of competitive differentiation arose a class of mining capitalists who began to turn diamond digging into a mining industry. In the third phase (1877–81) output soared as De Beers, Dutoitspan and Bultfontein began serious production for the first time. The use of steam machinery became the dominant motive-power in the industry, with the poorer mines investing for the first time and Kimberley buying larger engines. This investment in fixed capital culminated in 1881 in a joint-stock mining

Table 1 *Exports and imports of the Cape Colony increased by the export of diamonds: 1869–88*

	Exports exclusive of diamonds £	Diamonds exported carats	value £	av. price s d	Total computed exports £	Total computed imports £
1869	2,200,966	16,542	24,813	30/-	2,225,779	1,953,091
1870	2,416,039	102,500	153,460	30/-	2,569,499	2,352,043
1871	3,128,260	269,000	403,349	30/-	3,531,609	2,585,298
1872	4,451,453	1,080,000	1,618,076	30/-	6,069,529	4,388,728
1873	3,882,626	1,100,000	1,648,451	30/-	5,531,077	5,130,065
1869–73	16,079,344	2,568,042	3,848,149		19,927,493	16,409,225
1874	4,225,413	1,313,500	1,313,340	20/-	5,538,747	5,558,215
1875	4,206,544	1,380,000	1,548,634	22/6	5,755,178	5,731,319
1876	3,499,196	1,513,000	1,513,107	20/-	5,012,303	5,556,077
1877	3,633,743	1,765,000	1,723,145	19/6	5,356,888	5,158,348
1878	3,456,330	1,920,000	2,159,298	22/6	5,615,628	6,151,595
1874–78	19,021,226	7,891,500	8,247,490		27,278,744	28,155,554
1869–78	35,100,570	10,459,542	12,105,667		47,206,237	44,564,779
1879	3,805,637	2,110,000	2,579,859	24/6	6,385,496	7,083,810
1880	4,342,294	3,140,000	3,367,897	21/6	7,710,191	7,662,858
1881	4,220,706	3,090,000	4,176,202	27/-	8,396,909	9,227,171
1882	4,514,098	2,660,000	3,992,502	30/-	8,506,600	9,372,019
1883	4,408,828	2,413,953	2,742,470	22/8½	7,151,298	6,470,391
1879–83	21,291,563	13,413,953	16,858,930		38,150,493	39,816,249
1884	4,138,345	2,263,606	2,807,329	24/9½	6,945,674	5,249,000
1885	3,321,785	2,439,920	2,489,659	20/4¾	5,811,444	4,772,904
1886	3,620,600	3,135,061	3,504,756	22/4	7,125,356	3,799,261
1887	3,616,504	3,598,930	4,242,470	23/7½	7,858,974	5,036,135
1888	4,854,278	3,841,937	4,022,379	20/11¼	8,876,657	5,678,337
1884–88	19,551,512	15,279,454	17,066,593		36,618,105	24,535,637
1879–88	40,843,075	28,693,407	33,925,523		74,768,598	64,351,886
1869–88	75,943,645	39,152,949	46,031,190		121,974,835	108,916,665

Sources: Max Bauer, *Precious Stones* (London, 1904), p. 236; A. Michielsen, *De diamant-economie. Waarde, prijs en conjunctuur* (Antwerp, 1955), p. 125; CPP.G–15–'89m *Trade Returns*, p. 5; CPP. G11–'90, *Reports of the Inspectors of Diamond Mines for 1889*, p. 36.

company promotion boom. There was an enormous inflation in the market value of claims. Inevitably, it was followed by a slump.

The crisis was the result of over-production. In the fourth phase (1882–1885) the mining industry suffered an extended depression, the product of both problems in mining and a collapse in the European diamond market. During the depression the industry worked to between 60 and 70 per cent of capacity and a quarter of the capital was liquidated. Production in Kimberley Mine largely came to a halt as a result of the accumulation of reef and experiments in underground mining were begun. This paralysis provided a natural restriction on output and for the first and last time, Dutoitspan and Bultfontein produced more than 50 per cent of the value of production.

The depression accelerated the tendency towards the centralisation of production in the mines. In the fifth and final phase (1886–91) underground mining replaced open-cast production in Kimberley and De Beers and marked a new era in the diamond industry. The large companies experimented with different systems until a uniform method was adopted when the mines were brought under the control of the De Beers Consolidated Mines Limited.

HAULAGE

The river diggings on the Vaal River were similar to the alluvial deposits in India and Brazil. When the mines at Dutoitspan and Bultfontein were first discovered in 1869, it was assumed that they would be similar surface diggings. Digging to bed-rock, diggers thought, would be accomplished quite adequately with picks and shovels. But the mines did not 'bottom-out'. Before this was realised digging was conducted on a damaging, haphazard basis. Soil taken out of a claim was sorted on an adjacent one; water was struck after 40 feet and so each hole was filled in and another one begun. Dutoitspan mine was so badly worked, wrote one official, 'that there are not 10 full claims worked to a depth of 40 feet, although it has been worked for 18 months longer than Colesberg Kopje [Kimberley Mine] and there is not an average depth of 10 feet.'[22]

Sorting inside the mine obstructed digging as debris mounds were left upon productive soil. In an attempt to encourage diggers to take soil out of the mines, a central road, running across the pits, was left intact in Bultfontein and Dutoitspan, while in Kimberley Mine a road system was adopted on a grand scale. Across the pit from north to south 14 roads were laid. Each claim surrendered seven and a half feet along one side and backed with its adjacent claim made roads 15 feet in width. The soil was hauled out of the claims in buckets, loaded on to waiting carts or wheel barrows on the roadways and then taken out of the pit to diggers' encampments for sorting. But the roadway system could not last. Diggers undermined the roadways in their search for diamonds and by April 1872 the system had developed into a death trap. Roads were patched together with planks, as narrow as seven feet in some parts and towering 50 to 60 feet above the claims beneath. Falling carts and lumps of ground from the roadways became daily hazards.

Diggers had to devise a new system of haulage and were faced with a choice between a wire rope system or the development of an incline tramway. In November 1872, a digger, William Hall, bought a steam engine, the first on the Fields, and constructed an incline tramway across a number of his own claims. He proposed to charge diggers for removing their diamondiferous ground, but they feared the monopoly power that this would confer on Hall and preferred their own independent means of haulage.[23]

A wire rope aerial tramway system of considerable ingenuity was developed. Timber stagings, carrying three or four platforms, were built on the edge of the mine. Wire ropes, on which buckets or tubs were run, extended from the stagings to the claims beneath. The buckets or tubs were hauled up the wires by windlasses wound by hand. In 1874 there were 1,000 windlasses on the stagings, allowing as many separate units of production, or at least 10,000 men, to work in the pit. 'So numerous were the wires', wrote one pioneer digger, 'that the mine seemed a yawning pit over which some Titanic spider had woven its web'.[24]

Hand labour and windlasses were soon replaced by horse-power in haulage. In May 1874 a mania for horse whims and whips set in and windlasses, though still in use, became a technique of the past in Kimberley Mine. The horse-driven whim was a large timber wheel 14 or 18 feet in diameter, fixed horizontally seven or eight feet above the ground, and a wire went round the wheel into the pit. As one bucket or tub was hauled up an empty one was returned to the claims. Underneath the wheel the horse walked round and round in a modified circular tread mill. The whip was an alternative model in which the horse trod the zig-zag course of the whip's lash.[25]

In the late 1870s steam winding-engines came into general use in Kimberley Mine. Steam-power increased the number of loads hauled out of the pit and a comparison with earlier appliances illustrates the rapid development. An average windlass hauled from seven to ten loads a day. A horse whim hauled from 40 to 60 loads a day and the first six horse-power steam engines managed between 60 and 100 loads a day. In 1877 Kimberley Mine was worked by 16 steam winding-engines, 65 whims, two whips and 40 windlasses. This was an impressive display of steam-power compared to its larger neighbour, De Beers mine, where there were only two steam winding-engines, but 15 whims, six whips and 81 windlasses.[26]

Between 1877 and 1882 there was a revolution in steam-power in the rich mines. By the latter year there were only steam winding-engines in operation, 48 in Kimberley Mine and 26 in De Beers.[27] But in the poor mines steam, horse and hand-power continued to co-exist well into the 1880s. Progressive diggers in the poor mines began to invest in small steam

Plate 1 Kimberley Mine, south side, 1877, showing the depositing boxes on the edge of the mine. The blue ground was hauled up aerial tramways in sixteen cubic feet tubs by horse or steam-driven winding engines (out of picture), upended into the boxes and shovelled into waiting Scotch carts for transport to the depositing floors. Courtesy De Beers, London.

engines for the first time. Others found such powerful and expensive appliances unnecessary. One mining expert observed:

> Diamond soil is carted from the diggings to the top of the washing heap in bullock carts. About ten or twelve hundred weight to the load is drawn by four to six bullocks, with nearly as many drivers and assistants. To get those bullocks with their loads from the bottom to the top of the mine is no easy matter, and I have sometimes seen the teams of bullocks stuck in the middle of the hill and looking as if they were tied in a knot.[28]

Some parts of the poor mines were developed at the pace of the proverbial ox waggon.

Steam winding-engines facilitated a growth in output, but in Kimberley Mine only marginally more blue was hauled in 1888 from underground workings than had been raised by 1,000 windlasses from the open-cast mine in 1874. Of course, a shallow open pit was easier to work than a deep underground mine. Still, there was a middle period of prodigious production when the pit was open and deep. Between 1877 and 1882 the number of loads of blue hauled out of Kimberley Mine increased enormously, being twice that of the previous five years, but in the same period 20

13

times more reef was extracted than in the earlier years.[29] Kimberley Mine 'exhausted itself by overproduction of diamonds in its early days', said one prominent mining capitalist, 'and in its old age was unable to sustain its reputation'.[30]

TRANSPORT, DEPOSITING FLOORS AND WASHING

Horses were the mainstay of the mine transport networks. In the 1870s Scotch carts were the most popular form of transport, but in the 1880s carts, although not horses, were gradually replaced by tramways and trucks. Certainly fewer drivers and their assistants were required in Kimberley Mine, where locomotives and systems of mechanical haulage were in operation, but large numbers of horses, mules and oxen were in constant use in the other mines.[31]

The blue ground was transported to depositing floors where it was laid out to decompose through a natural process of weathering before it was processed for diamonds. For miles around the mines the blue was placed on floors, surrounding Kimberley with an artificial landscape of ploughed fields. Kimberley blue took one to four months to weather, while some De Beers blue took up to a year. The necessity of softening the blue by natural processes considerably lengthened the turn-over time of production. Imperfectly weathered blue yielded less carats and contributed to fears that diamonds were being stolen. Often companies tried to speed up the process of weathering by ploughing the floors with horse-drawn harrows or sending in a platoon of labourers to break up lumps of blue by hand. But these were primitive methods and the results failed to compare with what nature did for free. It was only in the late 1880s that a pulverising machine at De Beers and a six ton road roller at Bultfontein made mechanical appliances a viable and economic proposition.[32]

After 1874 washing replaced dry-sorting by hand as the method of winning diamonds from the blue ground. Smaller diamonds that had been missed before were uncovered in great quantities in this process and the lucrative occupation of debris-washing, that is, washing the tailings of the diamondiferous soil which had only been dry-sorted, became all the rage in Kimberley Mine. Washing machines were constructed 'on the general plan of puddling, i.e. reducing the mass to the consistency of thin mud, and then by agitation allowing the thin parts to run off and retaining the heavy portions of garnets, iron ore and diamond'.[33] The ripple cradle was the first machine used to wash diamonds, but it was soon replaced by the rotary washing machine. Driven by horse-power the rotary machine was capable of washing between 25 and 30 loads of blue a day, but driven by steam-power it processed anything between 400 and 800 loads a day, depending on the size of the pan. The great majority of diamonds now emerged in the wash-up, although stones continued to be found in the claims and on the floors.[34]

14

Plate 2 The first rotary washing machine to be used at Kimberley Mine in 1874. Courtesy De Beers, London.

FUEL, DYNAMITE AND WATER

The introduction of steam-power increased the amount of fuel required to run the mining industry. Unlike later on the Rand, where the supply and cost of coal – between 10 and 15 per cent of working costs – remained within manageable proportions,[35] the availability of fuel and its cost was a great problem on the Diamond Fields. Wood was the major fuel in use for the better part of the first two decades of mining. The countryside surrounding Kimberley was denuded of trees and some diggers and companies went to the length of buying farms simply for the supply of timber they provided. The further afield transport riders and tree farmers had to range to bring wood to the Kimberley market, the higher was the cost of fuel. In 1882, at the end of the first major production boom, 30 per cent of total working costs was spent on fuel.[36] Three years later in 1885, when the railway line was less than 100 miles away and the depression had reduced capacity, the fuel bill had been reduced to 16 per cent of production costs.[37] The railway meant that cheap coal imports from Wales became an economic proposition and, although most boilers had been built to burn wood, from 1886 coal began to compete with wood. Still, in the late 1880s wood remained in demand and contractors brought 8,000 lb. waggon loads to Kimberley from as far away as 200 miles, a journey which entailed a round trip of 35 days.[38]

15

Plate 3 A team of workers in Kimberley Mine in the late 1870s. One African holds an overhead drill; the tub is loaded ready to be hauled out of the claims on an aerial tramway. Courtesy De Beers, London.

In early digging the diamondiferous soil was excavated with picks and shovels. Once the blue ground was struck diggers found that it had to be blasted. Gunpowder was used but it was a remarkably unreliable blasting agent as its effects could not be adequately controlled. Although blasting was done during the lunch hour, flying lumps of blue ground damaged wires and equipment in surrounding claims. The well known figure of the digger, with a pick in one hand and writ in the other, was substantially shaped by attempts to recover the big diamond, the size of a man's fist, that may or may not have been blasted out of his claim.

Dynamite was a better blasting agent than powder. Once claims began to be blocked together it was used regularly. A case of dynamite (50 lbs) dislodged about 400 loads of blue. Although blasting certainly lightened the load of the labourer who picked the soil, it created the arduous task of drilling. In the open mine two 'drill boys' worked together on one blast hole with long overhand jumper drills sharpened at both ends. If the blue was hard, single-hand hammers were used in addition. Between 10 and 20 feet was the average rate of boring in a 12 hour day's work. Hand-drilling was the dominant method of work until the turn of the century and was only replaced by machine-drilling, roughly four times the cost of hand labour per foot, in sinking shafts through the hard rock.[39]

In the early days water for washing came from rain or spring water pumped out of the mines or from wells sunk in and around the camps. Well water was passable for human consumption and, as it was more expensive than mine water, it was not used for mine purposes. Once steam engines came into use, it was found that the mine water was hard and left a deposit in the boilers which reduced their firing efficiency. Although a false economy, diggers continued to risk a deterioration in their boilers and a higher fuel cost, until in 1883 water was laid on from the Vaal River. The Kimberley Waterworks Company piped water 17 miles from the river, filtered it and provided better quality at half the price of well water. In the middle 1880s the cost of water was only three per cent of working expenditure – dynamite consumed around five per cent – and was no longer the vital commodity that had been so scarce in the early days.[40]

UNDERGROUND MINING

Underground mining in blue ground presented new and unique problems for engineers. One key consultant found that 'conditions and circumstances' for underground mining were absent in Kimberley Mine, but when he witnessed a spectacular collapse of reef he was convinced of the need for urgent underground experimentation.[41] In fact, underground mining was first undertaken to remove reef but by 1883 it had become clear that blue would have to be excavated by shafts and tunnels.

In the 1880s two basic underground systems were experimented with in Kimberley Mine. The first was the pillar and stall method which was loosely copied from the haematite mines of Cumberland. It became known as the 'gallery' system in Kimberley as huge galleries or caverns, often 50 feet high, were carved out of the blue, chunks of which were left standing as pillars. The East End of Kimberley Mine (and De Beers Mine as well) became a gigantic honeycomb, with the excavated blue representing the honey and the pillars of remaining blue the comb. But it was inherently unstable. In November 1888 the honeycomb was crushed, as the pressure of the fallen reef in the open pit proved too heavy for the pillars, and there was a massive movement of West End blue towards the east of the mine. The second method known as long-wall mining, which had been developed in the West End, was destroyed in the collapse. Its singular difference to the gallery system was the fact that no pillars were left and all blue was excavated.[42]

After 1889 a uniform underground system was laid out in both Kimberley and De Beers Mines. The General Manager of the new monopoly company, De Beers Consolidated Mines, described the new system:

> When the numerous small tunnels had been driven to the margin of the mine, i.e. to the point where they reached the side of the crater, the blue ground was stoped on both sides of and above each tunnel until a chamber was formed extending along the face of the rock for 100 or more feet, with an average width of about 20 feet and about 20 feet high. The roof of the chamber or gallery was then blasted down or allowed to break down by the pressure of the overlying mass of broken diamond-bearing ground.[43]

17

Upper levels were excavated in advance of those which lay underneath, thus avoiding the danger of a general collapse. The basic principle of this system served the mines well until the end of the century.

CONCLUSION

Diamond mining was a labour-intensive industry. As early as 1872 there were as many as 10,000 Africans working in Kimberley Mine. Although there were constant fluctuations in supply throughout the 1870s, the trend was towards the greater employment of African labour. During the first boom period (1878–81) over 30,000 Africans were employed in all the mines, but numbers declined during the depression and remained low through the next boom period (1886–90) during which the pits were centralised under the ownership of De Beers Consolidated Mines. In 1889, with Dutoitspan and Bultfontein almost totally closed down, there were only 10,000 Africans employed in the mines. Although a new mine was discovered in 1890, the number of African mineworkers in the industry continued to fall to an all-time low of around 6,000 in 1895 before the South African War and the Siege of Kimberley at the end of the century.

The introduction of steam-power increased the intensity of labour in the mines. Dynamite, powerful winding-gears and large washing machines meant that workers had to drill more holes, load more tubs and wash more weathered blue ground. There was little mechanical substitution to lighten the labourer's load in the claims or in underground mining at the stope face. Even the mineowners' fear of diamond theft did little to induce technological innovation in the first two decades of diamond mining. In the 1890s electricity was first used for surveillance purposes before it replaced steam as the motive power. So, manual labour was the basis of the industry and steam-power was applied to haulage in the mines, transport to the floors and in the final process of winning the diamonds from the blue ground.

2

African labour in the early days

In the early days on the Diamond Fields the great majority of pioneers were African men predominantly from the interior of southern Africa where they had not as yet come into contact with Europeans. African men went south without their wives or before they were married and the few black women who made their way to the camps were mainly Griqua, Koranna or of 'mixed race'. In contrast very soon after the diggings were opened up roughly half the European men had their wives with them and overall there were three European women to every five European men. In 1872 the official number of Europeans was 13,000 out of a population variously estimated at between 28,000 and 50,000. The very different sex ratios of Europeans and non-Europeans and the great predominance of African men from the interior of South Africa were the most obvious and important sociological facts about early Kimberley.[1]

LABOUR MIGRATION

In the early days Africans spent between three and six months working on the Diamond Fields before returning home. From 1871 to 1875 between 50,000 and 80,000 Africans went to and left Kimberley each year. The great majority were Pedi, known on the Fields by Colonial officials initially as 'Mahawa' and later as 'Secocoeni Basuto'. Next in numbers were the Tsonga, known as 'Shangaan', who came overland from the Gaza Empire in Mozambique or through Natal to Kimberley. The third African people of importance on the Fields were the South Sotho. They were called simply 'Moshesh's people' and went to the Fields soon after they were opened up, often going with grain waggons. As they were closer to the Fields than Pedi or Tsonga they generally spent only three months at minework before returning home.[2]

There were numbers of other African peoples who went to the Fields. In early 1874 the Kalanga, a Shona people, known by European officials as 'Makalaka', arrived in Kimberley for the first time. Their arrival was noted because they were emaciated and unable to work after their long journey on foot from north of the Limpopo River.[3] The Ndebele and other Shona did not contribute greatly to labour in the mines, although a few did make the long trek south. Zulu from Natal came in noticeable numbers, although not

19

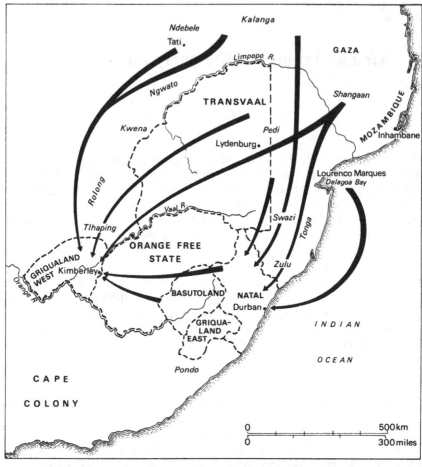

Map 2 Principal labour migration routes to Kimberley. In the Registrar's report on labour for 1876, he noted where labour-supplying African peoples lived and how far they had to travel to Kimberley:

    1. 'The *Secocoeni Basutos [Pedi]* inhabit that portion of country lying south of the Limpopo and bordering on the district of Lydenberg – Transvaal Republic, eastwards approaching the Comatie River and westwards till the *Bakwain [Kwena]* country is reached . . . the probable distance travelled by them to these Fields is from 500 to 600 miles.'

    2. The '*British Basutos*' travelled 200 miles.

    3. The '*Shangaan*' under Shoshangane lived east of the Zontpansberg, beyond the Transvaal Republic, in the territory between the Limpopo River and Delagoa Bay. 'The *Shangaans* under Umzile, [live] north of the Limpopo and at a distance of nearly 1,000 miles . . .'

    4. The *Kalanga*, conquered by the Ndebele 'and now pretty well fused', travelled over 800 miles.

    5. *Natal Zulu* travelled over 400 miles.

    6. The *Ngwato* under Khama lived 600 miles from Kimberley 'and some 18 days per bullock waggon south of Zambesi', but in the 1870s supplied very little labour. (Source: CAD,GLW 118, No. 944, W. J. Coleman to Colonial Secretary, 18 April 1878).

Zulu from Zululand. Natal Zulu were usually contracted in their home district and brought to Kimberley by their masters for a period of not shorter than six months. They earned the reputation of being the best mineworkers on the Fields and this was due, in no small measure, to their long contracts, payment on completion of service, (rather than monthly) and most often paid not in Kimberley but back in Natal. European diggers from Natal had this key initial advantage over diggers from the Cape as few Cape Colonial Africans could be induced to work in the mines as labourers.[4]

Like Cape Colonials, other African peoples went to the Fields but found work in the camps and not the mines. While there were no African peoples settled in the immediate vicinity of Kimberley, there were Rolong, Tlhaping, Griqua and Koranna chiefdoms occupying land between the Vaal and Harts Rivers. As they were so close to the Fields (50–250 miles) they were among the first to assess its economic possibilities and needs. For example, Koranna managed to monopolise the production, distribution and sale of milk in Kimberley. Similarly, the Tlhaping sold produce, particularly firewood, on the Kimberley market and avoided selling labour until well into the 1880s. The growth of the town market led to the migration of Tswana, Griqua and Koranna to Kimberley with their wives, dependents and cattle.[5]

Some Europeans also went to Kimberley to work as labourers in the pits. They were few, indeed, compared to the great majority of Africans, but the belief that Europeans would not work with their hands is an old historiographical myth.[6] Some diggers even preferred seasoned European labourers to 'raw' Africans unaccustomed to heavy manual work. There was certainly a lot to be said for the greater productivity of the Irishman who could take down a claim as fast as a gang of four Africans. Most often, Europeans were employed when African labour was scarce and before the growth of the production unit required the employment of overseers.[7]

Despite a relative profusion of evidence about Europeans in Kimberley, we know very little about where European manual workers came from, beyond the fact that the great majority were Colonial or Republican in origin. We know even less about the specific combination of social and economic circumstances that led to a journey to Kimberley. In contrast, thanks to the illuminating work of Delius,[8] Harries[9] and Kimble,[10] we have a much clearer idea of why Africans from the Pedi, Tsonga and South Sotho paramountcies went to Kimberley.

In general, they have made three important points about early African wage labour migration. First, labour migration did not begin with the discovery of diamonds in Kimberley. Pedi, Tsonga and South Sotho were in a majority on the Diamond Fields because they were deeply involved in migrant labour prior to 1870. As early as the 1840s, but more so in the following three decades, Pedi walked the 15 days' journey and more to work on the farms and public works of the Cape Colony. Similarly, in the 1850s and 1860s Tsonga began working for wages in Natal and in the Cape, and before 1870 South Sotho worked on farms in the Orange Free State. This wage labour on a migrant basis took place without the coercion of colonial laws or agents of the colonial state.

Secondly, there were a variety of reasons for labour migration from these non-capitalist economies. Although the desire to earn cash for bride-wealth or a plough was important, the Pedi were primarily after guns. The beginning of substantial Pedi migration in the 1850s was related to the need to arm against the growing threats of Zulu, Swazi and Boer military might in the Transvaal region. By the 1860s migration had become institutionalised so that 'each male youth, on reaching maturity, went to the Cape Colony for one or more years'.[11] By the 1870s the military threat to the Pedi polity had grown even stronger. Fortunately, the development of diamond mining opened up new opportunities for Pedi as Kimberley was a shorter walk than the eastern Cape, wages were higher and combined with earnings in the illicit market in diamonds, they found that they spent less time working for a gun than further south.

While the gun market in Kimberley was certainly a great enticement to Africans, it does not explain why Pedi sold their labour, rather than cattle and grain to buy weapons. The Mpondo and South Sotho sold cattle and grain to buy guns. Mpondo economic independence was based on their wealth in cattle. 'With these they could purchase the commodities they needed', writes Beinart, '[and] they had not found it necessary to go to Kimberley to work for firearms'.[12] In similar fashion, in the 1860s and 1870s the South Sotho expanded grain production to meet the demands of growing colonial markets and to earn cash to buy colonial commodities.

In contrast, prior to 1870 it appears that this sort of trade was not open to the Pedi. Grain markets were not accessible in the north-east Transvaal and by the 1860s ivory trading had largely passed to the Zoutpansberg. Moreover, cattle wealth was restricted to a few individuals, unlike among the Mpondo, and consequently the sale of cattle would not have enabled every man to own a gun. And a widespread ownership of guns was required in face of the growing military threat to the land of the Pedi. Even the discovery of alluvial gold fields in the eastern Transvaal in the 1870s did not provide an alternative labour or commodity market. On the one hand, wages were lower and guns more expensive than in Kimberley while, on the other hand, growing ecological pressures on land and food restricted market production. As a result, the Pedi remained committed to selling their labour in Kimberley.

The South Sotho were involved in both commodity production and migrant labour prior to 1870. After the discovery of diamonds this dual involvement in the colonial economy deepened. 'Not only do the men work at home', wrote one district magistrate in Basutoland:

> raising with the help of their women from 30 to 40 bags of grain per household, but the European communities get the benefit of the labour of 3 out of 4 of all who are able to work.[13]

The point was that commodity production and migrant labour were not mutually exclusive. Commodity producers, or rather members of market-oriented households, went to the Fields to earn cash which would enable them to engage more actively in agricultural export. Again, although the importance of bride-wealth cannot be underestimated, they went to Kimberley primarily to earn a gun and a plough.

The Tsonga had slightly different reasons for engaging in wage labour in Kimberley. The material base of Tsonga society was more threatened by internal and ecological processes than by the external military threats that faced the Pedi and the South Sotho. The Tsonga economy suffered from the hunting out of game and a re-orientation of trade routes. In addition, cattle herding and agriculture was adversely affected by capitalist penetration. Ecological upsets and warfare further undermined the rural economy. As a consequence, wage labour began to appear as the way to improve a young man's chances within the web of kinship relations. So Tsonga walked to Kimberley to earn wages for bridewealth and consumer goods like cloth and liquor. Unlike the Pedi and the South Sotho, their overriding interest was in cattle and women.

There was little that was voluntaristic in migrant labour. Africans were not individuals exercising free choices. A chasm separated the complex of social and economic relationships that pointed a European and an African in the direction of Kimberley. European 'free', that is wage, labour was fundamentally different to African 'free' labour. Africans were neither 'free' from the land nor 'free' as individuals to sell their capacity to labour. They were not free of kinship relations, which in Harries' words, 'tied labour to existing social obligations and means of production and consequently prevented the development of a force of free labourers or a market for free labour'.[14]

This brings us to the third point about migrant labour. It was initially subject to chiefly control. A number of implications can be drawn from this fact. It meant that, in the case of the Pedi and the South Sotho, the mass acquisition of guns was a political strategy pursued by paramount chiefs. It also meant that migrant labour was a political duty from which chiefs took tribute or tax in the form of wages, guns or stolen diamonds. But it did not mean that chiefly direction or control went unchallenged, for migrant labour also provided the avenue of potential, independent accumulation outside kinship and chiefly bonds.

Chiefs directed the labour of young men into the colonial economies. The Pedi paramount, Sekhukhune, and the Koena chief, Molapo, certainly initiated and supervised the migration of their young men to Kimberley. There is some evidence that men went to the Fields on a regimental basis and headmen acted as their representatives in negotiations over wages and labour conditions. In 1874 Marmaree, Sekhukhune's brother, fulfilled this role in Kimberley and he also acted as the interpreter to the Registrar of Servants.[15]

Initially colonial agents had rather less to do with labour migration than Chiefs. There were a few labour contractors who worked in a grey area between slavery and compulsory recruitment. In August 1873 one contractor, J. Edwards, made an arrangement with Sekhukhune 'to supply constant labour to the Fields at current wages'.[16] Edwards' fee was £1 per man per six month contract and while this was to be advanced out of wages, another £1 royalty or tribute was to be paid out of wages at the end of the contract to the paramount's headmen on the Fields. The agreement then stated 'that no man is to receive a permit for a gun without the sanction of Marmaree and Timan and not until after the royalty has been paid'.[17]

While it is unlikely that this arrangement was an attempt to reinforce the authority of the paramount, it was aimed more at employers and colonial authorities. Edwards was well aware of the harassment that Africans underwent on their way through the Boer region of the Transvaal and he needed British government intervention to establish a line of depots along the road for the succour and protection of Africans travelling to the Fields. But the British authorities in Kimberley refused to intervene with the Boer government and would have nothing to do with private labour schemes. The authorities did keep in contact with interior chiefs, although only to make representations regarding labour rather than becoming involved in active recruiting.[18]

The extent of chiefly control was exhibited most clearly when labourers on the Fields were required to become warriors in their paramount's army. In 1876, in response to the belligerence of Burger's Boers, Sekhukhune summoned his men back from the Fields. In May, June and July over 6,000 Africans left Kimberley and the mine work-force was halved. It was made crystal clear to diggers that wars were not good for mine production.[19]

Despite this dramatic display of loyalty, chiefly control was evaded at times. Precisely whether this was due to divisions within a paramountcy, colonial erosion of chiefly power, or the response to individual or household accumulation, only further research will tell. The evasion of chiefly control was most evident amongst the Tsonga. Chiefs and elders found that wages gave young men an independence that threatened their control of societal reproduction. Consequently, as sterling displaced cattle and hoes as the medium of bride-price, so the price of marriage was raised above the level of returning migrants' wages. This manipulation of bride-price, and the marriage age, gave rise to social and political dissatisfaction. The result was that many young men, unable to live off the local economy or unwilling to suffer increased exploitation, emigrated permanently to the colonial economies. The pressures against such a solution were great, but it is clear that it happened.[20]

The major significance of this analysis, according to Delius, Harries and Kimble, is that migrant labour was not forced on Africans by colonial capitalists. It was not thought out as a way of cheapening the maintenance and reproduction costs of labour, though it was to serve this function in the

twentieth century. Rather, migrant labour developed out of social relationships in non-capitalist economies and later became entrenched as a system
as a result of struggles between mining capitalists and elders over the control
of the labour-power of African men. While chiefs and elders tried to retain
control over land, cattle, marriage and tribute labour, direct access to
colonial labour markets enabled African men to circumvent chiefly control.
But migrant labour was not simply subversive of chiefly rule. 'These
struggles were extraordinarily diverse', writes Marks and Rathbone:

> and were shaped by ecology and forms of pre-capitalist production, the
> configuration of social classes in the rural social formation, the timing of
> colonial penetration and the nature of the colonial state, and the impact of
> Christian missionaries.[21]

DESERTION, DIAMOND THEFT AND VIOLENCE

Despite chiefly encouragement of African labour migration, diggers
complained about the shortage of labour. Irrespective of what they said,
their problem was not one of labour shortage but of labour turnover.
Kimberley's labour market was imperfect; mining development was uneven
and supply periodically failed to match demand. Migrancy created the
wider problem, but it was the frequency of desertion which upset the labour
market. Behind every desertion diggers saw diamond theft. To them it was a
case of hit and run.

In the 1870s most Africans met their masters through the medium of
labour touts. They intercepted Africans outside Kimberley at, for example,
Christiana or Potchefstroom and engaged them then and there or promised
them protection on the remainder of the journey and employment when
they reached the mines. In practice, this meant selling them to diggers at
labour auctions in Market Square. 'When I first came here', wrote Governor Richard Southey in 1873:

> it was the usual thing for claimholders to pay £1 a head for labourers, to
> persons who went out and brought them, and then they were not of much use
> until fed up for 2 or 3 weeks, which – food and wages – cost 2 or 3 pounds more
> than they engaged for only about 4 months.[22]

But convalescence was not followed by gratitude and faithful service, as
even many of these failed to stay the length of the contract.

Diggers contributed to the problem of desertion by competing for labour,
as combining to reduce wages had proved so ineffective. In May 1872 some
diggers had tried to reduce wages from 10s a week to 5s a week, and
although a Chief of the Pedi, representing 2,000 Africans apparently
accepted a reduction to 6s a week, he would not accept monthly wage
payment. By June Africans were refusing to work for 24s a month and
leaving for home.[23] So at a time like this a digger, who offered 5s a week
more than his neighbour, was unlikely to be idle in his claims. Moreover,

Plate 4 A gang of African mine labourers arriving at the outskirts of Kimberley. Interesting points to note are their youth, the pieces of European clothing they are wearing indicating that this was not their first visit to the Fields, and the absence of guns. It is probable that the well dressed, bearded gentleman in the background was the tout bringing them into Kimberley's labour market. Courtesy De Beers, London.

information on good and bad employers, rich and poor claims, and safe and dangerous occupations soon became common amongst different African peoples. Higher than average wages were the most important inducement to take up employment with a particular digger, and the most important inducement to desert was the non-payment of wages.

In general diggers did not intentionally defraud Africans of their wages. Default in wages, which were paid in cash and kind, resulted from factors over which diggers had little control. African labourers usually received 10s a week in cash and a further 10s in the form of food. The cash component of the wage was the first to suffer in the event of poor finds in the claim, and default was enough to lead to desertion and the end of production. Short of selling out, diggers had to wait for the next labour auction in Market Square, borrow to buy labour, pressurise raw recruits into accepting a monthly wage and pray that finds improved.[24]

The kind component of the wage was even further beyond the control of diggers. Shortage of food, and its inflation in price, also led to the desertion of African labourers. The problems of supplying Kimberley with food were immense. Even if food production in the granary areas of South Africa was abundant, there was always the problem of moving grain and produce to Kimberley. For example, in 1872 there was a good harvest in the Transvaal, Basutoland and Aliwal North (Wittenberg Reserve), but in the spring there was a drought in Griqualand West. As a result, without water and grass for oxen, carriage to Kimberley was impossible. In September the price of 'kaffir corn' rose by 50 per cent and diggers began buying 'mielies', the principal horse forage, for their workers. 'It was feared', wrote the Registrar of Servants, 'that thousands of natives would be dismissed because of the shortage of food'.[25] In December 1872 5,000 Africans (one-third of the work-force) deserted and set off for home. Five months later, they had still not been replaced and 6,000 Africans were required to satisfy the labour requirements of the mines.[26]

Such an understanding of the causes of desertion cut little ice with diggers. They were convinced that the major cause was diamond theft. If an African stole a diamond he would not need to work and could live on his illicit earnings in the warren of tents and tin shanties that made up the camps. The frustration at poor finds was often put down to wholesale theft. Colonial newspapers reported lurid stories of Africans, suspected of theft, being beaten to death by their masters. 'Instances of unauthorised and cruel punishments for diamond stealing have no doubt occurred', wrote the Cape Governor:

> and there is a disposition on the part of some masters, generally recent arrivals, to domineer over the natives as an inferior race and to make no allowance at all for the peculiar temptations to which they are exposed in digging and the enormous inducements held out to them by unscrupulous traders to act dishonestly. The great majority of the sensational stories which have gone the round of the papers have, I believe, but very little foundation in fact, and indeed the only case of the kind of which I could obtain certain information from the authorities was one in which a Mahowa, who had secreted a diamond purposely placed in his way succumbed under the repeated floggings which were inflicted by his master in order to make him confess. It is not satisfactory to be obliged to add, that public feeling on the Fields was so strongly in favour of the master, that the public prosecutor, who had first of all indicted him for murder, was obliged to rest content with his conviction by the jury for common assault.[27]

Despite this official view summary punishments were meted out by masters and, although there was a whipping post at the Police Court, it was little used.[28] In the absence of a fully-fledged colonial state there was little more to labour discipline than physical violence.[29] But violence was not a long-term solution. What was required was the majesty of British law and its acceptance by those over whom it held sway.

THE PASS SYSTEM

The first piece of labour legislation written for the Diamond Fields reflected the connection diggers made between desertion and diamond theft. In 1872, while the Fields were still under the administration of the three Commissioners, the Cape Governor, Sir Henry Barkly, proclaimed his famous Proclamation 14, which both laid down penalties – one year's hard labour and 50 lashes – for diamond theft and defined a labour contract.[30] The procedure of registering a labour contract became the basis of the notorious pass system, which has been remarkable for its longevity, and is still one of the main methods of African labour control today. It has become more sophisticated, but the essentials remain as they were then: movement for Africans was restricted, and without a valid pass Africans could be arrested and imprisoned.

The pass system on the Diamond Fields was based on the contract of service. Each labour contract showed the name of the servant, his wages, the name of his master and the period of service. Several servants were often registered on one contract at the new Servants' Registry, established under the Proclamation, and it was at the discretion of the employer that a pass or ticket was given to each employee. The pass was simply a piece of paper stating that a servant was contracted to a particular master. Without a pass signed by a master 'any person who shall be found wandering or loitering without being able to give a good and satisfactory account of himself', it stated in section 21 of the Proclamation, was liable to arrest and a £5 fine or imprisonment for up to three months.[31]

The language of the law was colour-blind and used the terms masters and servants. In August 1872 a Registrar of Servants was appointed and it certainly was the intention of the Proclamation that all employees should be contracted at the Registry, but four years later when an additional Registrar was appointed at the poor mines, in Dutoitspan, his title was simply 'Registrar of Natives'.[32] In practice only Africans had ever been contracted, while all others – whether artisan or labourer, man or woman – had refused to submit to a system of registration which they regarded as exclusively for 'natives'.[33] 'The distinction ... between native labourers and the other servants', wrote Sydney Shippard, the Attorney-General, 'is one which already virtually exists; it is one which is here not only necessary but inevitable'.[34]

In the early days the pass system did little to control desertion even though it was a criminal offence to break a contract of service. If servants broke their contracts they were liable to second rather than first offence penalties, an indication of how difficult labour discipline was on the Fields. The Proclamation also allowed masters to search their servants' property and to assume any diamonds they found to have been stolen. Despite these legal powers granted to employers registration was not an effective means of labour control.

The pass system was tightened up in the late 1870s. As early as 1872 it had been suggested that passes of different colours be issued to 'raw' Africans and those who had been previously contracted,[35] but it was only in 1879 that this idea was put into practise, albeit in a different form.[36] White passes were issued to mine servants; red passes to servants of Indians, 'persons of colour' and Africans; and green passes to domestic and town servants of Europeans. Such attention to the identification of town and mine employees and to the racial classification of masters was the product of the growth of large-scale mining and the attempt to subordinate Africans to rigorous industrial discipline. The police became more vigilant and the number of pass arrests and convictions more frequent and numerous. But in the early days the pass system was more honoured in the breach than in practise.

Not all Africans were subject to the pass system, as colonial officials took pains to distinguish between civilised and uncivilised Africans. 'There are many natives, half-castes, and others from the Colony, who are honest, intelligent and respectable men' wrote one important Commissioner:

> and these must of course be treated in every way similar to the whites, but the great mass of the labouring coloured population consists of raw Kaffirs, who come from the interior with every element of barbarism, and no touch of civilisation among them, in fact they must be treated as children incapable of governing themselves.[37]

Colonial officials reinforced this distinction by granting some Africans exemption from the pass laws. Africans who were their own masters, holding claim or cart licences, or engaged as independent traders, were granted 'protection passes'. But there were other Africans, whose 'civilisation' was more easily measured by literacy than property and in 1878 Cape certificates of citizenship were recognised in Griqualand West as an exemption from the pass laws.[38]

In short, Proclamation 14 applied the Cape's masters and servants laws to Griqualand West. Cape law had been written to regulate labour relations in an agricultural economy and it was only slightly modified for the mining industry. Most European diggers found the law wanting and remembered with nostalgia the period of Orange Free State rule, before the province was annexed by Britain in 1871, when servants knew their places and Europeans were able to enforce a purely racial colonial order.

RACISM

At the same time as the pass system was being instituted, European diggers demanded the abolition of claimownership by Africans, Indians and 'persons of colour'. Discrimination in the right to dig was demanded as a measure to prevent diamond theft. Claimownership entitled blacks to sell diamonds and, so the argument went, provided a facility for servants to rob their masters. Such a view assumed that all blacks were 'brothers', irrespective of whether they owned a claim or worked in one, and would happily conspire to defraud white masters of the fruits of exploitation. That such racial solidarity did not apply to patently colour-blind receivers of stolen diamonds did not bother those diggers concerned to appeal to the gut element of racism. Such European illicit dealers were, in any case, beyond the pale. The consequences of black claimownership appeared clear to European diggers. 'If niggers can dig for themselves and sell diamonds unquestioned', wrote Payton, a journalist, 'the employment of native labour becomes practically useless'.[39]

This view was compounded by the fact that only a few diggers made a fortune. The expectations of striking it rich before money and health ran out were high, but the reality was rather different. 'A very large number earn about as much or nearly what they would have made at their ordinary vocations at home', wrote Archdeacon Croghan, 'and many more, I fear, are unsuccessful'.[40] In such a situation diamond theft was a ready-made explanation for lack of success.

In July 1872 the British Commissioners were forced by white diggers to take action against black claimowners. They suspended the claim licences of 46 black diggers at Dutoitspan and Bultfontein, but the Cape Governor refused to allow such a blatantly discriminatory measure.[41] He replaced the proclamation with the requirement that diggers hold 'a certificate of good character' from a Justice of the Peace or the Resident Magistrate. Black diggers grew in numbers in the poor mines, while Europeans flocked to the rich Kimberley pit.[42]

White racism was instrumentally linked to competition over labour. 'The only chance is to bring up plenty of Caffres', wrote one digger from Natal, 'as labour is still very scarce'.[43] It was at times so scarce that, not only were labourers auctioned on Market Square, but they were also hired out on the basis of the labour contractor taking a percentage of the diamonds found through their labour. Men lost their claims through having no labour as they were forfeited if unworked for seven days.[44] 'If I had £1,000 to get and keep 50 Kaffirs going here', lamented one pioneer digger, 'my fortune would be made without a doubt'.[45]

Initially Afrikaans farmers (who were the first to dig Dutoitspan) had a great labour advantage over those Europeans who came from towns in the Colonies. 'Some of the deepest holes are made', wrote Payton, 'and the largest heaps thrown out by Duchmen with large families'.[46] He went on to explain, no doubt with a measure of prejudice, the advantages of the Afrikaner in this respect:

> Who digs so cheaply, who risks so little capital as he? . . . he has with him not only his "vrouw" and "kinders", i.e. wife and children, but a lot of kaffirs, who he has obtained in the interior at about the wages of a cow or £3 a year . . . See him dig – well you can hardly call it digging; the brutal old patriarch will sit at the sorting table all day with his pipe – perhaps allowing the "vrouw" to do likewise – while half naked Kaffir boys (aye and young girls too) and his own children . . . are all toiling hard under the broiling sun.[47]

While Afrikaners had command of family labour, related by blood and by different forms of rural bondage, the English digger at De Beers was at the mercy of market forces. As early as 1871 De Beers diggers were reputed to be 'men of capital, employing large parties of natives and consequently geting through much more work'[48] than in Dutoitspan. Acquiring gangs of African labourers was even more critical in the richer Kimberley Mine.

Afrikaans diggers did move to Kimberley Mine and 'used to work in strong parties'.[49] Some quickly made fortunes and left the mine to plough their winnings back into the land. Others were not so lucky and like so many other diggers found that their servants deserted into the labyrinthine tent town of Kimberley. Afrikaners had initially worked far more cheaply than other European diggers, but there was no movement to have their digging licences removed. Englishmen felt little respect for them as a people, but Afrikaners did not work in the mines as labourers. Racism was directed at black diggers because it was from the ranks of the migrant African population that labour was drawn.

CONCLUSION

Although Africans stole diamonds and left their masters, desertion was often the product of non-payment of wages or lack of adequate food. Only a few diggers made a fortune and everyone had to cope with hard labour conditions, bad food and disease. Labouring in Kimberley Mine was arduous and dangerous. By early 1872 the roads across the pit had begun to crumble and many Africans chose not to work in particular claims. Nearly everyone succumbed, at one time or another, to 'camp fever' which was 'malarial, aggravated by exposure to the sun, tent life, bad weather ... imperfectly tinned meat and fish, a scarcity of meat and vegetables and ... by strong drink'.[50] Nonetheless, Africans from Pediland, Tsongaland and Basutoland continued to come to the Fields in great numbers and certainly had a greater command over the sale of their labour than diggers had over its purchase.

3

The new colonial state, 1873–75

In January 1873 Griqualand West became a British Crown Colony. On 9 January Richard Southey, the Lieutenant-Governor, arrived in Kimberley and was received with fireworks, music and a banquet in the Theatre Royal. However, enthusiasm for the Governor was shortlived as he proceeded to rule by proclamation and the assistance of an unelected executive. Southey appointed John Blades Currey as Colonial Secretary, J. C. Thompson, one of the Commissioners, as Crown Prosecutor and R. W. H. Giddy as Treasurer-General. It was not until the end of 1873 that elections were held for an eight member Legislative Council and even then the four elected members found themselves in a permanent minority as the Governor had a casting vote and the right to veto any legislation. The constitution they received was not modelled on the Natal Legislature, as Governor Barkly of the Cape Colony had promised in 1872, and the actions of the executive majority gave rise to growing disaffection amongst diggers.

THE FIRST ELECTION

Governor Southey took office in a difficult year. In the second half of 1873 there was a severe drought in Griqualand West and the first major collapse in the price of diamonds. Both events created great hardship in Kimberley. Drought drove up the price of staple foods and in October 1873 the butchers of Kimberley combined to raise the price of beef and mutton by 15 per cent. On top of the increase in the cost of living, the enormous output of the mines depressed the price of rough diamonds in London. While it inaugurated the so-called 'Kaapse tijd' in the Amsterdam cutting industry, the one-third fall in diamond prices in late 1873 had a dramatic effect on Kimberley. Canteen and hotel-keepers suffered the worst in the ensuing depression – the consumption of liquor was a barometer of the prospects of digging – and auctioneers alone were kept busy selling off property from mine claims to merchant stock and from stands to household furniture. The population of the Fields began to fall sharply and the euphoria of the early days came to an abrupt end.[1]

When the constitution was promulgated in July 1873, it was not well received by the majority of diggers. The built in executive majority threatened the control that diggers had exercised over the social and

32

economic affairs of the mines and camps through Diggers' Committees. These were composed of popularly elected European diggers and the value of claim property carried no weight in the election of members. As a result the Committees opposed the growth of monopoly in claims or in any part of the labour process. The Committees were the bastions of what came to be called 'diggers' democracy' and this equality of representation was cherished against the executive majority in the Governor's constitution.[2]

The Members of the Committees rejected the constitution but decided to elect 'People's Candidates' to wreck the Legislative Council. The Diggers' Association of New Rush[3] was formed and Dale Buchanan, who had spent thirty years in the Cape Colony, was proposed as their candidate. A technical inaccuracy was uncovered in the requisition calling on him to stand for the Council, and he was disqualified. He was replaced by Henry Tucker, an experienced Colonial politician, who had been a Cape MLA for Cradock from 1861–66. He went to the fields soon after they were discovered and, as he was an uncertified insolvent at the time, he traded as a storekeeper under his wife's name. He also speculated in diamonds and worked some claims in Kimberley Mine. Tucker suffered with many other diggers when the depression struck and the change in his fortunes encouraged him to become a member of the Diggers' Association.[4]

Tucker's election manifesto was a clear expression of the Association's views. He spoke for a mobilisation of diggers to resist any increases in claim rents; for diggers' customary rights to free dwelling plots and sorting places; and for diggers' control of all mining matters through the Diggers' Committees. He also wanted all diggers' disputes removed from the courts for their adjudication, and he was in favour of the official endorsement of detective societies which were little more than vigilante groups aiming to suppress diamond theft. Finally, he wanted the land developed, not in the interest of capitalist farmers or land speculators, but for the provision of cheap bread and meat for the urban market.[5]

Tucker was opposed by two men who represented a different constituency in the mining camps. Dr Graham, an Irishman, was an advocate of the High Court and his support came from Dutoitspan merchants. He took pains to distance himself from the Diggers' Association and believed the Committees should be replaced by Mining Boards.[6] Henry Green, a Cape public servant of 40 years standing, represented the merchants of Kimberley. He was a digger in Kimberley Mine in partnership with George Paton, who had been a Californian forty-niner and prospector for gold in Australia. Although Green was a prominent digger he was not an Association man. This had a lot to do with his acquisition of 56,000 morgen of land in the disputed area of arable and possibly diamondiferous farms between the Vaal and the Harts rivers. The farms had Griqua titles and he was anxious to convert them to more marketable British ones. He was abused as a 'government man' and noted for his 'scrvilc adulation' of Richard Southey, whom he knew well from his days in the Cape Colonial service.[7]

In November 1873 the election took place and Tucker failed to win either of the two Kimberley seats. His support was strongest in Kimberley but virtually non-existent in Dutoitspan.[8] Both Graham and Green polled well in Dutoitspan and went through to the Council together with David Arnot, a 'person of colour', representing the Division of Hay and Francis Thompson, a trader, representing Barkly. The exclusion of the Association's candidate reinforced the faith of the majority of diggers in the Diggers' Committees. They became even more determined to extend their formal control from mining to municipal affairs. They wanted to control the construction of streets, squares and buildings; to levy rates for buildings and dwelling sites; and to oversee water and sanitary arrangements. All this was very threatening to the new Colonial state and, as J. B. Currey later recalled, he feared 'that given sufficient encouragement they would take sole charge and constitute themselves a Republican government'.[9]

THE DIGGERS' COMMITTEES

The new government set about undermining the power of the Diggers' Committees and the general belief in 'diggers' democracy'. One of the first steps it took was the modification of the system of 'jumping' claims. If a claim was unworked for three days, it was liable to be 'jumped' (taken over) by another digger. 'This system', in the words of one petition, 'gave poor men who were unable to purchase claims an opportunity of obtaining them'.[10] The 'jumping' rule was copied from the Gold Fields in California and Australia and was a rational system which contributed to methodical digging. It had two major purposes: to ensure a uniform working of the pit and to prevent speculators buying claims and holding them for sale in a good market. Uniform working was important as not only did unworked claims create problems of safety, but they also made the labour costs of digging more expensive. Diggers at greater depths than their neighbours worked in constant fear of falling ground and the litigation that automatically followed; and high claims between one in the centre of the mine and the stagings often meant that as many as four more Africans had to be employed to wind the windlass.

In 1873 a commission investigating affairs on the Diamond Fields reached the conclusion that 'jumping' did not ensure uniform working in the pits. While it recognised that there was a majority of diggers in favour of the principle of 'jumping', the commission recommended some modification to the practice. It suggested that claims should be forfeited and auctioned after a warning notice had been served, as it believed some security should be given to 'miners in the possession of their claims for which they have given valuable consideration in work and money'.[11] In diggings where the value of claims had not been established, the commission recommended that 'jumping' remain in its original form. Here the commission's thinking followed the tenets of 'diggers' democracy'. Unless 'jumping' was main-

34

tained in new diggings they would be dominated by 'a small number of diggers, who have an unlimited supply of native labour at their command, to the detriment of the great bulk of the mining community'.[12] These recommendations were proclaimed by Governor Southey and became law.

The 'jumping' system in its original form safeguarded the central plank of 'diggers' democracy', which was the opposition to the emergence of large claimowners. Each digger was not allowed to own more than two claims under the regime of the Diggers' Committees. Although this Committee rule had been sanctioned by Orange Free State law, it was not re-enacted under British law.[13] Still, even though it was not legal in Southey's Kimberley, it was a moral rule in the mines and budding monopolists went to some pains to disguise their spreading ownership. These men were well aware that 'jumping' posed the greatest threat to their consolidation of claims in the mines.[14]

The most articulate monopolist was William Hall, the owner of the first steam engine on the Fields and the incline tramway in the West End of Kimberley mine. 'As long as the claims are fairly worked', he wrote in a submission to the 1873 Diamond Fields Commission:

> the benefits to the community is the same whether the claims are owned by one man or a hundred. To restrain the investment of capital in the mine would be injurious to the present holders of ground, opposed to advancement and be adopting principles that are far behind the age and have always failed. It would also drive all our most intelligent and enterprising men from our midst and would be a permanent injury to a new state like this. By restricting what a man may acquire an end is put to all progress which is the very soul of a new country. If a man is only to hold two claims why not prevent him from holding more than two farms or two houses or two stores or two carts, in fact, if "individual levelling" is going to be adopted we had better at once call ourselves "Chartists" or "Fenians" or "Communists" or the latest improvement "Internationalists" and redivide the claims in "Colesberg Kopje" [Kimberley Mine] every month.[15]

It was clear to Hall that the Diggers' Committees interfered with progress, which required the application of capital and the introduction of steam machinery. John Blades Currey, the Colonial Secretary, was a powerful ally in the monopolists' campaign against the Diggers' Committees. 'As the best means of compassing my object of curbing or getting rid of the Diggers' Committees', wrote Currey in his memoirs, 'I proposed ... to substitute Mining Boards with defined and limited powers for the old Diggers' Committees'.[16]

In 1874, as part of the new Mining Ordinance, the Committees were replaced by Mining Boards with more limited powers. The Boards were strictly confined to mining affairs and an Inspector was appointed with responsibility for the safety of life and limb. Election to the Boards was by a system of loaded votes. Owners with three or more claims were allowed a maximum of three votes, while those with a quarter claim or less were allowed one vote only. It was the thin edge of the wedge: the

35

Boards introduced differentiation amongst diggers in terms of representation.

Still, for consolidating owners three votes was not enough and they wanted to tie representation to the value of claims. This would be the knot to throttle 'diggers' democracy'. They feared that the Mining Boards would be dominated by the popular diggers on the Committees. Indeed, in the first election for the Kimberley Mining Board in June 1874, seven of the nine members had been on the old Diggers' Committee.[17] A similar pattern of old Association men soundly beating aspiring monopolists to the seats on the Boards followed in the other mines.[18] In 1875 the tide began to turn but by then organisation of opposition to the new state had taken broader forms and was no longer based purely in the mines.

THE COMMITTEE OF PUBLIC SAFETY

Before the Diggers' Committees were replaced by the Boards, they organised a private force called the Vigilance Committee to police the camps. Between September 1873, when it first went into operation, and March 1874, it boasted a proud record of policing: 41 Africans convicted of diamond theft, 40 canteen-keepers convicted of illegally selling liquor to Africans, and the arrest of 'one hundred persons who were breaking the laws'.[19] Initially Southey's government approved of the Vigilance Committee and handed over half the fines inflicted on the convicted as an 'informer's reward'. But in early 1874, after the introduction of the new Mining Ordinance, the government began to review its support for the Committee. The *Diamond News*, then the goverment paper, fell to abusing the Committee as 'common informers', 'thief-takers' and a bunch of 'roughs'. In April 1874, after Resident Magistrate Gray had taken exception to the system of 'trapping', which was used to apprehend illicit diamond dealers, the government decided to withdraw the 'informer's reward' from the Vigilance Committee. With little to finance its activities it fell apart.[20]

The vacuum created by the demise of the Vigilance Committee was not filled by the forces of the state. Kimberley was badly underpoliced as the constabulary held few attractions when there was a prospective fortune to be had in the mines. Consequently, after a period of uncertainty, diggers and others decided to form a new organisation to protect their interests and property. On the 15 August 1874, 500 people gathered in Market Square and elected a body called the Committee of Public Safety, a deliberately provocative name which was intended to strike revolutionary terror into Southey's government. The members of the new Committee were, by now, well known in the camps: George Bean, John Birbeck, Gustavus Blanch, Fred English, John Gifford, William Ling, John Lawler, Christian Marias, J. J. 'Dan' O'Leary, Johan Rausch, Henry Tucker and George Tearnan.[21]

Southey took the Committee of Public Safety seriously but, as it began to show signs of constituting itself as an alternative government, he refused to recognise it as an authorised body. When he was threatened with a disturbance for his intransigence, he made preparations to meet a riot. 'The first thing done', he wrote to Sir Henry Barkly:

> has been to appoint 5 or 6 Justices of the Peace and to select for the office men of influence among the business people and in particular 3 belonging to the Jewish fraternity (and if I find it needful I shall authorize each J.P. to swear in a certain number of Special Constables).[22]

He called in men from the Frontier Armed and Mounted Police and predicted a 'decided movement on the part of the respectable portion of the community in opposition to the Roughs'.[23]

While he awaited the turn of events, Southey attempted to find out who and what motivated the Committee for Public Safety. 'I was at first very much surprised', he wrote:

> to find Henry Tucker's name published as having occupied the Chair at the "Mass Meeting" for I thought he had done well here and had something to lose but Green told me yesterday that this was not so and he (Tucker) had nothing to lose.[24]

Southey then instructed his Chief of Police, Inspector Percy, to keep him informed of what was growing into a serious opposition movement to his new government. Percy sent Mortimer Spurgin to spy on the Committee of Public Safety, not a difficult assignment in a canvas and corrugated iron camp, where the only problem lay in finding the right office, canteen or tent for their meetings.

The Committee met at various venues – Blanch's office, Cundill's canteen, Tucker's house – and Spurgin managed to overhear most of the closed discussions. The Committee had a core of between 25 and 50 members whose voices Spurgin spent some time learning to identify. His brief was to uncover a conspiracy to overthrow the British government, and he kept his ears peeled for talk of Republicanism or the intervention of foreign agents. He may well have misunderstood what was said, but he faithfully relayed to Inspector Percy splits amongst members over how to pursue particular forms of action. He did not smear any particular member as he knew that the majority of Committee activists were not roughs but men of respectable reputations in the community.

In August and September 1874 the Committee was preoccupied with writing and raising support for a monster petition to the Queen. The petition, which was a catalogue of their grievances, was left at the Blue Posts canteen for signature. The spy Spurgin alleged that signatures were bought by the Committee, and Governor Southey took the issue seriously enough to use it to discredit the petition when he eventually sent it on to Governor Barkly at Cape Town. Purchase of names there may well have been, but the hint of intimidation was more effective when and if support was required.[25]

The Committee kept abreast of all political affairs in the camps. The farm land issue was frequently debated and Spurgin was dismayed to hear of alleged government corruption and swindling land sales. In November the Committee took a dim view of the new Diamond Dealers Ordinance. This new piece of legislation raised the licence fees for dealing in diamonds and restricted the trade to the offices of diamond merchants. Its purpose was to cut out the '*kopje-wallopers*', the small-scale diamond dealers, whose business equipment was 'a pair of top boots, a courier bag and a half-a-crown'.[26] Not only did it attack small men earning money on small margins, but it also raised taxation without adequate representation. Even Spurgin was acquainted with the implications of this last assertion. He heard Tucker warn 'the Executive to be very careful how they treated the express wishes of the people'.[27] The warning was followed by the revolutionary threat that there was 'a storm brewing which would shake the present government to its very foundations'.[28]

In keeping with its constitution as an alternative government, the Committee of Public Safety bought a newspaper. The Committee had the option of buying out the proprietors of the *Diamond Field*, one of the earliest newspapers on the Fields started by, but no longer owned by, Vickers Brothers. Instead, they chose to pay £600 for its editorial control for 12 months. The reasoning behind this limited purchase was that the owners, J. S. Bold and I. R. Taylor, would remain liable for libel prosecutions. The cash for the editorial control was raised by a private subscription of £10 shares. Curiously enough the names of some loyal citizens, such as the large diamond merchant, J. B. Robinson, and the large claimholder, F. Baring Gould, appeared among the shareholders.[29] The new controllers sacked the editor, Dr P. H. Graham, the member of the Legislative Council, and replaced him with Alfred Aylward, an excellent journalist among other callings, who was to be closely identified with the turbulent opposition to Southey's government.[30]

Aylward was an ardent Republican and he was eager to convert the Committee of Public Safety to his views. He was Irish and had been connected with the Fenian movement. This experience had formed his abhorrence of British rule and he found many in Kimberley who shared his belief in Republicanism. He also found sympathetic listeners in the neighbouring Orange Free State. Early in October 1874 Aylward went to Bloemfontein for an audience with President Brand and five Volksraad members. Brand told him that he approved of the work of the Committee and Aylward used this endorsement to support his proposal for Republican government in Kimberley.

Republicanism became a burning issue within the Committee of Public Safety. In September Aylward raised the subject of new forms of government in a committee meeting. The spy Spurgin discovered that annexation to the Cape was dismissed out of hand and, although the advantages and disadvantages of Southey's government generated a heated discussion, it was also dismissed as unsuitable. Aylward was left with three alternative forms of Republicanism: a Republic with a Commissioner as President; a Federation with the South African Republic and the Orange Free State; or simply annexation to the Orange Free State. While Aylward would have been happy with any of these options, there were still many on the Committee who remained loyal to the Queen.[31]

In November 1874 the debate over Republicanism led to a split in the Committee. Spurgin caught the conflict in his reports to his superior. Gustavus Blanch, a claimholder and a claim agent, was committed to British rule. He did not want the Committee used as a standing Republican threat to the government, but rather as a pressure group arguing for reform of the constitution. He refused to negotiate 'with a revolver in his pocket and a rifle in his hand'.[32] In a rage he challenged Aylward to choose between reform or revolution. Aylward's reply was to submit that 'Mr Blanch's name be struck off the list of the Committee of Public Safety as a traitor to the cause'.[33] But Aylward did not carry the other members with him and, although he remained editor of the *Diamond Field*, he turned his Republican energies to another organisation.

THE DEFENCE LEAGUE

In November 1874 the Defence League and Protection Association was formed on the basis of a pledge not to pay taxes. It invoked the Anti-Convict League as an historical precedent, but the anti-colonial and anti-taxing rebellions in America were a far more poignant historical parallel. Aylward put all his Republican arguments into the formation of this organisation. He wrote a bill of demands which he called the 'cat-o-nine-tails'. The nine demands were: a licencing board to issue miners' certificates; the suspension of the new Diamond Dealing Ordinance; the suspension of the new Mining Ordinance; the publication of the revenue and expenditure of the government; reef extraction should be charged to the general revenue; severer penalties for illegal diamond dealing and expulsion from Griqualand West; a vagrant law; the withdrawal of the £25,000 government loan secured against the mines; and the removal of those interested in land speculation from the Land Commission. It was a formidable set of demands. Aylward was charitable enough to absolve Governor Southey from some of the responsibility for the situation in Griqualand West. 'But I do believe', he said, 'that there are enemies of the people, unfit and improper persons, permitted to be about the person of Her Majesty's Representative, who sway him against the interests of the people'.[34]

In the new year the interests of the people were threatened more by landowners than the government. The owners of Vooruitzicht farm, a syndicate of Port Elizabeth merchants led by Dunell, Ebden and Company, took William Ling, a well-known digger and member of the Committee of Public Safety, to court for the failure to pay rent. Ling believed that diggers were entitled to a dwelling stand as part of their claim licence. He had first been taken to court in October 1873, and when he lost he appealed to the Circuit Court, where he won. Then, he found himself arraigned under a new charge of trespass. In February 1875 he lost the third round and the Acting Recorder, J. C. Thompson, ruled that the proprietors could raise rents as they pleased.[35]

The issue of rents was of great moment to all diggers and standholders in the mining camps. In fact, Southey had tried to regulate the extraction of rent, but his ordinances to that effect had been vetoed by the Colonial Office.[36] Even before the vetoes were made public in March 1875, it was known throughout Kimberley. Immediately, diggers resolved to resist rent increases and events began to take a more threatening turn. On the 3 March, at a mass meeting of 800 people in Kimberley Hall, Aylward encouraged diggers to take up arms. 'If I erect the English ensign . . . with a black flag under it', he cried, 'I expect to see you with your rifles and your revolvers . . . [ready] in the name of heaven and your country, to protect yourselves from injustice'.[37]

THE DIGGERS' PROTECTION ASSOCIATION

Aylward's call to arms on 3 March was taken seriously by a number of dis-affected organisations on the fields. Ten days later the Diggers' Protection Association was formed at a joint meeting of the Committee of Public Safety, Committee Number One, the Delegates, the League and the Diggers' Association. The Protection Association was explicitly organised on a military basis of companies of men, whose captains formed the commanding body or *krygsraad* (war council). There were seven armed companies, five at Kimberley and a burgher guard at Dutoitspan and De Beers. 'Captain' William Ling commanded the Cavalry Patrol and 'Captain' Alfred Aylward commanded one of the infantry companies. Conrad von Schlickmann, a Prussian soldier, was in charge of the 'German Company' and Henry Tucker was 'Captain' of the Reserve. This latter company was directly armed by funds from the Protection Association, while all the others were armed and outfitted by their members. By the end of April 1875, 800 men were under arms and another 400 were waiting to be equipped. The seriousness of the Protection Association's intentions was underlined by the report that two Armstrong guns were on the road to Kimberley from Port Elizabeth.[38]

The mustering of such a force of men and arms was a forbidding prospect for Governor Southey. He felt that the lengths to which Aylward and his men were driving matters was 'beyond all proper liberty'.[39] Martial drilling on the cricket ground and in Market Square began to alarm the mercantile community of Kimberley. Loyal subjects, which included a 'respectable German portion', promised to co-operate with the government in 'putting down the nuisance'.[40] Their co-operation as volunteers was called on sooner than they had imagined.

In the middle of March the Protection Association announced that it intended to assume the coercive functions of government. The Association's statement appeared in the *Diamond Field* in the form of a Manifesto signed by Henry Tucker and William Ling. The Manifesto declared that 'the rights, property and liberty of the diggers' were threatened by a large number of Africans who were 'not gaining their living by honest labour' and were not under adequate police surveillance.[41] The Association declared that its members would see to the security of Europeans on the Fields. Its declaration harked back to the Vigilance Committee and its planned methods of private policing owed much to vigilante groups in mining camps elsewhere in the world.

As a result Governor Southey sent for British troops. His despatch to Sir Henry Barkly reached Cape Town on the 27 March, but on the following day Southey telegraphed and cancelled his request for reinforcements.[42] What occurred in the week between the despatch and the telegram? Sending for troops was an extreme measure and would be an immense financial drain on the new colonial state. It was the option that J. B. Currey, the Colonial Secretary, favoured; he believed that the 'little clique of desperate men, ex-convicts, bankrupts, and penniless adventurers, who have disturbed the tranquillity of the Province' should be put down once and for all.[43] But Southey disagreed with this characterisation of the opposition. He had discovered the true nature of the discontent a day or so before he cancelled his request for troops.

Southey was opposed not by a rabble, it appeared to him, but by a conspiracy of capitalists. 'I am getting a clearer insight into the movement', he wrote privately to Barkly:

> and the wires that are being pulled. My present conviction is that Hall (Walsh and Co.) is at the bottom of it and that the object is to endeavour to convince the Home authorities that there is nothing in the Province but the mines and that they ought to be in the possession of a Company of Capitalists ... The plan has been well laid. He and some others are told off to do the apparently friendly part, to stand between the government and the Rebels. The friendly ones' duties are to interview me and urge non-opposition to the violent party; "let things slide" as Hall tried to impress on me and so show that we are unable to maintain order while inviting other members of the Government to friendly tea parties etc. to cajole and make an impression on them that temporising is the proper thing. Others such as Tucker, Ling, Aylward and Co. are told off on the other side to endeavour to strike fear in the minds of the government and the well disposed by threatening to set fire to public and other buildings. I am assured that both parties are working in concert and when I look at who the open men are I get an amount of light that could not be acquired all at once. The leaders of the violent party are all men of straw, and I think it likely that they have been offered, as myself and others were indirectly offered last session, that if success follows and a company can get the mine they shall have shares in the company without paying for them.[44]

Southey's new understanding of the situation meant that aspirant capitalists need not be put down by arms as they were potentially government supporters. They could be dealt with by other means. What Southey had in mind was a state purchase of the most important farm, Vooruitzicht, as it was the fear of rising rents that galvanised capitalists and diggers into one disaffected movement of opposition to the state.

While Southey began negotiating for the purchase of the farm, the Protection Association patrolled the streets of Kimberley. The primary activity of patrols was to ensure that Africans went around the camps unarmed. Most Africans carried a stick of some kind and the Association took this as evidence of violent intentions. Sambo Mossambicha was one African who fell foul of a patrol from 'Captain' Aylward's company. One Sunday afternoon he and some friends were attacked by Frederick Wepenaar and four white men outside Kimberley Hall. Sambo's knob-kierie, which had cost 2s 6d at Gowie's store, was confiscated by the patrol. Normally, that would have been the end of the affair, but one of his companions was the servant of a government official and he encouraged Sambo to take the theft of his stick to court. It was an unusual event in the current state of the camps, but Sambo won the case and Wepenaar was fined £2 for his illegal action.[45] Most others suffered the attentions of the patrols without protest, but some Africans and 'persons of colour', particularly those who were their own masters, formed vigilante groups for their own protection. John Coverwell, a pugilist of colonial renown and canteen-keeper in the Malay Camp, was the best known leader of these self-defence groups. The Association branded them 'Parliament Men' and accused them of 'green leaf' atrocities.[46]

'Parliament Men' were poorly organised compared to the Diggers' Protection Association. The Association had bought the *Diamond Field* editorial column with subscriptions from claimholders and merchants, while a number of small canteen and shopkeepers supported the movement with cash or goods. Loyal merchants who refused to support the association were intimidated. Charles Sonnenberg was visited by Jacob Dahl, who demanded a subscription 'to further the objects of the Association' and when he was refused he warned Sonnenberg that 'he was a marked man and would be punished when the government was kicked out'.[47] Anton Dunkelsbuhler, 'a very respectable diamond merchant', was visited by a fellow German, Conrad von Schlickmann, who asked for a contribution and when he was refused calmly noted Dunkelsbuhler's name in a book.[48] As policing was in the hands of the Association, the refusal to subscribe laid merchants open to incendiarism and other acts of malicious violence.

The Griqualand West Constabulary was thin on the ground. It was composed of nine officers and 24 white privates aided by a fluctuating number of black auxiliaries. 'It is impossible to get sufficient white men to join the force who are trustworthy', wrote the *Diamond News*, 'as honest, sober white men on the Fields can earn as much in a day as is paid per week to constables'.[49] Consequently, to the distress of disaffected organisations, black constables were employed in growing numbers. In April 1875, the

Association decided it was time to put an end to this practice. Thomas, a government spy, reported that:

> the Association now numbered one thousand men, that they would be at the Police Camp this afternoon, and if they saw any Coloured People amongst the Volunteers drilling, or in any way mixed up with them, they had orders to fire on them.[50]

This display of Association strength impressed Southey enough to keep Africans and 'persons of colour' out of active policing in the camps, but Africans and Indians were armed to guard convicts in the overcrowded gaol. The threat of so-called 'class riots' in what had become armed camps encouraged Southey to attempt to restrict the distribution of rifles and guns.

THE BLACK FLAG REVOLT

The prosecution of a prominent Associationist for an alleged illegal arms sale precipitated the formal declaration of a state of rebellion. William Cowie, a hotel-keeper, was tried for failing to procure a permit to transfer 12 guns to Alfred Aylward. D'Arcy, the Resident Magistrate of Kimberley, gave evidence in court that the prosecution was the result of a routine check, as the supervision of the gun trade was part of his magisterial duties.[51] But there was little that was routine about selecting Cowie for bureaucratic investigation. In February 1875 Cowie had been elected Chairman of the Licensed Victuallers Association and, by refusing to pay tax increases, he led canteen and hotel-keepers into opposition to the government.[52] On the 24 March D'Arcy visited Cowie's hotel to collect evidence of illegal gun sales. On the following day, Southey wrote to Barkly:

> ... As I learnt there was a brisk trade in guns and ammunition I called upon the Magistrate to examine stocks and permits, and the result is to discover a good deal of illicit trade which has seriously alarmed some of the leaders who will be let in for heavy fines I fancy.[53]

Cowie later denied that he had ever bought the guns or passed them on to Aylward. While guns were certainly delivered by the gun-dealers, Reid and Wilson, Cowie claimed that he never paid for the consignment. He argued that he had been framed.

The trial of William Cowie on 12 April 1875 was a major political event. In the face of the threatening presence of Association men inside and outside the court room, the Resident Magistrate of Dutoitspan, R. W. Gray, showed considerable courage in convicting Cowie, fining him £50 and refusing him bail pending confirmation of his verdict by the Recorder. The immediate problem for court officials and police was to remove Cowie to gaol through the throng of men who opposed his conviction. With an escort of six constables, Cowie was taken from the Court House and marched the 250 yards to the gaol where they found their path blocked by Association men. 'When the escort with the prisoner reached the front of the gaol', wrote Resident Magistrate D'Arcy in an official report:

> they halted at about twenty paces from the gate, facing the armed men already posted there. At this time there were in all some 150 armed men obstructing the entrance to the prison. Immediately after the escort halted about 24 non-commissioned officers and men of the Griqualand Armed Constabulary, armed with rifles with fixed bayonets came round the lower corner of the gaol from the police barracks, and took up their position in front of the rebels. There were then probably 2,500 to 3,000 people armed and unarmed, assembled in the neighbourhood of the gaol and any firing must inevitably have caused great loss of life. Seeing that the odds against the police were about 15 to 1, I addressed the armed men, then mustering some 300 in number and asked who was their leader.[54]

William Ling stepped forward and D'Arcy warned him of the consequences of what he was doing. After a short conversation Ling demanded to see the Governor and, 'hoping to avoid a collision',[55] D'Arcy, Ling and Tucker set off for the government offices, leaving the confrontation outside the gaol in a state of suspense.

Southey refused to see the deputation and it fell to Currey to negotiate a compromise. It took some time but eventually Tucker agreed to sign a check for £50 which D'Arcy promised not to cash until after the Recorder's review. 'Mr Tucker gave me his cheque for the amount of the fine', D'Arcy continued in his official report:

> and I returned to the prison where I found everything as I had left it, except that the surrounding crowd was much larger and the Inspector of Constabu- lary had completed a flank movement of his men so as to place them on the left flank of the rebels where, however, they were again outflanked by a third body known as Schlickmann's Germans, who occupied some mounds of soil to their left. Cowie was still in the custody of the escort and I liberated him. Mr Tucker then addressed the men and dismissed them.[56]

Bloodshed had been avoided but the Association had crossed the consti- titional Rubicon. On the following day, 13 April, Governor Southey declared that 'certain evil disposed persons', who had continued to 'enrol themselves in illegal bodies and to arm and drill', were 'in rebellion against Her Majesty the Queen'.[57]

The proclamation of a rebellion was provoked by the interference with the due process of law in Cowie's trial, but the event which gave its name to the rebellion occurred on the afternoon of 12 April away from the main confrontation. Between three and four p.m. a black flag was hoisted on Frames' whim at the edge of Kimberley mine. The man who raised the flag, which most government officials remembered clearly as the signal of rebellion that Aylward had promised on 3 March, was Albany Paddon. But it was on Aylward that attention was focussed and against whom accu- sations were levelled afterwards. The police believed that he had master- minded the whole unpleasant occasion; he later asserted that he no longer belonged to the Association at the time and exercised no authority over the 30 or 40 men who congregated around the whim. There is little doubt that Aylward spent the afternoon at the whim, equipped with a sword, but precisely what function he fulfilled, perched above the throngs of people in the street below, is open to conjecture. Whatever his role, whether sinister or innocuous, it was the hoisting of a black flag on a whim on the debris mound they called Mount Ararat, that entered history as the decisive moment of the rebellion.[58]

The Association ruled the streets of the mining camps. Its members were rebels but they could not decide whether or not to overthrow the government by force of arms. Their indecision was reinforced by the establishment of the Moderate Party, an organisation of wealthy merchants. It was formed soon after the rebellion proclamation and, in an attempt to stop the despatch of troops from Cape Town, sent a deputation to see Sir Henry Barkly.[59] While the deputation was *en route* to Cape Town, G. R. Blanch tried to persuade Southey to take no action until the Moderate Party's case had been made to the Cape Governor. 'He was very excited', wrote Southey, 'walked in, was refused an audience by me, went out, rode off at a gallop, came back and saw Currey'.[60] Southey believed that he was one of the 'very worst of the lot with whom no parley should be held'.[61] Southey conceded that he was a very clever claim agent, but he thought Blanch was 'cracked'. Beside he felt threatened by Blanch's manner. 'He looked', wrote Southey, 'as if he could have taken a revolver out of his pocket in a moment'.[62]

Blanch had reason to be agitated as he believed that the intervention of the Moderate Party would persuade Sir Henry Barkly to grant an amnesty to the rebels. And he was right. Barkly promised an amnesty provided that the members of the Association disarmed. On the 9 May, Tucker claimed the Association had been dissolved, but on 12 May at a meeting in Tucker's compound the rebels resolved to remain under arms as troops had been sent from Cape Town.[63] Over the next month there was an uneasy calm in the camps as rebels and loyalists waited for the arrival of the military column. On the 12 June, Southey learnt that the rebels would protect their leaders, who had been excluded from the amnesty, against arrest on the arrival of Lieutenant-Colonel Cunnynghame and his troops. It appeared that 800 armed men could be called on to support the seven proscribed leaders.[64] But on 1 July, soon after Cunnynghame arrived with 250 men, Henry Tucker, William Ling, Gustavus Blanch, Conrad von Schlickmann and John Brien were arrested without any resistance. Alfred Aylward and John Sloane Fisher were arrested a few days later and all the leaders were released on £1,000 bail each. British troops had re-established Southey's authority after two and a half months of open rebellion.[65]

THE TRIAL

In September 1875, when the state trial took place, the arrested leaders of the Black Flag Revolt did not stand together in the dock. Four of them, Tucker, Blanch, Fisher and Brien, pleaded guilty to the minor charge of having unlawfully assembled on the 12 April and as a *quid pro quo* all other charges were withdrawn. In this fashion they escaped a possible death penalty. Judgement was reserved pending the trial of the other three leaders, Aylward, Ling and Schlickmann, who had refused to throw themselves on the mercy of the Court as the other leaders had done. They had pleaded not guilty to the charges of sedition, conspiracy and riot. Their defence revolved around their argument that British law had no jurisdiction in what they regarded as Orange Free State territory. Whether or not this carried any legal weight turned out to be irrelevant. No jury of diggers was going to convict men who had stood up for their rights on the Fields. After three days of evidence the jury took 23 minutes to return a verdict of not guilty.[66]

Aylward's precise role in the Black Flag Revolt was clarified more before the trial than in his evidence. In July 1875 he gave a lecture on rebellion to 250 people in Kimberley Hall. It was an impressive performance spiced with anecdotes from his own wide knowledge and experience of successful and abortive struggles against authorities in Ireland and America. The justification for rebellion, he argued, lay simply in the power of the people to overthrow the state. He openly stated that in Griqualand West he had proposed 'an armed resistance and was determined to get rid of the government'.[67] The failure of the 'so-called rebellion' he laid at the feet of Henry Tucker. It was Tucker who had persuaded the Association to give up its struggle before the 'just and legitimate demands of the people' had been conceded by the government.[68] It was Tucker who committed 'political suicide' by going over to the Moderate Party. And it was the Moderate Party which had negotiated the amnesty. In his analysis of the defects of Tucker's capitulation to the Moderate Party, Aylward appealed to the readers of history in the future to remark 'on the incompleteness of his sacrifice'.[69]

Historians have said next to nothing about Tucker's betrayal, but much about the opportunism and 'extremism' of Aylward.[70] While Aylward chose to stand trial, in the witness box he did not openly admit an intention to overthrow the state. He chose, in his eloquent defence, to pick a legal path through the problems of justification and proof of sedition:

> If I had intended a revolt I can assure you I would have gone about my object in a more secret manner. I certainly should not have taken the course I did. I would not have called a public meeting and explained my intentions, when I was well aware that from 60 to 100 government officials or justices formed part of that meeting. Looking at the dangerous state of the camp and the inability of the Mining Board to cope with the evil, an association was formed for

mutual protection and support. There had formerly been a Vigilance Committee, but on the retirement of Mr Buyskes from the office of magistrate that had been broken up. There was no police protection at night time, and although constables were stationed at the churches on Sunday in the day time they failed to keep order. All this you have in evidence and plainly shows the necessity which existed for some protective force. You have heard that the command of the Association's men was offered either to Mr Percy, the Police Inspector, or Mr Spurgin, the Chief Detective, and you have also heard that I have frequently assisted the police. Before the hoisting of the Black Flag, at which Mr Woollaston states I was present, I had given up my whistle, the badge of my office as adjutant, and my sword; and with regard to my being at the whim on the kopje, for all Mr Woollaston can say I might have been there merely as a spectator; he does not say he heard me give orders; and he admits that I apparently stopped some armed men from going down to the gaol. Had I still been a member of the Association on the 12 April my place would have been at the gaol among the other members. You have heard that the men at the gaol committed no violence, and in reality did not attempt any rescue; they merely stood between the police and the gaol. If then there was no attempt at rescue and no violence, I submit that there was no riot whatever and if there was no riot, I don't see what further question you have to take into consideration. Whatever occurred at the gaol has been greatly exaggerated and was provoked by the government people who were first seen with arms in their hands. The evidence has failed to attach me to the riot, if riot it can be called, and it is amply proved that I had no hand in any attempted rescue. On this I say that the charge against me has failed completely.[71]

Aylward was vindicated in his acquittal. He believed he had made his political point, even though there had been immense pressure on him to plead guilty. The other rebel leaders, by accepting the court's deal, had prejudiced his case. Still, the rebels were found not guilty and they had not sued for a pardon at the bidding of the Moderate Party.[72]

The subsequent careers of the three main rebel leaders were revealing. In the following year, 1876, Henry Tucker became a Member of the Legislative Council and soon after he had taken office he was maliciously imprisoned for a technical contravention of the diamond trading laws. After he was released he became the editor of the *Independent* newspaper, then owned by J. B. Robinson, the diamond merchant, and thereafter remained a respectable member of Kimberley's bourgeoisie. William Ling did not capitulate so readily to the growing power of mining capitalists and maintained his rebellion beliefs in 'diggers' democracy'. He had taken the issue of 'diggers' rights' to law and lost to the landowners. He fell heavily into debt. In June 1876, although he appeared to own claims worth £20,000, they were fully mortgaged. At the beginning of 1877 he went bankrupt and was arrested for debt.[73] Despite his financial problems he was much respected amongst the white Diamond Fields community. It was otherwise with Alfred Aylward. In early 1876 he became editor of the *Independent* newspaper, then owned by William Ling, but his brand of Republicanism was not appreciated by the majority of diggers. In Sepember 1876, when Ling was forced to part with his newspaper, Aylward left Kimberley to join the Lydenburgh Volunteer Corps in the South African Republic.[74] He devoted himself to another Republican cause.

4

The Black Flag Revolt: an analysis[1]

De Kiewiet has provided the most penetrating analysis of the Revolt in *The Imperial Factor in South Africa*.[2] 'For the first time in South African history', he wrote, the 'naked problem of capital and labour' emerged and the Revolt decided how 'mining enterprise ... was to be organised and controlled'.[3] De Kiewiet understood that Governor Southey defended the small independent digger against the growth of mining companies by restricting the number of claims that could be owned by one person or firm to ten. As a result he thwarted company promoters, setting himself 'resolutely in the path of the free play of those sovereign economic forces that gave Cobden's England its wealth and power'.[4] Southey's support for the small-scale producer, argued de Kiewiet, created the conditions for the rebellion, together with his defence of the rights of Africans and 'persons of colour' to own claims, to buy and sell diamonds and to sort debris. The outcome of the revolt marked the death knell of this 'radical industrial experiment'; Africans and 'persons of colour' were consigned to the status of labourers and the mines came to be owned and controlled by 'organised capital'.[5]

The strength of this analysis lies in the crucial determination assigned to the conflict over the consolidation of claim ownership. While this is certainly a convincing approach to the issues raised by the Revolt, de Kiewiet failed to explain why Southey opposed the growth of mining companies. This failure also obscures an understanding of the demise of the 'liberal policy'[6] that allowed Africans to own claims and be their own masters. An examination of these two gaps in de Kiewiet's argument provides a more illuminating view of what was a crucial period of transition on the Diamond Fields.

DIGGERS AND SHARE-WORKERS

One of the main reasons for the inadequacy of de Kiewiet's analysis was his failure to recognise the existence of share-working, that is, digging by men who did not own their claims. Share-workers arranged with claimowners to work their claims in return for a percentage, which could be from 50 per cent to 90 per cent of the net profit of enterprise. As the percentage varied, so did the specific arrangements of the sub-contract. Most commonly the owner simply paid the claim licence and any mining taxes, while the share-worker did the digging, hired labourers, bought tools, planned production and sold diamonds. Share-working was like share-cropping in agriculture: the share-worker or share-cropper took his share of the diamonds or the harvest in cash or kind. Share-workers did not own their claims, but they still called themselves diggers.

It is difficult to quantify the extent of share-working or to specify when it was first introduced into the mines, but the meteoric rise in Kimberley claim prices gives some indication of how difficult it was to buy a claim in the early days. In the first three months after discovery claim prices rose from £100 to £2,000.[7] This was prohibitive to newcomers without substantial initial capital and claims were divided into quarters or smaller parcels of ground. In 1872, by which time share-working was common, it was estimated that there were from 1,600 to 1,800 separate holdings in the 470 claim Kimberley Mine. In 1874, two years later, 1,500 licences were issued for the mine and this suggests that a quarter claim remained the basic unit of production, although there was a measure of concentration in ownership. Certainly, by April 1875 the number of owners in Kimberley Mine was significantly reduced and at the end of 1875 there were 381 owners of 405 claims.[8]

At the time of the Rebellion share-workers outnumbered claimowners. At most, in a population of 6,000 Europeans, only 757 men owned a total of 1,243 claims in the four mines and at least 120 of these owners were Africans, Indians or 'persons of colour'.[9] One missionary pointed out:

> Not all blacks on the Diamond Fields are servants. There are many quite well educated diggers or merchants. These are mostly from the Colony and they are mostly those who tend to remain and build up a nucleus of permanency to which newcomers adhere.[10]

Besides being owners, especially in the 'poor man's diggings' at Bultfontein, Africans and others were also share-workers. While the number of black share-workers was unknown, there were certainly enough to be the focus of white racism, as was apparent from the attempt in 1872 to abolish the digging rights of 'natives'.[11] In 1874 Alfred Alyward demanded that 'men who employed coloured labourers on shares while hundreds of honest men are in want of employment' should be excluded from Mining Board elections.[12] And Dr Matthews, who provided one of the most informative contemporary accounts of the period, put racism down to European jealousy of 'their black brethren digging at Dutoitspan and Bultfontein'.[13]

Share-working was simply a form of sub-contract suited to exploratory development in mines which many diggers feared would 'bottom out' or vary widely in richness. It limited a claimowner's responsibilities and risks. Responsibility for production and maintenance of the asset was delegated, while risks in the development of a claim were shared with the share-worker. Share-working flourished in Kimberley where the owner was otherwise engaged; a landed gentleman or a merchant could speculate in claims without it taking too much of his capital or his time. One owner explained the attraction of this arrangement:

> Digging moreover promised to afford an agreeable means of subsistence. It involves no personal labour, and makes no demands on one's time. If you have much ground you let out the greater portion on shares, in which case you have nothing to do but receive the proceeds. You reserve a good piece to work on your own account, and this you leave to your boys under a European overseer. Your time is accordingly all your own to dispose of as you list.[14]

Share-working encouraged the lateral extension of mining rather than its vertical integration in depth.

Share-working gave share-workers a measure of independence, freedom from supervision and the opportunity to strike it rich. For those escaping from relations of dependency in Colonial or European cities or those accustomed to positions of authority on farms in the Republics or the Cape, it was a system that provided a buffer against wage labour. It is worth while illustrating this point through the biography of Barend Christian van Buuren, whose career was similar to many other Afrikaners who composed over half of the rank and file of rebels.[15]

Van Buuren was born in 1845 in Cradock where his father had a business. When he was 22 years old his father died and he went to the Orange Free State to become an overseer on a farm, owned by B. L. Baintjies, between Bloemfontein and Fauresmith. In July 1871 he went to the Diamond Fields and Baintjies bought him a claim to work. Soon he was struck down by camp fever and, after selling the claim, he returned to Baintjies' farm for 18 months. In 1873 he went back to Kimberley with his wife and three children and lived with and worked for his brother-in-law, John von Abo, who kept a produce store. Then he became a share-worker for a short while before he made a trip into the interior. At the end of 1874 he returned and worked in a claim for Pat Murtha and then for Paddon Brothers, the largest claimowner in the mine. At the time of the Rebellion van Buuren was employed as an overseer by Paddon Brothers. His story shows the ambiguity in the prospects of success on the Diamond Fields, and the ever present possibility of depression into the ranks of the proletariat. Faced with this prospect, share-working was a system many Europeans wanted to protect.[16]

Although share-working was a system designed for the mutual benefit of both parties involved, it was the share-workers who were open to exploitation. They did not receive a good press in Kimberley as they were people of little political and social weight in the community, but they did find one champion for their cause in Alfred Aylward, then a share-worker. He wrote a letter to the *Diamond News*:

> ... the class I belong to, that is, "diggers not being claimholders", although they have really the largest interests, the employers of the greatest amount of labour and the workers of the greatest extent of ground, have no representation on the Mining Board whatever ... A man takes over ground to work on shares, he gives up a high percentage (say 40 per cent) to the claimholder, he

> by his presence and labour keeps that claim from the penalties of unworked claims in the Mining Ordinance, he feeds and pays Kaffirs, keeps gear in order, goes through bad layers and as occurs in a vast proportion of cases loses money, health, patience and time that will never return (and) an ungentlemanly claimholder may sell the claim over his head or from under his feet without giving him even an hour's notice, or worse he may let the digger on shares work through a bad layer, spend perhaps £200 in getting the claim in first class order and to a paying level and then he may – and but too frequently does – step in and work the claim himself.[17]

The share-workers' response to this situation was to conceal their total finds from their principals and to sell a portion on the illicit market.

As a result claimowners tried to tighten their control over share-workers. From 1874 it became the practice to contract share-workers as servants. This was undignified from the point of view of the worker, but what was more damaging to the relationship between workers and owners was a new ordinance which redefined the system. Share-working was defined as a partnership in the proceeds of the claim and not in the claim itself. The percentage taken by the share-worker was payment in lieu of wages. It was a redefinition which cut into the roots of the share-workers' conception of themselves as independent contractors or tenants. 'The workers on shares are tenants of the claims', wrote Aylward, 'and the claimholder's share is rent and nothing else'.[18] The extraction of rent was a very different thing to the payment of wages and this new understanding of share-working created growing tensions in the relationship.[19]

The differences between share-workers and owners became acute in the year before the Rebellion. This was largely due to consolidation in claimownership and the growth of larger units of production; share-working was gradually displaced as private firms organised digging purely on the basis of wage labour. Share-workers were often forced into the new and degraded position of overseer of labour. As such they were sometimes rewarded with a small percentage on finds, but they had lost the speculative benefits of profit-sharing that had existed in share-working. Still, share-working was the dominant relation of production in Kimberley Mine. But after 1874 digging was more difficult as the price of diamonds declined and problems in the process of production increased; those share-workers who survived took on more of the risks and costs of mining as the fortunes of mining grew worse.

MASTER AND SERVANT RELATIONS

The rebels complained of a deterioration in master and servant relations. They blamed the spread of illicit diamond buying, but a review of the conditions in the mines, particularly Kimberley Mine, suggests a different explanation. At the end of 1873 large chunks of the south reef in Kimberley Mine fell into the pit. In January 1874 torrential rains made mining in many parts of the mines impossible and diggers and labourers were thrown out of work. Prior to the initial reef disaster the Kimberley and De Beers Mines employed 13,000 Africans, but by June 1874 this number had been halved. At this time in June 40 per cent of Kimberley Mine (150 claims) was under water and William 'Tramway' Hall was given a pumping contract to clear the mine. In November 1874, as he was nearing the completion of his task, the reef fell in again on the south side of the mine. So, by the time of the Rebellion over half the claims in Kimberley Mine were unworkable because of reef or water problems. The value of the unworkable claims was £300,000 out of a total of £500,000 and included the rich claims on the south-west side, as well as the reef claims held for speculative purposes.[20]

While this created a powerful constituency of European diggers and share-workers who were prepared to blame Africans and the government for their problems, it was the prospect of an imminent improvement in conditions that induced a frantic demand for labour. In March 1875 the mine looked better than it had for the past 18 months. 'Tramway' Hall had renewed his pumping contract and was poised to conquer the water problems. But more labourers were needed in what had become an extended production process. Kimberley Mine had reached a deepest point of 160 feet and new techniques of haulage, such as horse whims, had been introduced by most claimowners. The average production unit was composed of 15 to 20 labourers who could extract 40 to 50 loads of blue ground a day. By now it was common practice to leave the blue on depositing floors to decompose and this led to an expanded sphere of labour in cartage and diamond winning. The system of dry-sorting diamonds was superceded by washing, initially in primitive ripple cradles, but by 1875 in sophisticated rotary washing machines.[21]

Diggers found there was a shortage of labour in Kimberley. Although the number of African mine labourers walking to Kimberley had declined since 1873,[22] it was not simply the reduced number of potential mineworkers that created the shortage. 'Old hands' selected rich employers and safe conditions in the mines and passed on such information to newcomers from their own kinship group. Such a system of market intelligence meant that Africans refused to work in third class claims and shunned dangerous claims near the reef. Both these categories of claim were most often worked on shares, the first as yet unproved and the second held purely as speculative investments by merchants and others. Consequently, share-workers felt the shortage of labour more severely than other diggers.[23]

There was also a new sphere of employment which drew labour out of the pits and affected all diggers, if not in terms of supply, certainly in terms of wages. In early 1875, debris-washing became an industry. All the soil that had been dry-sorted and dumped in heaps was washed for the first time. It was a re-processing industry with few overhead costs and Governor Southey estimated that 600 washing machines found diamonds worth £20,000 each week.[24] The growth of debris-washing provoked anger amongst diggers

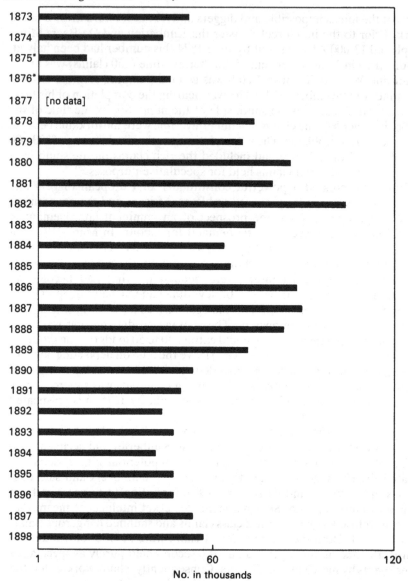

Fig. 2 Number of labour contracts registered in all mines, 1873–98. Note: Labour contracts registered were between two and six times in excess of labourers registered each year. (Sources: CAD, GLW, 55, 71 (1873–75); *Griqualand West Government Gazette*, 1877–80; *Blue Book on Native Affairs*, 1881–1900)

over the theft of diamondiferous soil and the avenue it provided for alternative work. 'There are at least 800 savages in the camp', Alfred Aylward told a public meeting, 'registered to other persons of indifferent character and similar colour, apparently for sorting debris'.[25]

Competition for labour facilitated a fundamental shift in master and servant relations. African labourers were in a position of strength and they imposed the 'board wages' system on their employers.[26] This meant that wages were forced up from 10s to 25s per week, and labourers fed themselves at the proliferation of boarding houses and 'kaffir eating-houses' in the main thoroughfares of the camps. The significance of this was twofold: it increased the real wage and it removed Africans from the 'immediate control of their masters'.[27] In the early 1870s contracted Africans (as well as white labourers) lived on diggers' compounds, but 'board wages' encouraged Africans to fend for themselves. They squatted in 'native camps' which sprang up on the outskirts of the main camps. The West End was one such area:

> The district lies to the west of the stretched out 'camp' and is bare and flat as the camp itself. It is almost exclusively inhabited by Blacks and Coloureds. The Blacks are mainly Basuto either subjects of Sekukuni or of other chieftains living beyond the Magaliesberg or they are Moshesh's people. Many of the latter have already worked for years in the Colony or in the Free State; the vast majority however are migrant labourers. The Coloureds are Koranna and Griqua from this area. Zulus, as other Black tribes and Bastards, are scarcely represented.[28]

Other Africans lived independently in the main townships, squatting or renting rooms in Bultfontein, the Malay Camp or Newton. As a result of this new development, white citizens demanded the 'localisation' in particular areas of all Africans not living on their employers' compounds, but Governor Southey refused to dictate where Africans should reside in Kimberley.[29]

This independence of Africans in the mining camps was not restricted by the system of labour registration. Diggers complained that the system did little to prevent desertion. By the end of 1874 it was common practice for diggers to contract only half their servants, giving passes only to those who worked in the mines, while the remainder at the sorting table or on the floors were unregistered. In February 1875, when an extra 1s per month was added to the registration of each servant as a hospital tax, diggers refused to contract their labourers. Registration became an issue of conflict. The Southey government decided to pursue employers who did not register their servants and picked out Henry Tucker and William Ling, rebel leaders, for police attention. Southey believed registration was a sufficient deterrent to desertion if all employers obeyed the law and refrained from poaching labourers from one another in periods of scarcity.[30]

Africans who claimed the freedom of the camps posed a threat to Europeans on the Fields. African independence threatened, in the words of the Association's Manifesto, European 'rights, property and liberty'.[31] At the source of the evil, it was believed, was the prevalence of diamond theft. Where policing was insufficient and labour unwilling, diggers took discipline into their own hands. In a number of cases murder was the result and one advocate argued in mitigation at one such trial:

> ... there may be a bias against the Coloured races; I will go further and say that a bias is only natural because in spite of Diggers' Committees, in spite of Vigilance Committees, and in defiance of all Government can do, diamond thieving continues to be the curse of the community.[32]

While there was no doubt that diggers were robbed of their diamonds, the scale of theft was open to speculation. European diggers complained about the lack of morality of their African servants and failed to deal with theft as part of a struggle over the terms and conditions of labour.

European diggers also suspected black claimowners and share-workers of diamond theft. Some Europeans went into partnership with Africans as claimowners so as to provide a legal channel through which to direct stolen diamonds. A number of court cases, which exposed this practice,[33] outraged struggling diggers and they wanted all Africans barred from claim-ownership, share-working and debris-washing. When Southey refused to agree they argued that 'the class who steal have the protection of the law, or at least the Government'.[34]

Racism developed around the issue of diamond theft. Although black and white diggers occupied similar positions in share-working, they failed to combine when under pressure from owners or the diamond or labour markets. Black share-workers were certainly able to work more cheaply than Europeans, and probably had easier access to labour, although we know very little about how blacks treated their servants; they did prosecute their servants for desertion and many were prosecuted for dumping dead employees in the veld to avoid mortuary fees. In any event, black diggers were outnumbered by Europeans. The only mine in which black diggers predominated was Bultfontein and there in 1874 they joined a small group of white diggers in forming a Diggers' Committee. This early example of co-operation was damaged when in 1875 they were again threatened with the revocation of their right to own claims. Blacks retreated into a separate organisation and, in a similar response to the 1872 attack on their digging rights, they petitioned the Cape Governor under the leadership of African clergymen and evangelists.[35]

While Africans never lost their right to own claims under the law, white racism persisted. Europeans regarded themselves as part of a superior race and the ideology of Social Darwinism supported this belief in themselves. On the Fields this ideology was buttressed by a complementary view of social relations in the mining camps. Europeans believed that they should all become masters in the pits and 'diggers' democracy' was the practical path to this order of society.

'Diggers' democracy' was exclusive to Europeans and was based on the enterprise of the small-scale producer. One new immigrant expressed the ideals of 'diggers' democracy' in a letter to the *Diamond Field*. He wrote of the danger of aspiring capitalists who saw a 'paradise of MONOPOLISTS being created by the enchanter's wand of CAPITAL in dusty Griqualand'.[36] He had been threatened by such men who wanted to reduce white diggers to servants, but they had forgotten that nearly every European left home in pursuit of independence and because he had revolted against 'social slavery – the class distinctions of Europe'.[37] They had come to Kimberley to create a new world:

> Born to labour, the multitude works and suffers, but we who have flung ourselves out from the ranks of the hopeless life-long toilers, who live only to multiply the luxuries of the rich, we who have become the mining and mercantile guerillas of a new state, will not permit ourselves to be brought back to the chain of the monopolist, from which we have so recently escaped.[38]

Both the new immigrant and the Afrikaner, whose experience lay largely in the customary racial order of the rural economy, found common ground in resistance to wage labour.

REBEL LEADERS

Men of political and social respectability gave the Committee of Public Safety and its successor organisations its strength and, when the choice between continued rebellion or disarmament was confronted, its weakness. These men were claimowners, but often also occupied in some trade, and had reached public prominence through the Diggers' Committees. They relished the management of their own affairs and were jealous of surrendering any control to the state.

The leader of the movement was Henry Tucker of Craddock. Both he and his brother, Kidger Tucker, were storekeepers as well as claimowners in Kimberley Mine. Henry's claims were not rich and he sold them to work on shares in his brother's property. In early 1875 he claimed to have 98 Africans in his service at wages of 5s to 9s a week, well below the ruling rate. This was an indication that they were 'raw' Africans, newly employed and prone to desertion once they were in a position to assess their opportunities on the Fields. Labour problems certainly added to the fact that he had not been able to make ends meet for some time. In contrast, his brother was a moderately successful digger. Kidger Tucker was elected to the first two Kimberley Mining Boards; as a share-worker, Henry Tucker was not eligible for membership. Instead, he joined the Committee of Public Safety and became its most prominent leader.[39]

William Ling was the most respected claimowner among the rebels. He was a staunch champion of diggers' rights and opponent of monopoly. He had arrived on the Fields in June 1871 from the Natal Midlands where he kept a roadside inn. He was popular among the Natalians who gathered on the south side of Kimberley Mine. They had two particular regional grievances against the Southey government which contributed powerfully to their disapproval of his rule. Southey attempted to implement the Cape system of African incorporation on class lines, whereas they were happier with Shepstonian segregation and reserves as a system of social control. And Southey did nothing to restrict the gun trade in Kimberley. Natalians called it the 'trade in blood' and regarded it as a direct cause of the Langalibalele Rebellion in Natal.

In common with many other Natalians, Ling suffered from declining fortunes in digging. In February 1875 William and his son, Edmund Ling, held eight claims in Kimberley Mine and four in De Beers Mine. Clearly some of these claims were out on shares, as their complement of labour varied between 20 and 70 Africans. But in April 1875 William Ling owned only three-quarters of a claim worth £75. As he was heavily in debt due to the costs of court cases, he transferred claims worth £1,000 to his son to avoid attachment.[40]

Claimowners had a powerful set of grievances against the Southey government. The major activists on the Committee of Public Safety – W. M. Frames, 'Dan' O'Leary, J. H. W. Rausch, G. R. Blanch, G. Tearnan, the Cotty Brothers and Fred English – were all claimowners. Their main complaint was that the 1874 Mining Ordinance placed significant areas of digging in the hands of a Surveyor, who was responsible to the government and not the newly elected Mining Boards. Claimowners wanted to adjudicate claim disputes, to decide where machinery should be placed, what rates to be levied and how monies were to be spent in the mines. What was particularly irksome to owners was the power of the Surveyor to prohibit the working of a claim if he thought danger existed to life and limb. They demanded the abolition of the Mining Ordinance and, in their petition to the Queen, they considered matters were so serious that a Commission of Enquiry was needed.[41]

The respectable rebels had little trouble in extending their quarrel with the government to various sections of the commercial community. Many claimowners were, like the Tuckers, storekeepers as well, but canteen-keepers and hotel-keepers were the most active in the rebel movement. Consumption of liquor went down with the falling fortunes of digging and canteen-keepers and hotel-keepers refused to pay the increased taxation demanded of them by government. This stand was organised through the Licensed Victuallers Association and the prosecution of their chairman, William Cowie, was the immediate catalyst to the outbreak of the Rebellion.[42]

Share-workers were often worse off than the respectable rebels. Their plight was best articulated by Alfred Aylward. He was a talented man, who worked as a Medical Officer in Dutoitspan before becoming a digger. In

1872 he bought five claims in De Beers Mine, employed 75 labourers and became chairman of the De Beers Diggers' Committee. He found that he had a lot in common with the Afrikaners who made up the majority of his fellow workers. He had learnt Dutch soon after he came to South Africa and spoke it fluently. In November 1872 he was convicted of assault and sentenced to 18 months hard labour, and as a result he lost his claims and his Committee position. On his early release in December 1873 he became a share-worker in De Beers Mine. In June 1874 he moved to Kimberley Mine as a share-worker, and employed 20 men under a 'respectable white man'. In August 1874, when he wrote a letter in defence of share-workers, he signed himself as an agent for 11 and a quarter claims.[43]

Share-working and his belief in Republicanism fused into a clear opposition to British rule. Respectable British claimowners found his Republicanism unacceptable, but he was an excellent journalist and his services to the rebel movement as editor of the *Diamond Field* were invaluable. After 13 April, when the claimowners in the Association were unclear about the path ahead, Aylward called for the expansion of the 'incipient local rebellion' into a union with colonial and Republican allies.[44] He proposed to promote:

> the holiest and greatest thought that can be conceived by colonial men – the creation of a South African Colonial Free and Republican Confederation.[45]

The leaders of the Association were stung into closing down this particular option and Tucker dismissed Aylward as editor. It was the breakpoint of the Rebellion. Troops were poised to march from Cape Town and small property owners saw the call for a Republic as opposed to their instinct for economic survival, as they preferred an amnesty in exchange for disarmament. Aylward lamented afterwards that he had 'rocked the late movement in its cradle' but had not been permitted 'to follow it to the grave'.[46]

MERCHANTS, MINING CAPITALISTS AND THE STATE

Although Governor Southey was an imperialist and an opponent of colonial self-government, he was committed to the development of colonial capitalism in Griqualand West. He chose a path of economic development, which favoured colonial accumulation in the mines and in agriculture, but did not restrict the expansion of British commerce into the interior of South Africa. De Kiewiet was incorrect when he wrote that Southey was opposed to the development of mining companies. Southey was not, but what he was opposed to was a non-colonial monopoly of the mines. This would be to the advantage of foreign shareholders and not colonial capitalists. Southey supported small-scale digging in the mines because it was the most beneficial pattern of economic activity for the expansion of the commodity market in Kimberley. De Kiewiet failed to emphasize that Southey's support for the small digger was, in fact, a support for colonial merchants.

Merchants were the most powerful group of men in Kimberley. The *Diamond News* went further and suggested that merchant capital was the dominant economic force in South Africa. 'It regulates almost everything', its editor wrote, 'and disposes of men and measures after its own supreme and semi-regal way'.[47] On the one hand, merchants 'disposed' of men through the economic power they exercised over traders whom they supplied with goods and to whom they extended credit. In Kimberley 34 general merchants, usually supported by firms on the coast, supplied 133 canteenkeepers and 258 storekeepers. On the other hand, merchants 'disposed' of measures through direct access to government and the ability to write legislation to suit their interests. In general, merchants remained loyal to Southey during the rebellion and called for troops to restore state authority. 'The injury to trade in one month is greater than the cost of transport for the troops', said one leading merchant, 'the mere digger does not feel this so much'.[48]

Kimberley very rapidly became the largest market town in South Africa. Port Elizabeth merchants, in particular, found the greater share of their trade moving north to the Kimberley which, in the words of the *Diamond News*, became a 'branch establishment' of the port town.[49] The nature of the relationship between coastal merchants and interior commerce is best illustrated by way of example. Adolph Mosenthal and Company was the leading Port Elizabeth general merchant. In the early 1870s the firm had a capital of £500,000, and it required only a small portion of this for trading as it had £300,000 on fixed deposit in various banks. They never discounted bills and only required banking services for bills of exchange on their London firm. They dealt in hides, mohair, wool and ostrich feathers, which they bought through an elaborate system of country trading constituents, whom they supplied with goods. Lilienfeld Brothers in Hopetown were their gateway house to the interior and it was through this small firm that Mosenthals first speculated in Diamond Field business and property. But in 1873 they appointed a specialist, Anton Dunkelsbuhler, as their diamond agent in Kimberley. In addition, they supported Alphonse Levy, a gun and general merchant, who in 1875 owned property worth £10,000. They supplied him with goods and credit on a six months basis. Like other large Port Elizabeth merchants, such as L. Lippert and Company, D. Blaine and Company and A. C. Stewart and Company, Mosenthals exemplified the dominant trend of supporting trading constituents in Kimberley.[50]

Kimberley merchants rapidly became men of property. The business activities of James Ferguson, the leading general merchant, extended from renting buildings to speculating in labour recruiting and claims. He owned stores, a steam flour mill, iron and brick houses and ten farms in the Transvaal. In late 1874 he sold 49 buildings, which included some excellent properties in Main Street: Vine Hotel, Richmond Dining Rooms, Vickers Brothers' offices, Milligan's Boot Depot, Crewes and Sons, and the Morning Star public house. Even after this sale of property Ferguson was an economic power in Kimberley. At the beginning of 1875 his stock of merchandise was worth £40,000 and his books showed him £30,000 in the black. A wide collection of small businessmen were dependent on his ability to discount their bills at banks in Kimberley. He in turn owed £20,000 to L. Lippert and Company of Port Elizabeth and, as the Rebellion was damaging his ability to pay off his debt, he was vociferous in demanding troops to put down the rebels.[51]

Still, the extension of credit did not place the creditor in a position of unrivalled power. Coastal merchants could not collect on bad debts. There was a firmly judged limit to credit based on the 'character' of the debtor; the power to inflict bankruptcy was sparingly used. Henry Tucker was a case in point. He was supported by a Port Elizabeth firm which had the power to wind up his business when it pleased because of unpaid debts. The firm's agent on the Fields, Charles Rudd, was loyal to Southey, but he did not 'dispose' of Tucker by forcing him into insolvency. Bankruptcy would have suited neither the economic interests of the supporting firm, nor the political interests of the Southey government in trying to find a peaceful solution to the Rebellion.[52]

Merchants approved of the liberal policy of the Southey government towards Africans. They praised the Governor for his 'paternal regard for the coloured races',[53] which manifested itself in an ideology of equal rights for all propertied men. The material basis of this ideology lay in the implications for the expansion of commerce of the large African population on the Fields:

> A people are being induced to work who never worked before and thousands of native men obtain an insight into the value of civilisation and industry.[54]

Africans spent wages worth between £250,000 and £500,000 a year in Kimberley and took manufactured goods back into the interior. Guns were the most popular commodity and a rapid migration of African labourers meant a rapid turnover in the sale of guns.[55]

Gun sales were one of the most striking sights in early Kimberley. 'At knock off time', wrote one pioneer digger:

> our Kaffirs used to pass down streets of tented shops owned by white traders and presided over by yelling black salesmen whirling guns above their heads. These they discharged in the air crying: *"Reka, reka, mona mtskeka"*. [Buy, buy, a gun]. A deafening din. A sight never to be forgotten.[56]

In the 15 months between April 1873 and June 1874, 75,000 guns were sold in Kimberley. The Tower musket, on sale for around £4 (it cost £2 in Cape Town), was the most popular model in the market, and Africans usually earned such a gun after three months minework. Some Africans bought more expensive breech-loading guns. In 1874 Sekhukhune's brother, Marmaree, took home a gun which had cost £25. The gun trade was a very profitable business and it was the one trade that Southey did not meddle with when he increased commercial taxation. In 1875 traders carried a stock of 200,000 guns and it was difficult to keep up sales in view of the decline in African labour migration.[57]

Southey's liberal African policy was appreciated by colonial blacks, 'persons of colour, Her Majesty's subjects who have come hither from the Cape Colony, Natal and Basutoland'.[58] Southey distinguished them from both Europeans and Africans from the interior. He estimated that most colonial blacks lived with their families, and with three to a family there were 3,000 to 4,000 on the Fields.[59] In April 1875 Southey wrote to Barkly that 1,000 men wanted to enrol as special constables:

> Basutos, Zulus, Griquas and other natives have tendered their services but I am sure you will agree with me that it would be a lamentable spectacle to see such men as compose the great body of the Rebels, put down by force of arms by means of these Coloured men, however loyal and respectable they may be . . . [60]

Other non-Europeans did not place their faith in Southey's government and chose to leave the Fields. Malay cab-owners, cab-drivers and skilled workers left for Cape Town loaded with moveable property. But Southey was disappointed where he did expect to find popular support. Europeans did not enrol in great numbers in support of his government; only some 200 'mechanics and old soldiers' volunteered as special constables.[61]

Southey's liberalism shaped his attitude to agriculture and mining in Griqualand West. He planned the even development of capitalism in the Province and wanted to capitalise the farming land before a company monopoly drove the population away from the mines. He wanted to build an irrigation scheme at Fourteen Streams, using the state to raise the necessary capital, but he was unable to issue British land titles which alone would lure young men from the eastern Cape. In his view, with the lands of the Province 'occupied and turned to account by industrious farmers, the Mines will be of less importance to the government than they have been or are'.[62]

The issue of British titles to land was a vexed one before 1875. New titles could not be issued before rival claims for farms had been settled and Southey, who had had previous experience in this field on the eastern frontier,[63] set up a Land Commission. Problems arose from the fact that British annexation had been based on the belief that Griqualand West belonged to the Griqua. When it came to an assessment of occupation on the ground it became clear that there were other African peoples involved, particularly in the richest area between the Vaal and Harts Rivers. There were 1,780 farms of 3,000 morgen each in Griqualand West. The farms differed widely in value, but there was an ever present expectation of finding new diamond mines. Fertile river farms were especially sought after and many men became active in land speculation. When the Land Commission was accused of corruption, a Land Court was established to adjudicate competing claims for land. This was a lengthy process and the result was that no British land titles had been issued before the rebellion. The government was held responsible and accused of corruption in favour of particular land jobbers.[64]

Southey's desire to capitalise the agricultural land of the Province was the basis of his policy in the mines. He was certainly more successful in restricting the growth of a monopoly of claims in the mines, and so maintaining a thriving economic centre to the colony, than in implementing his plans for the countryside. Southey's claim policy was revealed during the passage of the 1874 Mining Ordinance in the Legislative Council. Currey summed up what the Executive regarded as its most important clause:

> The Ordinance had been drafted several months ago, at a time when the general feeling seemed to be against working of mines by companies, and it had been thought desirable to restrict the issue of licences to dig to individuals. Since then public opinion had undergone a change and it was now felt some portions at least of the mines could not be worked other than by companies. At all events it was not now regarded as a dangerous doctrine to hold that companies might be of use.[65]

In fact, a number of public companies had been formed.[66] For example, in January 1874 R. E. Wallace and Company, in which Charles Rudd was a partner, bought 16 claims and formed the Old De Beers Company with a capital of £8,000. The directors of this company were interesting: Henry Green, Francis Baring Gould, George Manning, H. W. Hull, G. H. Hull, J. Birbeck, J. H. W. Rausch and Henry Tucker. By August the company had failed and its property was added to a block of 50 claims owned by Jones, Rudd, and Company and Bayly, Tarry and Company, two firms whose partners were to make their mark in the Kimberley mines. The other public companies also failed, although private partnerships thrived in the pits.[67]

Originally there was no restriction on claimownership in the 1874 Mining Bill. Any limit on the number of claims was left to the discretion of the Mining Boards. But this did not suit 'Tramway' Hall. He was one of the largest claimowners in Kimberley mine and valued his property at £20,000. He began a campaign for what he called the 'free trade' in claims, and wanted it actually stated in the Mining Bill that there was no restriction of the number of claims a man or a company could own. Southey became suspicious of Hall's insistence on this point and he discovered that Hall wanted to float a large company in London. He was told that Hall and others hoped to make a quarter of a million out of the promotion of the venture.[68] This speculative profit was galling to Southey in itself, but more importantly it threatened his development plans for Griqualand West. A British monopoly of Kimberley Mine would destroy the prosperity of the Province, 'for not only would far less labour and superintendence be employed but the profits whatever they were would go out of the country and into the pockets of foreign shareholders'.[69] This was precisely what had happened, as Southey knew, to the Namaqua copper mines.

Southey's solution was to inhibit the import of foreign and British capital. He did this by inserting the 18th clause into the Mining Ordinance. Instead of leaving it up to the Mining Boards, the clause restricted the number of claims that could be owned by an individual, firm or company to ten. Francis Oats, the Provincial Engineer, explained the effect of this restriction on ownership:

> The local capitalist knows very well how to evade the law, and it is done over and over again, while the claimholder who disposes of his ground suffers an injustice through the ground not realizing as much as it would undoubtedly had the home or foreign capitalist legitimate means of competing for the ground, for no one will be found to invest money in a mine (away from the place) under such a paltry restriction.[70]

While this allowed the local growth of companies, it placed a crucial obstacle in the path of the grandiose scheme of Hall and made him a bitter enemy of the government.

Hall sponsored a movement for the reform of the ten claim law. In late 1874 he bought the *Mining Gazette* and used it as his mouthpiece. He was not a popular man with diggers, but he won the support of members of the Executive. Both Sydney Shippard, the Attorney-General, and Richard Giddy, the Treasurer-General, believed Hall was an honest man with property at risk. Giddy even passed him the minutes of the Executive Council. Both men supported his company scheme and were bribed with the offer of shares if it ever came to fruition. Popular agitation and rebellion played into his hands by depreciating the value of claims, reducing competition in the diamond market and disrupting production through creating a shortage of labour.[71]

Hall argued that a large company would also rally the price of diamonds in London and he hoped to draw the principal diamond shippers into his scheme. The shippers in Kimberley represented the major London rough diamond importers. 'It is they who bring the capital to the Fields', wrote the *Diamond News*, '... and without [them] ... the mines must soon collapse.'[72] All diamonds eventually found their way into the hands of the shippers for export, but were bought and sold numerous times in the local Kimberley market by dealers and '*kopje-wallopers*'. The shippers were diamond specialists who knew the value of the stones and the vicissitudes of the seasonal European market. It was one of the most secretive commodity markets in the world, but subject to manipulation and combinations:

> ... the market riggers at home had begun to fear that they had done too much in forcing a fall, for they knew that every fall had a reaction on the Fields through which the local buyers got diamonds cheaper, and consequently obtained facilities for competing profitably even with those who were rigging the market.[73]

Most diggers did not understand the diamond market. They knew that they were dependent on the prices the shippers paid and that they could not refuse to sell diamonds or wait for a better market.

The shippers took different attitudes to the Rebellion. If they supported the government there was a sound economic reason. One major London diamond importer, M. J. Posno,[74] supported Southey. Posno was also the Chairman of the London and South African Exploration Company which by 1875 owned the two farms on which the Dutoitspan and Bultfontein mines were situated. Consequently, he had a stake in the maintenance of a large population on his property, which the ten claim clause would do much to ensure. Mosenthals also supported the Southey government. Their general merchant business was still, at this time, more important than dealing in diamonds or investing in claims.[75]

Other shippers had an interest in the abolition of the ten claim restriction on claimownership. Abolition was a necessary condition for the investment of British and foreign capital in the mines. This was an important issue for Jules Porges and Company, although the firm was never an open backer of the rebels. At the time Jules Porges and Company was the largest Cape diamond importer in London[76] with £30,000 invested in the business.[77] Jules Porges was the London partner, while Charles Mege lived in Kimberley and employed Julius Wernher as his clerk. Like other major diamond merchants, such as J. B. Robinson, Lewis and Marks, Paddon Brothers, Thomas Lynch and Isidore Gordon, Jules Porges could only see a future for the diamond industry based on a rapid consolidation of claimownership. Governor Southey referred to this group, when he wrote of 'German diamond merchants' as the 'wire-pullers' behind the Rebellion.[78]

While these diamond merchants preferred to keep a low profile, after the Rebellion had been declared their interests were represented publicly in Kimberley through the Moderate Party. Its best known member was J. B. Robinson, who had rapidly grown from a small town trader to a large diamond merchant with substantial investments in claims. When the Standard Bank had refused him an open credit for £60,000 to buy diamonds, he had secured the support of Joseph Brothers, experienced London diamond brokers.[79] Robinson was an economic power in the local diamond market and he had a lot in common with W. A. Hall. Both were on the Committee of the Moderate Party, which also included A. A. Rothschild, leading auctioneer, and P. L. Buyskes, the dismissed Magistrate. The Party entered the public arena when the Legislative Council decided to call for troops.[80]

The Moderate Party did not relish the arrival of British troops or the consequent enquiries into the causes of the Rebellion. They knew it would be suggested that Tucker was the tool of their Party. In the words of the radical rebels the Moderate Party was 'like a shield raised up to protect the breast of Tucker'.[81] This was one point on which both the Governor and the radical rebels agreed. Southey's privately expressed views to Barkly on the role of the 'wire-pullers' found its way into the government newspaper, the *Diamond News*:

> It is not the many that armed themselves that are to be blamed. They were misguided by the few who, under the pretence that they were patriotically bent on preserving the rights and liberties of the people, fanned the passions of the many into a blaze to serve a band of confederated conspirators. We know now who provided the sinews of war and under the cloak of "Moderation" worked the puppets that are branded rebels.[82]

And it was this version of capitalist conspiracy that de Kiewiet accepted in his analysis of the rebellion. But he made one major change to Southey and his government's view of the affair. Instead of the capitalists fanning 'the passions of the many', de Kiewiet found an agitator in the 'incredible personage' of Alfred Aylward, 'assassin, Fenian and correspondent of the *Daily Telegraph*'.[83] But, share-workers and radical rebels required no agitator to arouse their fears and frustrations about losing health and wealth on the richest diamond fields in the world.

MONEY-LENDERS

Money-lenders played an important part in precipitating the Rebellion through bankrupting diggers by lending to them at enormous rates of interest.[84] The period between late 1873 and June 1876 was one of uneven fortune for diggers. In 1873 and 1876 there were severe slumps in the price of diamonds and throughout the two and a half years mining was interrupted by falls of reef and heavy summer rains. Clearing a claim of reef or water was unproductive labour and diggers had to borrow working capital from usurers. They demanded a high rate of interest and often took over the claims of struggling diggers. Governor Southey explained what happened:

> A man wanted say £200: he had a claim worth £1,000: he could not get the money from a Bank because he could not mortgage his claim: he was therefore driven to a lender who could advance the money for a month or so at 10%, taking a cession of the claim which, in many cases I have been told, never got back to its owner: the 10% per month eat it up quite quickly.[85]

This was the position before the middle of 1874 when Southey changed the law to encourage banks to finance digging.

The 1874 Mining Ordinance made it possible to mortgage claims to banks. In the second half of 1874 the Cape of Good Hope Bank lent £35,000 to diggers at the moderate rate of 1 to 1.5 per cent per month, but the Standard Bank, the major imperial bank in the Cape, steered clear of the mines, regarding diggers as 'needy, unmoneyed customers'.[86] In general, the banks did not satisfy the needs of struggling diggers and largely confined their business to discounting commercial bills and advancing money against diamonds on confirmed credits. Consequently, the lack of available finance for digging restricted the development of the industry and forced diggers into the hands of usurers or private discounters.

'Tramway' Hall was the most notorious usurer in Kimberley. He had been a bankrupt in Bradford before he emigrated to the Cape Colony in 1872. He borrowed £3,200 from his sister-in-law, Margaret Walsh, and invested some of this sum in loans to diggers and the remainder in a tramway venture under the name of Walsh and Company. He discounted diggers' promissory notes at the Standard Bank, but at the end of 1872 the bank began to have doubts about the nature of Hall's security. He had taken the cession of claims from the men he lent money. Disliking claims as a security, the Standard Bank also considered that his capital was insufficient for the accommodation that he was receiving. As a result Hall took his business to the more amenable Cape of Good Hope Bank. He continued to lend money and to discount diggers' bills. He expanded his network of debt by employing agents to seek out business and to collect his interest. Johan de Beer, Accountant-General of the South African Republic, was one of his first agents and he had excellent contacts among needy Afrikaner diggers. J. H. W. Rausch, who was a prominent rebel leader, was another of his debt collecting agents. Hall was certainly well placed to promote a monster company in London, with his tramway in the West End and his money-lending bringing him claims by default.[87]

Numerous professional men pursued usury as a by-product of their legitimate business. Lawyers acted for principals living away from Kimberley while others established themselves as professional money-lenders. In 1873 J. J. G. Rhodes and L. P. Ford, both attorneys, formed the Kimberley Loan Company with a capital of £12,000 and earned a 60 per cent dividend in its first financial year. The prominent member of the Moderate Party, A. A. Rothschild, had £5,000 invested in his auctioneering business and a similar sum earning interest from diggers. Even middling men of moderate means lent money. A manager of a Port Elizabeth merchant firm, D. J. Bouwer, had £1,200 invested in claims and loans to diggers. Most of these men lent money to make money. They did not see usury as a way to take-over claims in the mines, as W. A. Hall did, and they sold claims if diggers defaulted.[88]

One prominent rebel leader, Gustavus Blanch, was driven to disaffection by usury. In 1873 he was associated with Hall's tramway company and he was in favour of consolidating claim ownership.[89] He was a claim agent and wanted to see a rise in the value of claims. But in 1874 he ran into financial problems:

> I had previously lent a friend of mine some money and also endorsed a bill for him. The sudden nature of the crisis prevented him from meeting it. I became liable and was arrested for the amount, which I paid from my own resources, and have never had one shilling back from the person who was the real debtor.[90]

Still, he managed to recover his position. In June 1875 he owned claims worth £2,000, mortgaged for £400, and his 'character' at the Standard Bank was a respectable one. They did not believe that his political offence would affect his financial position.[91] But prior to the rebellion he was in straightened circumstances, which were aggravated by the enormous interest taken and penalties imposed by usurers. Usury struck at the heart of his occupation as a claim agent. At the time of the rebellion it was very difficult to buy or sell a claim owing to the proportion which had fallen into the hands of money-lenders.

LANDED PROPRIETORS

Both Governors Southey and Barkly believed that the main cause of the Rebellion lay in the insecurity of claim tenure and the fear of rising rents.[92] At the root of the problem was the private ownership of the farms on which the mines were situated. Vooruitzicht was owned by a syndicate of colonial merchants led by Dunell, Ebden and Company of Port Elizabeth. At the time of the Rebellion the other two farms were owned by the London and South African Exploration Company, whose most important shareholders were the Posno and Mosenthal families. These landlords wanted to extract as much rent as possible from the mines. But the Southey government refused to recognise their ownership of the minerals in the soil, a dispute based on differences between Orange Free State and Cape quitrent tenure. While the adjudication of the dispute was pending, the government collected claim rents, leaving the landowners to collect revenue from renting stands for business and dwelling purposes.

The issue of rent proved to be a time bomb whose fuse was measured by the progress through the courts of the case of Alfred Ebden vs. William Ling. Ling believed that diggers were entitled to a dwelling stand as part of their claim licences. The owners of Vooruitzicht disagreed and in October 1873 took Ling to court over rent arrears. Ling's defence was that Ebden was not the legal owner of the farm; he had no contract with Ebden's 'fraudulent' syndicate; and that he had a 'digger's right' to a dwelling stand through custom and occupation. The Resident Magistrate did not find Ling's argument convincing and Ebden won the case. Ling appealed to a higher court amidst public demands that the government buy Vooruitzicht, but Southey could not move as it was still undecided whether the state or the landlords owned the minerals in the soil.[93]

On the strength of the proprietors' success in the Magistrate Court, they decided to raise stand rents. In February 1874, when their intentions of raising dwelling rents by 25 per cent and business rents by 100 per cent were published in a circular, there was a public outcry:

> The braggart insolence of this circular is only equalled by the unparalleled rapacity exhibited in it. No pack of wolves ever hunted down their prey more savagely than do this purse-proud inflated pack of hungry proprietors hunt down the men who are here to improve the condition of their lives by honest industry and fair dealing.[94]

Merchants and traders were the most important tenants on Vooruitzicht and they valued their stands and businesses at £600,000. They formed a Standholders Defence League to oppose the proprietors. It was led by the most influential general merchants on the Fields: Ferguson, West, Bayly, Gowie and Goodchild.[95] These men rented a good deal of property in Kimberley's diamond market and sub-let stands for diamond and other offices. In view of the 'handsome ransoms' made by merchants, one of the proprietors could not understand why they 'should be stigmatised as cormorants, robbers, bloodsuckers etc. because they thought fit to do what everyone else was doing'.[96]

Southey was forced to act on the rent issue by the result of Ling's appeal against the Magistrate's judgement. In February 1874 Recorder Barry sitting in the Circuit Court reversed the judgement in the case of Ebden vs. Ling in the lower court, but he opened the way for another case when he pronounced that Ling could be regarded as a trespasser as he had never paid rent or regarded the syndicate as his landlord. The judgement made it clear that Southey had to take steps to prevent a severe disruption of the peace in Kimberley. 'I find myself acting', he wrote, 'in opposition to the interests of some of my oldest and most intimate friends.'[97] In particular, Southey was thinking of John Merriman and Tom Barry, who were members of the landed syndicate. Southey passed an Ordinance which revoked a previous admission that the state had no right to minerals and precious stones. This gave the government legal control of claim rents, but in another Ordinance Southey went even further and limited the amount of rent that the proprietors could charge for stands.

For Southey these were popular measures which he hoped would defuse an explosive situation. 'I have received the support, morally, of the "people" ', he wrote:

> for I consider that the would-be rioters are but few as compared with the well-disposed and loyal inhabitants but an attempt made by the government in obedience to the demands of the proprietors would, I consider, reverse the order of things and range all persons interested in claims against us. The claimholders would refuse to pay and we have no force here to compel them. Our law courts will be laughed at for judgements could not be enforced and we shall be a people without a government, for I depend entirely upon the moral support of the people.[98]

While this pragmatic approach was certainly popular with diggers and merchants, it was totally inimical to the interests of the landed proprietors. They did not take this interference with their rent-rolls lightly, as a figure in the region of £30,000 per annum, their current claim and stand income, was the bottom-line for their shareholders.[99] The London and South African Exploration Company had close contact with the Colonial Office and Southey found out that some of its shareholders 'were too influential and powerful to have their interests interfered with'.[100] Acting in concert the landed proprietors succeeded in having both ordinances vetoed by the Colonial Office.

The rent issue remained a threatening one for aspirant capitalists. In February 1875 their worst fears were confirmed in the judgement of the re-trial of Ebden vs. Ling. The Acting Recorder found in favour of the landlords, but he also ruled that they were free to raise rents at their pleasure. An arbitrary increase in rents affected all diggers, and it would cripple the prospect of floating a company in London. Hall told a packed meeting after the judgement:

> If the government failed against the proprietors those gentlemen could charge as well £500 as £50. What makes men patriotic? An attack on their property. This might be a selfish motive, but it was a strong one. What ever must be done must be done gently. Politics must not be mixed up in business. These matters should be discussed only by men having an interest or a claim in the country. Claims or stands – men of property. It was unnecessary to talk of revolution. That might in due time become necessary but it was to be avoided till the last . . . [101]

Hall was a man of property with an enormous gamble about to go wrong. He knew that his company could only be floated if claims were capitalised at a fixed rental. Without such an essential legal title to the diamond property no European investor would take an interest in the mine. Talk of rent increases threatened to damage Hall's speculation once and for all. But Southey knew he could not enforce the exactions of the proprietors against the will of the people and it was in February 1875 that he began to negotiate for the state purchase of Vooruitzicht farm.

The landed proprietors of Vooruitzicht also had plans for a company monopoly in Kimberley mine. In 1874 they negotiated for the sale of the farm for about £150,000 to a London based company.[102] John Merriman conducted a long correspondence with King, Son and Company, who had been instrumental in forming a company to take over the Namaqua copper mines. Merriman explained that the best way to create a monopoly in Kimberley mine would be 'to starve them out by raising the licence'.[103] Alternatively, an alliance could be struck with the large claimowners, but the point of the scheme would be to clear diggers off the farm. King, Son and Company were not enthusiastic about the proposal, on account of the legal confusion over the land title, the restriction on claimownership and the weakness of the Southey government.

By the end of 1874 it was clear that a London company would not buy Vooruitzicht, and so the proprietors set about getting the best deal they could in the Cape Colony. Private talks with the Cape government began in February 1875, but formal negotiations between Merriman and Sir Henry Barkly only began in March. The landed syndicate put in an opening offer of £128,000. They agreed privately to accept £100,000 and to go to arbitration if Barkly offered less than £75,000, a figure which would still give a good profit to those who had bought into the syndicate at the highest price.[104]

The landed proprietors used devious means to force the Griqualand West state to pay their price for the farm. Southey was led to believe that there were other buyers in the market for the farm and it was James Ferguson, leading merchant, and R. W. Murray, loyal editor, who became paid agents of the landed proprietors. In March 1875, Ferguson and Murray left for Cape Town in pursuit of a contract to supply African labour to the Cape government. They went via Port Elizabeth where on the 19 March Ferguson dined with August Barsdorf, a partner in L. Lippert and Company, his supporting house. Barsdorf suggested that Ferguson could earn a commission from the land syndicate by selling the farm Vooruitzicht to the state. As Ferguson had refused to pay rent and owed £700 for the current year to the syndicate, discussion with Alfred Ebden promised to be difficult in view of pending court cases. But Barsdorf acted as mediator and Ebden was convinced that Ferguson could assist in pushing the sale of the farm through quickly and at the proprietors' price of £100,000. Ferguson signed an agreement with Ebden that he would 'save the proprietors from all expenses and delay of arbitration' over the price of the farm for the 'consideration' of £4,000.[105] Both Ferguson and Murray, who was apparently also party to the business, then went on to Cape Town ostensibly about the labour contract. Murray saw Governor Barkly and then he and Ferguson returned to Kimberley separately.

Once back in Kimberley Ferguson set about earning his 'consideration'. He selected men to guarantee the £100,000 purchase price, that is, if the sale was not ratified by Lord Carnarvon, he and his friends would take over the property at the proprietors' price.[106] George Paton, partner to Henry Green, first put the idea to Southey and by May the Governor was confident that the full sum was covered. He wrote to Barkly that 'it was most desirable' to 'close with the Proprietors' as a company had offered the same price and he feared they would lose the farm.[107]

The truth about the subscription pledge for the private purchase of the farm emerged a year and a half later. Murray, then a Member of the Legislative Council, sued Ferguson for his share of the £4,000 'consideration'. In his judgement, Recorder Barry said:

> The case is a painful and perplexing one. Whatever be the judgement of the court the conversations in evidence reflect no credit on either of the litigants or the two owners who took an active part in the sale. Secret services were unquestionably employed to screw up the price and unduly induce the government to pay the £100,000 demanded by the proprietors.[108]

Despite this exposition of dishonesty, the sale of the farm did defuse the rebellion. But the proprietors took no credit for that.

CONCLUSION

In the final analysis the Southey government placed a brake on the development of the productive forces through its restrictions on claim combination and its inability to regulate monopoly rents, both of which hindered the import of British and foreign capital. Local accumulation proceeded with some vigour under Southey's rule and his replacement in November 1875 cleared the way for metropolitan investment in claims and the final dispossession of share-workers. De Kiewiet's analysis pointed in this direction but his major errors lay in an identification of Southey's liberalism with 'diggers' democracy'; his failure to recognize share-working as the dominant relation of production; and his assertion that the rebellion consigned Africans to the status of labourers. Southey's liberalism was, in fact, based on the rule of merchant capital and an attempt to capitalise the agricultural land of Griqualand West. The passing of Southey's liberalism did not turn Africans into labourers, as Africans continued to own property in Kimberley. Rather, the emergence of a class of mining capitalists through the Rebellion began a new phase of production in which share-working was phased out and an attempt was made to subordinate labourers to rigorous industrial discipline.

5

Company mining

Southey lost his post as Governor as a result of the Black Flag Revolt. Before and after the rebellion he justified his action by pointing to the sense of insecurity felt by property owners and his inability to do anything about rents and land titles. However, Governor Barkly believed that Southey had misjudged events by prosecuting William Cowie and proclaiming a rebellion.[1] While Barkly regarded this as unfortunate, he found it more difficult to pass over the conduct and attitudes of J. B. Currey, the Secretary to Government. Currey had advocated martial law and minuted: 'I should deeply deplore bloodshed, but I should not shrink from it if it were necessary'.[2] It was sentiments such as these that spelt the end of Southey's rule in Griqualand West. In August Lord Carnarvon wrote to Sir Henry Barkly about the poor finances of the Province and, as part of a package of economies, he sacked Southey and Currey.

In November 1875 a new government under Major W. O. Lanyon as Administrator was introduced with a brief to clear up the land problems of Griqualand West and prepare the way for the annexation of the Province to the Cape. At the same time Colonel Crossman was appointed to enquire into both colonial finances and the grievances that had led to the Rebellion. In January 1876 he began his enquiry, reporting in February on the Province's finances and in May on the causes of the Black Flag Revolt.[3] His May report defused the grievances of the Moderate Party and the respectable rebels; there he spelt out a framework for a new order based on company mining. Crucially Crossman recommended that the ten claim restriction be abolished, and as Vooruitzicht now belonged to the state, the path was prepared for metropolitan investment.

After July 1876 British and foreign capital poured into the mines for investment in claims and mining machinery. Private companies rapidly came to dominate the mines beginning the first industrial boom-slump cycle of production on the Fields (1877–85). The acquisition of steam engines to cope with the growing depth of Kimberley Mine began the boom. In 1877 there were only 16 steam engines in operation in the mines, but by 1881 the total number had increased to 306 engines. Diamond output and labour productivity grew by leaps and bounds and by 1879 the average rate of profit of private companies in Kimberley Mine was a handsome 30 per cent. The new order over which Major Lanyon presided until 1878, followed by Sir

Company mining

Charles Warren in 1879 and James Rose-Innes in 1880 before annexation to the Cape in October, was more receptive to the requirements of accumulation based on company mining in which share-working was less and less common.[4]

Yet, the commitment of the administrators to mining capital was not unequivocal. The Province still had to balance its books and, in the face of continuing problems over settling land claims and selling farms, revenue from the mines remained crucial. In this respect echoes of Southey can be heard in the pages of Warren's despatches. Warren knew that 1,200 small holders in a mine paid six to eight times the revenue of a monopoly company. While he recognised that the age of mining capitalists had arrived he believed 'they should not be specially assisted in rolling and swallowing up all the small claim holders who are worth £20,000 to £30,000 each and who form the backbone of the community'. Moreover, small holders spent money in the Province, while under the rule of capital 'the diamond market will become a monopoly in the hands of a few foreign financiers, who will grow rich in impoverishing South Africa'.[5]

DIAMOND MERCHANTS AND THE DIAMOND TRADE

Diamond merchants, the most important group of men in the Kimberley diamond market, played a central role in the post-rebellion economic order. They were the specialists who bought diamonds for shipment to London and either brought capital into the Colony or arranged a credit in England through a colonial bank. Best known in the early days were Julius Pam, a partner in Julius Pam and Company, Moritz Joseph, a partner in the major London firm of Joseph Brothers, and Charles Mege, a partner in Jules Porges and Company, the largest diamond shipper through the Standard Bank.[6] Beneath the merchants in the hierarchy of the market were the accredited agents, who represented principals in Europe or the Cape and were originally 'clerks in large firms, commercial travellers or shopmen',[7] men like A. W. Davis for the London and Paris firm of brokers, Ochs Brothers, H. B. Webb for the Amsterdam firm of diamond factory owners, M. J. Posno and Company, Max Gammius for the Hamburg merchant, D. Lippert and Company and Henri Jacobs for the Parisian jeweller, Oulman and Company. The largest Port Elizabeth merchant, Adolph Mosenthal and Sons, was represented by Anton Dunkelsbuhler who was later to become one of the best-known diamond merchants associated with the Kimberley mines. Generally these agents knew little about the value of diamonds and less about the intricacies of the European markets; they traded on each other, on shippers and also sent diamonds directly to their principals.

While established diamond brokers formed part of the apex of the Kimberley diamond trade together with the agents and merchants, there was another type of diamond broker who possessed nowhere near the

74

£5,000 required to become established in the higher echelons of the trade.[8] These were the *kopje-wallopers*, who in the early days numbered amongst their members Barney Barnato, and who earned their name through living on their wits, cheating the Afrikaner diggers and scavenging the sorting-tables near the mines for diamonds to sell.[9] They rarely sold to shippers but to local dealers who speculated in small parcels of stones bought and sold as often as five times a day.[10]

The increase in the number of mining companies after the Rebellion led to a declining slice of the diamond trade for local dealers and *kopje-wallopers* as companies preferred to deal with respected agents and shippers. In the early 1880s 20 shippers exported the majority of diamonds from Kimberley to London, but only eight firms dominated the market each exporting around £300,000 worth of diamonds a year. These firms were in order of prominence: Jules Porges and Company, represented by Paul Keil and from 1884 by Alfred Beit; A. Mosenthal and Sons, represented by Paul Dreyfus; Anton Dunkelsbuhler, now a principal in his own right, represented by J. E. Abrahams; Barnato Brothers, established in London in only 1880, represented by Woolf Joel; Joseph Brothers, represented by Moritz Joseph; Isaac Lewis and Sammy Marks, represented by Barnet Lewis; Ochs Brothers, represented by Arthur Davis; and Julius Pam and Company, represented by Ludwig Breitmeyer. In the same league of export as these major firms was the mining company, Compagnie Française, represented by Otto Staib, who shipped its production directly to London. The remainder of the market was shared out between firms like Martin Lilienfeld and Company, represented by Sigismund Neumann, at the top end and Krauss Brothers at the bottom end.[11] Four of the big eight and seven of the remaining 12 firms had been in the diamond trade prior to the Cape discoveries: only two firms were formed in Kimberley, Barnato Brothers and Lewis and Marks; and two others, Mosenthal and Dunkelsbuhler, had a special advantage in the trade through their association with members of the Salamons family, which had been importing diamonds from India since the 1740s.[12]

The majority of diamonds were bought in the Kimberley market, but in the early 1880s some companies began to ship their production, or at least some of it, directly to London. This trend was not wholly supported by shippers, who usually specialised in particular types of diamonds and preferred to buy from a selection of dealers and companies. However, companies needed to sell their production as soon as possible, and as a whole; only rarely could they afford to wait for the market. As the 1880s progressed companies began to sell regularly in both markets, appointing agents in London to facilitate the turnover of sales. By the end of the decade the number of dealers in the Kimberley market had declined to 50; they were dominated by 10 to 15 shippers. In 1889, on the establishment of a production monopoly, the local market was closed in favour of London, but it was reopened in the following year to encourage competition between major and minor merchants.[13]

Diamond merchants' profits were closely guarded secrets. The general trend, though, seems to have been towards a declining rate of profit over the whole period punctuated by exceptional periods of prosperity and the successes of temporary merchant combinations. In the 1870s there were widely different profit margins before company mining led to an equalisation of rates.[14] In the 1880s seven London importers, who appeared 'to understand each other', controlled the diamonds sent directly to Hatton Garden by companies.[15] One of the major shippers in the 1880s averaged out his annual profits over the decade at seven per cent. In 1881 he had a capital of £20,000 which by 1887 had grown to £36,000. Before the slump (1883–85) he turned over £20,000 worth of diamonds each month. In bad times as in 1885 he made a loss of £5,000 on his year's trading. In good times as in 1891, the best year ever for rough merchants and an exceedingly poor one for producers, he made a £20,000 profit.[16]

By the 1890s the diamond trade was largely in the hands of five major London importers, known as the Diamond Syndicate. Their rate of profit in the good year of 1891 was 15 to 16 per cent on a turnover of around £3 million of diamonds; we do not know what all the Syndicate members made, but Barnato Brothers made a trading profit of £60,000. These profit rates, while substantial in absolute terms were small compared to the returns on capital invested in mining, which in the late 1870s and in the late 1880s were around 30 per cent climbing in the late 1890s to 40 per cent. Certainly, by the turn of the century trading profits had been severely reduced and under new profit-sharing agreements with the producer fell to as low as four per cent.[17]

Diamond merchants depended on the banks for credit and a whole range of commercial services. Diamonds were, for the most part, sent to London through the post by the banks. They were either insured by the banks or the shippers. Merchants drew bills on their London firms and the banks advanced money in Kimberley for the purchase of diamonds. Often advances were made before diamonds were delivered to the banks. As the invoice value of diamonds exported varied against the fluctuating price in London, the banks took a margin of safety on its advance from 10 per cent to as much as 40 per cent; the banks would seldom advance more than £27,000 against an invoice value of £30,000. However, selected customers were allowed to negotiate bills against diamonds of equal value. For example, in 1883 Barnet Lewis was authorised to pass drafts on his London firm for up to £31,000 at any one time and the security was a fixed deposit of the same value held at the Kimberley branch of the Standard Bank. Once a month or every six weeks Lewis shipped a parcel of diamonds. His normal practice was to take his parcel sorted into different packets to the Standard manager. Then, Lewis weighed each packet and the manager checked their value against the detailed invoice. The parcel was then placed in a strong tin box, sealed with Lewis' seal and sent off to the London office of the Standard Bank. Once there the diamonds were given up when the draft had been accepted by Lewis' London firm or retired by rebate.[18]

Drafts, better known as bills of exchange, confirmed or unconfirmed by the London offices of local banks were sold under letters of credit issued by London firms. In other cases London banks issued letters of credit to merchants whose Kimberley representatives drew through the local banks on the credit issuer. An example of this latter case was Porges' arrangement with the London merchant or accepting houses, Kleinwort, Sons and Company and J. H. Schröder and Company, for his Kimberley representatives, Paul Keil or Alfred Beit, to draw on them. This meant that Porges borrowed the names of these two merchant bankers to obtain his diamonds before his drafts matured enabling him to operate on a scale well beyond his capital. However, once he began to borrow the names of other banks, including the Deutsche Bank, the Standard Bank refused to advance up to the full invoice value and took a margin.[19]

When the London importers had taken possession of their parcels they arranged sights for continental jewellery and cutting factory representatives, who travelled across the channel to buy rough diamonds. In the 1870s shoals of small buyers came to London from Amsterdam and importers only went abroad when they were over-stocked; an importer on the continent meant cheap diamonds and forced sales. However, by the beginning of the 1880s there had been a substantial concentration of capital in the rough and finished goods trade which had important implications for the operation of the Dutch cutting industry.

In the nineteenth century diamond cutting underwent a long-drawn-out industrial revolution. Before the 1840s it was largely a domestic industry in which outwork accounted for the largest number of carats cut and polished. However, in the 1830s and 1840s factories began to be built with horse- and steam-driven mills which were rented out at fixed rates to diamond workers. Cutters and polishers were independent artisans who worked with their own tools, employed assistants or apprentices as setters and contracted with jewellers to cut and polish their stones. In 1845, in a significant innovation in the industry, nearly all the Amsterdam brilliant jewellers, dominated by the Posno family, formed the Diamantslijperij–Maatschappij to build a giant steam-mill factory. Here workers were required to cut the factory owners' rough diamonds before they were allowed to contract with other jewellers. The only large jewellers outside the company, both of whom owned factories, were M. E. Coster and B. & L. Arons.

In the 1870s the discovery of diamonds at Kimberley inaugurated the 'Kaapse tijd' in Amsterdam. It was a period of plentiful employment and new opportunities for diamond workers. So-called *eigenwerk-makers* went into business on their own account; they bought their own rough stones, cut and polished them and sold their finished goods to French cut merchants. Some *eigenwerk-makers* even established their own factories and worked them on co-operative principles. Thus, the vast increase in the supply of rough stones from South Africa enabled many workers to become small-scale entrepreneurs, but the secular decline in the price of cut diamonds after 1873 made it extremely difficult for polishers and cutters, other than master craftsmen , to make more than their earlier weekly returns under the indirect control of the jewellers.[20]

Nonetheless, the emergence and expansion of *eigenwerk-makers* combined with the concentration of capital in the rough and cut trades, led to the erosion of the position of the old jewellers in the cutting industry; by 1885 their elimination was practically complete. In their place emerged a group of manufacturing jewellers, who built factories and directly employed diamond workers. Polishers now worked for factory owners on piece-wages, earning between 40s and 120s a week, less than an artisan in Kimberley. In 1887 it was reported that:

> the earnings of workmen employed in the Amsterdam trade are gradually decreasing and probably will continue to do so, as the new system of large works conducted on wage payments and with powerful mechanical appliances develops.[21]

The reference to mechanisation was more with Antwerp than Amsterdam in mind; Antwerp cut large stones while Amsterdam specialised in small stones. Much of the work done in Amsterdam factories was not done on account of the new group of manufacturing jewellers. By the end of the 1880s working for London and Paris account became increasingly common and it was 'a known fact that much of the capital employed'[22] in Amsterdam was controlled by London and Paris houses. In fact, capital had accumulated in the rough and cut trades and by-passed the under-capitalised Amsterdam cutting industry.

The wealthy cut diamond merchants were based in Paris, although sales were not concentrated in this centre of European fashion. The trade was seasonal and based on fairs throughout Europe. At the Leipzig *Ostermesse* in March and April merchants bought diamonds for the East European and Asian markets; at the annual fair at Nisji-Nowgorod in June and July Russian merchants stocked up for their clients; in August and September the Leipzig *Michaelmesse* provided a second stock-taking for merchants in the eastern market; and in October and November merchants bought in Paris for the west European and US markets with an eye on Christmas sales. Such seasonality combined with the fact that diamonds were a luxury commodity meant that the market was very sensitive to wars, political disturbances and depressions. Luxury markets were very easily disturbed. For example, at the end of the 1875 Turkey, a major cut diamond market, defaulted on its loans and in 1877 Russia declared war on her. This led to the collapse of the diamond market and the failure of cut diamond merchants in Paris, notably Joseph Halpern. European wars were a fundamentally destabilising factor in the finished diamond market before the emergence of the US as the primary diamond market in the 1890s.[23]

MINING CAPITALISTS AND MINING COMPANIES

After the rebellion a class of mineowners emerged drawn mainly from diggers, merchants and diamond merchants. They formed a 'very small section of the public' in Kimberley.[24] From the ranks of the diggers arose mining capitalists like the Newberry brothers, William Hall, William Knight, John Stanford, Daniel Francis, the Baring Gould brothers, the Marais brothers, Richard Atkins and Cecil Rhodes. The best known merchant-claimowner was James Ferguson, who bought into De Beers mine. Edward Wallace Tarry was probably the richest merchant who owned claims; he was worth £150,000 in 1881.[25] He took Charles Rudd, another merchant-claimowner into partnership in E. W. Tarry and Company, the largest importer of mining machinery on the Fields. The sphere of mining machinery sales enriched other men like Reginald Fenton, who invested substantially in Kimberley claims. But of all the mineowners it was the diamond merchants, men like Jules Porges, Isaac Lewis, Anton Dunkelsbuhler, Barney Barnato, Harry Mosenthal, Joseph Robinson and Alfred Beit, who bought up most claims in all the mines. Capital accumulated in the sphere of exchange was ploughed back into production after the Rebellion.

The state purchase of the Vooruitzicht estate after the Rebellion unleashed a period of rapid claim speculation. Between 1875 and 1876 the assessed value of Kimberley Mine doubled – De Beers was worth only a fifth of its richer neighbour while the other mines were not even assessed (see Table 2, Assessment value of diamond mines, 1874–90). Second class Kimberley claims were more in demand than first class claims near the reef: the former returned a 10s to £1 profit per load all the year round compared to the £2 per load of the latter but only for a third of the year. In March 1876 claim speculation came to an end when the price of diamonds collapsed by between 30 and 40 per cent. In July the banks in Kimberley began to call in loans and raised the discount rate to 20 per cent which virtually put an end to the discounting of new bills. In August nearly half the miners stopped work and where the banks had feared to lend the usurers now foreclosed. Those men with capital, largely diamond merchants, picked up claims on forced sales; within the space of four years the number of claimowners in Kimberley Mine was halved.[26]

During the crisis there was a major attempt to monopolise production in Kimberley Mine. In July 1876, in the aftermath of the second major fall in diamond prices, Chevalier Thomas Lynch,[27] the representative of Blaine, MacDonald and Company,[28] began negotiations to form the Diamond Fields Association. He arranged for Kimberley claims worth £450,000, half the assessed value of the mine, to be put into a company to be floated in London with a capital of £1 million; the proposed company was similar to that of Hall's of the previous year. However, the time was not right for mining company promotions in London. Besides, the ten-claim restriction

Table 2 *Assessment value of diamond mines, 1874–90*

	Kimberley		De Beers		Dutoitspan		Bultfontein	
	£	C	£	C	£	C	£	C
1874	474,100		none		none		none	
1875	500,000	(400)	none		none		none	
1876	1,043,600		none		none		none	
1877	939,677		272,250	(612)	54,037	(1441)*	22,366	(1026)*
1878	1,313,487	(420)	none		321,950	(1652)**	353,450	(1073)**
1879	1,509,520	(410)	none		none		none	
1880	1,569,760		810,700		none		none	
1881	2,860,717	(390)	2,063,375	(610)	2,906,000	(1453)†	1,003,000	(1003)†
1882	none		2,000,875	(610)	none		none	
1883	none		1,982,553		none	(1501)	none	(1037)
1884	3,047,037	(365)	1,164,075	(594)	2,343,414	(1501)††	660,085	(983)††
1885	2,782,774	(333)	934,737	(591)	1,282,691	(1430)	682,266	(822)
1886	1,452,276	(345)	933,960	(583)	1,087,892	(1411)	415,845	(828)
1887	1,364,130	(320)	1,965,830	(469)	1,133,215	(1419)	492,275	(930)
1888	1,358,770	(342)	none		1,291,410	(1497)	574,900	(934)
1889	1,353,760	(289)	none		1,290,560	(1651)	581,232	(1037)
1890	none		none		1,310,243	(1651)	603,332	(1037)

C. = Claims.

* Source: CAD, GLW 104, No.1414. This figure represents the market, not assessed, value of Dutoitspan and Bultfontein, based on the sale of 639 claims for an average price of £37 10/-, in the case of the former, and 541 claims for an average price of £21 16/- in the case of the latter, being the last sales up to 16 June 1877.

** Source: CAD, GLW 12, Enclosure in No. 4, Frere to Lanyon, 1 Jan. 1879. List of claimholders and valuation of A. A. Rothschild: Dutoitspan, 1 Oct. 1878 and Bultfontein, 1 Dec. 1878.

† Estimate: Dutoitspan claims put in at an average of £2,000 each and Bultfontein at an average of £1,000 each.

†† First official assessment.

remained on the statute book, although the impending formation of Lynch's company led Lanyon to abolish the restriction in November 1876. In the following month J. B. Robinson tried to float a rival company but he was unable to draw enough claimowners from Lynch's group to form a viable block of claims. Before he abandoned his scheme he libelled Lynch, calling him a 'ruined gamester' who had 'gulled the claimholders by getting up a sham company'.[29] Robinson lost in the ensuing suit but Lynch's success did not enhance his prospects of floating the Diamond Fields Association on the London Stock Exchange.[30]

An additional reason for Lynch's failure lay in the arrival in Kimberley of Jules Porges, the leading London diamond importer and a keen rival in the company promotion stakes. He bought claims at depressed prices for a syndicate of English and French diamond merchants and brokers. The syndicate was made up of Jules Porges, Parke Pittar, George and James Leverson in London and Leopold Taub, Emile van der Heim and Charles Mege in Paris. By the time Porges left the Fields in April 1877 his spending spree of £90,000 had driven up the market value of claims again. In London he put the syndicate's claims into a private company called the Griqualand DMC with a nominal capital of £400,000 of which only £100,000 was called up. In his absence his new partner, Julius Wernher, was instructed to pick up first-class Kimberley claims whenever possible.[31]

Foreign diamond merchants were not the first to form private mining companies. Large British and colonial diamond merchants already established in the mine were amongst the earliest promoters of private mining companies. The two most important were Paddon Brothers and Lewis and Marks (Snr). In 1876 Paddon Brothers was the largest claimholder in Kimberley Mine with property valued at £70,000. Samuel and William Paddon, who left Okehampton in England for Kimberley soon after the discovery of diamonds, combined diamond buying with digging very successfully until the crisis of early 1876 during which they nearly went bankrupt. Their problem was a result of a mixture of business and politics. They had lent £15,000 to William Ling, the rebel leader, against a mortgage of his claims valued at £20,000. In turn, they discounted Ling's bills at the Cape of Good Hope Bank. During the crisis the bank called up its advances including Ling's bills, and Paddon Brothers were unable to pay. However, the firm was rescued by Blaine and Company, who were interested in the solvency of the largest holder in their prospective London-registered company.[32]

Lewis and Marks (Snr), whose partners were Sammy Marks, Isaac Lewis and Barnet Lewis, carried on a limited diamond buying business with around £10,000 invested in the trade. They had emigrated from Lithuania in 1868 and settled in the Cape where they earned a living as travelling pedlars. By the time the diamond mines had been opened up they had graduated to general traders and on the Diamond Fields soon became diamond dealers who invested shrewdly in claims. At the end of 1875 Lewis and Marks and Paddon Brothers combined a block of their claims to form the Kimberley Mining Company, one of the first viable private companies in the mine. Initially the company owned ten claims and the capital of £36,811 was divided equally between Paddon Brothers and Lewis and Marks. By March 1879 the company had grown and its value inflated to £200,000.[33]

At the beginning of 1880 the majority of claims in Kimberley Mine were in the hands of 12 private companies with an aggregate capital of £2.5 million. Diamond merchants, who owned most of these private companies, were the first to float joint-stock ventures in the mine. In 1879 the first private company to go public, the Cape DMC, was floated in Port Elizabeth by the diamond merchant firm, Martin Lilienfeld and Company. Martin Lilienfeld ran his firm from London, while his partner, Emil Castens, resided in Port Elizabeth. They were represented in Kimberley by Max Michaelis and Sigismund Neumann, both of whom were later to become major diamond merchants and financiers in their own right.[34] In 1880 the Paris-based Compagnie Française des Mines de Diamants du Cap (£560,000) was the first Kimberley joint-stock company to be floated in Europe. It was a combination of the Kimberley Mining Company, the Griqualand DMC (Porges and friends) and claims owned by Lewis and Marks, (Jnr)[35] and covered a quarter of Kimberley Mine.[36]

While some diamond merchants like Lilienfeld restricted their investments to Kimberley Mine, others were at the forefront of the scramble for the other mines. The assessments tell the story of financial leap-frogging in the poorer pits. While Kimberley Mine tripled in value between 1876 and 1881, De Beers increased seven times, Dutoitspan 60 times and Bultfontein 50 times in value. Although the average number of carats found in each load of soil was less than in Kimberley Mine, the poorer mines had the advantage of being cheaper to work. They were shallower, faced fewer physical problems and required a smaller investment in steam machinery for efficient production. Lewis and Marks (Snr & Jnr), Samuel Paddon, Jules Porges, Harry Mosenthal, the Ochs brothers, Anton Dunkelsbuhler, Jules Le Jeune, Alfred Beit and Joseph Robinson reinvested profits from Kimberley Mine in the other pits. Barney Barnato, who was to become one of Kimberley's richest financiers, began with the purchase of three claims in Kimberley Mine in 1878 and rapidly expanded into new ground in De Beers and Dutoitspan mines. While merchants invested in production primarily to ensure easy access to their chosen trading commodity – the Cape DMC like the Kimberley Mining Company and the Griqualand DMC shipped its production directly to its merchant owners in London – almost all of them acquired a detailed understanding of production and management through active involvement in the direction of companies. Only senior partners domiciled in London and Paris made the progression into the ranks of mining financiers.[37]

THE PRIMITIVE ACCUMULATION OF CECIL RHODES

Cecil Rhodes is by far the best-known mining capitalist to have made his fortune at Kimberley. As an ill-informed mythology surrounds his early years it is worthwhile examining how he established himself in De Beers mine. Rhodes was no ordinary digger seeking to enrich himself at Kimberley. Herbert and Frank, his two elder brothers, had been to Winchester and Eton respectively. Through such a schooling their clergyman father had bought them not only a good education but access to men of wealth and power. Herbert preceded Cecil to Kimberley and paved the way for his younger brother not only by buying claims and making money but also by introducing him to a select group of gentlemen on the Fields. When Herbert, a keen explorer of the interior of southern Africa, was in residence at the diggings, he lived and messed with the 'Twelve Apostles', who speculated in joint ventures concluded over cigars, port and whist in the congenial atmosphere of the Craven Club. Cecil met and became friends with John Merriman and John Currey amongst other politicians, lawyers and civil servants who moved in this circle. While he was certainly over-shadowed by his more social elder brother, Cecil mastered the business of digging and managed his brother's claims when he went off on his explor-ation trips. In fact, Cecil began his career as a share-worker on one of his brother's three claims. In January 1872 he said he was averaging £100 a week and the money he made in this period he took home to England at the end of 1873, where he invested it in landed property in Hampstead.

It is not known exactly when Herbert Rhodes sold his Kimberley claims; either he struck poor layers or succumbed to the blue ground scare that diggers thought meant the mine had 'bottomed out'. However, by 1873 Rhodes was working for Charles Rudd, a partner in R. E. Wallace and Company, which speculated in numerous ventures ranging from an attempt to buy 200 claims in De Beers Mine to a telegraph between Dutoitspan and Kimberley to an ice-making business.[38] Rhodes never entered a formal partnership with Rudd in any of these speculations, a common assumption in all the Rhodes literature, and was as Louis Cohen remembered him 'a clerk with Wallace and Rudd'.[39] Moreover, it was Rudd who recognised the future importance of the pumping contracts; his elder brother became the largest holder of claims in De Beers Mine in 1874 at precisely the time water began to become a serious problem for diggers in the pit.[40] Indeed, Edward Tarry was a partner of Rudd's brother in this venture and Tarry had begun to specialise in the importation of mining machinery. It was through this association that Rudd and Tarry decided to tender for the pumping contracts in the mines and enlisted Rhodes to do the leg-work.[41]

The pumping contractors were in a position of great power in the mines. While water in the claims was one of the hazards that drove failing diggers to rebellion, it was also a scarce commodity on the Fields and one that was essential for efficient production. It had been discovered that washing the soil in sophisticated machines captured those small diamonds which escaped the human eye. But washing with drinking-well water was expen-sive and a waste of a life-giving resource. Rain-water and spring-water from the mines was preferred and it was the pumping contractor who controlled the supply.

There was, however, another important advantage connected with the pumping contracts. The contractor needed to own some deep claims to form a reservoir for his pumping operations and they were often some of the most valuable properties in the mines. Moreover, through the organi-sation of his pumping operations he was able to regulate which claims were cleared of water and which remained submerged. The point was that submerged claims sold cheaply in the market and owners gained remission of rates and licence fees. Especially in the untested waters of the poorer mines submerged property possessed a dormant value which the contractor often had the first option of sampling.

Rudd and Rhodes first attempted to win the pumping contract for Kimberley Mine. William 'Tramway' Hall was the current contractor in 1874 and, as he owned the only effective pumping machinery on the Fields, he dictated the price for his services to the Kimberley Mining Board. He also owned, illegally, 18 claims in the mine which gave him a substantial representation on the Board through his nominees. In contrast, Rudd and Rhodes had no 'pull in their own ground' and after they failed to take the contract from Hall in late 1874 they turned their attention to Dutoitspan where Rudd's influence was far greater.[42]

There, John Fry, Chairman of the Mining Board, was a close business associate of Rudd's. Consequently, when Rudd's tender for the contract was preferred over that of Hall, charges of jobbery appeared in all the Diamond Field newspapers. On the evidence there was scant reason for the preference of Rudd over Hall. Not only did Hall tender to pump from three places in the mine compared to his rival's one, but he also pointed out that Rhodes, 'the poor schoolboy', and Rudd did not have pumping machinery on the Fields.[43]

This was a potentially fatal inadequacy for a prospective contractor. Consequently, in December 1874 Rhodes dashed off to Victoria West to drive an apparently hard bargain – popularly regarded as 'evidence of his early commercial genius – over a pumping engine with farmer Devenish. The fact was that farmer Devenish's six h.p. engine had been on sale for £1,000 in Kimberley for some time and was not regarded with enthusiasm by any progressive claimholder. Ironically, Rudd had recently bought an eight h.p. engine from Cape Town for £450 and sold it to the De Beers Mining Board for £1,000; the Board had preferred Rudd's new machine to Devenish's second hand one. Caught short over the Dutoitspan contract, Rudd was forced to pay £1,000 for an inferior engine worth a quarter of the price. All Rhodes had to do was collect it.

Nonetheless, Rhodes did manage, run and make a profit out of the £500 per month Dutoitspan pumping contract. After a year and a half the contract was used to provide working capital for a mining venture in the mine. In May 1876 a three-year partnership was formed between Rhodes, Henry Barlow Webb, representative of the Posno family, owner of 200 Dutoitspan claims and large shareholder in the London and South African Exploration Company, Samuel Woolf, a diamond dealer, and Jules Le Jeune, a diamond merchant. Le Jeune owned ten claims which were valued at £800 and each of the other three put in a similar amount in cash making a capital of £3,200. By this time Rhodes alone held the pumping contract and he agreed to use its profits for mining the claims of the partnership which was styled Le Jeune and Company.[44]

When the partnership deed was drawn up Rhodes was no longer on the Fields and the reason for this lay in the drama that surrounded the De Beers pumping contract. In July 1874 the De Beers Mining Board had a choice of two possible methods of clearing their mine of water: under their own direction or through a contractor. They chose to buy pumping machinery at an estimated cost of £1,600 rather than offer the contract to a private party as in the case of Dutoitspan. The pumping engine, which Rudd had turned a handsome profit by selling to the Board, answered well until the rainy season at the end of 1874 when it failed to clear the mine. Then, Rhodes and James Mckenzie, engineer to the Kimberley Mining Board, won a contract to clear the mine in two months and to keep it dry for the next two months. This was the time when the diggers' discontent with most things connected with the mines reached boiling point and bubbled over into rebellion against Her Majesty the Queen. Rhodes himself made a substantial contribution to the discontent. By May 1875 it was evident to all that he had failed to keep the mine dry; as the most visible contractor he was not a popular man about the mine. Undaunted he ordered new pumps from England through Rudd's brother and entered a conditional contract which was due to begin on the arrival of the pumps in Kimberley.[45]

In the interim the pumping task reverted to the De Beers Mining Board. In July 1875 E. Huteau, a 35-year-old Mauritian engineer, was appointed to superintend the pumping operations in the Mine. He kept the mine dry during the wettest months at the end of 1875 and kept working expenditure below Rhodes' £400 a month contract price. In the face of this performance Rhodes' contract began to appear unnecessary. On 26 December 1875 the engine was sabotaged by persons unknown and the claims were flooded. Soon after it was discovered that an attempt had been made to bribe Huteau to damage the engine. Angry diggers, whose claims were under water, insisted that Huteau expose the perpetrator of the bribe. On the 5 January the propitious moment arrived before the open court held by Colonel Crossman, who was investigating diggers' grievances. Huteau named Rhodes as the guilty party and when Rhodes was called to account he denied the charge. To emphasise his innocence he had Huteau arraigned on a charge of perjury and committed for trial in the High Court. However, at the end of January Sydney Shippard, the Attorney-General, declined to prosecute and dismissed the case.[46]

This was a curious affair which none of Rhodes' biographers have taken time to examine. The one historian who does deal with the affair, Brian Roberts, finds the incident interesting but claims the charge against Rhodes was unproven.[47] While he has his suspicions about the integrity of Rhodes, Roberts still weighed the scales of doubt against Huteau in the belief that the engineer stood to lose his job when Rhodes took up the contract. Yet, it is now clear that Huteau had proved to the Board that his pumping was cheaper and more efficient than that of Rhodes; Huteau stood to gain nothing by destroying his own work and the livelihood of those diggers who depended on his water extraction. Moreover, Rhodes messed with Sydney Shippard, the Attorney-General, and Recorder Barry, who presided over the High Court, and it was probably their idea to file a case against Huteau, effectively ending public discussion of Rhodes' conduct. The fact that his honour was not pursued to a legal judgement in a society where such concepts were important, and under the advice of legal men at the hub of colonial law, is very damning evidence. In March 1876 he left Kimberley for Oxford under a cloud. 'My character was so battered at the Diamond Fields', he wrote from Oxford, 'that I like to preserve the few remnants.'[48]

Before Rhodes left for England he had to fight for the pumping contract. In February 1876 De Beers diggers voted to have Rhodes' contract annulled if his pumps did not arrive within the month. They also demanded that he pump from two reservoirs in the mine, one in Baxter's Gully and the other in Schwab's Gully; for this they recognised that new pumping equipment was needed. Rhodes guaranteed the arrival of his pumps within the month and, in partnership with Rudd and Tarry, was granted a contract for nine months for £650 a month. There is little doubt that Rhodes' association with respected merchants like Tarry and Rudd carried the weight that his own personal and business reputation in the mine lacked.

Effectively banished from the Fields he did not lose interest in the pumping contracts. While he was in England he shipped a 12 h.p. steam engine and pump through Rudd and Company in London. It satisfied the Board with its performance until the end of 1877 when James Ferguson won the contract. He then failed to conquer the water problem and the contract passed back to Rhodes and Rudd in April 1878. However, as Rudd would not sign in the hope of securing a higher fee, the Board began pumping under its own auspices again. Rhodes sued the Board for breach of contract and won back the contract. During the trial it was revealed that his working expenses were £256 a month, which left a monthly profit of £294 or an annual profit of £3,528.[49]

It is not known for certain whether this tidy profit went to pay working expenses for mining in De Beers, as happened in Dutoitspan. For one thing Rhodes and Rudd were in partnership in claims with Robert Graham in De Beers and not Edward Tarry; it is not known if Graham was involved in the pumping contract. Nonetheless, it appears that Rhodes and Rudd bought claims in De Beers before they won their first De Beers contract in early 1875. The first documented purchase by Rhodes was in October 1875 when he paid £8 for a claim. In the following year he and Graham brought a block of abandoned claims in Baxter's Gully which by September 1876 were worth £600. Before this time the prospects of the mine were jaundiced to say the least, but in 1877 the mine began to be systematically explored for the first time. 'The time when a "gully" was sunk in an immense mass of ground', wrote the *Diamond News*, 'and none but the enchanted hole touched is past'.[50] The mine began to take on the form of a basin, although the gullies still remained the richest sections of the mine. In 1878 the value of Rhodes' block of claims was £9,000 and over the next two years the partnership accumulated 40 claims, some in Baxter's Gully but most in the poor ground in the West End, all of which were capitalised in March 1880 for £200,000 in the De Beers DMC. At this time they were the second largest claimowner in the mine, next to the Diamant Commandit Gesellschaft George Lippert which held 116 claims based on the nucleus created by the Old De Beers Company and expanded by James Ferguson.[51]

It is likely that the pumping contract put the Rhodes partnership in a key position to acquire claims outside the proven gullies. After 1876 claims were certainly cheaper to buy in De Beers than Kimberley. More importantly De Beers, where it was worked, was a quarter of the depth of its richer neighbour. It was, thus, cheaper to dig. 'We are in as good a position' argued Rhodes in 1876, 'as North and Tarry block with Francis (D. Francis and Company in Kimberley Mine) and average the ground through as rich.'[52] Profits from ground value at £1,000 in De Beers equalled the profits from claims valued at £3,000 in Kimberley. In short, then, Rhodes combined luck and good connections with hard work in his university holidays to build up a commanding position in a cheap mine between 1878 and 1880.

THE WHITE WORKING CLASS

In the late 1870s the growth of company mining transformed the majority of white share-workers into waged overseers; a few men became contract workers and managers. Steam machinery and larger African labour forces in the mines required bands of overseers to watch and to drive men to work. Overseers wages quadrupled from £5 a month to £5 a week and white families supported by the uncertainties of share-work became dependent on the greater regularity of wage income. The decline of share-working was an uneven process in the mines as was the growth of company mining. Share-working lasted longer in the poorer mines where Kimberley capitalists were often content simply to hold claims for a rise in the market rather than to organise production. It was given a second lease of life during the depression of 1882–85, co-existing with formal leases of claims and contract work for loading and washing. However, even in Kimberley Mine share-working continued to exist in the late 1870s. Stanford, a large claimowner, looked on share-workers as partners. 'They have the privilege of selling the diamonds they find after I have seen them', he said in evidence at a trial, 'they are known in the trade as working for me'.[53] Nonetheless, forms of profit-sharing generally declined in favour in wage labour.

By 1880 the stratum of white overseers was large enough to organise in defence of their interests on the basis of a privileged position in supervisory labour. In that year overseers fought a proposal to have them searched on entry to and exit from the mines. The planned introduction of a searching system meant a number of things to white overseers. First, it implied a possible reduction in numbers of overseers; overseers would only be required to drive labourers rather than to prevent theft if there was an effective search before and after labouring in the mines. Secondly, searching whites and Africans alike involved the 'classing of intelligent and honest white men with raw and thievish natives' and this was a degradation which lowered 'the moral tone and social status of hundreds of citizens to the detriment of all concerned'.[54] Thirdly, searching involved a redefinition of the status of supervisory labour. Colonial legislators had some difficulty in defining the meaning of 'servant' for the new searching ordinance:

> Mr Green said the definition of a servant read by His Honour was one employed in bodily labour, that hardly applied to overseers.
> His Honour: Handicraft.
> The Attorney-General: They don't work with their brains.
> Mr Bottomley: They work with their eyes and ears.[55]

His Honour the Administrator, Mr Rose-Innes, carried the day for a non-racial definition of servants, which included overseers and excluded only managers. 'He would never consent to the introduction of a clause', he was reported as saying, 'which made a man a scoundrel because he had a black skin, and laid it down as a principle that because he had a white skin he was altogether beyond the range of temptation'.[56]

While the Searching Ordinance was intended to prevent theft, its implementation promised to have more insidious effects on labour relations. It threatened both to drive a wedge between overseers and owners and to abolish crucial distinctions between overseers and labourers. In the words of overseers themselves:

> relations between capital and labour have hitherto been harmonious and mutual confidence has as a rule existed between claimholders and their overseers which the proposed law will completely destroy.[57]

They argued that their transformation from small claimholders and share-workers into overseers had been too rapid and they appealed to the respect that had been theirs in the era of 'diggers' democracy'. They warned that they would ally with African labourers if they were to be rejected as equals by owners. 'The Kafir until this time regarded the overseer as his enemy', agreed the *Diamond Fields Advertiser*, '[but] would look upon searching as a sign that the owner was suspected, as well as himself, of readiness to steal'.[58] This appeal to the bonds of racial equality between overseers and owners, combined with the past evidence of and future fears for large-scale African desertion, was effective enough in preventing the promulgation of the Searching Ordinance.

Three crucial distinctions existed between white overseers and labourers. The first related to different degrees of dependence on mining for a living. 'Natives could if they pleased leave if they objected to searching', commented one digger, '[but] overseers who had wives and families with them would be obliged to remain'.[59] The second distinction related to methods of payment for work. Some company overseers were paid a commission on diamonds found in picking or in vigilant supervision of attempted theft. In the 1880s this practice became more common and, although it was extended to African labourers as well, overseers were given an economic incentive over and against the majority of the work force. The third distinction was the most important. White overseers, earning around £240 a year when fully employed, qualified for the vote whereas African labourers did not. In fact, white miners made up a half of the Kimberley Division electorate, although their numbers declined dramatically in the later 1880s.[60]

While the majority of white workers, over 60 per cent, were overseers, the remainder were skilled workers. In the 1870s skilled workers were largely confined to those crafts which had been practised before the development of mining. Carpenters, masons and blacksmiths earned £1 a day with blacksmiths at the top of the artisanal league of earnings. They were in great demand when the building industry went through a boom during the company mania of 1880 and 1881. Over £200,000 was spent on construction in central Kimberley; some carpenters became speculative builders while others lived well on high contract wages. Carpenters and smiths of all kinds were also employed in the mines, working largely as independent artisans or employed in workshops run by master craftsmen. After joint-stock companies were formed many carpenters and smiths became full-time employees.

Initially the only skilled work in the mining industry lay in the driving of carts and horse whims. Such drivers were 'chiefly drawn from Colonial men, such as Malays, Bastards, Hottentots etc.' who earned from 30s to 60s a week (storeboys earned 25s a week) and found food and accommodation for themselves.[61] Jobs in engineering trades, like mechanics, fitters and turners, expanded with the growth in the number of steam engines on the Fields. By 1881 the 300 steam engines needed a good deal of maintenance. In addition engine-driving required skill and sobriety; it was an occupation of responsibility with control over the whole pace of production and the safety of workers in the claims or on the floors. Engine-driving required little technical expertise and came to be dominated by Europeans who displaced 'men of colour' whim drivers; they never made up more than 20 per cent of the white and 'men of colour' working in the mining industry. They were highly paid often earning more than skilled men; they commanded £300 a year in wages and could earn up to £500 through over-time.[62]

THE SUPPLY OF AFRICAN LABOUR

One of the most important aspects of the systematic development of mining was the attempt to organise a reliable supply of African labourers, who remained migrant labourers through to the end of the century. In 1876 Major Lanyon set up a Labour Commission to investigate how this could be done. The conclusions the Commission came to were based on practices in force in India, Mauritius and, in particular, in Natal.[63] The Commission made three basic recommendations for the 'immediate attention of the government'.[64] The first recommendation was for no legislation on wages as it was recognised that high wages 'were the surest means of encouraging the introduction of labour'.[65] The second recommendation was for government aid in securing the safe passage of African migrants to the fields and providing their 'means of subsistence along the line of route'.[66] The Commission was in favour of government agencies among the labour supplying chiefdoms and government depots along the migration routes to provide food, shelter and security. The third recommendation was for the establishment of a labour depot in Kimberley itself.

The central depot in Kimberley was conceived as the one and only distributor of African labour to the camps and mines. It was believed that such a system would cut out employer competition for labour. The Superintendent of the depot was to have wide-ranging powers. His main task was to contract all 'natives' in Kimberley and new hands, 'mere apprentices learning the use of mining implements',[67] were to be contracted for a minimum period of three months. A subsidiary, but more problematic task, was to be the Superintendent's role as judge in all cases of conflict between master and servant. He was also to relieve the Resident Magistrate of his duty in issuing gun permits to 'natives'. His final task was to dispose of 'natives', who failed to find employment after five days:

> The compulsory employment of those natives who at the end of 5 days sojourn at a depot are unable to obtain employment, cannot be considered a hardship, when such natives are at liberty to contract themselves, and if unable to do so, may very reasonably be looked upon as paupers unable otherwise to obtain their subsistence. If such men were to be turned out of the depot they would be forced into vagrancy and possible crime.[68]

It was here that the depot system showed its true colours as an institution of forced labour, but the Commission reminded the Administrator that this was more apparent than real for 'the compulsion proposed is absolute liberty as compared with the tyrannical rule of their own chiefs'.[69]

These central recommendations of the Labour Commission were embodied in the 1876 Native Labour Ordinance. Objecting to specific laws for 'natives', the Colonial Office vetoed it and destroyed hopes for a colonial regulation of African labour supply. Instead, a central depot was established under an 1874 Ordinance, which had never been promulgated, as it was expensive and Africans were suspicious of its purpose. It provided for the establishment of depots, where all 'natives' could be located until contracted, and was also designed to ensure the compulsory clothing of African labourers. The problem with the 1874 depot system was that it was optional and Africans in search of employment were at liberty to locate themselves where they pleased in the camps. Diggers and companies found this unsatisfactory and pursued systematic, government-aided recruiting as a means of ensuring a constant supply of labour.[70]

The colonial state steered clear of formal involvement in recruiting schemes. Southey and Lanyon had a restricted conception of the role of government in capital accumulation, but Major Lanyon did send Alexander Bailie, a surveyor, on a journey to Lobengula in the hope of finding new sources of labour. Despite this exception, government policy on recruitment was relatively clear: '... employers of labour should make their own arrangements as the work is certainly not that of a government'.[71] While it was understood that chiefs would prefer to make recruiting arrangements with government rather than individuals, there was the additional fear about a humanitarian outcry over slavery. It was for this reason that in 1876 Major Lanyon refused to endorse a scheme to recruit Africans from the Zoutpansberg and beyond. Its sponsors were J. W. Crowley, a Kimberley mechant, and Joao Albasini, an old Portuguese slave dealer, who exercised 'a sort of chieftainship over certain portions of the tribe of Knobneus Kafirs on the extreme north eastern border of the Transvaal'.[72] Their scheme was based on the much desired depot system with three stations – one at Albasini's, another at Mosilikatzi's Nek and a third at Bloemhof – between the north-eastern Transvaal and Kimberley.

The Cape Government was, however, amenable to private applications for labour provided it was not required to guarantee any scheme. In 1878 Julius Wernher and Samuel Paddon, representing the two largest private companies in Kimberley Mine, wrote to the Secretary of Native Affairs asking for his aid in drawing labour from the eastern Cape. On receiving some encouragement, they approached the Griqualand West government believing that the support of both colonial executives would lead to a satisfactory recruiting scheme. But the 1878 Griqualand West Rebellion had just broken out and there seemed to be dangerous links between unrest on the eastern frontier and in the diamond province. '"Native" is a "big word"', commented Lanyon, 'I should think that the presence of a large number of "Kaal" Kaffirs hardly desirable just now'.[73] He refused to write to the Cape Government in support of the mineowners' application.

While the colonial state regarded aided-recruitment as outside its legitimate function, the conquest of African chiefdoms or even unruly Republican polities was most certainly within its recognised sphere of action. The annexation of the South African Republic in 1877, central to Carnarvon's South African confederation scheme, was in part a response to the demands of Kimberley mining capitalists for a regional system of labour supply.[74] Once the Transvaal was in British hands, the Administrator made frequent private appeals for labour. In early 1880, for example, Colonel Lanyon, then Administrator of the Transvaal, replied to such a request from James Rose-Innes, Administrator of Griqualand West:

> This province as also the rest of South Africa has doubtless benefitted greatly since the opening of the Diamond Fields. But at the same time the fact that it has suffered considerably from the consequent loss of its labour cannot be ignored. The amount of land under cultivation has certainly become less from this cause for the native prefers to go to Kimberley for work even though he be offered higher wages here. The illicit trade in diamonds accounts for this, as

thereby the native can supplement his wages to a large extent. Recent events, however, have made the labour question more simple and capable of being dealt with.[75]

Lanyon was referring to the recent conquest of the Pedi and from September to the end of 1880 he sent 12,000 Africans to Kimberley, the product of a tour of hut tax collection.[76]

In the south Griqualand West had to compete with the Cape for labour. While the Cape had difficulty in drawing labour from the eastern frontier for its public works, it had managed to compete successfully with Griqualand West for a share of South Sotho labour. After the 1876 commercial crisis on the Diamond Fields there was a considerable transfer of Sotho labour to the Cape. In 1875 Griffith, the Basutoland Government Agent, isolated the Colony as a preferential labour area and refused to endorse passes for the Diamond Fields. He also enlisted the support of some chiefs. 'You diggers hear!', Chief Lerothodi told a *pitso* in November 1875,

I have been to the Diamond Fields and know. The thefts of that place make me afraid . . . I was on the Wellington Railway which travels with wonderful swiftness. You thieving fellows from the Diamond Fields you would do much better to go to the public works . . . I repeat go to the government *letsima*.[77]

His appeal did not fall on deaf ears for two material reasons. Guns could be bought as easily in the eastern Cape as in Kimberley, and often more cheaply, while travelling to the old Colony was not as tortuous an undertaking as walking across land owned by hostile Orange Free State farmers.

The South Sotho had been one of the earliest African peoples to work in the mines. They did not work in significant numbers in the Kimberley and De Beers mines, dominated by the Pedi, and preferred the poorer and safer mines, where chances of share-working and claimownership were greater. After the 1876 slump, despite the precipitous decline in their contribution to the number of 'new hands' contracted, South Sotho continued to work in the poorer mines until the outbreak of the 'Gun War' in June 1880, when 4,000 men deserted to fight for their chiefs against the Cape Colony. The scale of this military desertion suggested that South Sotho made up a major share of the 'old hands' in the mines. It should be remembered that we do not know how many South Sotho, or any other African people for that matter, actually remained on the fields as 'old hands', although we know their aggregate numbers.[78]

The Tsonga, better know as 'Shangaan', now displaced the South Sotho as the major supplier of 'new hands' in the poorer mines where the demand for labour was growing rapidly. Between 1878 and 1881 the African work force expanded from 4,000 to 12,000 as a result of the growth in the size of both mining units and in the amount of ground worked for the first time. 'Shangaans' were not alone in flocking to the poorer mines as the Pedi continued to provide around a third of the new hands. However, the increase in 'Shangaan' numbers to a similar third was in inverse proportion

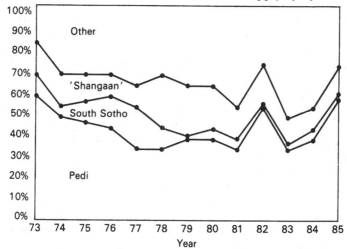

Fig. 3 'New hand' contracts registered in Kimberley and De Beers Mines, 1873–85. Note: *Pedi* includes, in the Registrar's terminology, 'Secocoeni Basuto'; 'Matabella (Mapoch, Zebedella, Matiega, Makapan)' that is, Ndzundza Ndebele; 'Transvaal Basuto'; and 'Magata Basuto'. *Other* includes Tlharo, Kwena (Secheli, Gamayan), Ngwato (Khama), Tlhaping (Mankurwane, Botlasitse, Jantjie), Rolong (Maontshiwa, Moroka, Moswete), Swazi, 'Portuguese Zulu', Ndebele, Kalanga, Shona, Cape Colonial, Griqua, Koranna. (Sources: CAD, GLW, 55, 71 (1873–75)' *Griqualand West Government Gazette*, 1877–80; *Blue Books on Native Affairs*, 1881–83; CAD, NA 195, 198, 202, 1884–85)

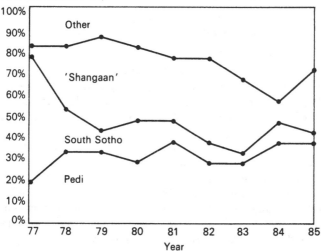

Fig. 4 'New hand' contracts registered in Dutoitspan and Bulfontein Mines, 1877–85. Note: See fig. 3. (Sources: *Griqualand West Government Gazette*, 1877–80; *Blue Books on Native Affairs*, 1881–83; CAD, NA, 195, 198, 202, 1884–85)

to the South Sotho. In many cases 'Shangaans' may well have deserted from Kimberley Mine and presented themselves as 'new hands' at the pan: the Registrar's correspondence was full of such suspicions. Still, 'Shangaans' were more actively recruited after the development of private companies, particularly making use of John Dunn's coastal corridor through Zululand and Natal for the protection of migrants.[79]

The importance of Pedi and 'Shangaan' labourers was evident from the pattern of circular migration. 'New hands' began arriving in spring and left for home again at the beginning of winter. Usually the winter shortage was made up by the supply of men from Basutoland 'which used to be inexhaustible' until the outbreak of the Gun War 1880–81.[80] However, the supply was never predictable. In February 1880, for example, there were 12,000 Africans in the mines and W. J. Coleman, the Registrar of Natives, estimated that 20,000 Africans were required to work the mines properly.[81] In July, rumours of war in Basutoland led to the desertion of 4,000 Sotho producing a winter labour-shortage crisis in the middle of a mining boom.[82] It was at this point that Lanyon began to direct Africans from the northern Transvaal to Kimberley; between September and December 12,000 men went to Kimberley. At the end of 1880 Coleman estimated that there were 22,000 African labourers working in the mines, but wanted another 10,000 men to reduce wages from 30s to 10s a week.[83] Still, the number of labourers in the pits had doubled over one year. 'African labour is the life of the Diamond Fields', wrote the *Daily Independent*, 'and just as in proportion as the supply and demand of this commodity varies so in great measure is the prosperity of the community gauged.'[84]

THE SOCIAL GEOGRAPHY OF KIMBERLEY

Under Governor Southey (1873–75) and Administrator Lanyon (1875–78) there was no official policy of racial, residential segregation in the mining camps. For Lanyon such a policy was 'repugnant to British law and custom'.[85] Besides, in the beginning there was little call for it; many diggers accommodated both black and white workers on their compounds or encampments in sheds or tents.[86] The growth of 'board wages' and of mining companies broke this close physical proximity between diggers and their labourers. Diggers' compounds became the sites of barrack-type accommodation for Africans, although not all African labourers chose to live in the housing provided. In addition, whites and 'persons of colour', who had lived on diggers' compounds, moved into boarding houses or rented rooms in the camps. The term compound no longer referred to a place where a digger lived; work and living space were now physically separated.

The separation of a digger's work-place from his residence gave the first meaningful shape to racial, residential segregation in Kimberley. On the one hand, wealthy diggers sought a measure of tranquillity and opulence in

Plate 5 A diggers' compound in Kimberley in the 1870s. Three diggers are seated: one on a chaise longue, one in a chair and the other on a barrel. Their overseer holds the greyhound. They are surrounded by their gang of twelve Africans who also lived on the compound. Courtesy De Beers, London.

exclusive areas. As early as 1875 a residential 'suburb', hopefully named Belgravia, was laid out around the Public Gardens on the London Company estate. At its heart was Governor Southey's residence; it attracted 'leading merchants and men of leisure'.[87] Many Belgravia houses were built in brick and furnished with all the trappings and comfort of Victorian bourgeois elegance, although as late as 1895 the majority of houses in Kimberley as a whole were made of 'principally wood frames, clad with corrugated iron, lined with wood or canvas'.[88] In 1883 another 'suburb', called Gladstone, was laid out along the cricket ground on the Vooruitzicht government estate.[89] Both Belgravia and Gladstone were exclusive white residential areas.

On the other hand, the compounds diggers left, while remaining sites of production for washing and sorting, were now exclusively used as accommodation for African labourers. 'The compound is under the shade of the Three Camel Thorn Trees', announced one advertisement, '. . . and the Buildings erected thereon are commodious and the Native Branch is capable of accommodating 100 Native servants . . . .'[90] As depositing floors expanded production was moved to them, and the compound became simply the place Africans were housed. New private companies either had

95

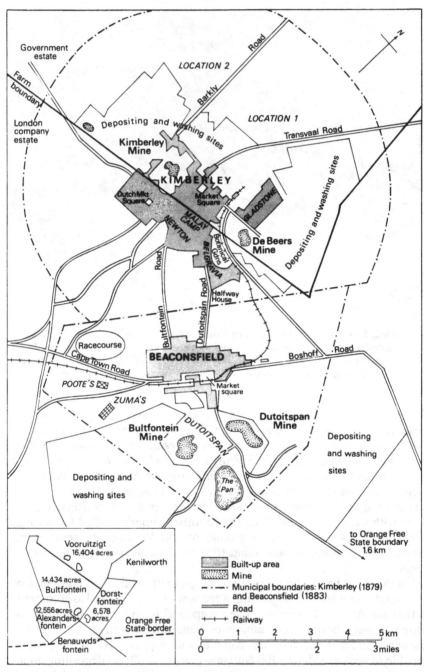

Map 3 Kimberley in the 1880s [Based on the London and South African Exploration Company 'Plan of the Diamond Fields' drawn for the Colonial and Indian Exhibition, 1886]

to buy existing compounds or build for themselves. 'We have the honour to request you will allot us', wrote the manager of the Kimberley Mining Company to the Mining Surveyor in 1877:

> a space behind our Engine House for the erection of a Building to accommodate our Kaffirs, say about 50 feet in length and 16 feet wide, to house between 60 and 80 men. When our Kaffirs sleep away, we find they are seldom to their work in proper time and more especially so on Monday mornings, when they have the excuse of being apprehended for drunkenness or other causes ... We trust you will give the matter due consideration, as the loss to us for the want of accommodation for our Kaffirs means a large difference in the working expenses.[91]

The quality of company accommodation seems to have been generally poor, although we do not know how compounds compared to 'board wage' housing. However, whether compound or rented rooms, inadequate shelter contributed to the high African death-rate which was seldom less than double the European figure. Lung-diseases were prevalent during the winter months, though it became a generally more serious danger with the development of underground mining.[92] Still, there were many in Kimberley who were ready to point a finger at mining companies for their standards of accommodation. In 1883 when Dennis Doyle, the Kimberley Sanitary Inspector, blamed the large number of African deaths from pneumonia on alcohol, Louis Diering, a major liquor wholesaler, was quick to retort that inadequate housing was the cause. 'The farmers make better provision for their cattle', he claimed, 'than the companies for their natives.'[93]

After 1876 mineowners tried to tie labourers more effectively to one master for three to six months; they wanted to reduce desertion from one employer to another, and between mines. The 1876 Labour Commission had attacked the prevalence of the 'board wages' system and had recommended that employers should be forced to house and feed their servants. At the time, however, such an idea had been regarded as 'absurd' by the Attorney-General,[94] but over the next four years as private companies and mining capitalists grew in size the idea became more appealing.

The initial picture of the compound as a site of labour control was provided by T. C. Kitto, an English Mining Inspector. He compared Kimberley diamond mine to Brazilian Diamond Field labour. 'The labour question here is, in my opinion, a matter of very great importance', reported Kitto to Administrator Warren in July 1879:

> and I think every possible means should be adopted to secure to owners of mines a constant supply ... I must say the quality of labour here is the worst I have seen in any part of the world, and I cannot help contrasting it with the black labour of Brazil. I am very certain that one of the Brazilian blacks will do as much work on an average as three Kimberley blacks. The Brazilian blacks are classed from one to four, and are hired out to English companies ... The companies have to feed them ... The blacks are lodged in barracks, which are built in the form of a square, the outer wall being much higher than the inner

> wall; the roof slopes inside. The entrance to the place is by a large gate, over which at night stands a powerful lamp which lights up the whole place. Men and women answer to the call of their names while passing out at the gate in the morning and in the evening when entering. They retire to rest early, and an overseer locks up the premises each night and unlocks them in the morning. There is a very good feeling between the Brazilian slaves and the owners ... in another 22 years, or thereabouts, all will be free; by which time, if they continue in their present state of progression, they will be ripe for the occasion.
>
> I believe the natives of South Africa, under European supervision, are capable of being made almost – if not quite – as good as the blacks of Brazil, provided they are dealt with in the same manner.[95]

Kitto was quick to point out that he did not advocate slavery, but the conclusions to be drawn from the comparison with Brazilian slave labour lay precisely in the disadvantages for mining capital of a migrant labour force. 'If natives could be bound to masters for say seven years', Kitto wrote, 'it would be for the infinite benefit of the natives themselves ...'[96]

In August 1879 board and lodging of African labourers in compounds was made compulsory although, as it turned out, it was unenforceable against the wishes of Africans and in the booming state of the mining industry.[97] At the same time its corollary was an attempt to segregate those Africans who were not compounded from the main camps. Sir Charles Warren, the Acting Administrator, became the architect of racial, residential segregation in Kimberley, although there had been moves in this direction prior to 1879.

The first private initiative for 'native' residential segregation came at the time of the Black Flag Revolt. The proprietor of the Vooruitzicht estate allocated a space between Gladstone and the Kimberley cemetery for a 'native' location and a rent reduction from 10s to 2s 6d a month for a lot was held out as an inducement for 'natives' to move out of the centre of Kimberley. Apparently numbers of Africans responded to this rent reduction, but most remained where they were or congregated in 'native camps' in, most noticeably, the West End where they did not have to pay any rent at all.[98]

By the late 1870s some 'native camps' were, nonetheless, known as locations and contained at least 3,500 people, when the official black population figure was 10,485 and in all likelihood double that figure.[99] Residents fell into three categories: 'those natives not residing on their masters' premises, those engaged in independent occupations, and the Bechuana, Kaal Kaffirs, Fingoes, Korannas etc. who have wives and families ...'[100] In early 1879 there were four locations on the Government estate and two on the Company estate. They were all on the outskirts of the main camps with only the eight slaughtering poles, replete with large sheep and cattle kraals, further away from the centre of Kimberley. Each location was identified with a particular people. On the Barkly Road was the 'Bechuana and Fingoe' location (160 lots, 100 occupied); close by were the smaller 'Kaffir' location (48 lots, 14 occupied) and the 'Koranna' location (96 lots, 24 occupied); and the largest location on the Transvaal Road (172 lots, 130 occupied) was also dominated by Korannas. These locations were 'laid out in regular order and suitable localities', but those on the Company estate were spread out and characterised by an 'air of neglect and disorder'.[101]

In addition, other 'native camps' closer to Kimberley Market Square were known as villages. Their distinguishing feature was that African residents were rent-paying standholders. They were named after clergymen, whose churches provided the focal point for village life. Gway's village, named after Gwayi Tyamzashe, the Congregational Minister and first African to be ordained in Kimberley, was situated on the Transvaal Road. Bevan's village, named after an English Anglican missionary, was on the Barkly Road to the north-west of Kimberley Mine. The remaining two villages were near the Race Course at Bultfontein: Poote's was named after James Poote, the Independent Minister, and Zuma's after John Zuma, a Wesleyan evangelist.[102]

In mid-1879 informal segregation by choice was over-taken by the adoption of an official policy of 'localising natives'. Official policy was determined, in this case, by the situation in the countryside. The establishment of locations in Griqualand West had been a central objective of Lanyon's administration; once Africans were confined to specific areas, white settlers could buy and occupy farms. However, it was only after the 1878 Griqualand Rebellion, a reaction on the part of the Griqua to the legal expropriation of their land and the loss of political independence, that there was effective white occupation of the agricultural hinterland of Kimberley. Sir Charles Warren, Acting Administrator in 1879, now emphasised the desirability of 'localisation' over and above the revenue possibilities of hut-tax.[103]

Thus, in June 1879 the Cape Location Acts were applied to Griqualand West and from July the Kimberley Town Council, after asking for the Act to be applied in the mining camps, began to enforce the new law within the municipality.[104] The new urban policy had largely been inspired by white fears of a black uprising in Kimberley during the 1878 Griqualand West Rebellion. In the following year such fears were exacerbated by the Zulu victories in the opening phases of the Anglo-Zulu War; it was rumoured that African labourers expected the imminent expulsion of Britain from South Africa. 'The colonists lost their heads', wrote the Anglican priest, Rev. Bevan, 'and took fright and treated every black man as an enemy, no matter of what race.'[105]

However, 'localisation' was not simply a policy of containment. It was also a response to demands for control of those Africans 'living at large', who were 'lazy', possible deserters from the pits and who lived in 'dirt and plenty without work or visible means of support'.[106] In other words, having long complained of the freedom that the system of 'board wages' allowed

African labourers, mineowners moved official policy into line with their prescriptions on both compounds and locations.

Location regulations were published in September 1880. A location was defined as:

> any number of huts or dwellings exceeding five within an area of one square mile occupied by any of the native races such as Kaffirs, Fingoes, Basutos, Hottentots, Bushmen and the like such occupants in case such huts or dwellings shall be situated on land which is private property, not being in the *bona fide* and continuous employment of the owner of such land either as his domestic servants or in or about the farming operations, or any trade, business or handicraft by him carried upon such land.[107]

'People of colour' and Indians were not included in the list of 'native races'. In 1881 there were six locations with a population of, at least, 2,380 (938 men, 585 women and 857 children) in the Kimberley Borough.[108] The earlier locations lost their specific ethnic identities and the villages their church and class-based origins. In fact, both were absorbed by the new municipal locations; the 'principal Becoana location' and Bevan's village became part of Location No. 2, which was composed of a 'few families from most of the tribes of South Africa' with a constantly growing but constantly changing migrant population.[109] Around the original houses built of clay, stone and brick clustered 'miserable huts formed of old sacks, rugs and skins'.[110]

Municipal locations were more difficult to establish on the Company estate. The landed proprietor preferred the higher rents from standholders compared to the devaluation of some of their central property through the proclamation of locations and the extraction of hut-rent. In 1883 the issue of locations on Company land was tested in the courts.[111] The Kimberley Location Inspector arrested Jim Squire, an African tenant living in Newton, for refusing to pay hut-rent. The Company encouraged Squire to challenge the Location Inspector's authority over Newton and financed his suit for wrongful arrest. The court ruled that there was no location in Newton and, as the area had never been exclusively occupied by 'native races', there never had been a location in that part of Kimberley. In fact, as late as 1888, the Beaconsfield Magistrate, who had a nominal watching brief over locations, claimed that no locations had ever been proclaimed on Company property and that the people were 'all mixed up'.[112]

There were some parts of the Company estate where there was little ethnic or racial diversity. In the 1870s the Malay Camp near the Jewish synagogue was exclusively occupied by Malays, who lived in 'good permanent clean houses, many of them built in brick'.[113] Some Malays, like Antonie Abdol, acquired great wealth as cab-owners; there were more stables in this part of Kimberley than any other. Abdol had been one of the 47 black claimholders who lost their digging licences in Bultfontein in the white purge of 1872.[114] However, through Governor Barkly's refusal to discriminate against black owners, Abdol continued to dig and in 1878 he owned ten claims in Dutoitspan. (His brother owned another seven, and half of these were among the richest in the mine.) In 1879 Abdol was worth £5,000; he had £1,000 on fixed deposit with the Standard Bank and 'considerable sums' with other banks. In 1881 he indulged in the 'share mania' and sold his claims. He then became a transport rider between Worcester and Kimberley and had £5,000 invested in transport stock. In 1883 he went bankrupt as a result of his share speculations and ended a promising career on the Fields.[115] By this time the Malay camp had lost its exclusive character; it became host to Indians, a colony of 'native' Christians and Europeans. It was, as Sister Catherine reported, very cosmopolitan with 'all nationalities congregated together in odd little houses of every description and made of all kinds of materials – wood, canvas, iron and even tin linings of packing cases neatly patched together'.[116]

A similar situation of ethnic and racial diversity came to exist in the locations. During the depression (1881–85) in particular, they were infiltrated by large numbers of European squatters in search of rent-free accommodation.[117] Moreover, if the locations were designed to control desertion from the mines, they singularly failed to fulfill their function. They remained 'hot beds of vice' and the 'resort of all the deserters, loafers and vagabonds of Kimberley'.[118] Still, the failure was not for want of trying on the part of the police. In December 1881, for example, the police made no fewer than 15 pass raids on the locations and shuffled their captives through the courts in batches of 20 or more.[119] These raids became so annoying to African householders in the locations that they complained to the Kimberley Town Council. Malata Mooika, a brick-maker, made an affidavit about a dawn raid in which his door was broken down and his pass demanded. As it turned out this raid had been carried out by the constabulary, rather than the municipal police who had enforced the municipal bye-laws since 1881.[120]

The Town Council was sympathetic to Mooika and other respectable location residents. Councillors were unhappy with the way Zulu headmen, to whom location control had been delegated (for £12 a month), discharged their duties. They had the power to evict people for 'having no means of subsistence' and in one case a headman ruled his fief in a 'harsh and over-bearing manner'.[121] Councillors were most often commercial men and they had a market interest in the settlement of a stable location community. Moreover, the Town Council owned no land in Kimberley and taking an interest in the tribulations of respectable location residents was part of a campaign to have the locations and the commonages of the borough handed over to the Council, a campaign which was only successful at the end of the decade.

In addition, pass raids became a local issue because an important group of location residents were exempt from the pass laws which applied only to 'native foreigners'.[122] Exemption was granted to those Africans from the eastern Cape who carried certificates of citizenship;[123] Africans who owned claims and held miner's certificates; and Africans who were their own masters. The latter group were issued protection passes and they pursued a variety of occupations: well-owners, standholders, eating-house keepers, cart-owners, cab-owners, wood-riders, transport riders, produce-sellers, hawkers, ginger-beer makers, debris-washers, milk-vendors, fruit-sellers, bottle-sellers, masons, brick-makers, carpenters, painters, tailors, harness-makers, tinsmiths, well-sinkers, jewellers and rug-makers.[124] Other Africans qualified for exemption on the basis of literacy or the ability to speak English: teachers like Henry Mayafi, Elisha Moroka and Charles Mbete, clergymen like John Roberts Parkie and civil servants in the Post Office like Nelson Lindie.[125]

Some Africans accumulated capital in Kimberley. Africa Kinde, for example, made a substantial sum out of mining (in 1881 he had £4,600 on fixed deposit at the Standard Bank), sold his claims during the 'share mania' and invested the proceeds in land in Barkly West. By 1890 he was a prosperous farmer with unmortgaged farms of considerable value and herds of cattle the envy of many of his neighbours.[126] Both James Poote, the Independent Minister, and Gwayi Tyamzashe, the Congregational Minister, owned claims in Dutoitspan Mine but made little money out of them.[127] Perhaps, the most successful African in Kimberley was a Mfengu, Joseph Moss, the High Court Interpreter. Moss lived with his family in Bultfontein Road, Newton, on the Company Estate. He employed servants, not only grooms for his horses, but domestic servants as well. In 1883 he sold his second house, which had stables for 12 horses, in the Malay camp and bought land with the proceeds near Taungs. He wrote superb English and spoke with a disarming eloquence. He was apparently above corruption; it was well known that interpeters often had control over conviction or acquittal in cases and were subject to the temptations of bribes. He was a man of means, a substantial intellect and in the mid-1880s played an important role in mobilising the black vote in Parliamentary elections.[128]

Other Africans and 'people of colour' displayed their success in a more flamboyant fashion. The 'swell nigger' could be found in Newton, the Malay Camp and the locations. He attracted a lot of venom from white citizens and envy from Africans impressed by the riches of Kimberley. 'His every day costume is a black clerical looking coat', wrote one correspondent:

> white flannel pants, pipe clayed boots and his woolly head surmounted with a black tile profusely enveloped with several yards of gilt-edged muslin; added to this a few pounds of Abyssinian gold indiscriminately distributed about his person and we have the ready made "gentleman". On Sundays our friend may be seen in his cab taking a quiet drive into the country when . . . he can with his bottle of "French" (nothing less than "French" does for this fellow) and bundle of choice cigars thoroughly enjoy himself.[129]

This opulence was taken by Europeans to be the conspicuous consumption indulged in by IDBs and there is little doubt that this flashiness was generally the uniform of touts and middle-men in the illicit trade. The term 'swell nigger' was American slang and applied to 'people of colour' as well as Africans.

Much more research needs to be done into the social history of Kimberley before a detailed landscape of race and class can be presented in our period. What little evidence that has come to light suggests some fluid lines of racial association. Colonial Africans, 'people of colour' and Europeans who lived in Newton, the Malay Camp and the locations had more in common with each other than with Africans from the interior. Most of the former spoke English, wore European clothes and were well acquainted with colonial capitalism. Attendance at churches and schools was suggestive of social and racial stratification. Both were divided into three categories: white colonial 'upper and middle classes'; 'half-castes and civilised natives' and poor whites; and mission schools and churches for 'raw Kaffirs'. Education was in the hands of the churches and the Anglicans, in particular, regarded the education of 'half-castes', 'civilized natives' and poor whites as 'rescuing the first generation of the labouring classes'.[130]

Another snapshot of racial integration was provided by a petition to Parliament in 1885. 'The Coloured population of Kimberley and adjoining locations' petitioned because they considered themselves 'heavy oppressed through heavy taxation'. They complained of ten taxes, some of which were only applied to Africans: the protection pass, the labour contract, house duty, stand rates, sanitary rates, commonage tax on cattle, cab tax, water cart tax, scotch cart tax and the dog tax. They demanded the modification of the pass system so as to afford 'more facility and freedom', and most importantly feared that heavy taxation damaged the prospect of a basic education for their children.[131]

Of all the racial groups in Kimberley the Indians were the butt of the most overt white racism. Not only were Indians obstructed in the courts and in the practice of the Hindu religion (although a majority were Catholic), but it was also suggested that the laws of supply and demand in the local produce market should be suspended. 'It appears to us that our local morning market exists principally for the coolies', wrote the editor of the *Independent*:

> Under the present system these people are enabled to outbid most other buyers and buy in as large quantities as they choose and by hawking the produce about the camp they gain a profit of three or four hundred per cent on the outlay . . . We know that it is not advisable generally to interfere with the principles of supply and demand, as it is a question that is self-regulating, but we do not think that our market should be carried on for the benefit of a certain section of the inhabitants, who have little or no stake in the place and whose chief ambition is to amass a fortune and return to their native country.[132]

This hypocrisy lay behind an attempt to create a 'coolie location' well out of reach of the produce market. Pressure for Indian segregation was built up through the 'imagery of infectious disease';[133] Indians were associated with insanitary habits.[134] In 1879 a site for a 'coolie location' was marked out near Otto's compound, but Indians were not legally compelled to live there and as it was too far from the market no stands were taken up. In 1884 another site was selected parallel to and west of Gway's village and this remained empty as well. In May 1885 Indians were moved from Tacoon Square near the old municipal compound to make way for the railway terminus and they moved into Newton or the Malay Camp. Indians managed to avoid segregation and the sabotage of their market operations until the end of the century.[135]

CONCLUSION

In the late 1870s a class of mining capitalists emerged who developed the productive forces in leaps and bounds. At the same time the African working class expanded in response to the prodigious demand for labour and developed a stake in the locations and townships on the Company estate. By the turn of the decade the transformation of small diggers and share-workers into overseers and managers was complete in the richer mines. Overseers began to organise as a stratum of supervisory workers with interests opposed to both labourers and managers. They had to suffer the indignity of a plan to have them searched together with African labourers. This plan was part of a strategy to subject both black and white workers to industrial discipline. The most important aspect of this strategy was to achieve greater control over the supply of African labour coming to Kimberley and their productivity in the mines. While Southey and Lanyon upheld the principles of government non-intervention in the production process, the Griqualand West Rebellion and the spate of colonial wars at the turn of the decade raised the issue of African control in Kimberley in a dramatic fashion. In 1879 Sir Charles Warren introduced policies of compulsory compounding and localisation of Africans. He took the first major steps – beyond the pass laws and discrimination in the sale of liquor – down the road to official, racial segregation in the mining economy. Moreover, in the full flush of investment in steam machinery and systematic production, it was what the mining capitalists demanded. 'This is now the richest community in the world for its size', wrote Cecil Rhodes, 'and . . . it shows every sign of permanency [and it] would take at our present rate of working 100 years to work out.'[136]

6

The 'share mania'

In October 1880 Griqualand West was annexed to the Cape Colony. Annexation had been on the cards since 1877, but had been delayed because of Cape fears over the increasing Griqualand West debt. In 1880 the debt stood at over £500,000 of which £200,000 was war expenditure. To overcome the Cape's reluctance to annex the diamond province, Britain agreed to waive the war expenditure, although the Cape would have preferred an imperial loan or guarantee for a railway to Kimberley. The strongest British pressure for annexation came from the Crown Agents and the Bank of England; the latter had raised the £90,000 loan to compensate the Orange Free State for the loss of the Diamond Fields. 'If it were not for the debt to the Bank of England and the Crown Agents', commented the Colonial Office:

> it would serve the Cape right to say we would practically have nothing more to do with the Province, but throw the reins on the horses' necks by giving the Diggers responsible government and leaving them to fight it out with their creditors and the [London and South African] Company.[1]

The Colonial Office had promised either to repay the Bank's loan or to improve its security. As it was unable to ensure the repayment of the loan, the Colonial Office did all it could to improve its security by encouraging annexation to the Cape. Annexation in 1880 primarily meant the attachment of a debtor province to the Cape's better credit rating in the London capital markets.

In Kimberley the most immediate financial effect of annexation was the 'share mania', which developed out of a phase of rapid mining company formation. Beginning in late 1880, but largely concentrated in the first half of 1881, the majority of private companies and small holdings in the mines were put into joint-stock mining companies. By April 1881 66 companies, including seven in the Orange Free State mines of Jagersfontein and Koffyfontein, had been floated on the Fields with a total nominal capital of £7,365,390. By the end of the year there were 71 companies in the Kimberley mines alone, with a nominal capital of £9,658,960.[2]

It is impossible to assess with accuracy the proportion of colonial to metropolitan capital speculated in the mines. Frankel made the claim that for the first 15 years of diamond production the mines were financed out of

Table 3 *Vendors' and invested capital, and fixed and circulating capital, in non-colonial and colonial DMCs formed in 1881*[3]

Companies	Vendors	Cash		Claims	Machinery	
	%	%		%	%	
Kimberley	84.1	15.9		84.9	10.6	
De Beers	85.2	14.8	100%	91.4	8.6	100%
Dutoitspan	65.6	34.4		84.4	15.6	
Bultfontein	60.6	39.4		78.9	21.1	
Non-colonial	67.5	32.5		83.6	16.4	

their own surplus and through inflation in the Cape.[4] On the whole this was true, but it should be noted that 15 of the 71 companies formed in 1881 were incorporated in London and Paris, and these 15 accounted for one-third of the total nominal capital of the mines. While this indicated where some company promoters hoped to raise capital, shares were not taken up by a wide public and remained restricted to the diamond brokers and merchants of Hatton Garden.[5]

The proportion of vendors' shares in issued capital is easier to prise from the statistics. Claim vendors often took payment in cash and scrip and, therefore, the actual cash invested was likely to have been even smaller. Despite the heavy weight of vendors' shares, there were marked differences between the richer and poorer mines (see Table 3). The majority of claim vendors kept their property in Kimberley and De Beers mines, where only a small proportion of capital was issued for cash. In contrast, a greater share of the poorer mines, where the majority of the non-colonial companies were formed, was taken up by the outside public. This was due to three main reasons: Kimberley residents knew the best properties and poor companies were sold to Colonial and European speculators; Kimberley capital, realised from the sale of claims and shares, was used to buy up poorer claims in the other mines and then sold for cash at inflated prices; and more working capital was required in the poorer mines, where the rate of development was slower, and investment in machinery was limited.

THE KIMBERLEY SHARE MARKET

Throughout 1880 claim prices rose rapidly in all the mines. In April the banks reported that money was becoming more plentiful in Kimberley and that residents had a greater confidence in the future of the mining town. This confidence was expressed through a sharp increase in mortgage investment.[6] At the same time claim consolidation progressed rapidly in Kimberley Mine. In August half of the pit was owned by seven joint-stock companies and by the end of 1880 ten companies had been formed in Kimberley Mine with a capital of £1,713,050.[7] The majority of claims were put into these companies 'at a valuation about 30 per cent above market rates'.[8] A similar situation existed in De Beers Mine where the Diament Commandit Gesellschaft and the De Beers Mining Company had been floated. The shares of these early joint-stock pioneers were generally well held and rapidly rose to premiums. But some stock was realised and speculation in the claims of the poorer mines began in earnest.[9] Between the beginning and the end of 1880 claim prices rose 50 per cent in Dutoitspan and 75 per cent in Bultfontein, despite the serious litigation over the proprietoral rights of the London and South African Exploration Company to raise claim licence fees.[10]

The 'share mania' took place in the first six months of 1881. In February the Royal Stock Exchange was established so that brokers and others could meet for business 'without the trouble of going round the camps to enquire for shares or to offer them for sale'.[11] The Exchange opened with 100 members in temporary premises in Beit's Buildings before moving to a new location in Ebden Street, where desks were provided for brokers as well as newspapers and telegraphic facilities. In the beginning all share transactions were for cash, but with the speculation of individuals at the coast shares began to take unprecedented jumps in price and this encouraged purchases on credit.[12] Time bargains became the order of the day. A time bargain was the promise to pay for a share in the future at an agreed price. In the interim the bargain or call could be bought and sold. However, if the market value of the share dropped before the agreed delivery date, the purchaser often refused to pay.[13]

Between April and June the engagements for the delivery of scrip 'assumed unusual proportions'.[14] The boom was fuelled by bank advances for the purchase of scrip, with the Cape of Good Hope Bank taking the bulk of the business, but being itself helped out with credit from the Standard Bank. In April the latter bank began to restrict its advances, as it found it 'necessary to check the speculative mania before it assumed greater dimensions'.[15] Advances were rejected at Port Elizabeth and Cape Town, which caused dissatisfaction amongst speculators. The Standard Bank partially succeeded in checking the 'share mania' in May and by June the bubble had burst.

The first companies were honestly promoted, but it was under the cover of their success that indifferent companies were formed. Shares in these companies were forced up to premiums on the backs of their betters:

> There appears to be a "ring" here, and every person in it has received an allotment of shares from each company, while the capital of the general public is received and politely returned. Immediately the shares are quoted at a premium and the outsiders are glad to pay it to get into what is apparently a good thing, but which has only been made to appear such by the chicancry of the promoters and their supporters.[16]

Shares were allotted – with a minimal sum payable in the first instance – to catch premiums and sold before calls were made. When the boom broke many premium catchers were stuck with a heavy amount of scrip which was a 'property difficult to get rid of and expensive to keep'.[17] It was the liberal allotment of shares to 'men of straw' without means, that led to the charges of an 'immense amount of swindling' taking place in Kimberley.[18]

The game of catching premiums was played on one of the most dangerous fields for speculation. Mining was generally regarded as a risky sector for investment and, for those not interested in quick stag profits, a higher rate of return on capital was expected. 'No investment can be considered safe and good in these diamond mines', wrote the *Diamond News*, 'that will not give 20 per cent per annum clear profit'.[19] But the majority of companies floated during the 'share mania' were over-capitalised and promised only modest dividends. There were a number of rich companies, which were well known to local capitalists and sharedealers, but the greatest volume of dealing took place in the shares of the dubious concerns. The large Kimberley sharedealers took advantage of the ignorance of speculators in the colonies and amassed a fortune at the height of the boom, but found that they had to retire bills 'receiving in return the scrip (now of a much depreciated nature) which they had sold at a vast premium and probably at a handsome profit'.[20]

The accounts of three leading firms of stockbrokers provide a good illustration of the growth and collapse of sharedealing during and after the 'share mania'. In 1879, A. Goldschmidt and Company, a partnership between Anthony Goldschmidt and Charles Sonnenberg, was a claim-holder in Dutoitspan with property worth £20,000, but by the end of 1881 the firm had become leading sharedealers in Kimberley, having amassed £180,000 over their liabilities, mostly in diamond scrip. They held shares in almost every company floated on the Fields and had promoted three, the mammoth Anglo-African DMC[21] and the smaller Alliance and Beaconsfield DMCs. But they were paper diamond kings, as the Standard Bank explained:

> They are speculative characters and Sonnenberg especially is unscrupulous. The large capital they once showed was purely fictitious and whatever they had they lost in mining claims and scrip which are now worthless. Both partners are here at present doing next to nothing beyond earning a small commission.[22]

By the end of 1884 they were barely solvent and their only material assets were a half-share in a powder factory and farms in the Transvaal.[23]

Another major firm of sharebrokers, S. Isaacs and Company, also went bankrupt after the boom was broken. In November 1881, the partners in the firm, Samuel Isaacs, Adolph Gates and Henry Hertog, were £307,000 to the good and had recently sold their interest in the Anglo-French DMC to Charles Roulina, wealthy Parisian diamond cutting factory owner, for £95,000. Like A. Goldschmidt and Company they held shares in every

DMC formed on the Fields, but their major interests were in the International, the London and South African, the Beaconsfield and the Alliance. By the end of 1883 their diamond scrip assets were worthless and the firm went bankrupt.[24]

August Rothschild, the best known auctioneer in Kimberley, became an important sharedealer during the 'mania'. He managed to stave off bankruptcy longer than the major firms of sharedealers:

> In the end of 1880 his statement [wrote the Standard Bank Manager] made up to that date showed him £40,000 to the good of which about one third had connection with diamonds. He speculated largely during the excitement and made £57,000. At the beginning of the reaction he had large liabilities with us and very large parcels of scrip on hand, but he would not sell imagining the 'drop' was only temporary. He continued however and certain parcels had to be sacrificed to enable him to reduce (which he has done to a large extent) and upon making up his books for the end of December 1881 the £57,000 profit had been reduced by £53,000.[25]

By the end of 1884 Rothschild regarded himself as 'irretrievably ruined in consequence of his share speculations and giving credit too freely'.[26] In 1885 he went bankrupt, but he was soon rehabilitated by friends and in 1888 he was worth £50,000.[27]

COLONIAL AND LONDON SPECULATORS

In the immediate aftermath of the boom Kimberley sharedealers viewed with indifference the paralysis of Colonial speculators. With the exception of the few companies, like Baxter's Gully and the Cape DMCs, which were floated in the Cape Colony, colonial speculators were chiefly buyers of diamond scrip when share prices were high. They bought into mining companies about which little was known outside Kimberley. The largest Cape Town plunger was Andrew McKenzie, a dock agent and building contractor.[28] At the end of 1881 his commitments were so large that his bankruptcy detonated a commercial crisis that exploded throughout the Cape and lasted well into 1885. In early 1881 McKenzie began speculating in diamond shares on a 'gigantic scale':

> It appears to have been his misfortune that his first speculations proved successful [wrote his liquidator] for ... misled thereby or prompted by a natural love of speculation he plunged madly into the excitement. He appears to have bought into every company ... in many instances beyond the highest market rates giving his bills with pledges of shares in payment of his purchases which altogether amounted to £300,000.[29]

McKenzie met his bills until June 1881, but from then until the 15 October he had to take up bills worth £94,378. By this time the 'share mania' had collapsed and McKenzie was unable to pay. He was forced to meet his creditors and he went bankrupt in December with liabilities of £451,570 against assets of £217,135.[30]

What was striking about colonial speculation was the amount of credit on offer to men with relatively little capital. Goodliffe and Company was a Port Elizabeth firm operating as a general merchant on a credit of £10,000 from a supporting firm in London. The business apparently never paid, but in April 1880 Goodliffe began to speculate in diamond shares with an initial £800 provided by his wife:

> Finding probably, however, that far greater facilities were given for carrying on this speculation than he could command in his legitimate business, and that there was a wide field for speculations, he carried on to a considerable extent, his purchases in 16 months amounting to over £80,000.[31]

When he was declared insolvent in 1882 his assets amounted to £5,031. Other Port Elizabeth businessmen suffered a similar fate. Fairbridge and Petit, well-known sharebrokers, lost their capital in diamond speculation.[32] Andrew Gloag, a saddler, crippled himself in diamond share speculation and only finished paying off his debts in 1888.[33] Peter Heugh, a medium-sized dock agent, worth £20,000 in 1881, speculated in Kimberley shares and went bankrupt two years later as a result.[34] William Jones, a leading tanner, held £21,000 worth of the shares of the Orion DMC, a good investment, but lost all he had by supporting the poorly informed speculations of his sons.[35] And these examples could be multiplied to cover the good majority of coastal merchants and business men impressed by the lure of diamond wealth.

There was a limited arbitrage business between the Kimberley and London diamond share markets. In particular, companies registered in Europe found a market for their shares in both London and Kimberley.[36] The London share market was in Hatton Garden, where the diamond importers and jewellers did their business. Few diamond mining companies had official quotations on the London Stock Exchange.[37] Its regulations required 50 per cent of the capital of a company to be offered to the public, and not many mining companies managed to satisfy this ruling. Thus, the Hatton Garden share market was an outside, street market with few formalities and little protection for uninformed investors.

Even though the London share market was restricted to those in the diamond business, Kimberley market operators attempted to relieve the pressure of their commitments by selling in London. In March 1881 there were heavy transmissions of scrip between the Cape and London.[38] In May, when the pressure of calls began to mount in Kimberley and colonial capital accumulation proved inadequate, speculators looked desperately to the London market, where there was a boom in Cornish mines. But the boom collapsed and the chance of attracting small investors to diamond companies was lost.[39]

The failure to attract European capital to the diamond mines was, in the view of the Standard Bank, at the heart of the collapse of the 'share mania'. The General Manager summed up the situation:

... the main reason for the widespread recession in prices is ... that the South African community thoroughly impressed with the 'payability' of the Fields, were immoderate in their desire to retain as large an interest as possible therein. Hence shares were bought for cash while it lasted, but afterwards on credit to an enormous extent, and this endeavour to hold more than they could afford to hold, has not only weakened the market to a disastrous extent, but has prevented the introduction of European capital without which the diamond industry cannot permanently be conducted on its present scale. No immediate improvement can be expected, as the diamond share market is now thoroughly discredited and prices will probably be worse before they are better. Relief will, however, we think be experienced in time, by foreign capitalists filling the place of weak colonial proprietors.[40]

Indeed, hardly had the 'share mania' collapsed, before promoters began sorting over the wreckage with an eye to reconstruction in Europe.[41] However, it was a piecemeal process as the European capital markets were struck by an international depression.

COMPANY PROMOTERS

Some individual claimholders made fortunes during the 'share mania'. One celebrated diamond magnate, William Knight, sold out completely and left for England £120,000 richer.[42] Among the few Afrikaners to make money out of company formation were the Marais brothers. While Christian Marais held on to his shares and a seat on the board of the most important Kimberley company, the Kimberley Central, Pieter Marais sold out and invested in the surrounding countryside. He bought 15 farms near the Vaal River and became a dominant figure in the Afrikaner Bond in Griqualand West.[43] Other claimowners took shares in companies, rather than selling out, and took a keen interest in board room politics and the secondary market.

In 1880/1 there were five major constellations of claimowners who promoted companies during the 'share mania'. First and foremost there was the group of diamond merchants and brokers led by Jules Porges and Company. This leading firm had, as we have already noted, combined their Kimberley claims with the local diamond merchants, Lewis and Marks and Paddon Brothers. Lewis and Marks was believed to be the wealthiest firm on the Fields, worth over £300,000 at the end of 1881 and 'interested in almost every good venture' on offer in Kimberley.[44] A second group was led by Charles Posno, whose family had originally been in the Amsterdam diamond industry, but whose interests were now in the rents extracted from the landed estate of the London and South African Exploration Company.[45] As the majority of European registered companies were formed in the Dutoitspan and Bultfontein mines, it was not surprising that Posno was a director of nine companies, one of the leading directors in the mines, and a fellow director of the London Company, Harry Mosenthal, was a director of five companies.

111

Table 4 *Selected directors, non-colonial DMCs, 1881–83*

Companies	Cie. Française (1880)	North Block (1881)	London & S. A'n (1881)	Victoria (1881)	African (1881)	Anglo-African (1881)	Anglo-French (1881)	Cape ... Hope (1881)	Central Mining (1880)	Cie. Generale (1883)	Gordon (1881)	Kimb'y Mining (1880)	Orion (1881)	Phoenix (1882)	West End (1882)	Adamant (1881)	Bu. Homestead (1880)	Bu. Mining (1880)	Franco-Afr'ne (1883)	Le Diamant (1882)*	Central Jag'tein (1881)*	London & Jag'tein (1881)*	Total Director-ships
Alderson, W.			x																				1
Barkly, Sir H.						x	x																2
Blaine, D. P.								x			x												2
Dunk'buhler, A.				x												x		x					3
Giddy, R. W. H.						x	x																2
Graham, R. D.			x																				1
Herz, C.															x								1
Herz, F	x					x	x																3
King, H. J.																					x	x	2
Leverson, J.				x				x								x							3
Lewis, I.	x					x	x						x			x							5
Lilienfeld, M.																					x	x	2
Litkie, V. A.		x																				x	2
MacDonald, A. J.				x							x												2
Marks, S.													x			x							2
Mayne, Adm.								x			x					x							3
Mosenthal, A.													x			x							2
Mosenthal, H.				x	x				x							x		x					5
Ochs, S.																		x	x				2
Paddon, S. W.						x	x						x	x	x								5
Porges, J.	x																				x		2
Posno, C. J.				x	x				x		x	x	x		x	x	x						9
Rhodes, C. J.			x													x							2
Roulina, C.									x											x			2
Webb, H. B.									x		x					x							2
Wernher, J.				x												x							2

Source: *The Directory of Directors* (1881–83)
* In the Orange Free State

Both Porges and Posno drew capital from European investors, but whereas Posno's contacts were limited to diamond merchants and brokers in London and Amsterdam, Porges had well established links with European financiers, Parisian bankers and mining brokers. The firm's key contact in Paris was Herz Fils et Compagnie, the leading mining broker on the Coulisse. The companies they promoted had been earmarked in Kimberley by Lewis and Marks.[46]

There is little doubt that these men made spectacular profits by floating companies in Europe. Jules Porges' promotion of the Anglo–African Company is a case in point. In 1880 Lewis and Marks, Senior, and Lewis and Marks, Junior, owned the Incorporated DMC in Dutoitspan mine. In 1881 this company was divided into two: the Anglo–African was floated in London and the Anglo–French[47] in Paris. The Anglo–African was formed with a capital of £650,000 and, next to the De Beers DMC, was the most highly capitalised company on the Fields. What was remarkable about this large company was the very high proportion of shares offered to the public, in stark contrast to the number of Compagnie Française shares offered for subscription. The vendors took £390,000 in cash and £216,000 in shares of which 1,110 were founders' shares. Few investors stopped to wonder why the vendors were so eager to dispose of their property, but it became evident later when the company failed to pay dividends. Still the shares of the company remained marketable and it became a force to be reckoned with in the process of amalgamation in the later 1880s.[48]

N. M. Rothschild and Sons and Rothschild Frères were induced to invest in the Anglo–African after the 'share mania' had collapsed. It came about in the following fashion. Anthony Goldschmidt sold £65,000 worth of Anglo–African shares to Lewis and Marks and they arranged to sell them to the Union Generale, a French corporate bank. The Union Generale went bankrupt before it was able to take delivery of the scrip. As a result the brokers, Herz Fils, looked around for alternative buyers. They offered 5,000 shares to N. M. Rothschild and Sons for £8 each. The firm's diamond correspondent, Albert Gansl, recommended the speculation and predicted that the Anglo–African's net profit would be £100,000 a year. On the strength of Gansl's advice the English and French Rothschilds bought 6,000 Anglo–African shares on joint account at £7 10s each, a speculation of £45,000. Gansl further reported that the shares would increase 50 per cent in value in one year and such a capital gain would mean a 20 per cent dividend at the below par purchase price.[49]

But the company did not declare any dividend at all. At the end of 1882 Gansl was sent to Kimberley to ascertain for the Rothschilds whether it was 'advisable to buy some more of the Anglo–African shares in order to reduce the cost of the first purchase'[50] or to sell the shares at a loss. Gansl soon discovered that the Anglo–African was 'unsatisfactory in every respect'[51] and that Dutoitspan Mine as a whole was barely self-supporting and could not 'be expected to yield any profit under present circumstances'.[52] Despite

113

Table 5 *Selected directors, colonial DMCs, 1880–81*

	Kimb'y & De Beers	Barnato (1881)	Beaconsfield (1881)	British (1880)	Cape (1881)	Gem (1881)	North-East (1880)	Octahedron (1880)	Rose-Innes (1880)	South East (1880)	Standard (1880)	Vulcan (1881)	Birbeck (1881)	De Beers (1880)	De Beers Central (1881)	Elma (1881)	Eagle (1881)	Frere (1881)	International (1881)	Oriental (1881)	Pleiades (1881)	Schwab's Gully (1881)
Abraham, H.	1	x												x			x					
Abrahams, J. E.	2																				x	
Alderson, W.	3						x						x							x		
Astleford, J.	4															x						
Barnato, B.	5	x												x			x					
Beit, A.	6															x						x
Birbeck, J.	7		x										x					x	x	x		
De Pass, J.	8					x					x					x						
Doveton, D. E.	9																					
Fenton, R.	10					x					x	x			x							
Gates, A.	11																					
Gervers, F.	12																			x		
Goldschmidt, A.	13		x															x				
Graham, R. D.	14		x		x	x								x					x			
Hart, H. B.	15																					
Hartog, H.	16		x															x				
Knight, W.	17			x					x													
Levy, A.	18				x															x		
Litkie, E. M.	19			x																		
McGreggor, A.	20			x												x						x
Richter, P. J.	21																					
Rhodes, C. J.	22		x											x				x				
Robinson, I.	23																	x				x
Robinson, J. B.	24							x	x													
Rothschild, A. A.	25					x		x		x										x		
Slater, T. G.	26																					
Tarry, E. W.	27											x										
Wallis, H. B.	28																					
Ward, H. A.	29																					

Table: Companies and directorships. Source: *Prospectuses of Diamond Mining and Other Companies*, Kimberley, 1881.

Companies: Du'pan & Bu'tein	Adamanta (1881)	British (1881)	Caledonian (1881)	Consolidated (1881)	Dutoitspan (1881)	Eldorado (1881)	European (1881)	Fry's Gully (1881)	Globe (1881)	G'land West (1880)	Hercules (1881)	Ne Plus Ultra (1881)	Royal (1881)	Standard (1881)	Victoria (1881)	Aegis (1881)	Alliance (1881)	Atlas (1881)	Bu. Central (1881)	Bu. Colonial (1881)	Cosmopolitan (1881)	Crown (1881)	Equitable (1881)	Fr & D'Esterre (1880)	Lilienstein (1880)	Union (1881)	Total Directorships
1	.	.	.	.	.	.	.	.	x	.	.	.	.	.	.	.	.	.	.	.	.	.	.	.	.	.	4
2	.	.	.	.	.	.	.	.	.	.	.	.	x	.	.	.	.	.	.	.	.	.	x	.	.	.	3
3	.	.	.	.	.	.	.	.	.	.	.	.	.	.	.	.	.	.	.	.	.	.	.	.	.	.	3
4	.	x	.	x	.	.	.	.	.	.	.	.	x	.	x	.	.	x	.	.	.	.	.	.	.	.	6
5	.	.	.	.	.	.	.	x	x	.	.	.	.	.	.	.	.	.	.	.	.	.	.	.	.	.	5
6	.	.	x	.	.	.	.	.	.	.	.	.	.	.	.	.	.	.	.	.	.	.	.	.	.	.	3
7	.	.	.	.	.	x	x	.	.	.	.	.	.	.	.	.	.	.	.	.	.	.	.	.	.	.	7
8	.	.	.	.	.	.	.	.	.	.	.	.	.	.	.	.	.	.	.	.	.	.	.	'	.	.	3
9	.	.	x	x	.	.	.	.	.	.	.	.	.	.	.	x	.	.	.	.	.	.	.	x	.	.	4
10	.	x	.	.	.	.	.	.	.	.	.	.	.	.	.	.	.	.	.	.	.	.	.	.	.	.	5
11	.	x	.	.	.	.	.	x	.	.	.	.	x	.	x	.	.	.	.	.	.	.	.	.	.	.	4
12	.	.	.	.	.	.	.	.	.	.	.	.	.	.	.	x	.	.	.	.	.	.	.	x	.	.	3
13	.	.	.	.	.	.	.	x	.	.	.	.	.	x	.	.	.	.	.	.	x	x	.	.	.	.	6
14	.	.	.	x	.	x	.	.	.	.	.	.	.	.	.	.	.	.	.	.	x	.	x	.	.	.	9
15	.	.	.	.	.	.	.	.	.	.	x	x	.	x	.	.	.	.	.	.	.	x	.	.	.	.	4
16	x	x	.	.	.	x	.	.	.	.	.	.	x	.	x	.	.	.	.	.	.	x	.	.	.	.	8
17	.	.	.	.	.	.	.	.	.	.	.	.	.	.	.	.	.	.	.	.	.	.	.	.	.	.	2
18	.	.	.	.	.	x	.	.	x	.	.	.	.	.	.	.	.	.	.	.	.	.	.	.	.	.	4
19	x	.	.	.	.	x	.	.	.	.	.	.	.	.	.	.	.	.	.	.	.	.	.	.	',	.	3
20	.	.	.	.	.	.	.	.	.	.	.	.	.	.	.	.	.	.	.	.	.	.	.	.	.	.	3
21	x	.	.	.	.	x	.	.	.	.	.	x	.	.	.	.	.	.	.	.	.	.	.	.	.	.	3
22	.	.	.	.	.	.	.	.	.	.	.	.	.	.	.	.	.	.	.	.	x	.	x	x	.	.	6
23	.	.	.	.	.	.	.	.	.	.	.	.	.	.	.	.	.	.	.	.	.	.	.	.	.	.	2
24	.	.	.	.	x	.	x	.	.	.	.	.	x	.	.	.	.	.	.	.	x	x	.	.	.	.	7
25	.	.	.	x	x	.	.	x	.	.	.	.	.	.	.	.	.	.	.	.	.	.	.	.	.	.	7
26	.	.	.	.	.	.	.	.	.	.	.	x	.	x	.	x	x	.	.	.	.	.	.	x	5
27	.	.	.	.	.	.	.	x	.	.	.	.	.	.	.	.	.	.	.	.	.	.	.	.	.	.	2
28	.	.	x	.	.	x	.	.	.	.	.	.	x	x	.	.	.	.	.	.	x	.	.	.	.	.	5
29	.	x	.	.	.	x	.	.	.	.	.	.	.	x	.	.	x	.	.	.	.	.	.	.	.	.	4

Source: *Prospectuses of Diamond Mining and Other Companies*, Kimberley, 1881.

Gansl's findings the Rothschilds did not sell their shares. Instead, they provided working capital for the company in the same way as the merchant bank, J. H. Schröder and Company, supported the Victoria DMC in De Beers Mine.[53]

The investment of European diamond merchants, like Jules Porges, had begun the boom, but it was Kimberley claimowners who spun the catherine wheel of company promotion. There were three major groups of Kimberley capitalists. J. B. Robinson was a capital force on his own with substantial interests in the Kimberley and Dutoitspan Mines. He was largely supported by the Cape of Good Hope Bank, which had to borrow from the Standard Bank to meet Robinson's financial requirements. The second group was dominated by the diamond merchant firm, Barnato Brothers. This firm promoted five companies in the thick of the 'share mania' and was closely associated with Hyam Abraham, David Symons and Charles Moses. The last group, of which Cecil Rhodes became the best known representative, was composed of professional men, merchants and diggers.

Joseph Robinson was a powerful diamond magnate in Kimberley. In 1880 he was instrumental in forming two of the earliest joint-stock companies in Kimberley Mine: the Standard and the Rose-Innes DMCs. In March 1881 both companies added claims to their property. The Standard took over claims Robinson had bought from the Compagnie Française and the Rose-Innes absorbed the claims of the Danish digger, Hans Olsen. Through these transactions Robinson made a fortune in the secondary market. For example, in March he sold 913 £100 Standard shares for £194,640 over double their nominal value.[54] Robinson also had an important foothold in Dutoitspan Mine. In September 1880, he promoted the Griqualand West DMC with a capital of £283,000, in which he and Henry Wallis owned two-thirds of the shares. The claims were put in at £2,000 each, which compared reasonably with the much inflated £6,000 of the Anglo–African DMC.[55] These two companies dominated Dutoitspan Mine.

Three genuine and valuable promotions made Robinson a capitalist to be reckoned with on the Diamond Fields, but he also owned some poor ground in Kimberley Mine which he tried to off-load on an ignorant public. Robinson and his London partner, Maurice Marcus, floated the Crystal DMC, capital £160,000, at three times its assessed value, and drew some sharp criticism both from experts with a keen eye to claim values and from the wider community over whom he presided as mayor. In September 1880, Gustavus Blanch, one-time rebel and well-known claim agent, assessed the prospects of the Crystal DMC as part of a review of a number of new companies for the *Dutoitspan Herald*. He commented that even the assessed value of the Crystal was high as some of the claims were 'worse than valueless'.[56] Robinson immediately instructed his attorney, Frederic Stow, to demand an apology from Blanch. The demand was strongly criticised by the *Diamond News* which believed Robinson was forcing an unwarranted retraction through legal terrorism.[57] In response, Robinson made a swingeing attack on the integrity of Blanch in his own newspaper, the *Daily Independent*:

> We would merely express our surprise at the audacity of an individual who has within a very short period several times compounded with his creditors, and suffered imprisonment for debt presuming to give his opinion upon the value of his neighbours' property.[58]

Blanch was stung into the reply, which was to form part of a libel suit a year later, that he promised to expose fraud regardless of the wealth or position of those involved. Blanch was supported by the *Diamond News* which published a simulated report of a Crystal Company Board meeting showing Robinson making all the decisions and surrounded by nominal directors. The editor referred to H. B. Wallis and Lionel Phillips as 'two gentlemen who can scarcely be considered, when we look at their past and present business relations with Mr Robinson, as forming an independent element on the Board of Directors'.[59]

The Crystal Company attracted public attention because of Robinson's attempt to force an amalgamation between it and the Cape DMC. Between June and August 1880 Robinson bought 1,000 Cape shares from Emil Castens, 570 shares from Martin Lilienfeld and 180 from the Goldscheider Brothers. These shares were bought partly for speculation but by November Robinson was the largest holder in the Cape DMC with 2,250 shares.[60] As early as July the Cape's manager, Mr Grellert, had warned the directors in Port Elizabeth that amalgamation with Robinson's Crystal would spell disaster for the Cape DMC. As a result the directors considered a number of proposals for the amalgamation of claims from Pieter Marais, from George Simpson, from Walter Stanford and from Julius Wernher on behalf of the Compagnie Française. But all these proposals fell through as Joseph Robinson used his influence for a plan of his own. The Cape directors feared that Robinson was using his shares in their company to acquire rich central ground for the Crystal, but they were wrong because Robinson did not intend to torpedo the Cape. Rather, he planned to improve the value of the Crystal by putting it into the richer Cape DMC. In January 1881 Robinson secured the sale of 16 Crystal claims to the Cape for £110,000, as well as Stanford's three and a quarter claims, which he had bought himself, for £25,000 in Cape shares.[61]

This was a one-sided merger and the Cape DMC failed to flourish. In late 1881 Robinson was forced to divide the company and the delayed libel suit against the *Diamond News* was intended to clear the air for this purpose.[62] Two new companies were formed – the North-West and the South-West DMCs – and the Cape DMC was left with the worthless Crystal claims.[63] This development benefited none of the companies concerned. The South-West never paid, was sub-let to contractors and then liquidated in 1884, while the North-West suffered the same fate, laying the foundations for Robinson's later bankruptcy.[64] Robinson's machinations did not only

117

have detrimental consequences for himself. 'Old and tried servants' of the Cape DMC were sacked 'without a day's notice and others comparatively untried put in to occupy their positions'.[65] In July 1881 the remaining overseers, engineers, cart-drivers and labourers went on strike and refused to work under Robinson's managerial staff. At the other end of the scale the Port Elizabeth directors became incensed with the 'dictatorial impertinence' they received from Robinson. Most of them sold out and resigned. John Holland, one director and a leading Port Elizabeth auctioneer, wrote: 'The game is not worth the candle and I blow mine out'.[66]

The second group of local mining capitalists, the Barnato Brothers and friends, survived the 'share mania' with a modest fortune. In early 1881 the newly formed firm of Barnato Brothers floated five companies with a total capital of £493,000 through the Royal Stock Exchange. They lost £28,000 in their two Dutoitspan ventures, the Globe and Fry's Gully, and the Frere in De Beers was an equally dismal failure. Their fourth promotion, the De Beers Central, fared a little better and was absorbed by the De Beers DMC on fair terms in 1883.[67]

The jewel in their collection of companies was the Barnato DMC in Kimberley Mine. This four-claim company was capitalised at £25,000 per claim – the highest claim valuation on the Fields – and Barnato Brothers held nearly all the £115,000 nominal capital. During the 'share mania' they sold half their holding at a premium and when shares collapsed to a tenth of their par value in the aftermath of the boom, they bought in again until they held three-quarters of the scrip. It was a valuable investment. In its first two years, before its claims were covered with reef, dividends amounted to 54 per cent. This equalled the performance of the Kimberley Central DMC and was only surpassed by William Knight's British DMC, which repaid its capital in two and a half years.[68] There were rumours that the Barnato's prodigious output was not wholly the proceeds of its own production, but the company was the hinge on which the firm swung to great wealth. In 1881 Barnato Brothers kept £30,000 on fixed deposit at the Standard Bank and were worth £100,000.[69]

The last group, led by Cecil Rhodes, was in many ways the most successful, although least acquainted with the woof and warp of share markets. Rhodes in partnership with Robert Graham and Charles Rudd had established his mining base in De Beers Mine.[70] In May 1879 he planned to sell his property and go to the bar in London, but a year later, after he had promoted the De Beers DMC, capital £200,000, he was still on the Fields:

> I have had to stop here for two years working at mining matters with head rather than hands and have been very successful though I have not sold out and mining transactions I own with candour are risky. Yet I have such confidence in the company I am in doubling itself during the ensuing year that I shall hold on. The only thing I am afraid of is a new mine and there have been none yet found like these first ones. I represent a large amount of shares

though as I do not sell ready money is scarce. It has been very heavy brain work forming one's block and has taken great time and trouble.[71]

As Rhodes predicted the nominal value of De Beers doubled inside a year. In March 1881 the claims of Frederic Stow, Robert English and George Compton were merged with the De Beers and the value of the original De Beers claims, without its poorer West End ground, was increased to £424,300, an increase of 84.5 per cent. Stow's claims were put into the company for £241,250 and the De Beers DMC with a nominal value of £665,550 in £10 shares was the most highly capitalised company on the Fields.[72]

Over 80 per cent of the original De Beers DMC was owned by five shareholders, and all of them were unable to resist the temptations of the 'share mania'.[73] Rhodes, who was worried by increasing costs of production, sold nearly all his shares for £37,500 in February 1881, but soon bought back in again.[74] Rudd also sold heavily and by the time of the merger with Stow held only half of his original stake of 280 £100 shares. Even though the value of Stow's claims in the new company was half that of the original company, he came out of the merger in March 1881 as the largest individual holder in De Beers. Stow held 16,114 shares; Alderson ranked next with 10,810 shares; English followed with 5,608 shares; while Rhodes, Graham and Rudd held 4,560, 4,316 and 2,955 shares respectively. By December 1881 Stow had sold 5,900 shares, the majority at high premiums in the 'share mania'. At this time Alderson was in severe trouble through rash speculation in the Jagersfontein Mine in the Orange Free State. In September 1883 the Bank of Africa forced him into insolvency and placed an interdict on the 10,946 De Beers shares he had transferred into his father's name. Robert Graham had also run into difficulties and was forced into bankruptcy in September 1883 by the Cape of Good Hope Bank. Stow, Rhodes and Rudd weathered the collapse in share prices and held on to their shareholdings in De Beers.[75]

During the 'share mania' Rhodes and Graham were the most prestigious company promoters on the Fields. In 1881, Rhodes and Graham were the directors of seven and ten diamond mining companies respectively, but they also sat on the boards of tramway, steam laundry, theatre, water, loan and coal companies.[76] Looked at from the point of view of age, Rhodes' ascent to company promoter of these proportions was remarkable. Only in 1876, aged 23, he had bemoaned his lack of a career and promised that he would become a 'most perfect speculator' in two years, if he obtained a profession.[77] Four years later, still lacking a profession, but having served a fruitful apprenticeship with some of the most influential colonial lawyers and merchants, he became a director of the Kimberley Share Exchange Company.[78] He was associated with it from its formation in October 1880, and when he became a member of the Cape Parliament in April 1881, it was the debt dabblings in company promotion of this small undertaking that had raised Rhodes to prominence. But as with other promoters Rhodes turned his hand to some dishonest dealings. While Joseph Robinson had his Crystal, Rhodes had his Beaconsfield.

The Beaconsfield DMC was formed out of 12 claims bought from the Compagnie Française. The claims were put into the Beaconsfield for £10,000 each and the promoters were paid three-quarters of the £132,000 capital. To those who knew the value of the claims it was a case of buying discarded claims and selling them to a public company under the cover of the 'share mania'.[79] Inspector Rennie of the Standard Bank wrote of such bogus concerns:

> ... such companies should be sorted out as soon as possible and an example made of a promoter here and there. One of the notorious companies under this head is the 'Beaconsfield' amongst the promoters and directors of which is the Bank's solicitor R. D. Graham.[80]

Graham held 1,406 £10 shares, while the other promoters, Rhodes, Alderson, Rothschild, Goldschmidt and Octavius Skill, the Manager of the Kimberley Share Exchange company, also held large blocks of shares.[81] This was only one poor venture that Skill's promotion company brought into the market place. It floated ten diamond mining companies during the 'share mania' only one of which, the French and d'Esterre, managed to survive into the second half of the 1880s. All the others liquidated.

Through the Kimberley Share Exchange Company Rhodes speculated in a wide range of companies. In Bultfontein Mine, he had a nominal interest in the Lilienstein, so-named after the Countess wife of Henry Green, and a larger interest in the French and d'Esterre. In Dutoitspan Mine he had a share in the Le Jeune,[82] which in 1882 was refloated in London as the West End DMC. In De Beers Mine the majority of the poor claims shed by the De Beers DMC, under the influence of Stow, were put into the International. Its claims were floated at the high figure of £3,700 each and the company was capitalised at £131,700. The International slipped into debt, failed to pay dividends, liquidated in June 1883 and fell back into the hands of De Beers for the knock-down price £18,974. Rhodes also had a substantial stake in the London and South African which was a hold-all for the poor ground in the West End. The company was promoted by Rhodes, Rudd, Alderson and Goldschmidt in London and its 96 claims were put in for £1,500 each. But it was a bogus company, which never went into production, and its working capital was lent to the South-East DMC in Kimberley Mine for a fixed rate of interest. In 1883 the De Beers DMC bought over a third of the London and South African at a bargain price and in 1884 absorbed the company. Finally, Rhodes speculated in the Jagersfontein Mine in the OFS with Tarry and Alderson and he also bought farms in Barkly West, which contained river diamond claims, with Tarry and Rudd. All in all Rhodes certainly worked hard to form his block of valuable claims, but in common with other company promoters he tried to shuffle off poor property at inflated prices.[83]

CONCLUSION

These then were the mining capitalists who took the best advantage of the 'share mania'. With the exception of Robinson, who went bankrupt in 1886 and moved to the Rand, they were all to play important roles in the formation of a monopoly in diamond production. While Rhodes did not have a clean record in financial dealings on the Fields prior to the final amalgamation, Barnato's reputation, as will be shown in chapter nine, was considerably worse. In the case of Rhodes his biographers have largely been content to bury dishonest dealings under the magical wand of imperialism. In the case of Barnato, his biographers have referred quaintly to his lack of a reputation.[84] There is little value in chronicling swindles in themselves, though they tarnish the conventional historical image of Rhodes, the great imperialist. But they do focus attention on the speculative profits that were made and which exacerbated the condition of the mining industry during the following slump. The inflated capitalisation of most companies, the product of the greed of promoters, contributed substantially to the failure of many companies to pay dividends and was as much a crime of common theft as illicit diamond buying. But while the promoters were responsible for the parlous state of the mining industry during the depression, it was the black working class that was held culpable for the situation, on the strength of the spread of diamond theft, and who eventually paid the due wages of their sins in closed compounds.

7

The depression and strikes of 1883 and 1884

In the 1880s the diamond mining industry went through a crisis followed by a rapid centralisation of capital. The crisis came hard on the heels of the promotion of joint-stock mining companies and was a product of both problems in mining and a collapse in the European diamond market. During the crisis, which manifested itself as a traditional depression in Kimberley, the mineowners made a concerted attempt to reduce wages and to tighten up the industrial discipline of their work-forces. This initiative resulted in two strikes. The first appeared to be a victory for mineworkers, but turned out to be only a prelude to the second, which was a clear success for the mineowners. The defeat of the second strike prepared the way for closed compounds and the centralisation of capital in one giant company, the De Beers Consolidated Mines.

The depression made the greatest impact on the division of labour by narrowing the differentials between grades of work. The mine wage structure was based on a hierarchy fixed by custom and not market calculations in the pre-mining economy. Artisans such as smiths, masons and carpenters, whose occupations had not been created by the mining industry, had fairly clear ideas of traditional differentials and how to defend their position; but the unskilled and semi-skilled operatives such as engine-drivers and overseers, whose jobs had been created in the growth of the mining industry, had no craft traditions to defend. Their wages and the competition of cheaper labour became an issue of bitter contention.

What was at stake during the strikes was a modification of the traditional racial division of labour in which Europeans generally earned more, and had better work conditions, than Indians, Africans and 'persons of colour'. For a period of three to four years it seemed that the mineowners had resolved to ignore some important distinctions between artisans and labourers, between overseers and workers and between Europeans and others. It appeared that white workers were to have their positions of authority eroded in the mining economy. Ten years before, when white men faced a fundamental threat to their position in the mine economy they resorted to insurrectionary tactics in the Black Flag Revolt, while in 1883–84 it was a measure of the development of the Kimberley mines that recently created white proletarians took up the traditional industrial weapon of a strike.

122

THE IMPACT OF THE DEPRESSION ON PROFIT IN THE MINING INDUSTRY

Between 1882 and 1885 the price of diamonds collapsed by 42 per cent in the London rough market and the enormous wealth of close to £4 million produced by the mines in 1882 was reduced to an all-time low of £2.5 million in 1885. This collapse led to the liquidation of 30 of the 71 joint-stock mining companies, most of them in the poorer mines of Bultfontein and Dutoitspan, and the reduction of the total capitalisation of the mines from £9.6 to £7.8 million.[1]

Between 1882 and 1885 mining profits scarcely reached four per cent of total capital while dividends were even less given interest payments, depreciation costs and reserve fund provisions.[2] This poor profit profile presents some interesting features of the mining economy. First, most of the profits were made by only ten companies, that is, a quarter of those enterprises that survived into 1886. Secondly, despite the deepening depression in 1884 and 1885, profits were better than in the two preceding years. Finally, it was in the poorer mines that profits improved the most over the depression and in 1884 and 1885, for the first and last time, they produced over 50 per cent of the total value of production.

The key to understanding these three features lies in the difference between the costs and prices of mine production. In 1883 it cost, on average, 20s to produce a value of 23s 6d from each load of blue ground in Kimberley Mine, while it cost 9s to produce a value of 13s 4d in De Beers Mine. While there was a wide difference in production costs in these two mines there was a comparable margin of profit measured in shillings. In the poorer mines, staying in the black was not a question of shillings but of pence. In Dutoitspan it cost 5s to produce a value of 5s 2d and in Bultfontein 5s to make 5s 4d. Such was the crucial ratio of costs and prices, determined by the quality of diamonds, quantity of carats in a load, depth of a mine, reef falls and state of the labour and diamond markets.[3]

Of immense importance at this time was the difficulty facing companies in Kimberley Mine. Potentially the richest pit, it was overburdened with fallen reef – to every load of blue (diamondiferous ground) extracted they had to take out three loads of dead ground – and in the throes of transforming itself from an opencast into an underground mine. While this immensely complicated and expensive experiment was under way, the poorer mines had to make money while their wealthier competitor was out of contention. In such a situation the mineowners, particularly in the poor mines where the margin of profit was so narrow, also began to experiment with the division of labour.

Table 6 *Mining production and profits 1 Sept. 1882–1 Sept. 1885*

	Profits 1.9.1882 – 1.3.1884 (18 months)						
	cts.	av. price	value	cts/lds	loads	expend.	profits
Kimberley	1,429,726	19/11½	£1,399,404	1.20	1,191,440	£1,191,440	£207,964
De Beers	656,427	21/4¼	£ 700,944	.66	1,050,280	£ 472,626	£228,318
Dutoitspan	709,877	28/7½	£1,016,404	.18	3,943,761	£ 985,940	£ 30,464
Bultfontein	738,230¼	21/5	£ 791,023	.25	2,952,920	£ 738,230	£ 52,793
Total	3,534,261¼	22/1¼	£3,907,775		9,138,401	£3,388,236	£519,539[1]

	Profits 1.3.1884 – 1.9.1885 (18 months)						
	cts.	av. price	value	cts/lds	loads	expend.	profits
Kimberley	850,396¼	18/10¼	£ 811,835	1.25	680,316	£ 680,316	£131,515
De Beers	790,968¾	20/11	£ 815,409	.75	1,054,544	£ 527,272	£288,137
Dutoitspan	733,306¾	28/1	£1,083,262	.20	3,866,530	£ 966,632	£116,630
Bultfontein	877,647½	19/9¼	£ 867,047	.28	3,134,453.	£ 783,613	£ 83,434
Total	3,292,259	21/11	£3,577,553		8,735,843	£2,957,833	£619,716[2]

1. SAL, 'To the President and Members of the Board of Directors of the Compagnie Française', p. 4. These figures are taken from the reports of the most important companies. The profit averaged out to 12 months in this period was £346,358.
2. *Ibid.* The profit averaged out to 12 months in this period was £413,145.

A WHITE LABOUR POLICY FOR THE MINES?

During the depression there was a shortage of Africans and a surplus of Europeans seeking situations in the mines. Disbanded volunteers from the Basutoland and Transvaal wars, unemployed railway workers and unemployed men from the port towns poured into Kimberley and created a reserve army of labour. The wars, which had ended and increased the ranks of the European unemployed, had originally created the shortage of African labour.

The mines required over 20,000 labourers to work to capacity. Generally, the supply of African labour increased over the summer and declined during the winter when hours were shorter and less work was done. In the summer of 1881 the 'Gun War' in Basutoland and the Transvaal War cut into the labour supply and Coleman, the Registrar of Natives, reported that 10,000 Africans were needed to make up the full mine work-force.[4]

In such a situation companies employed some Europeans as labourers. The British DMC reported, for example, in June 1881:

> Fuel has been and still is very dear and to counterbalance the effects of the want of Kafir labour a large number of white labourers had to be constantly employed.[5]

One consequence was that African wages were also higher and combined with expensive European labour this had different effects on companies. While the British DMC, one of the most profitable on the Fields, could stand the extra expense, finding 57s 3d in each load of soil which cost only 14s 2d to produce, the De Beers Company found it had to account for every last shilling. In 1882 the latter company spent 13s 2d to produce each load of soil but found, on average, only 21s 8d worth of diamonds, a comfortable margin although one which was reduced through the cost of European labour.[6]

The employment of white men as labourers in the mines, and the presence of a reservoir of unemployed Europeans in Kimberley, created a white labour debate or a debate over the advantages and disadvantages of employing a 'superior class of labour', a curtain raiser to the much more detailed 'civilised labour' debate and experiment that took place on the Rand after the War.[7] Merchants and tradesmen argued the case for the employment of unskilled white colonials and recruited Italians or Irish. They weighed the advantages of a white proletarian as against a black migrant labour policy.

White working class families settled on the Fields, it was argued, would expand the circulation of commodities in Kimberley as long as the value of their labour-power was not depressed below its historically constituted level in the Cape. 'Let us have European labour by all means', argued the *Diamond News*:

> if we can get it on a fair and equitable basis and then it will be a success, but any scheme which treats human beings like brute beasts and even white men like barbarous savages will surely fail.[8]

The point was that Italians might work for a pittance in Piedmont, or Irishmen get by in Cape Town on 2s a day, but such a wage was too little for a European to live on in Kimberley. The *Diamond News* feared that 'rendered desperate by disappointed hopes and animated by race hatred, which undoubtedly does exist between the uneducated white and the native barbarian, they might prove an element of extreme trouble'.[9] Moreover, and more importantly, Irish and Italians were not Chinese and nor were they 'Negroes' and working in the mines for an African labourer's wage, it was argued, would reduce them to little better than slaves.

The case was made that the higher cost of European labour, compared to African migrant labour, would be compensated for by its greater productivity. Immigrant Italians or Irish would be accustomed to manual labour

125

and consequently able to haul more loads or break up blue more rapidly on the floors than unskilled Africans. Such a view was fairly common amongst mineowners and had been frequently commented on by visiting mining specialists. Even the Inspector of Mines, Captain Erskine, agreed:

> I am inclined to think from observation in frequently watching working gangs, that Mining Companies would get a much better return for the employment chiefly of white labour. From my own observation I opine that white labour, though highly paid as compared with typical Kaffir-dawdling would prove the more economical and reliable.[10]

Labour productivity, that is the output per man-hour, changed due to the introduction of new machinery or new forms of organisation that improved the utilisation of the time, effort and skill of the workers. But the economics of labour productivity in Kimberley were closely bound up with reliability of labourers themselves, and not simply in the sense of turning up for work sober on Monday morning.

The supporters of European labour argued that whites were more honest and less likely to steal diamonds. The extra cost in wages could be off-set against improved finds and some mineowners, notably the last of the individual diggers in the poorer mines, paid higher than average 'honesty' wages to white labourers and overseers, and prospered. The majority of mineowners, however, found such a system unpalatable.

The opposition of most mineowners to 'honesty' wages was revealing, because the prevalence of African theft was the main argument they put forward in the political struggle to establish closed compounds in Kimberley, institutions which would exclude white workers. Sammy Marks, a major mineowner whose companies employed close on 3,000 African labourers, expressed the majority view to a Select Committee investigating IDB in 1882. 'Do people consider that what they pay the native, and what they steal, is not more than they pay a white man?' Marks was asked, and he replied:

> If we were sure when Europeans were engaged that they were straightforward and honest and we felt we could trust them then we could go into figures. I have tried white labour. I engaged 50 white men as labourers but it would not answer, they worked one day and got drunk the next. You can always depend on the Kaffirs.[11]

What Marks meant was that Europeans were as susceptible to theft as Africans, were more problematical to control and were too expensive. 'You cannot give white men less than £4 a week in a place like Kimberley', Marks argued, 'and it would not pay us to do that; you might as well close up the diggings'.[12] The cost of white labour at three or four times the price of black labour tipped the scales against the merchant case of Europeans as more reliable, more productive and politically more secure than African labourers.

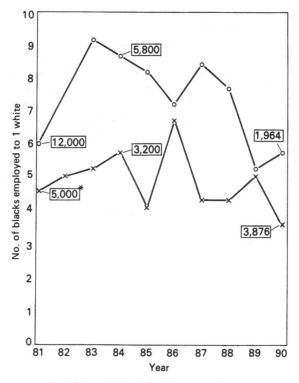

Fig. 5 Ratio of white to black workers employed in the mines, 1881–90. (Source: Cape *Statistical Registers*))

THE REORGANISATION OF THE DIVISION OF LABOUR

Having won the argument, mineowners proceeded to cope with the depression on two fronts: first, a parliamentary programme to enforce a tighter control of workers in and outside the work-place and, secondly, a reduction in wages and a reorganisation of the division of labour.

The bare statistics of employment during the depression illustrate clearly the changing ratio of white to black labour with whites being laid off to cut costs. Between 1881 and 1884 white employment was reduced most sharply in proportion to African employment in the poorer mines. In 1881 the ratio of European to African employees in the richer mines (Kimberley and De Beers) was 1:5 and in the poorer mines (Dutoitspan and Bultfontein) 1:6. As the depression began to bite the ratio shifted significantly. In 1884 the ratio in the richer mines was 1:6 while in the poorer mines it had widened to

1:9, at a time when profits and the value of production were greater in the latter than the former mines for the first and last time.

A more detailed profile of the work-force puts this changing ratio into perspective. Africans made up between 83 and 88 per cent of mineworkers and were paid 30s per week on average. The remaining workers, mainly Europeans and 'persons of colour',[13] were occupied as overseers and labourers (68 per cent) earning up to £5 a week, steam engine-drivers (20 per cent) earning between £6 and £8 a week, and the rest (12 per cent) were artisans such as mechanics, smiths, miners and carpenters, commanding the highest wages of around £8 a week. In addition, the mine transport networks were dominated by 'persons of colour', who were accustomed to handling Scotch carts and other animal-drawn conveyances. Although statistics are lacking for their exact numbers – and they are not included in the above profile – the replacement of animal-drawn transport by steam-driven tramways was under way during the depression and deprived a considerable number of their livelihoods.[14]

Overall, between 1881 and 1884, the number of Europeans employed fell by 61 per cent to 1,210, whereas the number of Africans employed fell by only 47 per cent to 9,000. While the employment of artisans and engine-drivers was, to some extent, guaranteed by the need to perform essential tasks around the mines and floors, the employment of overseers, a stratum of unskilled supervisory workers, was continually threatened by shortages of African labourers. Overseers were retrenched if labourers deserted or were in short supply, although some mines needed more overseers than others. In Kimberley Mine the ratio of overseers to labourers was 1:8 on average over the depression, while in Bultfontein, where the stones were generally very small, the ratio was 1:16. Overseers worked with their eyes, employed to prevent theft and to drive labourers to work harder. However, shortages or retrenchment of labourers were not the only causes of the decline of European employment as overseers.[15]

An active policy of employing black overseers was followed by cost-paring companies in the poorer mines. Throughout the 1870s it had been the rule for white claimowners to police their black workers with white overseers. The racial and cultural differences between white overseer and African labourer reinforced the pattern of authority in the work-place. However, in 1882 Sammy Marks, opponent of white labour, took the innovatory step of replacing his white overseers with Africans. Arthur Shepstone, a Natal railway labour recruiter, supplied Marks' companies with Tsonga labourers who were contracted to work naked under their own headmen in the claims.[16]

A similar policy was pursued by the Bultfontein Mining Company, one of the most profitable companies on the Fields, paying 25 per cent per annum in dividends throughout the 1880s. The Company was managed by Arthur Davis and largely owned by Ochs Brothers, the London diamond brokers. Like the British DMC Davis found no problem in employing European labourers, but he also employed recruited Tsonga labourers and worked them under Zulu overseers, who besides earning a higher wage than their gangs, were paid commissions on found diamonds, a reward which encouraged them to look after their master's property rather than risk the illicit diamond market.[17]

The squeeze on European employment as overseers came not only from Africans but also from children. There are no records of the ages of European employees, but the general impression that few miners were over 40 years old can be garnered from voters lists, censuses and death notices. At the other end of the age scale European boys of 12 years old worked as miners and overseers in the pits. A boy became a man as soon as he was into his teens and for poor white boys even earlier. The exact extent of the substitution of white boys for white men is unknown, but there is evidence from the few company pay-sheets that have survived and from memoirs that it became more important during the depression than before.[18]

Even European children were not so cheap as to be cossetted at all costs. When the Bultfontein Company found out that its boy sorters were stealing diamonds, they were replaced by Zulu men on six month contracts. Women, it seems, who had been prominent sorters in the early days were not recalled to the breach at this time of crisis.[19]

The search for cheaper labour extended to engine-drivers as well. Engine-driving was an occupation which required certain engineering skills, but technical knowledge was less important than 'general steadiness and sobriety'.[20] It was a job of great responsibility as careless driving threatened the lives of workers in the pits or in the vicinity of the engine-houses. Nonetheless, many engine-drivers were poorly qualified for their jobs, especially in Dutoitspan and Bultfontein. 'Not one-half of the engine-drivers, boiler attendants etc.,' observed the Inspector of Machinery, 'would pass muster in England'.[21]

In the normal pattern of engine-driving before the depression, a European was in charge of each engine-house. He was assisted by an African stoker whose job it was to fire-up the boiler in the mornings and to keep it going while the engine-driver drove the engine and made sure that tubs did not fall off the wires or blocks of earth fall on labourers' heads. Both driving and stoking were sought after jobs, carrying higher pay than overseers and labourers and also providing a pleasant occupational warmth that was so important during winter.

This neat racial division of labour in the engine-house changed during the depression and the substitution of black – Indian, African or 'persons of colour' – for white engine-drivers was widespread in De Beers and the two the poorer mines. Whether they displayed the artisanal virtues of 'general steadiness and sobriety' or not, black engine-drivers were employed and wages were reduced.[22]

That the European wage bill was a source of grave concern is best illustrated by the numerous company amalgamation schemes proposed

Table 7 *Kimberley Central DMC – labour complements, 1882 and 1883*

1882	1883		1882	1883	
–	1	general manager	15	14	engine-driver
1	2	claim manager	4	5	fitter
4	4	floor manager	7	10	carpenter
1	1	engineer	3	8	blacksmith
1	1	paymaster	–	2	apprentice
1	1	timekeeper	2	–	striker
1	1	clerk	1	1	wire splicer
4	4	gear manager	1	5	watcher
1	1	accountant	58	51	cart/tram
1	1	secretary			driver
–	1	traffic manager	1	1	harness maker
93	82	overseer	902	771	natives
5	3	miner	1	1	inspector of
11	6	labourer			natives
4	3	platelayer	1	1	messenger

Total: 1882 = 1,124   1883 = 982

during the depression and, in particular, the 1882 scheme prepared for De Beers Mine by Alderson, Dunsmure and Rhodes. In that year total European wages in De Beers Mine amounted to £95,000 and African wages to £121,680. In the projected amalgamation of the mine it was estimated that European wages could be reduced by two-thirds to £33,100, largely through the retrenchment of half the overseers, while African wages could be reduced by one-quarter to £90,090. The means to achieve this saving were systematic underground mining and the introduction of a closed compound system.[23] The ideas were current in the Kimberley Club by the turn of the decade but the resistance of workers and their allies in town and in Parliament had to be overcome.

The reduction of white labour was a more intractable problem in Kimberley Mine than in its poorer neighbours. Buttressed by its greater wealth, before fallen reef began to take its toll on production, the mine employed a higher proportion of white labour compared to the other mines. The largest company in the mine, the Kimberley Central DMC, showed this trend in the wages it paid to its workers. In 1882 overseers and engine-drivers were paid £40,877 and Africans £42,781. In 1883 there was a remarkable change in the wage bills: £62,561 and £52,612 respectively and this despite the fact that less labour was employed all round.

In 1883 enraged shareholders demanded that overseers be sacked to cut the soaring costs of production, but wages in Kimberley were high as the mine was deep and dangerous. While companies whose property lay in the open could often command labour freely, others near the reef or underground suffered a constant shortage of labour. More and more of the Central's claims were covered by reef and European and African wages rose sharply.[24]

Displaced Europeans, who were unable to leave Kimberley, were left with the limited and competitive option of contract work. It was a fairly attractive option, which required a certain spirit of entrepreneurship and carried potential rewards far greater than supervisory or artisanal labour. Companies offered contracts for specific jobs such as filling trucks or hauling ground from the claims. The contractors were paid a set rate for the work and employed company labourers. Although Africans were housed in the company's open compounds they were paid by and registered to the contractors.[25]

Contracting out mining tasks was not a universal system on the Fields after the formation of joint-stock companies. Some companies like the French and D'Esterre and the Anglo–African tried it for some years and then abolished it as part of the vertical integration of production. Other companies like the De Beers DMC found that the contract system answered well. It spread the risks of company mining and guaranteed production targets. It was also important in introducing piece-wages which became the general method of payment after the systematic development of underground mining.[26]

'Persons of colour' also took advantage of the proliferation of company contracts on offer during the depression, but for them most of the opportunities turned up in the poorer mines. In 1885, for example, Stephen Springhaan, described as a 'low set Hottentot, barefoot and somewhat "dishevelled" in appearance but speaking good English', had a contract to fill trucks for a Dutoitspan company. *The Diamond Fields Advertiser* commented that some diggers found 'the employment of coloured contractors, native overseers, and in some cases allowing boys of 14 years to act in the important latter capacity a satisfactory arrangement' but they considered it a dubious one.[27]

In short, a number of points can be made about the division of labour in the mines. First, while there was an undoubtedly clear racial division of labour in fact, in individual perceptions and in colonial ideology, it was not institutionalised through regulation and law as it was to become after the strikes. There was an ideology of 'kaffir work' but it did not prevent some Europeans doing the work of labourers, for a higher wage. Similarly, Africans were substituted for Europeans as overseers, engine-drivers and sorters. Secondly, there were substantial economic differences between mines and companies, but the greatest difference lay between the two poorer mines and the two richer mines. Where the profit margins were tighter, less European workers were employed and, as we shall see, the greatest militancy amongst workers was found in the poorer mines. Lastly, the reorganisation of the division of labour and the attempt to reduce wage levels were successful in De Beers, Dutoitspan and Bultfontein Mines. It was not successful in Kimberley where wage costs rose continuously through the depression. The necessity of underground mining made it important that European and African wage costs were reduced. It was no surprise that, despite the production paralysis of Kimberley Mine, the company leadership during the strikes came from large concerns, in all four mines, who stood to gain most from the recovery.

THE MINEOWNERS' LEGISLATIVE PROGRAMME

The 1883 strike was precipitated by wage reductions and the introduction of the searching system. Both were emergency measures in response to the depression, but the searching system was a second-best option implemented on the failure of the mineowners to secure legislative support from Parliament.

In April 1881, after the annexation of Griqualand West to the Cape Colony, the Province sent three members to the Cape Legislature. Once in Parliament the three representatives, Cecil Rhodes, Joseph Robinson and Dr Josiah Matthews, initiated an investigation of the diamond industry. In September 1881 a Diamond Mining Commission was appointed which was chaired by John Merriman, Commissioner of Crown Lands, Public Works and Mines, and consisted largely of managers and directors of mining companies.[28] The Commission dealt mainly with the land rights and the internal organisation of the industry. In addition in April 1882 a Select Committee was appointed to look into the issue of illicit diamond buying (IDB). It was chaired by Cecil Rhodes and consisted of some members who had no direct stake in the industry: Saul Solomon, James Irvine, John Ayliff, and J. H. Hofmeyr. The main purpose of the Select Committee was to report on the Bill drawn up by the Diamond Protection Society for a stricter control of the possession of diamonds. Together the Commission and the Committee revealed the demands that the mineowners made on the Cape state.

The mineowners sought to establish the infrastructure for the expanded reproduction of mining capital. First and foremost, they wanted a railway from the Cape; this was their primary reason for agreeing to annexation to the Colony and the railway reached the Orange River at the end of 1884 and Kimberley a year later.[29] Secondly, they wanted to ensure a constant labour supply through control, directly or indirectly, of the labour catchment areas and migration routes. Thirdly they sought a fortress of protective legislation for the diamond industry, central to which was a new diamond law. Lastly, they asked for legislative sanction for the increased coercion of African labour in Kimberley, the most important institutional device being the compound system. This essential demand made of the Cape Parliament was succinctly summed up by Charles Rudd, a founder member of the De Beers DMC: 'I gave eight of the best years of my life night and day to De Beers unpaid and served five years in Parliament to carry the compound system'.[30]

Labour supply was the most pressing problem of the mineowners. Atmore and Marks have emphasised that Carnarvon's confederation schemes for South Africa in the middle 1870s were based on a need for a uniform 'native policy'.[31] Etherington expanded this argument to highlight the particular influences on Carnarvon of Shepstone in Natal and Southey in Griqualand West.[32] The political fragmentation of the southern African region posed problems for the movement of Africans to the mines; they were harassed by white farmers and officials in the Transvaal and the Orange Free State. But the annexation of the Transvaal by Britain in 1877, the repression of the Griqualand West Rebellion in 1878 and the destruction of the Zulu and Pedi polities in 1879 made the migration of labourers to the mines easier than before. Then, the new decade opened with a series of disastrous colonial wars, in particular the independence struggle of the Transvaal Boers and the 'Gun War' in Basutoland. Both these wars disrupted the labour supply to the diamond mines. Faced with this situation the mineowners looked to a quick solution to the unsettled situation in Basutoland and the Transvaal and turned to Bechuanaland and the north for labour. Ironically, in the 1870s the Carnarvon schemes had run aground on the Cape's refusal to incorporate Griqualand West, and in the 1880s the mineowners went into the Cape with firm plans to use the old Colony for precisely those integrative purposes previously outlined by the Colonial Secretary.

The colonial African policy of the Kimberley representatives in Parliament was shaped by their mining interests. As early as 1881, for example, Rhodes had formulated the basic idea of the future Glen-Grey system and suggested its application to an unsubdued Basutoland. 'I should not support', he pledged in his first election manifesto:

> a measure for confiscation of territory, but would advocate that the chief's power be broken, the Russian village system introduced, namely a headman, agricultural land held individually and a general commonage – and that the cost of the war should be represented by a loan, chargeable on the revenues of Basutoland.[33]

And Basutoland was not simply important as a reservoir of labour. It was primarily the granary of the Diamond Fields and Dr Matthews estimated that the 'Gun War' cost Kimberley an added £480,000 in inflated grain prices. In addition, Basutoland provided a considerable amount of firewood for the Kimberley market. In July 1882, while Rhodes sat on the compensation commission for loyal Basuto, he traversed the country valuing trees for export to Kimberley.[34] Rhodes believed that the only political solution to the Cape's debacle lay in imperial intervention and, indeed, in 1883 Britain resumed direct responsibility for the country.

Similar concerns shaped Rhodes' political manoevres in Bechuanaland. It has too often been taken for granted that Rhodes' interest in the 'Road to the North' was simply of strategic importance for the expansion of British influence.[35] Rather, it is important to emphasise that he had specific interests in the 'Road to the North' as a mineowner; that merchants did as well; and that merchant and mining penetration into the interior was not simply dictated by the El Dorado they hoped to find across the Limpopo. The free-booters in the renegade Republics of Stellaland and Goshen threatened to obstruct labour migration down the western route to Kimberley, and Rhodes wanted to make sure that they fell under either British or Cape influence rather than that of the Transvaal. Then, as an astute politician preparing alliances with merchants and farmers, Rhodes was quick to emphasise the importance of maintaining easy access to the vast commercial market of the interior. In addition, Bechuanaland was a major source of fire-wood for Kimberley.[36] Most importantly, Rhodes and all mineowners were terrified of the discovery of new diamond mines. This fear directed Rhodes' speculation in the Orange Free State mines; his land speculation in Barkly West; and his desire to have mineral information about Bechuanaland, Mashonaland and Matabeleland. Seen from this perspective Rhodes did not acquire a fortune in order to expand to the north; he was forced to go north because his capital was invested in the Kimberley diamond mines.

The mineowners had limited success with their programme of protective legislation and closed compounds for the diamond industry. They presented diamond theft to Parliament as a haemorrhage the mining companies could no longer bear and, as it was the proper function of the state to protect private property, a new diamond law was enacted. The Diamond Trade Act of 1882 laid down stricter controls and penalties for theft and illicit diamond buying. A Special Court without a jury system was established to try only contraventions of the Act. But for the mineowners it was not enough. They wanted the enforcement of the pass law, the enactment of a new liquor law, the promulgation of the searching law, the extension of the Cape's vagrant law to Kimberley and the compulsory compounding of Africans.[37]

There was a struggle in Parliament over all these measures. They were demanded in the name of the suppression of illicit diamond theft and buying, which threatened to 'jeopardise the entire industry of diamond mining'.[38] The mineowners won on the pass law, but lost in the face of mercantile and farming opposition on the liquor law, the vagrant law and closed compounds. Parliament decided that mineowners were not doing enough to protect themselves and refused to interfere with the 'free market' in African labour. Consequently, with closed compounds blocked for the moment, mineowners resorted to the searching system and organised reductions in wages.

THE 1883 STRIKE

Wage reductions created a spirit of rebellion amongst workers before the searching system was introduced in 1883. Reductions in African wages had always played havoc with labour supply and what happened in late 1881 was a repetition of what had happened before. A mineowners' combination was announced to reduce wages to 25s a week without food and 20s with food, but only 35 companies agreed to do so. It was this partial response – which showed the inability of mineowners to reduce wages – that had encouraged large companies to seek further state intervention in the labour market.[39]

Cuts in European wages appeared easier to achieve owing to the glut of Europeans in Kimberley. In November 1882, reductions were announced in overseers' and artisans' wages. Immediately, a Working Men's Association was formed to resist wage reductions, but it did not last long and was more important for its intentions than its longevity, though the latter may have been determined by the former. This earliest of worker combinations officially formed on the Fields was open to all, but not African labourers, and to every branch of industry for a subscription of 2s 6d a week. It was founded by artisans, who had learnt their trade unionism in England. 'I came here to save enough money to go home', said a founder member, 'and the majority of us do the same'.[40] The Association did not only want to prevent wage reductions but also to reduce the long labouring day of 13 hours in the sun.

The Association, conceived as an industrial union covering all grades of mining, was not successful in its objects and gave way to craft-based unions. In 1883 the Artisans and Engine-drivers Association was formed on the basis of a £1 membership fee and a 2s 6d weekly subscription. After a three month membership they were entitled to a £2 a week unemployment benefit, an important consideration in Kimberley where mechanics, 'as a class out of employment' and 'weighted with families', were unable 'to remove to distant railway works'.[41] As a consequence the pressure on artisanal wages was considerable with talk of reducing the differential between artisans and labourers from four times or more to only twice the wages of the unskilled man. But skilled wages never fell that low.[42]

The prevalence of unemployment and wage reductions were aggravated by the introduction of the searching system. Its purpose was to prevent theft and it applied, with the exception of managers, to both black and white workers in the mines. Before its introduction on 1 March 1883 the mines were enclosed by wire fences and segregated search houses were built on the edges of the mines.

In practice, searching did little to prevent theft. In 1885, an investigation of the system concluded that searching was 'quite useless and enormously expensive'.[43] The reasons for this lay in the negative attitudes of companies and the Mining Boards to the system. On the one hand, the companies refused to allow adequate time for searching: 'the one thought uppermost in the majority of manager's minds is the number of loads that should be hauled during the day'.[44] On the other hand, the Mining Boards, which initially administered the system and the 80 searching officers, were unenthusiastic and in the case of Dutoitspan failed to provide the cash to pay the guards. In addition, structural security was less than adequate. The search houses were built some distance from the entrance to the mines and the passage ways were enclosed with wire fences. All the mineworker had to do to steal a diamond was to drop it through the fence: 'a native is not a fool; he is not likely to go to the trouble of swallowing a diamond if he can get it through in any other way'.[45]

Nonetheless, searching did perform a disciplinary function by ensuring a stricter control of the time spent working in the mines. All mineworkers now had to go through the search houses on entry to and exit from the mines. Searching meant a greater regimentation of labour and, in the case of Africans, it meant the wearing of a new uniform in the pits. The search houses were also change houses where Africans were required to don grain sacks which made it difficult to conceal stones in their clothing. While Africans did not initially resist searching, many refused to work in sacks and wore their own clothes or stripped naked in the claims. They jeered at those who submitted: 'why are you sent without clothes like a parcel of prisoners'.[46]

It was significant that overseers in the mines did not go on strike in March 1883 when the searching system was introduced. They certainly made it known that they resented searching and that they thought it would undermine the position of authority that overseers held over labourers, but they did not form a union as the artisans had done and most submitted to the system. Those who thought that searching degraded their labour, and were strong-minded enough to make a stand, were simply dismissed and were then 'glad to get a job at less money than before'.[47]

Searching became an explosive issue in September 1883 when it was announced that the searching system would be applied to the floors, work-shops and engine-houses and that Europeans would be required to wear a uniform and change in the search houses. The artisans organised to resist this new regulation unlike the more vulnerable overseers. Originally the Artisans Association was centred in Dutoitspan, where black substitution and wage reductions were most severe, but it spread to Kimberley and De Beers and each mine had its own branch. Under the threat of the new regulations the branches formed an action group called the Combined Working Men's Committee and conducted a campaign to have themselves exempted from searching.

Artisans regarded searching and the change of clothing in the search houses, the so-called 'stripping clause', as an assault on the respectability and dignity of their occupations. The notion of respectability was the product of skill and the power to exclude unqualified workers from their trades. Searching placed artisans and labourers on the same level and it was a small step in the politicisation of the conflict to see this division in racial terms. The public struggle over 'stripping' was conducted in terms of 'white degradation' as opposed to Africans whose 'state of nature' was one of nudity. While competition between black and white workers underlay the racial ideology, artisans were well aware that the searching system would entail more rigorous supervision.

The mineowners refused to budge over the 'stripping clause' and when, on the 15 October 1883, the new regulations were due to be implemented by the Detective Department, having taken over the responsibility from the Mining Boards, the Combined Committee called out its members on strike. The mines ceased production as overseers came out under the guidance of the artisans and carried most of their African labourers with them. Africans undoubtedly had their own organisations in the compounds and pits and, although specifically excluded from formal participation in the Combined Committee, would have found it extremely difficult to go to work in defiance of European strikers.

The strike lasted under a week, longer in Dutoitspan and Bultfontein than in Kimberley, because the mineowners turned out to be keen to seek a settlement. The speed with which they agreed to waive the 'stripping clause', once workers had shown their resolve to close down production, was only partially a consequence of inexperience in dealing with an organised strike for the first time. More important was their fear that they would lose their African labour. 'The employers of labour were of the opinion', said a director of De Beers, 'that if work once stopped, all the natives would leave for their kraals'.[48]

The settlement that was reached relied heavily on the word of the mineowners and state officials that 'stripping' would not be necessary in the process of searching Europeans. The Crown Prosecutor, Leigh Hoskyns, gave the opinion that the law did not require 'stripping'. On the strength of this John Fry, the Chief of the Detective Department, told the Association:

> I cannot attempt to strip you until the law is altered to have you stripped. I have to act on Mr. Hoskyn's instructions. I should be a great fool to go against them.[49]

Having extracted a fairly clear statement of how the officials would interpret the law, the Association agreed to drop its demand that the clause be taken out of the regulations. That was the essence of the compromise: 'stripping' would remain part of the rules but it would not be enforced.[50] And for six months the officials and the mineowners kept their word.

In short, the searching system was implemented at a time when the social and economic position of European workers was being substantially eroded. The decision to search all workers irrespective of skill or supervisory position degraded the value of European labour. First, it appeared the thin edge of the wedge in the gradual homogenisation of black and white labour. Secondly, it was the final blow in a rapid passage from independent digger to proletarian status. Many overseers in 1883 had been respectable claimholders in the past and it was only, they argued, the turn of fortune's wheel that had reduced them to wage labourers. Instead of placing trust in overseers and other Europeans, mineowners emphasised the new, dependent status of European workers by searching them in the same way as the labourers over whom they exercised authority. As in Europe, it was artisans who took the lead in trade union organisation and resisted the new policy of the mineowners and their managers. And in the first flexing of their union muscle they appeared to have won the day.

THE 1884 STRIKE

The mineowners rapid capitulation to the artisans was determined by another factor over which workers had no control. The fear of African desertion to their homes was a very real one in view of an outbreak of smallpox on the Fields. This episode of the epidemic that many denied existed was a very curious one and one which left a legacy of bitterness and of death.

In late 1882 smallpox broke out in Cape Town and the civil authorities in Kimberley feared it would spread into Griqualand West. A fumigation station was set up at the junction of the Riet and Modder rivers, but in October 1883 the threat appeared in the north. Some African workers travelling through the Transvaal from Mozambique were suspected of the disease and isolated at Felsteads farm nine miles from Kimberley. Others soon joined them and in November, six doctors paid an official visit to the quarantine station in an attempt to decide authoritatively on the disease. On the one hand, doctors Jameson, Matthews and Murphy decided it was not smallpox and called it a 'bulbous disease of the skin allied to pemphigus'. On the other hand, doctors Grimmer, Otto and Smith believed it was smallpox, warned that it was contagious and recommended continued quarantine.[51]

Professional disagreement of this kind did not allay public fears. At the time, in November and January, it was confirmed independently by a Cape Government doctor and by the *British Medical Journal* that the disease was in fact the dreaded smallpox.[52] But there was powerful opposition to the acceptance of this fact. Edward Judge, the Civil Commissioner of Kimberley, explained what happened in his autobiography:

> The Board [of Health] then established a lazaretto outside the towns and removed to it all patients who could not be quarantined in their own homes. These consisted almost entirely at first of natives, but after a short time the Indians, of whom there were a great many on the Diamond Fields, were attacked and then the Europeans. The Board did all it could to check the spread of the disease by vaccination, quarantine, fumigation ... but the two doctors, who had expressed the opinion that it was neither infectious nor contagious influenced people not to take precautions and the disease spread alarmingly and many Europeans were attacked. *The Diamond Fields Advertiser* had also used its influence in opposition to the measures taken by the Board. This state of things continued for about six months and then the funds of the Board were nearly exhausted and it had to curtail its operations. As a consequence the disease spread still more rapidly, especially among Euro-

peans . . . But for the opposition, and the expenditure, the number of persons attacked and the deaths would probably have been divided by at least three, as is evidenced by the immediate diminution of cases when the opposition became frightened and was withdrawn, and by the fact that a fresh outbreak at the end of 1885, in which 26 persons were involved, was immediately stamped out.[53]

The opposition of doctors and newspapers to the recognition of the epidemic covered up the true extent of mortality. Despite the questionable authenticity of the official figures they clearly showed that Africans had the worst of it. From October 1883 to January 1885 there were 2,311 cases recorded in a population of approximately 40,000 people and the mortality rate from the African cases was 35 per cent while the remainder suffered only a death rate of 12 per cent. These figures of 700 dead in 16 months were very dubious when compared with the 4,000 dead in Cape Town in a few months and without a public quarrel over the seriousness of the disease.[54]

The opposition to the naming of smallpox as the disease came from fears that the struggling mining economy would suffer the twin blows of a rise in the cost of basic supplies and of labour. And there is little doubt that the mineowners were behind the opposition and bought the professional reputations of doctors and editors.[55] While they did an enormous amount of human damage, they were unable to prevent what they feared would happen to the costs of production in the mines.

In December 1883 the Orange Free State quarantined Basutoland prohibiting 'trade and intercourse' because of the 'Diamond Field smallpox' among the Sotho.[56] They also set up fumigation sheds on the Griqualand West border. In 1884 only 12,000 people suffered the ordeal of being fumigated at the border and the commercial traffic was drastically cut. 'No people feared the disease more than the Boers', wrote John Angove, 'most of whom allowed their produce to perish rather than risk taking it to market at Kimberley or Dutoitspan for sale'.[57] The result was that wheat and wood prices went up and wages as well.[58]

It was in such a situation, with a worsening epidemic and a worsening mining economy, that the mineowners decided to confront the strength of their white workers. They went back on their word given to settle the 1883 strike and demanded a rigorous search of all workers. The incident that reactivated the 'stripping' controversy occurred on 26 March 1884. Two overseers, a miner, an engine-driver and a fitter in Kimberley Mine refused to open their mouths for a digital search or to remove their boots in the search house. They were arrested and sent for trial. Thereafter, others were also arrested but the majority were simply dismissed. A new policy of employee retrenchment on top of wage reductions was being pursued by the mineowners.[59]

Artisans took to the public meeting places and aired their displeasure at the new turn of events. They encouraged unskilled white workers to set up their own organisation and the Overseers and Miners Association was duly formed with branches at Dutoitspan and Kimberley.[60] As in 1883 a Combined Committee coordinated the strategy of mineworkers and it also co-opted non-association members, notably from the mercantile community, to strengthen its representation.[61] On 22 April the Committee resolved to abide by the October compromise and to ignore the new searching rules. But before they went on strike they agreed to wait for the ruling in the 'test case' of those who had refused to submit to 'stripping' and they resolved to try constitutional measures by sending a petition to Parliament to have the 'obnoxious clause' removed from the searching law.[62]

The mineowners were prepared for the organised opposition of their workers and had formed the Mining Protection Association to strengthen and unify their actions. The Protection Association was dominated by the larger companies, such as De Beers, Kimberley Central, French and Bultfontein Mining, and their directors took the key strategic decisions during the 'stripping' confrontation. Many had direct access to government, notably John X. Merriman, the Commissioner of Crown Lands and Mines, who had a keen understanding of and sympathy for mineowners' problems. It was Merriman himself who had visited Kimberley and ordered the changes in searching procedure. Even more important was the recent appointment of Cecil Rhodes, Chairman of the De Beers DMC, to the post of Treasurer-General in the government. Both men were to play key roles in rejecting any form of compromise with mineworkers.

The mineowners precipitated events. On the 23 April, the day after the Committee resolved to stand by the October compromise, the Protection Association set out a circular stating their resolve to search all workers without distinction and requiring all workers to sign an agreement in which searching, or rather the 'stripping clause', was a condition of contract.[63] On 24 April, when Europeans in the large companies refused to sign they were locked out, with De Beers and the French taking the lead. The same day the Committee sent a telegram to two non-mining Kimberley representatives in Parliament:

> Petition sent by yesterday's post. No alternative if request of petition be not granted but to strike – within 24 hours. Prevailing opinion that Merriman is urging on Fry to raise disturbances amongst the men to prevent petition being considered by Governor. De Beers Mining Company locked out; supposed at the instigation of Rhodes.[64]

The petition was rejected out of hand by the Government and on the following day, the 25 April, the Committee called its second strike.[65]

The first day of the strike was a Friday and not all companies stopped work. Some in De Beers and Dutoitspan continued to work under the armed protection of the police. The following day the Civil Commissioner prepared himself for the worst eventualities: he ordered all canteens to close and commandeered all ammunition in the stores. Sunday, being the day of rest, passed off quietly with the exception of a horse parade of 200 special constables riding through the streets of Dutoitspan. The message was clear – the Protection Association was prepared for the organised opposition of the Workers' Committee.[66]

The new week opened with a mass rally at the race course, where commercial support was pledged to the working men's struggle. White and black workers were the most important customers of retailers of all kinds, but in particular of licensed victuallers. They knew that if workers were defeated wages would be further reduced and there was the possibility of the introduction of closed compounds. William Eaglestone, an English artisan employed in Dutoitspan and one of the three Committee leaders, put the case for the worker–mercantile alliance:

> He thought that the present crisis was brought about by the larger companies who, baulked in their endeavours to bring about amalgamation sought to ruin the smaller companies and force them to come in by a long-continued strike. Amalgamation would mean the ruin of the merchant and therefore the men called on the merchant for practical aid and not sympathy alone.[67]

Practical aid came most significantly in the form of a petition from the Chamber of Commerce, representing large wholesale merchants, to the Mining Boards and Protection Association asking them to suspend mining until Parliament could discuss the 'stripping clause'.[68] In Parliament itself it was the commercial members, now dominating Kimberley representation, who championed the workers' cause. In turn, it had largely been European workers who had elected them to Parliament.[69]

The mineowners rejected the Chamber of Commerce's petition as impertinent and, as a result, the Committee attempted to tighten the strike by circularising men to come out in those companies still at work. On Tuesday the strike was almost complete with the exception of work, under armed guard, in the Standard DMC (Kimberley Mine) and the Victoria DMC (De Beers Mine) and the pumping of water in Kimberley Mine. The strikers targeted the Victoria DMC and at mid-day 'a large number of white men, accompanied by about 1,500 natives' surrounded the new shaft of the company.[70] They forced management to agree to suspend work and to blow off steam. Flushed with this success against an armed guard the strikers repaired to Half-Way House in the Dutoitspan Road.

Strike leaders knew that they had to bring the Kimberley Central's water gear in Kimberley Mine to a halt. It was there that new experiments in underground mining were under way and where the strike had to be won or lost. It was where most capital was at stake and where most white men were still employed. But the underground experiment was being conducted not by the company but by a private contractor, Edward Jones, who begged the Committee to allow the water gear to continue in operation. Some workers argued that Jones was not a capitalist, but the general feeling of the Committee was that his actions and structural position placed him on the side of the employers. The strike leaders perceived their position as the product of capitalist exploitation and polarised issues into workers against managers and owners. Jones was condemned to suffer with the mine-owners.[71]

On Tuesday afternoon at about half past two 'a long line of white men and natives' set off from Half-Way House in the direction of Kimberley Mine.[72] But they were unable to get near the Kimberley Central's water gear. They found a barricade of overturned trucks stretching from the margin of the mine to the engine-houses of the French Company. Behind the trucks Captain Christian, the Police Commissioner, was in command of 'some 10 police and 20 to 30 armed specials'.[73]

The march on Kimberley Mine was led by a 28-year-old overseer, Frederick Holmes, while Committee leaders were negotiating with civil authorities. The strikers were determined to draw the fire of the Kimberley Central water gear but they were warned that they would be attacked if they crossed the barricade. Before Holmes could negotiate with Christian, some trucks were overturned and he was shot dead. It was not the regular police but the special constables, under the command of Kimberley Central and French directors, who opened fire on the strikers. Four men fell dead and another eight were wounded of whom two later died. In the Cape's first major industrial dispute six European workers lost their lives.[74]

On the day after the shooting 'there was complete tranquillity throughout the camps'.[75] That afternoon two hearses bore four of the dead strikers from the Oddfellows Hall to the cemetery. 'Four abreast, dressed in mourning garb', wrote the *Daily Independent*, 'the men to the number of 1,400 followed the hearses; after them came 48 horsemen and the procession closed with 34 carts.'[76] At the cemetery the crowd grew to between 4 and 5,000 people. The funeral ceremony was performed by three clergymen to minister to two Englishmen, Frederick Holmes and Frederick Pollitt, an Austrian, Alexander Vucinovitch, and the colonial-born Louis Kettelson. Another Austrian, Joseph Sablitch, died that evening and a month later a young Afrikaner, Paul Roos, died as a result of his injuries. Three of the dead strikers were overseers and the others were a blaster, a boxman and an engine-driver.[77]

After the funeral of the four, a meeting was held at Half-Way House as 'murmurings' of disapproval had been expressed at the conduct of the Committee. James Brown, an artisan at Dutoitspan and one of the three Committee leaders, prevailed on the men not to resort to violent vengeance. He regained their confidence after the unforeseen outcome of the confrontation with the special constables and urged them to honour the dead by staying out.[78] On Thursday only the Standard and the Victoria DMCs went back to work, but shops re-opened while canteens remained closed. On Friday several companies restarted work at Dutoitspan and Bultfontein, but strikers drew their fires. The strike was led from the poorer mines, where production was only possible in the following week under armed guard, and was less successful in De Beers and Kimberley where many companies went back to work on the Friday. Still, the air was tense and the Civil Commissioner drafted Border Police and troops from the Cape Mounted Rifles into Kimberley and kept up a solid military presence at the mines over the next month.[79]

One of the most interesting questions about the strike concerned the relationship between black and white workers. Was there an alliance between the two groups? Cecil Rhodes thought there was and he told Parliament so:

> ... he contended that the defence of these 'specials' of the property of the mine was justifiable, especially when it was remembered that behind this peaceable and orderly crowd were some 600 or 800 natives, armed with kerries. It was not a contest between whites, but what he hoped never to see in this colony again, white men supported by natives in a struggle against whites.[80]

Europeans took the brunt of the fatal fusillade at the barricade and no Africans sought medical treatment after the shooting. But at other times during the strike gangs of Africans were the vanguard in keeping the mines out of production.

Without the support of Africans a strike of Europeans and 'persons of colour' comprising around 15 per cent of the work-force, despite their crucial control over the running and maintenance of steam machinery, would have been less than successful. The racist rhetoric of the Committee made it fairly clear that a formal alliance with African labourers was out of the question. Strike leaders certainly feared that Africans would take advantage of the strike and declared their opposition to putting themselves at 'the head of a lot of niggers with the intention of smashing the property of the employers'.[81] They feared they would not be able to control the excesses of Africans on the rampage, hence their emphasis on drawing fires alone, but they certainly needed their disciplined support and in many cases overseers were able to deliver this.

Despite the structural position of antagonism between overseer and labourer, their economic fortunes were locked together. 'At present it is not in the interests of white men', commented the *Daily Independent*:

> that the Kafir wages should be reduced. On the contrary if the Kafirs resent it and clear, the white employees must expect a stoppage of the companies and an end of their occupation.[82]

Instead of decoupling this symbiotic relationship, through bonuses or other forms of profit incentives and greater job security, the large companies chose to emphasise what their workers had in common through the undifferentiated introduction of the searching system. The majority of

143

Africans saw little reason to stand by their companies – for if the Europeans succeeded Africans could insist on the same law for all.[83]

Before the strikes Africans held meetings in their compounds to discuss what they would do in the event of European industrial action. Such meetings were not, of course, reported in the newspapers and only filtered back to employers through the Detective Department and trusted African headmen. Searching was not as important to them as it was to Europeans, but the strikes certainly provided an opportunity to express their views on the drudgery of minework. And they took to the streets in large numbers, armed with hoops of iron and knob-kieries, drawing fires and persuading their weaker minded brethren of the follies of working while their masters were on strike.[84]

Not all European workers in Kimberley supported the strike. Support was strongest from artisans in the poorer mines who had learnt their trade unionism in Europe[85] and weakest from colonial-born overseers. There were also those Europeans who were prepared to act as special constables. The Kimberley Central directors admitted they were 'mostly men of unreliable character',[86] but they were exonerated at the inquest into the strike deaths. Their indiscriminate firing of 80 shots into the crowd, without being under the effective command of Captain Christian, was the most distressing legal aspect of the shooting. The Cape was not at this point blessed with a riot act. 'It seemed to him', one MLA was reported as saying in Parliament, 'that the proper precautions were not taken to prevent the loss of life; that weapons were placed in the hands of "specials" simply because their interests were in danger; and that no provision was made for exercising proper control over them.'[87] This confrontation had been explicitly provoked by the largest companies in the mines, the Kimberley Central, the French, the De Beers and the Bultfontein Company, all of which had a great deal of capital at stake, planned a radical underground experiment in the mines and precipitated events by locking out their workers. Their directors sat on each others Boards during the strike to co-ordinate defences against workers. Of particular importance was their inability to reduce wages of expensive Europeans in Kimberley Mine. But they did not have the total commitment of smaller companies in their policy of confrontation. Hans Olsen, a director of the North-East DMC in Kimberley Mine, made the position of the smaller companies clear to workers and mineowners. He spoke at all the workers' and employers' meetings emphasising the importance of granting white workers a share in management. He perceived that mineowners, being a minority in the Kimberley community, needed the political support of their European workers: 'what voting powers had the community got without the workmen?'[88]

In short, the strikes were the major piece of resistance to a reorganisation of the division of labour during the depression. The position of authority and respectability of supervisors and skilled men was threatened by the application of searching to all mineworkers in the pits and on the floors. For the first time men who regarded themselves as masters were made to feel the reality of their position as wage labourers, aligned more with Africans than the new stratum of managers and foremen that company mining had produced. It was an unpleasant salutary experience and one which was driven home by the mineowners' success in the strike.

The shooting of European workers was a dramatic warning to Africans. If European managers and directors were able to shoot their immediate subordinates with legal impunity, they would have no compunction in doing similarly with their African work-force. The mineowners victory in the strikes created the right intimidatory atmosphere for the introduction of closed compounds in 1885, the means to control African labour more effectively. Once the 80 per cent of the mine work-force was at heel, the authority of Europeans was reinforced. They were not compounded and it was this system that institutionalised a rigid racial division of labour in the mines.

8

The closed compound system

In 1885, 15 years after diamonds were first mined at Kimberley, mining companies began to introduce closed compounds. In January the Compagnie Française began the system with 110 Africans recruited in Natal. In April the Kimberley Central followed suit with 400 Africans recruited from Inhambane in Mozambique. They promptly struck, but once the strike leaders had been dismissed the men went to work. Similarly, before the De Beers DMC closed its compound on 1,500 Africans in July 1886, F. R. Thompson, the compound manager, made recruiting arrangements with chiefs in Basutoland, Bechuanaland and the Transvaal. Nonetheless, Africans rejected the system by going on strike, but found their will quickly broken.[1]

The introduction of the closed compound system by the Kimberley Central was treated with great interest in the local press. One observer, who is worth quoting in full, described the physical layout of the compound:

> The Compound is situated on the north side of the North Circular Road, at the point where the bridge crosses from the Central Company's works. It is a rectangular enclosure and covers several acres of ground. The Compound itself is again surrounded a few yards away from its walls by a railing, indicating unmistakeably that the property is private property and trespassers will be prosecuted. No unauthorised person will be able to approach the walls of the compound unless to be able to elude the vigilance of the guard. In this way also the whole of the Central Company's works have been wired in so that the Kaffir will never be off his employer's ground. He will betake himself to the mine on a pathway well inside this fence and will never, without a permit, go outside it. One of the searching houses has recently been moved from the edge of the mine to the vicinity of the compound on the other side of the bridge, and he will pass through it and will be subjected to a thorough search whenever he leaves the compound. At first sight, the new compound strikes the observer as admirably adapted to the purpose it is intended for. In the words of one of our honourable judges, it may well be described as (for the Kaffir) an 'eligible residential situation'. Plenty of breathing space is granted him within its four walls, and room for the full indulgence of the antics in which he delights to disport his supple limbs. Entry is obtained through a guard-house at the corner, which is turretted, and on the summit a big 'C' is a landmark. Along one of the four sides of the enclosure are ranged the offices and sleeping rooms for such white employees as choose to avail themselves of the accommodation, the general store, refreshment room, Kaffir dining room, dispensary, infirmary etc., whilst the remaining three sides are devoted to the Kaffir sleeping rooms, capable of housing about 400 boys. Clean urinals and latrines are

146

provided, and also the unusual luxury of a bath in the centre of the enclosure, the use of which the boys were not slow to appreciate.[2]

The basic structure of the compound was similar in all cases, and they only varied in size. The largest was the De Beers West End compound, which covered four acres and was built for 3,000 men.[3]

The introduction of closed compounds has been put down to the desire of mineowners to prevent theft.[4] However, we will argue that things were somewhat more complex. The prevention of theft was only one factor influencing the introduction of compounds. Most importantly, they were introduced as an integral part of the development of underground mining. In order to test the validity of this new explanation, the effect of the compound system on African labourers will have to be assessed over the 1890s. By this time the mines had been monopolised by one giant company, De Beers Consolidated Mines. Furthermore, this chapter concentrates on the compound system from the point of view of the mining industry alone, and the following chapter examines the groundswell of opposition to the system from the town community.

IMPROVEMENT IN YIELD AND THEFT: THE MINEOWNERS' CASE
UNMASKED

The mineowners chose to ignore two important material facts about diamond mining and emphasised, for class interests of their own, the social aspect of theft in the production process. The first important factor was the general rule that the diamond yield improved with depth. In fact, from the late 1870s, well before the introduction of closed compounds, yield had begun to improve in Kimberley Mine. While mineowners were lamenting in Parliament that theft was a haemorrhage the diamond industry could no longer bear, the mines at their deepest points were yielding greater riches than ever before. This made it difficult to assess the extent of theft, but it also made it difficult to argue convincingly that closed compounds reduced theft.

The second factor, the washing of undecomposed blue ground, had an even more crucial bearing on yield and one which mineowners were anxious to diminish in importance. The factor became critical in the post 'share mania' period. The over-capitalisation of companies formed during the 'share mania' contributed, as we have seen in chapter 6, to the poor profile of profit in the industry. But, this was not all. Over-capitalisation was the product of the predominance of vendor and 'watered' stock in the majority of companies. In turn, this led to a shortage of working capital, which forced companies to shorten the time of production so as to realize diamonds quickly to pay expenses. The process of washing was the phase of production in which time could most easily be saved, but only at the expense of washing inadequately decomposed blue ground. While some blue decomposed on the floors in two weeks under a favourable combination of

Plate 6 De Beers West End compound in the early 1900s. The swimming pool is in the enclosure in the centre. The sleeping quarters are on the right-hand side of the compound to which is attached a covering of wire mesh. Courtesy De Beers, London.

repeated rain and brilliant sunshine, other blue took between six months and a year to disintegrate into a washable form. If inadequately weathered blue was washed, unknown quantities of diamonds were lost to the tailings heaps. Company directors knew this, but their cupidity had led them to make less than adequate provision for working capital.

The duplicity of the mineowners is illustrated by their public use of African theft as the most powerful weapon in their argument for the introduction of closed compounds, and their private admission that bad management and the washing of badly weathered blue, rather than theft, accounted for the major loss of diamonds. In April 1882, Sammy Marks told the Select Committee on IDB that diamond theft not only jeopardised the industry, but also prevented the investment of European capital in the mines. Even if African theft prevented investment, rather than the prevailing depression, Marks' own solution to the problem was novel. He discharged white overseers and employed African labourers under their own headmen. Nevertheless, Parliament could be expected to be sympathetic to an issue concerning the protection of private property.[5]

In contrast, in August 1882 Marks told Albert Gansl, the representative of the Rothschilds, that companies lost half their diamonds by washing undecomposed ground. Marks hoped that Lord Rothschild would back up his speculation in the Anglo–African DMC with the provision of working capital. Soon after Gansl arrived in Kimberley to inspect the Anglo–African, he sacked the General Manager, Walter Ward, and appointed Sammy Marks in his place. Under Gansl's direction the company's staff was reduced; salaries were cut by 25 to 40 per cent; and the company joined a group of others in a plan to reduce African wages. These changes would, Gansl predicted, reduce working costs from 8s 6d to 7s a load and save £40,000 a year, which in itself equalled a six per cent dividend. He reported to Lord Rothschild that 'extravagant and unbusiness-like management' had brought the company 'to the verge of ruin' and he asked for working capital to prevent the suspension of operations.[6]

The washing of inadequately decomposed blue and the improvement in yield with depth certainly made it difficult to argue convincingly that the closed compound system reduced the incidence of theft. In fact, some mineowners had accepted a simpler and more effective way of preventing theft than closed compounds. They paid workers, who found diamonds in working in the mines or picking on the floors, a percentage of the value of the found diamond. The percentages or 'premiums on honesty' varied from company to company, but an overseer was usually rewarded with around five per cent while an African labourer was given a 'present' which amounted to one or two per cent of the value of the stone.[7] These pecentages were about the prices stolen diamonds fetched on the illicit market; the original thief received only a fraction of the true market value. Some companies found it worth their while to pay even more. 'One company at Dutoitspan', wrote Dr Matthews, 'by this means improved their returns to such an extent that they found it paid them to promise each "Happy child of Ham" 25 per cent commission on whatever gem he might unearth.'[8] A popular song of the time called 'I would rather be a nigger and get 25 per cent' celebrated and questioned the practice; it was believed that it encouraged stolen diamonds to be legitimately offered to premium-paying companies.[9] Despite the controversy surrounding the system, premiums did off-set the temptation to steal and was a realistic compromise struck on the peculiar conditions of exploitation in the diamond industry.

UNDERGROUND MINING AND THE INTRODUCTION OF CLOSED
COMPOUNDS

Underground mining entailed a fundamental change in the social organisation of production and, in particular, in the exercise of authority and supervision in the work-place. The essence of this change lay in the concentration of the means of production in shafts and tunnels and the shedding of excess labour and plant that this allowed. Moreover, the concentration of means of production also applied to African accommodation and the building of large compounds was an intrinsic part of the reconstruction of the production process in the development of under-ground mining.

Both the Kimberley Central and the De Beers companies made the connection between underground mining and compounds clear to their shareholders. When the Kimberley Central first developed systematic underground mining after 1884, the closed compound system was an essential part of the new method of production.[10] Earlier, in 1882, the De Beers plan for the amalgamation of the mine proposed two essential innovations:

> FIRSTLY: 4 large engines should be erected (East, West, North and South) to work on the shaft and tunnel system, and capable of pulling out 8,000 loads per day ... this would reduce the number of 2,000 boys at present employed to 1,500. For the last ten years not more than one-third of the Mine has actually been worked; but in the course of a month the new company's machinery will be at work thus bringing the greater part of the Mine into play ...

> SECONDLY: Barracks should be built for lodging the boys.
> At seven o'clock in the morning the boys should be down in the Mine, return for dinner, go to the Mine again till 6 p.m. On their return they would be searched (for the first time that day) by the overseers and gatekeeper. Each journey between the barracks and the Mine would be performed by the boys marching in columns. After supper or after being searched the boys would be at liberty to go into town until 9 p.m. This plan would prevent the stealing of diamonds which prevails to such an extent that it is estimated 25% of the total are stolen.
> One of the present drawbacks on the Fields has been and is at the present time, the native labour question. By adopting the barracks system all competition would be obviated by entering into a contract with the Kaffir Chiefs for a constant supply of boys for the Company only; the company to establish depots along the road and pay for all food or requirements the boys needed (the boys holding the Company's pass) to and from the Fields. The contract might be so much per hundred, or an handsome present – a petty chief might reside on the Fields to represent the boys of his tribe.[11]

Here, the conception of compounds was reworked from a pool of ideas current in Kimberley since the 1876 Labour Commission. While the labour control intentions of mineowners were clear enough, the basic trans-formation of barracks into compounds incarcerating Africans for the length of a contract became vitally important with the development of under-ground mining.

Mining underground was initially undertaken to remove reef. In 1882 T. P. Watson, a government engineer estimated that nearly £1 million had already been spent in sinking shafts, driving tunnels and passes, and laying down railways solely for the purpose of removing reef.[12] By this time, despite the prodigious hauling of reef, it had become clear that under-ground mining had to be undertaken for the extraction of the blue. In May the Kimberley Central commissioned the construction of a shaft through the fallen reef inside the mine. It was built on the cofferdam principle by

Edward Jones, earlier the Manager of the De Beers DMC. Such a system, although successful, proved to be only a temporary measure.

The Kimberley Central planned a permanent underground works and engaged a firm of Manchester consulting engineers, J. & P. Higson. In mid-1884 the firm sent William Kenrick to Kimberley to make a report. He found the Jones shaft underground workings totally inadequate and warned that it would depreciate the value of the Company's property. His report advised the continuation of the open-cast working if the mine was unified; but with or without amalgamation a permanent rock shaft outside the mine had to be built. Kenrick also found the then current gallery or chamber method of underground mining unsatisfactory and recommended the development of the longwall system. As if to emphasise the validity of Kenrick's report, the fallen reef moved in September 1884 and destroyed the Jones shaft and its underground works. The output of the Kimberley Central fell to 600 loads a day and all future hopes then hung on the development of outside shafts.[13]

The make or break year for Kimberley Mine was 1885. In this year all three major mining companies, the Central, the French and the Standard, moved to systematic underground mining.[14] At the end of 1885 the Kimberley Central DMC was the first to complete its rock shaft and to begin underground mining. 'If their shaft and tunnel prove a success', wrote the Manager of the Standard Bank:

> together with their new scheme recently adopted for working out the blue instead of the old chamber system, then the success of the Central is ensured and the effects upon other mines may be disastrous. The cost connected with this undertaking has been vast, but the Company through their shaft within the mine have been enabled to turn out so much ground, that were it not for external obligation, law costs, etc. etc. they would almost have carried on without asking for additional funds. When they get their outside shaft in full working order and succeed – as they are most sanguine of doing – in hauling 1,000 loads a day, the time necessary for them to pay off all their debts and recommence paying dividends should not extend beyond the end of 1886.[15]

This prediction was accurate. In the company's 1887 financial year a dividend of 34.5 per cent was declared. The total capacity of the mine, which was owned by the Central by the end of 1887, was between 6,000 and 8,000 loads a day, and the man who was largely responsible for the conception and direction of this prodigious output was William McHardy, one of the unsung mining engineers of the diamond industry. At the end of 1887 the Kimberley Central reverted to an open system in combination with uniform underground works.[16]

The De Beers DMC lagged behind the Kimberley Central in the development of underground mining. In November 1884 the company began to sink a rock shaft outside the mine, but at a depth of 300 feet sinking was suspended owing to the hardness of the rock. The company approached the well-known London firm of engineers, John Taylor and Sons, for a mining engineer to superintend the development of shafts and tunnels, estimated to cost £60,000. Not finding anyone suitable, Rudd re-engaged Edward Jones to sink a shaft inside the mine and to work on the chamber system that the Kimberley Central had recently rejected.[17] According to Stow, Rudd indulged in some 'jobbery' in this appointment, for Jones had been sacked in 1881 at the instigation of Stow, who had a low opinion of his professional ability. Jones was in debt to E. W. Tarry and Company, a mining machinery firm in which Rudd was a partner, and the 1s per load that Jones earned on each load hauled between June 1885 and March 1887 (£23,500) substantially helped him out of insolvency. In contrast to Stow, Rhodes believed that Jones' engineering helped the company over its crucial transition from full open-working in 1884 to full underground mining in 1887.[18]

In April 1887 a new post of General Manager was created in the De Beers Company. Gardner Williams, an American mining engineer, who had been a consultant with the Exploration Company, a Rothschild mining finance intermediary, was appointed to the post at a salary of £3,000 a year.[19] He instituted a modified version of the Kimberley Central's longwall system, which he claimed was 'based essentially on a method suggested by the miners themselves and without reference to any other system'.[20] Under his management output increased to 3,000 loads a day by November 1887 and 6,000 loads by June 1888.

In both De Beers and Kimberley Mines increased output was the result of important changes in the organisation of production. Mining was now generally undertaken by contractors, who were paid to deliver the blue to the waggons at the shaft head for a set rate per load. The growth of this new system can be seen from the accounts of the Kimberley Central (see Table 8).[21]

Out of the contract price of around 5s a load of hauled blue, the contractor paid the wages of the men he employed (miners, overseers and labourers) and bought all the mining materials including explosives. For its part, the company supplied the necessary plant, steam-power, fuel and labour. Contracts were also offered for tramming the blue to the floors and for filling trucks. The company continued to have mineworkers in its direct employ for maintenance work and the preparation of the blue for washing.

Underground mining required skilled miners, in contrast to mining under the open system in which the engineering trades and craft work around the mines had been the only skilled occupations in the industry. Skilled miners directed the extraction of the blue ground. They had to listen to the roofs of drives, stopes and tunnels to assess safety; they had to know how to extract the greatest amount of blue in the most economical manner; and they had to know how to blast. Such miners were in short supply during the early development of shafts and tunnels. Shaft sinkers had to be imported from Lancashire to build the Kimberley Central rock shaft. The Compagnie Française was hampered by the shortage of skilled men in its development

Table 8 *Kimberley Central DMC, Wages*

	Year ending 30.4.1886	30.4.1887	30.6.1888
White wages	£ 29,188	£ 27,721	£ 61,257
African wages	£ 22,494	£ 35,750	£ 51,002
Contractors	£ 20,178	£ 54,331	£153,140

work. Once systematic underground mining became the major method of production skilled miners were imported from the haematite mines of Cumberland and the hard rock mines of Cornwall; the workshops of the companies were dominated by British and, in particular, Scottish artisans.[22]

The introduction of British miners and the reduction in the number of overseers necessary for underground working drastically reduced the employment of colonial whites in the mines. From well over half the white work force in 1885, the share of colonial whites was reduced to just over ten per cent in 1889. The biggest drop came between 1888 and 1889, when both underground mining was reconstructed on a uniform basis after amalgamation and the poorer mines were closed down. The consequence of this change in the composition of the white work force was the emergence of a stratum of poor whites in Kimberley. The size of this group was augmented by Afrikaner squatters, who had been evicted from farms in the surrounding countryside. They first moved to the river diggings and then into the squalor of the tailings heaps and locations in Kimberley. In 1887 the District Surgeon drew attention to their plight and commented that 'privation has without doubt in many instances contributed to bring on disease and accelerated a fatal issue'.[23] In the following year the Anglican priest, J. C. Todd, reported that he knew no coloured family 'so low as the most degraded whites'.[24]

At the same time as the problem of 'poor whiteism' was emerging, the first legal colour bar was introduced in the mining industry. After resisting discrimination in access to claims, in the time of Southey's governorship, and in labour legislation, during Lanyon's administration, discrimination was now introduced into mining with respect to blasting. Under the rules and regulations of the 1883 Mining Act, promulgated in December 1885, blasting was to be 'carried on under the supervision of a European experienced in blasting' and 'no person under 18 years of age and no native is to be permitted to manipulate explosives or prepare the same for blasting or other purposes'.[25] Furthermore, the General Regulations of the Kimberley Central DMC made Europeans responsible for all 'natives' working in the mine. They had to supply a daily attendance ticket to 'natives under their supervision' with the name of the supervisory miner or contractor on it and to ensure that each 'native' had a pass 'as provided by Government regulations for that purpose'.[26] In 1889 this provision found its way into legislated regulations: 'No native shall work or be allowed to work in any mine, whether in open or underground workings, excepting under the responsible charge of some particular white man as his master or "baas".'[27]

This was one of a number of measures, the introduction of closed compounds being most important, which bolstered the superior position of Europeans in the labour process. The searching system, as we have seen in chapter 7, implied that Europeans were not to be trusted in respect to theft. It is worth noting that it was openly admitted in commissions and private letters that white workers, and even managers, were as much involved in IDB as black workers.[28] Initially, mineowners had been committed to subjecting all their workers to the searching system, but when closed compounds were introduced, the preferred solution to diamond theft, white workers were excluded and allowed to live in the towns. This enhanced their authority in the mines and on the floors. 'If we were to dispute the white man's honesty', commented Joseph Gouldie, De Beers Mine Manager, 'we might lose more than by putting confidence in him.'[29] This was a point of view that he and other managers had not entertained before the 1883 and 1884 strikes.

Segregated compounds had a divisive effect on the labour force in a simple and instrumental way. European authority in the mines was endorsed by their exclusion from closed compounds; they were trusted by management whereas African mineworkers were treated as potential criminals. While it was politically difficult to compound Europeans,[30] a positive strategy emerged from their separate housing and privileged treatment, which benefitted both management and European mineworkers. Overseers, whose employment had been so dependent on the fluctuations in the supply of African labour, found fewer positions but greater security and regularity of earnings. Skilled workers, whose attempts at control of entry into their trades had been foiled, were co-opted with higher wages and in effect granted a sectional weapon that increased differentials. White workers of different skills became an entrenched group of supervisors in collaboration with management in disciplining the African labour force.

African mineworkers had to adapt to a new labour process of stoping, loading and drilling in underground workings. They worked in teams, usually formed on ethnic grounds, of 20 to 30 men. Shifts were 12 hours long until 1892, when they were shortened to eight hours. Each shift was divided by an hour-long dinner break and half-an-hour was allowed for shift changes which involved a 500 to 1,000 feet climb down the shaft by ladders. Overall, underground labour was more arduous than the longer sunrise-to-sunset routine in open mining during summer. Although the mines were worked by fewer Africans, production increased through round-the-clock shift work and greater demands made by contractors and management.[31]

For the first time Africans were paid piece-wages. Such a method of payment was inefficient in open working, as 'raw natives', unaccustomed to mine labour, could not be relied on to work under such an indirect system of control. According to mine managers Africans had to be driven to work by the close attention of overseers.[32] But with the development of underground mining, piece-wages were introduced to overcome the difficulties of supervision underground. 'We had an open system, where we had more control over the natives and overseers', said William McHardy, General Manager of the Kimberley Central, 'now they are comparatively spread about in underground workings in such a way it is impossible to have an efficient check'.[33] The ratio of one overseer to six African labourers in open mining widened to one to 30 in underground works.[34] Piece-work increased productivity and reduced the costs of supervision.

In short, the introduction of closed compounds was an integral part of the development of underground mining. The social division of labour was fundamentally altered: skilled miners were imported, colonial whites were made redundant as the need for supervision declined, a colour bar became part of mine regulations and Africans were paid piece-wages. Only Africans were compounded despite the fact that all workers were potential thieves.

THE DE BEERS CONVICT STATION: THE MODEL FOR THE CLOSED COMPOUND

The closed compound was modelled on the De Beers convict station. In October 1884, before the introduction of the first closed compound, the De Beers DMC began negotiations with the Cape government for convict labour. From November 1884 to May 1885 the company employed around 200 convicts, who were hired from the Law Department and maintained in the Kimberley gaols. De Beers found the employment of convicts so advantageous that they offered to build a convict station and to take 200 and more convicts 'completely off the hands of the government'.[35] The offer was accepted and, while the company provided the building materials at a cost of £5,200, free convict labour was supplied by the state for the construction of the station. In January 1886 De Beers was granted a two year contract for the free service of 300 convicts and the company undertook to maintain and discipline them in its convict station. In 1888 the Law Department renegotiated the contract and charged the company 3d per day per man, a sum De Beers was glad to pay.[36] The company showed its confidence in convicts by increasing the number employed from 200 in 1885 to over 800 in 1894. The availability of convict workers was limited by the number of prisoners and the requirements of the Public Works Department, which had a first option on labour. De Beers found convict labour so satisfactory that convicts were employed until 1932.[37]

The De Beers management was convinced that convicts were superior to free labour in almost every respect. There were advantages over free workers in five spheres: labour efficiency; labour discipline; labour cost; economies of scale in maintenance; and the prevention of diamond theft. In time free labour in compounds and prison labour in the convict station became similar with the only important difference being that between compulsory and voluntary service. 'In these convict barracks, or branch gaol', wrote the Mine Inspector, 'the perfection of the compound system may be said to have been reached.'[38]

The first major advantage of convict labour over free labour lay in its efficiency. 'It is by far the best native labour we have', reported Gardner Williams, 'owing to the fact that the convicts are obliged to remain for a considerable length of time, while the free natives only work two months at a time.'[39] Long-term convicts had enough time to become accustomed to the hard regime of working about a mine. However, the majority of Kimberley prisoners were short-term because of the enormous number of Africans convicted of pass offences and sentenced to up to one month's hard labour.[40] The Kimberley Gaol had been built to hold 400 convicts but in the late 1880s held twice that number.[41] For many 'raw' Africans their introduction to the diamond city was a transit through the Kimberley Gaol to the De Beers convict station. While this provided a regular supply of labour, pass offenders did not become the trained mine labourers that De Beers required. As a result the De Beers convict station seldom accommodated its full quota of prisoners before 1889, although it was forced to take convicts sentenced to less than two months hard labour. In the 1890s, as the number of pass convictions and the prison population of Kimberley declined, De Beers looked to other convict stations in the Cape Colony and drew the majority of its long-term prisoners from the Transkei, Dordrecht and Middelburg.[42]

The rigorous discipline and supervision that it was possible to impose on convict labour was its second advantage. Convicts were employed at the sorting tables and in breaking up the blue ground on the depositing floors. They were not employed underground, where even close supervision of free labourers was difficult. Convicts worked 13 hours a day in summer and nine and a half hours in winter, two hours longer than the hard labour regulations of the Prison Department, but no longer than the hours worked by free labour. They were controlled by government-appointed, but company-paid Zulu guards, initially one to every five convicts, a ratio which by 1891 had widened to one to every ten convicts.[43]

The relaxation in supervision in the 1890s was a product of the expansion in convict employment and the use of some incentives to accompany the stick of prison discipline. Even though discipline was tight there were always ways in which convicts could sabotage their gaoler's property. As diamonds were high in value and small in size, a convict coming across a diamond while working on the floors or at the sorting tables had it 'completely in his power to revenge himself on his employers either by sweeping the diamonds from the sorting tables or by burying them in the soil with his heel . . .'[44] To discourage such acts of vengeance, convicts were paid rewards of 3d to 10d per carat on found diamonds. Some convicts even left their periods of hard labour with more money than free labourers. When this came to the notice of the public there was an outcry, and a £15 limit per period of service was placed on rewards.[45]

A third advantage of convict labour was its cheapness. Between 1887 and 1894 the annual cost of discipline, maintenance and rent of convict labour fell from £58 to £39 10s per man. In 1887 free labour cost as much as £65 per man per year, but by 1894 this figure had fallen to about £40.[46] The decline in the cost of free labour was partly determined by the employment of convict labour. In 1890, for example, when the number of convicts employed was doubled to 700, the result was 'a large decrease in the number of free labourers'.[47] However, of even greater importance in the decline of free wages were the amalgamation of the mines and the introduction of closed compounds.

Although convicts were cheaper to employ than free labour, their maintenance standards were comparatively higher. The death rate, the most extreme index of social welfare, was 18 per thousand from 1891 to 1899 at the De Beers convict station, well under half the remainder of the African mine work-force.[48] Convicts were issued with thick jumpers, moleskin trousers, felt hats, boots 'when necessary', three blankets in winter and two in summer, and two sacks sewn together which formed a pillow and pallaise for bedding. The station diet had a generous meat component suitable to hard labour. Convicts were scheduled to receive a pound of meat a day, a half-pound of bread, eight ounces of meal, a pound of vegetables, an ounce of salt and a quart of soup.[49] This diet was certainly superior to the rations on offer in the Kimberley gaols. There, short-term convicts were given a mielie-meal diet, and long-term convicts were scheduled to receive some meat during each week. In 1884 gaol rations were reduced because of the high price of food and 350 long-term prisoners went on strike. In response the authorities reduced rations to below subsistence and scurvy broke out in the gaols. Rations were generally so poor that bad health kept a quarter of the hard-labour convicts on the sick list. In contrast, De Beers found it more economical to feed its convicts adequately.[50]

The final advantage that De Beers derived from convict labour lay in the prevention of theft. Convicts were searched on entry to and exit from the station. They stripped in the search houses and went naked to their cells where blankets were worn to keep warm. When their term of imprisonment was over they were held in solitary confinement for five days, naked and with large leather gloves locked on their hands. This was to ensure that they had not swallowed any diamonds in the hope of selling them once they were free. There is little doubt that such precautions made the theft of diamonds more difficult, and combined with rewards for found diamonds reduced the extent of theft.[51]

Closed compounds were not totalitarian institutions from their intro-duction. The Kimberley Central closed its compound on recruited Africans to force them into underground works. It still had to rely on others to replace its recruits and unlike De Beers did not have convict labourers as a reserve supply. The Kimberley Central induced Africans into its compound through the provision of liquor and the promise of time off on Sundays to go on the town. The Bultfontein Mining Company followed the same policy and other companies let it be known that tobacco, coffee and food were provided for free. In the late 1880s these compounds did not introduce the theft prevention refinements of wire mesh, detention cells and electric lighting, though they would have followed the lead of De Beers had they survived into the 1890s.[52]

Similarly, closed compounds were not functionally integrated into the organisation of the labour process from their introduction. The Kimberley Central did not separate its surface and underground workers, and its 'Cape boy' tram drivers remained at liberty in the towns. De Beers was more efficient in its labour management after it had monopolised production. Not only were surface and underground workers segregated, but accommodation was centralised on a grand scale. In 1896 De Beers had two mine compounds for over 4,000 Africans and one floor compound for under 1,000 men. In addition, there was a stable compound for 245 transport workers, 'mostly Cape Boys and Colonial Kaffirs', and a smaller workshop compound.[53]

CLOSED COMPOUNDS AND SOCIAL WELFARE

By 1889 all 10,000 African mineworkers were accommodated in closed compounds.[54] Even before all mineworkers were subjected to the system, Gardner Williams, General Manager of De Beers Consolidated, was convinced that closed compounds improved the welfare of African miners. 'Our natives are better housed and better fed than uncompounded natives', he told his shareholders:

> and are better paid than miners in any of the European countries. Those unfit for work, either through sickness or on account of injuries received in the mine are taken free of cost in the Company's hospital which adjoins the compound. There are fewer accidents under the present system than there were in the open workings. A very large majority of the accidents in the mine are due either to carelessness or the stupidity of natives themselves. A large percentage of the deaths in the compound has been caused by receiving natives who come in companies from countries north of the Transvaal, many of whom are so starved and emaciated as to be beyond help.[55]

While the comparison with European miners is difficult to test, other elements of this statement are open to question. Most problematic is Williams' understanding of why Africans under his control in compounds and in the mines died.

There is little doubt that there were fewer accidents in open working than in underground mining. There is also little doubt that underground diamond mining was more dangerous than mining elsewhere in the world.

Some statistics illustrate the point. In late nineteenth-century British mining a rate of over three persons killed per 1,000 was considered unacceptable. On the Witwatersrand between 1896 and 1905, after the development of deep-level mining, the mine accident death-rate averaged a little over 4 per 1,000. In Southern Rhodesia the mine accident death-rate never went over 5 per 1,000 between 1907 and 1933. For the latter half of this period it averaged around 2.5 deaths per 1,000. Worst of all, the Kimberley mine death-rate was very high during the experimental stage of underground mining, but settled down to 6.2 per 1,000 between 1890 and 1899.[56]

In part, this high death-rate was the product of the novel and treacherous nature of underground mining in diamondiferous ground. Vast caverns were excavated in the blue and the Kimberley and De Beers mines were transformed into gigantic honeycombs. The blue left as pillars was inherently unsafe, as it disintegrated on exposure to the atmosphere and to water. There were also greasy slides between large blocks of blue which slipped without warning. Consequently, the roofs of underground workings were constant sources of danger. In addition, firedamp was a threat while candles were the major means of underground lighting. Finally, mud rushes became the most feared underground hazard, bursting into tunnels and filling them up with terrifying speed.

In part, accidents in underground mining were caused by the competition to increase production in the struggle for the total control of the four mines in the late 1880s. The De Beers DMC pushed its workers to the limit to catch up with the greater productive capacity of the Kimberley Central DMC. In 1886, the Mining Inspector commented that 'the majority of employers of labour in these mines look upon regulations for safety as mere harassing restrictions'.[57] Such an attitude on the part of the De Beers management led to catastrophic results. In July 1888 a fire broke out underground in De Beers Mine. Out of a work-force of 67 Europeans and 625 Africans, 24 Europeans and 178 Africans died. The Lutheran Minister, Brother Arndt, described the disaster:

> The overseers above ground heard the Christian blacks singing and soon the smoke confirmed the news of fire. These Christian labourers realising their hopeless situation prepared themselves for death by singing. One heathen black saved the lives of three white men. One he found unconscious and carried him 300 steps through the suffocating smoke to safety. He then returned and fetched the other two. A Zulu, John, carried his master through the smoke, stepping over mounds of corpses, up a ladder and to safety. When both were offered a reward (a watch and a chain) by the mining company, Jim started to cry that he had not done this for the sake of a reward but only to save their masters. When Jim was asked why he went back twice risking his life, he answered: 'it is nothing if I die, but if the whites die it is a big thing'.[58]

The Commission that investigated the disaster found that there were no fire extinguishers in the mine, that there was a lack of adequate ladderways, and that, as the escape shaft had been closed at the time of the accident, mining should have been stopped. Those who survived were rescued through opening up a tunnel into the open mine. Although Gardner Williams received absolution from the directors of De Beers, he was held culpable by the Commission of Enquiry.[59]

Yet, accidents accounted for only a small proportion of the death-rate of the diamond mines. Disease rather than accidents claimed the lion's share of African lives. Mortality statistics of the time are certainly unreliable by twentieth-century standards, but enough can be gleaned from fragmented figures to establish trends. But first, a number of *caveats* have to be made. The population of Kimberley could only be roughly estimated given transient African labourers and the maze-like nature of the mining camps. Moreover, the mortality rates for the 1870s and 1880s apply to the whole population and not simply to those who worked in the mines. Still, it should be remembered that the African population was overwhelmingly male, that African males were predominantly employed in the mining industry and that the death-rate was highest among African male adults.

A further problem relates to the depression and smallpox epidemic period (1882–85). While privation and smallpox during the depression years must have increased the death rate, the mineowners and several doctors, as we have seen in chapter 7, tried to conceal the nature of the epidemic and the extent of its deadly legacy. It was openly admitted by officials and doctors after the epidemic had passed that many Africans had died without any death registration. After 1885 registration became more systematic and mortality figures more reliable. Consequently, the extent of death in Kimberley became an issue of public concern for the first time. In 1887 one Parliamentary Commission discovered the fact that four convicts were fully employed in picking up African corpses from the compounds and streets, while another 10 to 30 were employed full-time in digging graves.[60]

Even so, it is possible to compare the mortality rate in the two boom periods of the late 1870s and the late 1880s. In 1878, when African labourers lived in open compounds and in the camps, the African death-rate was 80 per 1,000. This was a mortality rate that was, according to Dr Matthews:

> sufficiently large to rank Kimberley among the most unhealthy towns in existence. This is about three times the proportionate rate of mortality in London and is considerably greater than the average number of deaths per 1,000 in large and crowded cities of the East.[61]

But a decade later, even after allowing for improved death registration, matters were worse. In 1888, when almost all African mineworkers lived in closed compounds, the death rate was over 100 per 1,000, more than double the Rhodesian mortality rate in a comparable period of mining development.[62] Even if we take into account the unreliability of total Kimberley population figures, we know that the trend in the earlier period was towards an increase in population while the converse was true of the second period. This tends to improve the mortality rate of the late 1870s but worsens it in the late 1880s. 'The death rate is not as low as might have been expected', wrote the Registrar of Natives, 'especially considering the increased compound accommodation'.[63]

It appears, then, that Gardner Williams was off the mark in his claim that closed compounds increased the social welfare of African miners. But on such unreliable mortality and population figures Williams' case is not conclusively disproved. What does cast a dark shadow of doubt over his claims is a comparison of the causes of death during the two eras of open and closed compounds. In the former era twice as many Africans died of sanitation-related diseases, such as fever, dysentery and diarrhoea, as died of lung-related diseases, such as bronchitis, pneumonia, pthisis and pleurisy.[64] In the era of closed compounds the reverse was true, and the majority of Africans died of lung diseases caused by overcrowded accommodation, poor diet and inadequate protection against major changes in temperature, exacerbated by underground mining. While sanitation and public health improved over the 1880s and 1890s, De Beers and the few marginal companies which survived amalgamation did little to improve their compound accommodation. Throughout the 1890s pneumonia continued to be the most feared killer in the compounds. 'This disease will continue to be our most serious cause of death in the ordinary course of events', wrote Dr Stoney in 1900, 'so long as overcrowding in the compounds continues . . .'[65]

Overcrowding was exacerbated by the centralisation of compound accommodation after the monopolisation of the mines. In 1889 there were 17 compounds for 10,000 Africans; but in 1896 De Beers used only three compounds for 5,000 Africans.[66] As the work force had fallen Africans were concentrated in fewer but larger compounds. The model De Beers West End compound, described so well by Gardner Williams in his book, covered four acres, contained the much-vaunted swimming bath and housed 3,000 Africans.[67] Yet, wide open spaces could not compensate for the congestion in the sleeping compartments. At the beginning of the 1890s De Beers compounds infringed the minimum public health standards of 300 cubic feet per man.[68] The situation worsened over the decade. Systematic shiftwork encouraged the illusion that accommodation could be provided on shares, one shift sleeping while the two others worked or took time out. After 1896, when the minework force began to expand again, there was an inadequate increase in compound accommodation. In 1900, Dr Stoney reported that until the compounds were 'extended and re-modelled with an increased air-space, proper lighting and impermeable floors, this terrible disease (pneumonia) amongst the natives will continue its ravages'.[69]

Besides being overcrowded, compounds were also cold. Africans slept on the ground in blankets in quarters without doors and with an open space around the top of the walls. While this aided ventilation during summer and during the day, it did not exclude the intense cold at night and during winter. Kimberley was and is notorious for its savage inversions of temperature. In fact, despite the provision of 'free' wood, compounds were so cold

161

that 'natives for the night shift were in the habit of going down into the mine early in the afternoon because it was warmer there than in their compound ...'[70] Wood may well have been 'free', but the quantity provided was certainly inadequate for keeping Africans warm. 'In the face of the great amounts of profits made out of these natives', the Protector of Natives doubted whether 'they receive anything for nothing.'[71]

Medical care was also, according to Gardner Williams, provided 'free of cost'. A review of the history of health care in Kimberley suggests otherwise. In the early days sick Africans were most often sent to the Kimberley gaols. Prisons were not only lock-ups, but also 'asylums for lunatics, hospitals for prisoners and chronic sick paupers and refuges for the destitute'.[72] While their facilities were certainly free, medical care was minimal. In the 1880s better treatment was available in the Kimberley Hospital, but beds for Africans were limited. This was so despite the fact that Africans paid a special hospital tax as part of the fee for the registration of a labour contract. This tax, which only Africans paid, provided the largest subsidy to the Kimberley Hospital throughout the 1880s and 1890s. The benefit of this funding went to white patients. Nonetheless, Africans paid 12s a year for medical care, and were entitled to it, whether in mine or municipal hospitals.[73]

Were Africans compensated in the mine hospital for the care they were entitled to at the Kimberley Hospital? Before monopolisation, companies varied in their standards of health care, ranging from none at all to visiting doctors, dispensaries and infirmaries. Whatever services were provided, they were not as adequate as the improving standards of medicine in the Kimberley Hospital. Compound managers did not take advantage of this. In fact, hospital authorities complained that Africans were sent to them merely to die.[74] At the turn of the decade, a more humane policy of earlier admission to the hospital led to a significant decline in the death-rate. However, in the 1890s, as security in the compounds was tightened against diamond theft, all African workers were treated in compound hospitals. And it is in mine hospital deaths that a clear-cut mortality rate for mineworkers can be established (see Table 9). Although the death-rate declined over the 1890s, it was still appalling compared to the considerable improvement to around 20 per 1,000 in the decade after 1903. In 1903 the compound system underwent fundamental reconstruction. The most important facet of the improvements were the building of new dormitories with double the cubic space per man of the old enclosures.[75]

In the 1890s an inadequate diet also contributed to this high death-rate. Diamond mineworkers were not rationed as was the practice on Southern Rhodesian mines. Compound dwellers had to pay for their food indi-vidually or in food clubs, and cook it for themselves or have it cooked for them by injured Africans unable to do minework. There was a simple reason for this management practice. 'If you were to ration the natives', said F. R. Thompson, 'you would either find them all sick, or not wanting to

162

Table 9 *Death-rates of Africans in diamond mines, 1897–1905*

Year	Average number of workers[a]	Total deaths	Total death rate per 1,000
1897	6,942	333	47.97
1898	7,934	343	43.23
1899	8,022	368	45.87
1900	5,468	365	66.75
1901	6,292	684	108.70
1902	6,603	497	75.27
1903	7,273	317	43.59
1904	7,858	129	16.42
1905	11,243	387	34.42

[a] Excludes Wesselton mine

Source: *Statistical Registers of the Colony of the Cape of Good Hope, 1897–1905*. Mine-hospital death-rates were first recorded in 1897.

work, because they would get their food all the same, whereas now they say we must work to get food.'[76] Yet, as we will see below, work was often not available, as more Africans were compounded than were required for a full work-force. Management control over work, wages and food prices in the compounds amounted to a formidable array of coercive power.

In short, the social welfare provided in Kimberley's closed compounds before 1903 was poor. After 30 years and more of diamond mining and 15 under the closed compound system, African mortality was still' unacceptably high. Sanitation had improved and a section of the African work-force had become acclimatised and accustomed to minework. Yet, pneumonia was still the greatest killer in the compounds, accounting for as much as 75 per cent of African mortality. Death-rates are blunt measures and we do not know which people or age group suffered most on the mines. Nonetheless, the broad figures remain and show a substantial improvement, a two-thirds reduction in the rate of mortality, after the reconstruction of the compounds in 1903. Before this time management merely massaged shareholders' sensibilities over welfare with a misplaced paternalism, and perfected coercive control of African labourers.

MORTALITY IN COMPARATIVE PERSPECTIVE

In 1903 a private commission of Rand compound managers visited the Kimberley diamond mine compounds to see if they could improve their own system.[77] By this time Kimberley had a reputation for model compounds amongst mineowners. They believed that good accommodation, healthy food and competent medical care were responsible for keeping up the labour supply to the diamond mines. Unlike on the Rand after the war, there was no major labour shortage in Kimberley. 'The De Beers Company have set an example of just and reasonable treatment of their Native employees', wrote *Outlook*, famous organ of Christian mission opinion, in 1906, 'which might with advantage be followed at other South African labour centres.'[78] While De Beers was not without problems over labour supply, its shining example lay in its low mortality rate of 20 per 1,000 between 1903 and 1912.[79]

After the South African war the new British administration was deeply concerned – a concern which led to the compound commission to Kimberley – over the high rate of African mortality on the gold mines. In 1903 the rate was 71.25 per 1,000 and had been as bad, if not worse, in the 1890s.[80] 'I do not see', wrote Lyttleton, the Colonial Secretary, to Lord Milner, Governor of the Transvaal, 'how a death rate of between 50 and 100 per 1,000 can be defended . . .'[81] This mortality rate became an important issue in the debate over the introduction of Chinese workers to the Rand mines. Milner did all he could to improve compound conditions in view of the British and Chinese governments' negotiations over the conditions regulating the importation of Chinese into the Transvaal.[82] Rand mine doctors believed that the death-rate could be reduced to 40 per 1,000 and, it seems, this was acceptable to Lyttleton in the circumstances.[83] The mine doctors and compound managers introduced improvements, on the basis of what they had learnt in Kimberley, in the matters of sanitation, impervious floors, open stoves, diet, housing and hospitals.[84] As an immediate result the mortality rate dropped to 42.62 per 1,000 in 1904, but thereafter never matched Kimberley.

Rhodesian mine managers also looked to Kimberley for ideas in compound improvements. A Rhodesian representative joined the 1903 Rand compound commission to Kimberley, but Southern Rhodesian compounds derived no immediate benefit from the visit. In fact, van Onselen has argued that the Rhodesian mines had 'for many years an even more appalling health record than the Rand . . .'[85] Standards of health cannot, of course, simply be assessed by the death-rate, but it is the only meaningful indicator of physical welfare that can be adequately measured. In Southern Rhodesia, African mortality on the mines steadily declined over the first half of the twentieth century. It was at its worst between 1906 and 1915 when mortality averaged 43.40 per 1,000 each year.[86] The causes of death were quite clear. 'The greatest killers of all on Rhodesian mines', wrote van Onselen, 'were diseases which could be directly attributable to the inadequate diet and poor standards of accommodation for workers.'[87] As at Kimberley and on the Rand, pneumonia accounted for the greatest number of deaths. And pneumonia was a 'disease of employment' which was found comparatively rarely in the rural catchment areas of southern and central Africa.

The culpability for mortality on the Katangan copper mines is less clear. 'It is, of course, impossible to determine', wrote Perrings, 'just how much mortality rates among particular age groups were increased by their presence on the mines since it is certain that even in rural areas mortality was high.'[88] What is clear is that Africans died in greater numbers on Katangan mines at their most dangerous than at any other mining centre in southern and central Africa. Between 1913 and 1922 the average mortality rate was 71 per 1,000 each year. These figures conceal sharp variations in death-rates of different African peoples and of recruited as opposed to voluntary workers. As sections of the labour force were stabilised there was greater investment in medical care, housing and rations. After 1932 the rate of mortality due to disease remained consistently below 10 per 1,000 each year. Katanga came to rival Kimberley in the humanity of its health record.[89]

PROLETARIAN, STABILISED OR MIGRANT WORKERS?

Did the closed compound system encourage the proletarianisation of male workers? 'The term proletarianisation', writes Sharon Stichter, 'refers to the increasingly economically necessary character of participation in the wage labour market.'[90] A fully proleterianised male worker is one who has been divorced from the means of production and from the kinship bonds which determine their use. What we need to know is whether the predominantly voluntary nature (that is, without capitalist direction) of migrant wage labour of the early days of diamond mining gave way to the economic compulsion of proletarianisation after the introduction of closed compounds. Certainly, by this time the wholesale conquest of African chiefdoms in southern Africa had pushed a considerable number of Africans into the colonial economy; some land had been expropriated and income from agriculture reduced. But in a complex regional economy, and on the basis of fragmentary evidence, we still know very little about how different African peoples were divorced from the land and the social bonds of kinship or how they were incorporated into the mining industry. Nonetheless, it is probable that only a minority of mine workers – town workers apart – were fully proletarianised between 1870 and 1900.

It is perhaps more useful to ask whether the compound system stabilised the mine work force rather than helped to create proletarians. Charles Perrings has analysed the differences between a stabilised and a proleterianised work-force in his history of black workers in the copper mines of the Belgian Congo (now Zaire) and Northern Rhodesia (now Zambia) between 1911 and 1941. 'Stabilization meant the establishment of conditions', writes Perrings:

> adequate to the maintenance of the worker and his dependants in the urban milieu over an extended period, and a necessary effect of this was a reduction in the mobility of workers not only within the industrial labour market but also between wage labour and peasant or subsistence production.[91]

Stabilisation established the preconditions of proletarianisation; it provided capitalists with the benefits of proletarianisation without the social costs of a settled working class of men and dependent women. Controlled mobility between mine and area of origin was encouraged, not as a subsistence subsidy on lines of the famous Wolpe thesis,[92] but so that the costs of retirement would be borne by workers and not capitalists. Thus, a stabilised work-force of male mineworkers was consistent with a pattern of circular migration between both wage labour and peasant or subsistence production.

If closed compounds encouraged a stabilised work-force in the 1890s, we need to know a lot more than we do about the way Africans from different chiefdoms were incorporated into the work-force. Here again Sharon Stichter's analytical clarity illuminates the issue.[93] She identifies three types of rural economies which in turn condition the manner in which Africans were incorporated into mine labour. The first type of economy is so impoverished that there is no hope of agricultural or pastoral subsistence. Families are dependent on wage labour even if some members have access to land. Certainly, some Tswana had been reduced to this position by the 1890s and entered Kimberley as proletarians to work in the town if not in the mines.[94] The second type of rural economy is one which is based on the extensive farming of cash crops. Migrants from these economies choose to participate full-time in wage labour; they are not forced into the labour market. They are fully incorporated into wage work but they have the option of investing in land and livestock outside the cities. Usually it is those with education or technical skills who take this option and they are not proleterianised in the sense of being separated from the means of production. In fact, accumulation in the cities enables them to reinvest in rural areas, to maintain extended familial ties and to become successful farmers. Many who lived in Kimberley's locations and worked in the towns fell into this category, although it is not clear to what extent labourers in the mine economy were able to reinvest in their areas of origin.

The final type of economy was a functioning system of production for use and exchange value, but it was not based on an expanding market for cash crops. Male migrants from these economies genuinely straddled two modes of production; they moved between a waged and a non-waged sector of work. These are the classic migrant labourers, and the majority of diamond labourers fell into this category. Their desertion in the face of low pay, poor conditions or at the command of their chiefs had led to the call for closed compounds in the first place. It will be suggested that the irregular pattern of migration in the 1870s and 1880s gave way to a regular cycle of circular migration under the closed compound system that is immediately recognisable as the enforced variant common in twentieth-century South Africa.

By most accounts the majority of Africans who came to Kimberley did not settle permanently. Yet, the precise pattern of migration is unclear. In 1876 one editor guessed that after three working visits Africans settled on the Fields.[95] This is hardly illuminating or authoritative, but evidence for

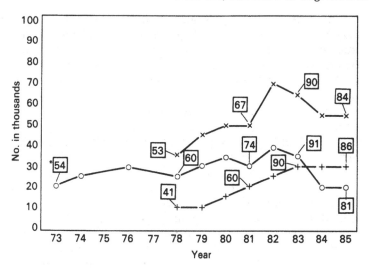

x Total number of 'old hand' contracts registered

o Total number of 'old hand' contracts registered in Kimberley and De Beers Mines

+ Total number of 'old hand' contracts registered in Bultfontein and Dutoitspan Mines

· Indicates per cent of total contracts registered; of Kimberley and De Beers total; and of Dutoitspan and Bultfontein total

Fig. 6 'Old hand' contracts registered in all mines, 1873–85. (Sources: CAD, GLW, 55, 77, (1873–75); *Griqualand West Government Gazette*, 1877–80; *Blue Book on Native Affairs*, 1881–83; CAD, NA 195, 198, 202, 1883–85)

growth of a settled population of Africans in Kimberley is going to require an imaginative and laborious search through court records. What we do know is that the number of 'old hands' re-registering for work grew rapidly as the mining economy expanded at the turn of the decade, and that 'new hands', those who had never worked on the Fields before, grew fewer. In 1878, 53 per cent of those contracted were 'old hands' and by 1883 the proportion had risen to 90 per cent. Yet, we do not know how long 'old hands' remained at the mines. Edward Judge, the Civil Commissioner, summed up the situation in early 1883:

> ... a very large native population, numbering probably some 40,000 is congregated about the mines, and demands the attention of the Government. It would appear from the returns of the Registrars of Natives that over 30,000 new hands were registered during the year 1882, from which it may be inferred that about the same number had arrived at the mines; and as the population has not been largely increased, it may be further assumed that about the same number have returned to their homes during the year.[96]

167

At the same time the Acting Registrar of Natives, Edward Hosmer, suggested that there were about 9,220 'resident Native labourers' and as this was more than his estimate for 1881 he took it to mean that the 'number of labourers more or less settled in the place is largely on the increase . . .' He found further evidence to support his supposition in the large number of protection passes issued 'and which are only given to Natives of good character, and on the recommendation of the Inspector of Locations'.[97] Elsewhere, I took this to mean that 9,000 Africans were 'permanently resident' on the Fields.[98] But we have no certain evidence that the same 9,000 Africans remained on the Fields; all we can say is that the annual turnover of Africans was less than the total African population in Kimberley. Nonetheless, as the 1880s progressed fewer and fewer 'raw' Africans went to Kimberley; most of them were recontracted.

The growth of re-contracting certainly suggests the consolidation of a pool of experienced mineworkers. In the 1880s contracts commonly ran for two months in De Beers and Bultfontein mines, while they lasted for three months in Kimberley Mine. According to the Mine Inspector Africans re-contracted for additional time in all the mines. In Kimberley Mine 'the majority re-engage for further periods up to nine months, in some cases remaining for 18 months'.[99] This was certainly a longer period of continuous service than in the early days of digging, although Africans might well have spent 18 months in Kimberley and then returned home forever.

Nonetheless, from the early 1880s a number of Africans became full-time mineworkers. In 1888 Arthur Davis of the Bultfontein Mining Company noted that Africans had worked for his company for seven or eight years.[100] In 1902 Gardner Williams wrote that some Africans had remained in the compounds continuously for ten years or more.[101] Still, we do not know whether these apparently proletarianised workers were Pedi, South Sotho, 'Shangaan' or Chopi, or what jobs they did in the mines, although it is likely that these were Africans with special skills in leading gangs or driving machinery. However, it is clear that after the introduction of closed compounds a pattern emerged of a stint of mine labour followed by a short period of 'resting' in the locations. Landlords made a living out of letting rooms for two to six weeks to recuperating mineworkers.[102]

An indication of stabilisation, if not proletarianisation, is provided in the number of women living in the locations and dependent on mineworkers in compounds. 'It must not be forgotten that the wives of these men live in the locations', wrote the Civil Commissioner, 'as do also their mothers, aunts and female cousins . . . [who] form a very large proportion of the unemployed inhabitants of the Locations'.[103] We do not have any reliable statistics to measure this relation between compound and location in any systematic way; both the mission and official records reveal very little about the number of dependent families in the locations (see Table 10).[104]

By this time De Beers had become the owners of the Beaconsfield estate

Table 10 *Kimberley location population, 1903*

Greenpoint and Flenter's Locations, under control of Beaconsfield Municipality, the Town Clerk of which contends that it has control only in sanitary matters, while the De Beers Company appoints and pays the Headmen:

Population, about	8,000
Men, mostly employed	2,000
Men, unemployed	3,000
Women, children, aged, decrepit, male and female unemployed	3,000

No. 2 Location, under control of the Kimberley Town Council:

Population	8,000
Men, employed in town	1,800
Balance: women, children, aged and decrepits, unemployed	6,200

and it may well have become a service centre for the mining economy; it is difficult to know whether the unemployed men were recuperating mineworkers or men looking for jobs in the towns. In contrast, it appears that the Kimberley location serviced the town economy. There, the number of women and children was double that in Beaconsfield, suggesting that town employed Africans were permanently settled in the area. All in all, the population of the locations at around 16,000 people, including Indians and 'people of colour', was twice that of the compounds, and that was a significant change from the 1880s.[105]

There is not enough evidence to say whether this amounted to a minework-force more stabilised or proleterianised than migrant. Yet, there is strong evidence that oscillating migrant labour between source areas and the mines became more marked in the 1890s. Throughout the decade the Protector of Natives noted a seasonal scarcity of labour, not in winter as in the 1880s but in November and December of each year, which was the time of the ploughing season in the lowlands of Basutoland. South Sotho labourers had largely replaced Mozambiquan and Pedi labourers, who were now attracted to the booming gold fields on the Rand. In addition, in the middle 1890s large numbers of Tswana came to work in the mines and became dependent on minework for the first time. Seasonal migrancy from areas closer to the Diamond Fields than Mozambique and the northern Transvaal led to a more regulated turnover of labourers.[106]

During the 1890s De Beers Consolidated had to recruit 'new hands' to make up for seasonal scarcity. For the first time the diamond mining industry had to compete in a regional labour market of which it was not the centre. Labour touts came to Kimberley and enticed Africans away to the Rand with the promises of higher wages, open compounds and healthier

169

working conditions. Consequently, attempts were made to recruit from the Transkei, although Colonial Africans were regarded with grave suspicion by mine management, and from north of the Limpopo. The size of the Kimberley work-force contracted in the mid-1890s and then expanded before and after the war, which in itself may have necessitated recruitment. Yet, even after the labour shortage following the South African War, De Beers continued to recruit about ten per cent of its work-force.[107]

What part, then, did compound coercion play in stabilising Africans in the mines? Re-contracting was seldom attended without some pressure from managers, but overt physical coercion would have resulted in a dwindling supply to the mines.[108] While the length of the average contract was extended to four months in closed compounds, the mines still had to rely on voluntary re-registration. The Kimberley Central compound manager, James Gifford, described what normally happened:

> Every Saturday as the shifts come in from work, every boy's pass is examined and if it has expired it is taken from him; if he wishes to stop on he pays three shillings for re-registration, for which I give him a receipt, and I take the names to the registry office, and a clerk is sent down with passes, and as they hand in their receipts for three shillings they receive their passes. Those whose time has expired and who don't wish to re-contract are discharged.[109]

Despite this apparently reasonable treatment, matters were not that simple. Large numbers of Africans remained uncontracted inside the barrack gates. In the largest compound, the De Beers West End compound, which increased its complement from 400 Africans in 1886 to 2,900 in 1895 (over half the De Beers work-force), at least one-third to one-half of the labourers were continually uncontracted.[110] A labour contract had always been a mixed blessing to Africans. Breaking a contract on the part of a labourer was a criminal offence, but it did offer some protection against employers. Legally contracts came to an end, at which point servants could withdraw their labour from one employer and offer it to another or some could leave for home. Without a contract recourse to the Registrar was impossible. Africans were incarcerated in compounds in a legal no man's land.

In the long run, though, economic rather than physical coercion in compounds was more important in extending the length of a mineworker's contract. Piece-work was punitive and not rewarding in underground mining. Although Africans were contracted at a wage of between 15s and 21s a week, paid fortnightly by the contractors, they had to earn the wage by delivering a set number of loads to the shaft flat-sheet each day. If they did not reach the target set by the contractor, they lost a portion of the week's wage. Frequently Africans were penalised because of the hardness of the blue ground. Lumps of blasted blue took two to three days to be broken up before loading, but this was unpaid labour. They were only paid according to the number of trucks loaded. Although gangs put in a full week's work, they often found that they received only half a week's pay. While this was a uniform source of grievance, it certainly extended the time spent working for the contractors. They took a different view: 'Natives worked much harder for themselves than they would for the company'.[111]

Economic coercion went beyond part-time pay to part-time work. Residence in a compound did not guarantee full-time minework as more Africans were compounded than were required for a full complement of labour. In the late 1880s, for example, the Kimberley Central generally employed 1,000 out of 1,200 Africans in their compounds.[112] A similar situation existed in the De Beers DMC. 'To work 900 men we want 1,400 or 1,500 men', commented F. Thompson, 'for natives won't stand the whole week with the white miner'.[113] This underlined the importance of having a constant supply of African labour. Not only did closed compounds maintain such a supply, but they also provided a reserve pool of labour to fall back on in times of strikes or disasters. In addition, a compound reserve provided a cushion in periods of social tension between African miners and guards or contractors.

There is abundant evidence that conflict between contractors and their men was rife underground. Close supervision was impossible below the surface and piece-wages had been introduced to ensure that mineworkers kept to production targets. Yet, piece-wages created new problems. Competition between contractors in search of bonuses in experimental underground working led to violence between contractors and their men. There were numerous assaults of African workers on white contractors. In 1890 the situation became so bad that the Mine Inspector feared an African uprising underground and the wholesale slaughter of European contractors and supervisors.[114] Contractors seldom charged Africans with assault as the Mine Inspector explained:

> It is with the greatest difficulty that a sufficient supply of Kaffir labour can be obtained, and to dismiss from his work every Kaffir who disobeys orders for safety, or is mutinous, would simply mean a very large reduction daily of the underground mining labour and (2) if the Kaffirs knew that they would be turned out of the compound immediately on committing any such act of insubordination, many who desired to break their engagement or to escape with stolen diamonds would commit some offence in order to be discharged.[115]

There were fewer reported assaults of whites on their men. The evidence comes from the Mine Inspector, but he does seem to have taken pains to prosecute those contractors who threw Africans down mine shafts in fits of anger. Nonetheless, on balance, underground workings provided a refuge for workers from mine authorities, and created discipline problems for supervisors and contractors.[116]

Above ground in closed compounds the situation was reversed. Management and guards held all the cudgels of coercion in their hands. They usurped the judicial functions of punishment reserved to the state in the Masters and Servants Acts; they had their 'own way of treating natives' and adopted their own 'method of maintaining order'.[117] Almost all compounds practised a system of fines, which were inflicted to protect companies 'against the natural impulse of human nature, white and black, to do as little work as possible and get drunk whenever the occasion offers'.[118] When fines failed to discipline, more drastic measures were taken by compound management. In 1894 there was a dispute over work and wages in the Wesselton compound, which 'grew to such proportions that a riot ensued, during which the natives were fired on by the police and others, with the result that three of them were killed and seven wounded'.[119]

Most disputes that ended in compound violence were over unfairly docked wages or unsatisfactory work conditions. For example, Africans refused to work in dangerous tunnels or stopes. Such a refusal to work when commanded was a punishable offence, although workers could remain unemployed and unpaid in the compounds. Before 1896, after which it improved its reputation, the De Beers compounds had the worst name amongst Africans for guard assaults. In one typical case, Charles Riordan, Head Guard of the De Beers West End compound, flogged a team of 22 Africans for refusing to work, confined them in a detention cell for five days and then dismissed them. The evidence of this corporal punishment – 'the scars or wounds were still raw and about four inches in length' – was still apparent a week later.[120] The Protector of Natives pointed out that this indignity was 'perpetrated on men between the ages of 40 and 50 years, Colonial Kaffirs and of the most civilised bearing'. In his view such a flogging was a bitter humiliation for Colonial Africans, but not for 'Inhambanes or Shangaans' who took 'these things as a matter of course'.[121]

In short, the closed compound system was the effective form in which mineowners came to terms with migrant labour. It was an essential part of the centralisation of ownership in the industry; it contributed to lower wages, and a more disciplined and experienced work-force. We do not know how many African mineworkers were permanently settled in Kimberley or how many were migrant labourers. While the exact nature of stabilisation remains unclear, we do know that regular migrancy replaced the uncontrolled desertions that occurred in the open mining economy. Even though the monopoly of De Beers Consolidated Mines eliminated competition in the local labour market, recruitment and labour touting continued because of the powerful attractions of the gold mines on the Rand. Closed compounds were part of a monopolistic system that coerced Africans into longer spells of minework than before through three practices: no contract, part-time pay and part-time work.

CONCLUSION

Before 1903 Kimberley's compounds were planned more for labour control than social welfare. The reason for this lay not so much in callousness or the economics of mining companies, although both played a part, as in the historical position that diamond mining occupied in South Africa's mineral revolution. Diamond mining began that revolution and had to prise a work-force out of a pre-capitalist rural hinterland ruled by independent African chiefs. 'It may well be', wrote Perrings, 'that where an industry did not have the means to exercise the necessary controls over labour in the supplying areas, controls at the work place (in the compounds) were of heightened significance.'[122] Controls in the compounds were of even greater significance when production was monopolised by one leviathan company like De Beers Consolidated Mines. Not only did this facilitate control over the labour supply, but it also minimised African organisation against exploitation in the mines. Kimberley had a more totalitarian system of labour control than imitators on mines further to the north. Kimberley's compounds differed from those on the Rand and in Southern Rhodesia in being closed, whereas they in varying degrees were not. Yet, the greater compound self-sufficiency that this entailed in Kimberley did not lead to markedly higher standards of accommodation, diet and health care until after 1903. Kimberley's compounds were as bad as those mine compounds on the Rand, in Southern Rhodesia and in Katanga in encouraging a death-rate of enormous proportions. And that death-rate has been hidden for far too long under the justification of compound philanthropy and the great weight of mineowners' claims to protection against theft.

9

Illicit diamond buying and the town economy

The traffic in illicit diamonds was the most contentious of the bonds that tied the towns to the mines. As we have seen, the long-established right to the protection of private property was converted into a powerful argument for the incarceration of African mineworkers in closed compounds. But this did not suit the majority of Kimberley's citizens. In the 1880s an organised opposition to the closed compound system and the diamond laws grew in strength in Kimberley. The small group of mineowners, desperately trying to protect their coveted property and to construct the best conditions for the maximum exploitation of labour, found themselves isolated in a hostile community.

GONIVAS

The extent of IDB was as difficult for the mineowners to establish at the time as it is for the historian today. During the 1870s the extent of the illicit trade was open to conjecture as no official returns were required and production was in the hands of many diggers. In the 1880s the concentration of production by mining companies provided the basis for a closer quantification. The difference between the figures provided by the Treasurer-General of the value of diamonds sent to England and the value contained in company statements – excluding individual diggers – roughly equalled the illicit export. It seems surprising that the Diamond Mining Protection Board never did this.

The failure of the Protection Board to compare returns with exports was not simply part of a propaganda war to blow up the threat of IDB. Undeclared diamonds left the Cape with travellers and were taken not only to London but to the Continent. Within production itself company statements were not subject to the unbiased controls of accountants and auditors. Assessment was further complicated by a slower turn-over of diamond production under the company regime; individual diggers had had to produce a certain value of diamonds each week to pay working costs, while companies if they could raise loans could hold diamonds for a rise in the market. Moreover, washing inadequately decomposed ground gave a return of fewer carats per load than properly weathered soil. However, most important, in concealing the extent of the illicit traffic was the difficulty of knowing whether output declined as a result of theft or a change in the

174

quality of the blue ground. 'The conclusion I have worked up to in my own mind', wrote Charles Nind, Director of De Beers Consolidated, in 1892, 'is, that, robbed or not, our mines are not producing the same amount of fine goods as formerly, and they are producing a much larger quantity of inferior goods'.[1]

Nonetheless, the unknown leakage of diamonds into illicit channels of commerce was used to advantage by the mineowners. It allowed for the speculative magnification of the crime. In 1881 the mineowners argued from data collected from diamond merchant shippers, that only £60,000 of the £100,000 of diamonds exported each week was legitimate.[2] However, Basil Roper, Chief of the Detective Department from 1885 to 1888, did not believe that a quarter of company production had ever been stolen. But Roper was trying to argue the past effectiveness of his Department in preventing theft.[3]

The Standard Bank, which shipped a half to a third of the diamond exports, was unable to estimate the illicit proportion.[4] In fact the banks were often told that they could stop the IDB trade by withdrawing credit from IDB suspects. Lewis Michell, the General Manager of the Standard Bank, explained that this was easier said than done:

> It is comparatively easy for me to instruct branches not to advance on diamonds to parties under suspicion, but it should not be overlooked that this would only catch the subordinate sinners. Traders of a high grade possess and act under undoubted home credits, and the banks are often entirely unable to know whether the diamonds against which these accredited drafts are drawn have been legitimately purchased or not.[5]

The diamond shippers legally bought stones which had initially entered the local diamond market illegally and passed through numerous hands before their final sale. Consequently, where legal and illegal exports flowed together in the bank transactions of the large dealers, this curious alchemy preserved the secrets of the extent of the illicit trade.

The chain of illicit distribution was well-known in the Kimberley community. The labourer, picking in the claims or working on the floors, stole diamonds which he sold well below market rates to a tout, who frequented canteens, compounds, locations and gaols. The tout worked for a receiver of stolen goods and he in turn was funded by an illicit capitalist. The links in the chain were most visible in the first stage but faded to invisibility at the end. There were a few well-worn ways of performing this vanishing trick. Before 1875 it was common for the IDB to buy straight from mine labourers without the intervention of intermediaries. The employment of a tout or a 'swell nigger' developed later. Most commonly the latter frequented canteens and 'Kaffir eating-houses' in which drink and food was paid for in diamonds and the touts acquainted new boarders with the disposition of the proprietor. A more devious system was the direct employment of African labourers planted in the mines, 'whose sole object was to rob and bring diamonds to their real master'.[6]

The most sophisticated mode of operation was the purchase of a claim, which acted as a blind for the purchase of illicit stones. This was not foolproof as many came to know the productivity of which particular claims were capable – even in the poorer mines.[7] Mathilda Contat held on to a solitary claim in Kimberley Mine and the Civil Commissioner commented baldly in 1890: 'The owner is dead and the executor testamentary in her estate is in gaol for IDB'.[8] Another form of blind was to take out a diamond dealer's licence and pretend to transact legal business when in fact illicit dealing was conducted in 'the dead waist and middle of the night'.[9] After 1882 this became problematic as the registration of each purchase and sale was enforced and subject to detective inspection. But even here there were loopholes. Dealers kept bort (diamonds for industrial use) on hand, which was registered and thrown away to accommodate illicit stones: carats were recorded, while value below £100 for a single stone was secret.

Part of the attraction of the Diamond Fields for Africans was the possibility of supplementing wages through theft and sale of diamonds on the illicit market. Coleman, the Registrar of Natives, provided the best summary:

> That natives still come from the Interior might perhaps be advanced as evidence that upon the whole the treatment they receive and the working of the laws cannot be very bad or irksome. But is it not on the other hand open to look for the cause of attraction in a different direction – the chance of acquiring diamonds, which induces natives, who hear about this in his country, to brave the perils connected with his coming hither, in the shape of accidents in the mines, robbery and violence, entanglement in the meshes of the law, and being occasionally cheated out of his earnings – for the sake of this hoped for gain.[10]

Even stronger is the evidence of Judge Laurence, who was the most influential interpreter of the diamond laws in the Special Court set up in 1880 to try only IDB cases. 'Of course I stole that diamond', he remembered being told in one case by an African, 'Do you think I was going down into that dangerous mine for a morsel of pap, or perhaps to lose my soul.'[11] And even Judge Laurence had to admit that 'there was considerable force in that argument'.[12]

Some Europeans believed that chiefs required their subjects to pay tribute in diamonds on their return to their country. Certainly Africans took diamonds with them on their return home, but in the 1870s they preferred to leave the Fields with gold, as it was an easier currency of exchange in rural areas.[13] It was only after the gun trade was abolished in Kimberley in 1879, that Africans began to leave the Fields with diamonds to a significant extent. Rather than running the risks of the illicit market at the mines they exchanged diamonds for guns with canteen and storekeepers in the Transvaal and elsewhere. In 1880 one merchant in Kuruman was reported to have made £30,000 in a short space of time by buying diamonds from Africans returning home from the mines.[14] The abolition of the gun trade and closer

Plate 7 Kimberley Market Square from the Old De Beers Road in the 1880s. Ox waggons carrying firewood and other materials or commodities fill the square. Louis Diering, a leading liquor wholesaler, can be seen on the left, Goodchilds auction mart in the centre, and Peach, an important general merchant, near the Transvaal Road exit. Courtesy De Beers, London.

supervision of the diamond trade in Kimberley at the turn of the decade were more important than tribute in increasing the number of illicit diamonds taken away from the mines by labourers.[15]

If Africans were labelled diamond thieves by the mineowners, 'Cape boys' and Jews were most commonly associated with illicit dealing. 'Black' Abrahams was the best known IDB of the first group. He operated from a stronghold in the Malay Camp with an elaborate system of counter detective surveillance at his command. As late as 1906 he had illicit agents buying diamonds from him as far afield as Mafeking.[16] Dr Matthews pinpointed Whitechapel as the point of origin of the second group but also spoke of men 'drawn from the purlieues of European cities'.[17] Lewis Michell, General Manager of the Standard Bank, had strong views on this section of the community:

> The departure of hordes of hook-nosed Polish and Lithuanian Jews whose evil countenances now peer from every little shanty and cigar divan would be a distinct gain to the community. Under cover of keeping a 'winkel' they at present flock to Kimberley from afar, like asvogels to a dead ox, and their villainous faces enable one easily to understand the depth of hatred borne to them in Russia and elsewhere.[18]

177

This was virulent anti-semitism coming from a Protestant, well aware of the different classes into which Jews fell. Louis Cohen, an English Jew, made the same charges about the 'scum of Germany and Whitechapel', with a lighter touch and a sense of self parody.[19]

Hawking jewellery on Market Square was the characteristic apprenticeship for a novice IDB. The next level in the hierarchy of the trade was to keep a store or a canteen, which raised a man's status and gave good access to a constant supply of 'gonivas'.[20] The employment of a tout and the acquisition of a mistress were the next essential steps. Women were sometimes IDB principals but more often combined in themselves the 'capacities of mistress, drudge and go-between'. European men employed 'Kafir females, on the one hand as touts for their trade, and on the other to minister to the basest lusts of their nature'.[21] Henry Koski, a Polish Jew known as the 'High Gentleman', was a man whose career illustrated this 'making of an IDB'. In 1879 he came to Kimberley when he was 19 years old. He was a tailor by trade and he took work in Cornwall's clothing establishment where he earned £7 10s a week. This was not good enough, however, and he took to hawking 'fancy goods' on Market Square. Here he fell in with 'bad company' and began his career in the illicit trade. He tried to set up a store-keeping business with a partner but it failed. By this time Koski was well versed in the intricacies of the traffic and had organised a measure of protection for his illicit transactions. A Sergeant, returned from the war in the Transvaal in 1881, had crossed Koski's path on Market Square with watches to sell. A little later he joined the police force and became confidant and accomplice to the 'High Gentleman'. This arrangement worked well for a while until, as thieves fall out, he participated in trapping Koski in 1882 and in despatching him to the Cape Town breakwater for penal servitude.[22]

The illicit capitalist, the unseen hand of illicit supply and demand, was often suspected of his irregular dealings. 'The respectable portion of the community do not avoid them absolutely in the street', said Harry Caldecott, Stow's legal partner, 'and pass over to the other side, but they don't take them into their houses.'[23] The heads of the 'prevailing industry' were supposed to be all well-known.[24] The reduction in the number of dealers in the legitimate trade as a result of concentration in company production also reduced the number of large illicit dealers. By 1888, Basil Roper, Chief of the Detective Department, could say: '... there are only one or two capitalists in the illicit market; the others, and there are any number of them, are men who simply buy from hand to mouth'.[25]

From the early 1870s it had been illegal to buy from unlicensed sellers, but unless caught in the act, illicit dealing had always been difficult to prove. The major piece of legislation in this connection was the Diamond Trade Act of 1882, which introduced a crucial innovation in the so-called *onus probandi* clause. This thrust the *onus* of proof of legal possession of a diamond on to the diamond owner. In so doing it made illicit dealing in

Kimberley easier to monitor and consequently more dangerous for operators. As a result, where the illicit traffic did not move through the bank accounts of the licensed dealers it moved across the provincial borders into the Orange Free State. Here the Griqualand West laws did not apply.

Even though the Orange Free State had two producing diamond mines the crime of IDB was 'somewhat lightly regarded by the mining community' at those mines.[26] Both mines, Jagersfontein and Koffyfontein, were dominated by capital from Kimberley. Nonetheless, in 1882 the Volksraad passed a stringent IDB law, which provided for 20 years imprisonment, banishment, £5,000 fine, or 100 lashes. But the law was only operative within six miles of proclaimed diggings. The illicit traffic then plied a circuitous route through the Orange Free State to the Cape. In 1885 the Diamond Trade Act was extended to the Colony and the centre of the illicit trade moved to the Transvaal. From there diamonds were exported through Natal, which became 'a thieves' highway'.[27] At the end of the 1880s detectives in Griqualand West believed Transvaal officials assisted IDBs and that the Orange Free State was apathetic.[28] In the case of Natal, suppression of the IDB traffic became involved with a conflict over custom dues with the Cape.[29]

The proximity of the republican border was a great advantage to IDBs and an ironic Orange Free State revenge for the loss of the Diamond Fields. In the words of a popular song:

> Over the Free State Line,
> Whatever is yours is mine.[30]

Free Town was five miles from Dutoitspan on the Boshoff Road and a few hundred yards inside the Orange Free State border. It was the 'rendezvous of the IDBs, highwaymen and escaped convicts'.[31] Another small town with a similar reputation sprang up at Oliphantsfontein. Africans were employed as 'runners' and whites as 'troopers' to take diamonds across the border, in many cases with detectives in 'hot pursuit'.[32] Sometimes it was easier to swallow diamonds and ride or walk across the 'Free State line' and wait for the stones to reappear in 'the course of nature'. Dogs, horses, oxen and even carrier pigeons were used to send illicit stones to Free Town and Oliphantsfontein.[33] These towns flourished tantalisingly outside the official reach of the Griqualand West authorities and no check was applied by the government of the Orange Free State.

Although safe from the law, IDBs in Free Town and Oliphantsfontein were not safe from illegal possés of men raiding across the border. In these cases the Orange Free State could do little more than complain officially to the authorities in Kimberley.[34] The appearance of organised groups of highwaymen underlined 'the insecurity of life and property' in these border lands.[35] Samuel Weil, a well known IDB and one time Jagersfontein speculator, fell foul of a celebrated group of highwaymen led by Scotty Smith and Arthur Leigh, a Kimberley Police sergeant. Samuel Weil was taking £4,000 of diamonds to Julius Weil in Cape Town in 1885 when he was robbed and nearly murdered by Scotty Smith and his band on the road to the Orange River. The hold-up had been planned by a German IDB, Thomas Welford, who was well acquainted with Weil's operations, as he divided his time between the homestead at Oliphantsfontein and the Malay Camp in Kimberley. Welford and the highwaymen were sentenced to four years hard labour and Scotty Smith had to suffer 25 lashes in addition. Smith had also been active in running diamonds across the Transvaal border to Christiana. He had become notorious in this connection when, together with Sergeant Walter Mays, policeman turned highwayman, he had double-crossed his masters, the Van Praagh brothers, best-known Christiana IDB residents.[36]

From Christiana the illicit stones were run through Pretoria and down to Durban. The volume of stones on this route increased after the Diamond Trade Act was applied to the whole of the Cape in 1885.[37] Adolph Fass and Company of Pietermaritzburg supported Z. L. A. Rocher as an IDB trader at Christiana. 'They make no secret of it', wrote the Standard's Pietermaritzburg Manager, 'but admit that Rocher deals very largely in diamonds, they supplying the funds and shipping the diamonds.'[38] Adolph Fass and Company was a business which took 'something like a quarter of a million of pounds to work it with' in 1885.[39] Adolph Fass was an enormously wealthy man and had just floated the Barrett Brothers Gold Mining Company on the London Stock Exchange, in which he had induced Baron Grant to invest.[40] It is difficult to know just how large this trade was but in another case, 'the most notorious operator' showed deposits of £156,000 in the first half of 1889.[41]

Throughout the 1880s it was comparatively easy to deal illicitly in Port Elizabeth and Cape Town. It was always difficult to convict in these cities. The extension of the Diamond Trade Act to the Cape did make some impact. 'There is very little done in the IDB line in Cape Town', wrote Detective Chadwick in March 1886, 'owing to the passing of the last act – and that in consequence has made Trade (especially the Hotel business) very dull'.[42] The flow of diamonds from Kimberley, however, continued to worry the detectives. A number of stratagems were employed to evade the law. The railway may have cheapened mine production but it made it easier to export illicit stones. Runners were sent down the line to Beaufort West or Worcester, from where diamonds were registered and posted to Cape Town to avoid the railway detectives. 'The Malays as a rule transmit theirs by women and children', reported Detective Beaton, 'their organisation is perfect and their faithfulness worthy of a better cause.'[43] Diamonds were hidden in all forms of merchandise and passed surreptitiously through the hands of dock agents on to the ships of the Castle line or Union Steamship Company.

Illicit diamonds were shipped to London in a mirror image of the legitimate trade. In London Rosenthal Cronon was named as a well-known receiver of illicit goods.[44] The Van Praagh brothers had a London office and sold such large stones in Antwerp that it was widely commented on.[45] Diamond merchants in London argued that illicit importers undermined the trade as they could sell cheaper to the continental buyers. The great lure of the illicit traffic lay in the wider profit margins, but there was little reason for illicits to sell under the ruling rates. 'I don't know that they undersell me', said Rudolph Heinrichsen, 'but they get the goods, and it is generally very large and more saleable than the other goods.'[46] More difficult to assess was the quantitative impact of illicit stones on the market. Here the best measure was the impact of De Beers Consolidated's secret reserve on the European market in the 1890s. In 1891 the market did not 'suffer from the selling of surplus stock to the extent of about half a million £'.[47] It was a remarkable year for importers and it is probable that the charges of unfair competition from the illicit trade became voluble in bad years. Whatever the effect on the European market, there is little doubt that the illicit importers were the 'Fagans of the Diamond Fields'.[48]

THE DIAMOND TRADE ACT OF 1882

After the collapse of the 'share mania', as we have already outlined in chapter 7, the mineowners went to Parliament to write the legislation essential for a reconstruction of Kimberley in their own image. They obtained the enforcement of the pass law and the searching law, but failed over the compulsory housing of Africans in compounds. They asked for the police force to be increased and for the Detective Department to concentrate specifically on diamond offences. In addition they wanted a new diamond law suited to 'the exceptional circumstances' of the mining industry. The result was the Diamond Trade Act of 1882, which made illicit diamond dealing more difficult, but fundamentally undermined the legal rights of British subjects. In the view of the United States Consul, the law was 'repugnant to every sense of right and justice'.[49]

The Act upheld the practice, instituted in 1880, of trial without jury for IDB defendants as the mineowners believed it would be impossible to convict in these cases. Originally magistrates had dealt with these offences, but as the penalties were increased from £500 and three years in 1877 to £500 and five years in 1880 for a first offence, special provisions had been created. A Special Court was established in 1880 and was presided over by a Special Magistrate, sitting with the Magistrates of Kimberley and Dutoitspan. As the promulgation of the Diamond Trade Act coincided with the formation of a three judge High Court in Kimberley, one judge took over the position of President of the Special Court. He was empowered to mete out a maximum penalty of 15 years or five years and banishment from Griqualand West.

The Act discarded another tenet of British law: the presumption of innocence until proved guilty. The Act placed the *onus probandi* of legal

181

possession of a diamond on the suspected party. Furthermore the officers of the law were given wide powers of search in public and private places. A Detective Department was created to investigate IDB offences alone. Although constituted as a State Department – it was largely funded by a registration fee of ½ per cent on diamond exports – it was privately subsidised by mining capitalists through the Board for the Protection of Mining Interests, which was given a legal status in the Act. The Department worked closely with the mineowners, and the use and abuse of detective surveillance for political purposes and labour intimidation was soon to excite strong protests from the wider Diamond Fields community. By placing strict controls on the diamond trade and sanctioning the 'trapping system' the Act created fear and suspicion among Kimberley's citizens.

The 'trapping system' first came into public condemnation when it was used by the Vigilance Committee before the 1875 Rebellion. The detectives in the Griqualand West Constabulary continued to use it in the late 1870s. In 1879 an eloquent statement against the system was made by 130 IDB convicts:

> While your petitioners are fully aware that in a digging community strenuous efforts require to be made to stop the market for stolen diamonds, yet they would point out to Your Excellency that the practises adopted by no means compass the end required. Hitherto legislation has been somewhat one-sided; claimholders in this community naturally represent capital, and the laws made by them to protect that capital have left many loopholes for abuse; unprincipled men not satisfied with the law, have resorted to the most un-English and diabolical system of 'Trapping', so as to gain convictions against men of all classes. According to the practice at present employed, no man, however respectable is safe from the private *pique* of an enemy, as at any moment he may be thrown into prison and summarily convicted by the Resident Magistrate upon the evidence of one or two Kaffirs who do not know the nature of an oath. Every case of 'Trapping' may be traced to some personal jealousy or spite as a very great power has been given to men of little standing or education to act as detectives, a word from whom is sufficient to destroy the character of any respectable man, whilst so strong is the feeling of the diggers that to arrest a man is almost to convict him.[50]

The Acting Administrator believed that this petition was worthy of 'very serious consideration'. He had doubts about the legality of the trapping system, which he viewed 'with the greatest repugnance'. He charged the mineowners with failing to take 'necessary precautions' for the protection of their property and pointed out that it was 'undesirable that laws should be enacted which would fetter the whole population'. It was clear that although the mineowners were 'extremely wealthy and influential', they did not represent 'the larger portion of the public'.[51] Still, the mineowners managed to maintain the trapping system in a hostile Kimberley community.

The detectives argued that the practice of trapping was subject to strict controls. Only well-known IDBs were trapped; several trial trappings were undertaken before the detectives moved in; and the traps themselves were subject to a rigorous procedure. It is worth while illustrating this procedure through the controversial trapping of Frans Junker, a canteen-keeper:

> According to the evidence for the Crown [said Judge Laurence in his judgement], John Dunn and two other natives, named Sixpence and Lange, were on the day in question searched by Detective Muller, in the presence of Detective Chadwick. A rough diamond was then given to John Dunn, and the three natives then proceeded, in charge of Muller, to the prisoner's premises, a house and canteen in the Transvaal Road, which was being watched by other detectives – Burgess, Mays, McIntosh, and Human. On entering the place the traps met the prisoner and ultimately agreed to sell the diamond to him for £10, and he told them to call for the money later on, on the same afternoon, at the same time giving them 4/6 and some brandy in a bottle, as a present. The traps then left, and signalled to the detectives, who came in and arrested the prisoner. The traps were searched and the money above referred to, and the bottle of brandy, were given by John Dunn to the Detectives. At this time no diamond was found either on the prisoner or on the traps . . . The next day the search was resumed by the detectives and the trap-stone was found by Burgess in a box, attached to the counter on the inner side, and used for the purposes of opening bottles of soda-water and lemonade.[52]

Junker had a 'good character' but he was sentenced to five years hard labour. He appealed and new evidence about the planting of the diamond after the initial search was sufficient to clear his name.[53] This case seemed to prove the common belief that IDBs were convicted 'on suspicion' before a private tribunal of the Chief of the Detective Department and the two chief detectives. Once convinced of a man's guilt they did not care whether he was guilty of the crime of which he was convicted.

The Special Court did not have a high conviction rate, which lent support to its impartiality, but left much to be desired in trap evidence. Between September 1882 and 1888 only 60 per cent of the accused were convicted and the majority of acquittals were the result of unsatisfactory trap evidence.[54] The white Kimberley community was indignant at the ease with which an African trap swore 'a white man's life away'.[55] In fact, the Detective Department and the Judges of the Special Court regarded this as the virtue of African traps. Judge Laurence found that Africans went into 'this matter as a regular means of earning a livelihood'[56] and saw no disgrace in it. They were employed by the Detective Department for 30s a week (a little more than a mine labourer), and they mingled with runners and others to gain the confidence of particular men and women dealing illicitly. The Department employed 40 or 50 traps at any one time. Generally, they were not paid rewards for successful trappings and they were constantly changed to avoid recognition. The working life of an African trap was a short one. When it was over he was catapulted back into the world of the location or compound better equipped to avoid the diamond laws.

European traps entered into the spirit of trapping in a different fashion. Judge Laurence always felt with white traps 'a doubt whether there may not be some secret motive' for trapping an individual.[57] White traps usually demanded a greater price for their work 'for they well knew they were doing a dirty and dishonourable and in some cases a dangerous thing'.[58] For example, Andries Posno, asked for £2,000 and the cost of a trip to Australia to trap a friend.[59] During the depression white traps were prepared to trap for less. In early 1884, Williams trapped the jeweller, David Cohen. Six weeks before, Williams had been discharged from the Victoria DMC after a work spell of four weeks. He had refused to work a night shift. He had also worked for the Birbeck DMC before it liquidated and the Pleiades DMC from where he was dismissed as drunk. Immediately prior to trapping Cohen, he had spent a stretch in jail for theft.[60] Living on the margins of the mine economy traps were open to inducement and bribery from all quarters. 'They are often bribed', said Inspector Ramsay Steuart, 'that is a risk we have to run either white or black'.[61]

Trapping was often associated with violence. Andries Posno had his shoulder broken by a group of Africans when his trapping intentions were discovered. Woolsack, who worked for Detective Fox in the late 1870s, was thrashed for trapping IDBs.[62] Many believed this was the just dessert for tempting men into crime, even if the punishment was meted out by IDBs.[63] Some traps were even murdered for their treachery.[64] In fact the *Diamond Fields Advertiser* made the case that IDB was the Procrustean bed out of which all Kimberley crime grew:

> There is something terribly revolting about the extent of crime arising out of the IDB calling in all its ramifications. Inducing servants to steal, murder, perjury, receiving stolen goods, white women prostituting themselves to Kafirs for payment in diamonds, little boys employed by mining companies taught to steal and supplied with false pockets in which to conceal the gems, bribes attempted on officers of the law and a thousand other crimes are gloried in by gangs of ruffians whom the law never reaches.[65]

The charge of murder was the most serious. In early 1882 Francis Baring Gould, director of the Kimberley Central DMC, noticed that 47 men had been taken up for culpable homicide in two months. 'That is entirely owing to the stealing of diamonds', he said, 'and the bad liquor they get.'[66] On similar lines Basil Roper, who took over as Police Commissioner as well as Chief of the Detective Department in 1885, agreed with his police predecessor's belief that the 'cause' of the crime of murder was 'in nearly every case, drink'.[67]

TOWN VS. MINE

If IDB polluted Kimberley society in the ways the mineowners described, it was perhaps surprising that there was so much opposition to the trapping system and the operations of the detectives. Many of Kimberley's 'honest' citizens however made the connection between the mineowners' morality and their economic interests. The mineowners were unable to present their interests and ideology as the common ideology of the whole diamond community. Within the bourgeoisie and petty bourgeoisie there was a clearly defined fracture which is best illuminated by a comparison with the mining communities in the Orange Free State.

In Jagersfontein and Koffyfontein the town–mine division was as stark as in Kimberley, but the major difference lay in the access of the mineowners to the state and state policy. Merchants and landowners struck an alliance in the Volksraad over the Diamond Trade Act: it was not enforced even within proclaimed diggings. In addition, the Detective Department, run by Major Maxwell, former Kimberley Gaol Superintendent, was abolished as an expense the state could ill afford to bear. Throughout the 1880s the ability of the mineowners to 'influence' the Volksraad varied, but on the whole it was weak. The major reason for this was the way in which mining capital was seen as foreign, while the local bourgeoisie identified the interest of the Republic with the store-keepers, landowners and mining town economies.[68]

A similar, but more complex, configuration of economic interests existed in Kimberley, but the outcome of their political struggle was a very different one. The Kimberley mineowners attempted to show that there was no division between mine and town. They argued that the shareholders standpoint was identical with the 'commercial point of view' on IDB, as 'such a very large number of our local merchants are also shareholders'.[69] However, this was not true, as it was 'well known that the trading community of Kimberley . . . kept very clear of the mania'.[70]

This division in proprietorial involvement in the mines was reinforced by contradictory interests in relation to African labour. The mineowners wanted to reduce wages to a minimum. In contrast, the commercial community profited from a large amount of money in circulation. This broke into an open conflict when the mineowners wanted to enforce or re-enact the compulsory compounding of African labour in 1882. Merchants petitioned Parliament:

> The general spirit and tenor of these rules seem to imply an intention to unduly and unfairly curtail the liberty of the natives engaged in the mines, as well as to foster the establishment of retail shops by Mining Companies, for by entrusting employers with the power to prohibit the natives from leaving their compounds after working hours, it will be in the power of the employers to prevent their servants from going into the open market to spend their wages, and so indirectly compel them to deal with such shops they might themselves establish in the compounds.[71]

Here the tradespeople of Kimberley presented themselves as the protectors of African liberty and placed themselves in the path of the mineowners' attempt to reconstruct the industry. It was, however, the political strength of coastal merchants, who had been so badly hit by the collapse of the 'share mania', together with the 'brandy interest' in the Cape Parliament, which managed to keep compounds off the statute book.

The mineowners treated with contempt the argument that the local economy benefitted from the generous expenditure of IDBs. It was, however, substantially true as Inspector Rennie of the Standard Bank reported:

> Illicit diamond buying although very ruinous to the diamond industry is remarkably profitable to the storekeepers. It is very rife at present and many hundreds of hands are believed to be engaged in it. Men of this nature are simply gamblers, to whom money comes easily and goes easily also. They all of them live in 'good style', at any rate in an 'expensive style' and are all 'good pays'. Herman Willigerod one of the merchant petitioners who has a magnificent business here has informed me that few people have any idea of the immense amount of money expended by 'Illicits' upon these Fields, and he attributes his large cash sales of liquor very much to the custom of these illicits to the various canteens and houses throughout the camps, to which he finds the supplies.[72]

Not only did IDBs contribute to a booming town economy, but a flush working class boosted consumer sales. As we have seen in relation to the strikes, the close economic relationship between, on the one hand, liquor and general retailers and, on the other, the black and white working class crystallised into a sympathetic alliance. It was not surprising that the mineowners treated the commercial petty bourgeoisie with suspicion and tried to restrict its political influence and commercial contacts, which provided opportunities for IDB.

The provision of food had always been a contentious issue between mineowners and labourers. On the payment of 'board wages' Africans frequented 'Kaffir eating-houses'. While some were run by Africans, the most popular, situated close to the edge of the mines to cater for the labourer's midday meal were 'generally kept by the lowest class of whites'.[73] The eating-house keepers tried to resist state regulation, but the mineowners were determined to circumscribe their activities as closely as possible. In 1879 the Legislative Council passed the Registered Servants Ordinance which provided a penalty of three years hard labour for the discovery of IDB taking place on an eating-house keeper's premises. In the following year rules and regulations were promulgated: two claimholders had to support the application for a licence; the possession of a diamond dealer's, broker's, liquor, retail or mining licence was forbidden to an eating-house keeper; a register had to be kept of all Africans boarding at an eating-house and no liquor was allowed to be consumed on the premises.[74]

Eating-house keepers petitioned Parliament over these rules which they termed 'oppressive'.[75] They objected to the need to be sanctioned by two claimowners as by the beginning of the 1880s most of the mines were in the hands of companies. They argued that the rules deprived them of their privileges as citizens by debarring them from other trades. Lastly, they professed that it was 'utterly impossible to keep a correct register' of table boarders, as Africans resented such surveillance and the exposure to police intimidation that it invited. In all, the rules were 'bad for business', a conclusion which could only please the mineowners.

The great volume of evidence relating to eating-house keepers came from the mineowners. None of it was complimentary. They failed, however, to close the business down and in 1882 there were 20 eating-houses in Kimberley. Some claimholders were prepared to support their licence applications. 'I have hardly seen a respectable person's name', said William Brown, company director, 'for the recommendation to open a Kafir eating-house.'[76] The vehement distaste which the mineowners particularly reserved for eating-house keepers was an expression of class disgust, linked to the lack of control employers exercised over their labour. Even though it was suggested that respectable men should contract to feed servants 'as a speculation on their own account' – Judge Laurence suggested clubs on the model of Besant's 'Palaces of Delight' in London's East End – it was quite clear that mineowners looked to closed compounds as a preferred solution.[77] Food and housing were integrally related to the labour process. The support for eating-houses has to be inferred from the preferences of their customers. When Sammy Marks tried to lodge and feed his labourers on his compounds in 1882 'they would not stand it, and preferred serving masters where they could be free men'.[78]

One branch of shop-keeping specialised in what was termed 'Kaffir truck', that is, the provision of blankets and clothing suited to the African market.[79] The character of 'Kaffir shop-keepers' was collectively assassinated by the mineowners. Some of them were Indians; in the locations others were Africans. They shared their customers with those dealing in the 'necessaries of life'.[80] These traders, generally with £1,000 in stock and fixed property, did not feel the pressure of the crisis until 1883.[81] As the credit system for the retail trade was one month, the amount of loss through insolvency was very small. The many shop-keepers who survived began to receive support directly from the coast or Britain, by-passing the local wholesalers.[82] Profit margins in the retail trade were narrow and direct importing was an attempt to remain competitive. The structural situation of depression and concentration in claim ownership induced some 'Kafir shop keepers' to take a share in the 'vast increase' of illicit traffic in the middle 1880s.[83]

Liquor traders, more than any other section of the mercantile community, were involved or ensnared in the illicit web that the IDB traffic spun across Kimberley. If all Africans were seen as potential thieves by the mineowners, all hotels and canteens were seen as potential illicit markets or, more intimately, fences. The liquor trade came under specific attack from the mineowners for this and a complex of other reasons. Liquor, in the mineowners' view, was unlike food, in that it could only be classed as a 'necessary of life' under certain conditions, namely, as a reward for and not a precondition of labour in the mine. There was some debate about this. Some mineowners believed that liquor kept a 'certain number' of Africans on the Fields, and held 'the labour market more steady'.[84] The Kimberley Central DMC, however, disapproved of employing 'natives who have been a long time on the Fields, and who do not return to their country'.[85]

The liquor trade, most importantly, threatened the profits of the mining industry. Captain Erskine, the Inspector of Mines, estimated that one-third of the labour force was absent on Mondays; clergymen reported the horrors of drunken revelries in the locations on Sundays.[86] In the early days of digging it was estimated that there was one canteen to every 48 people in Kimberley.[87] The ratio of population to canteens changed with the waves of migration to and from Kimberley. By the end of the 1880s the ratio had increased to one canteen to 300 people in Kimberley and one to 600 people in Dutoitspan.[88] The number of convictions for drunkenness increased steadily throughout this period and were certainly the highest in the whole of Cape Colony.

The black population made up the greater part of the canteen clientele but the attempt of the mineowners to tag Africans with the label of drunkards was belied by medical history. Dr Matthews, who largely tended white people, claimed that 70 per cent of the cases he treated between 1871 and 1886 could be 'traced either directly, or indirectly to excessive indulgence in alcohol'.[89] The mark of a good artisan was sobriety, the better part of 'respectability', but the white working class as a whole imbibed a good share of the liquor sold on the Fields. The literate section of the white Kimberley community was able to express most vigorously their fears of drunken hordes of men, and particularly black men, who made scenes 'which would put the worst part of Ratcliffe Highway completely into the shade'.[90]

Cape brandy made up the better part of liquor consumed in Kimberley and it was the cheapest drink on the retail market.[91] Two-fifths of the Cape wine production was normally distilled into spirits. 'Dop brandy' and 'cango' was made from the husks of the grapes after they had been pressed. If the husks were not used to make brandy they were fed to pigs or used as manure.[92] In Kimberley Cape brandy was transformed into 'Cape Smoke' for the African market. The formula for this 'villainous compound' was the addition of two pounds of tobacco, one pound of cayenne pepper and three gallons of Natal rum to 13 gallons of Cape brandy making 16 gallons of 'Cape Smoke'.[93] The adulteration of the brandy in this fashion strengthened the spirits. In contrast, colonial and imported wines were aimed at the European market. This split preference in the market was maintained throughout the 1870s and 1880s. By the 1890s there was a slight change as 'many of the natives' were 'getting more civilised' and took to 'wines and lighter liquors'.[94]

The structure of the liquor market was reinforced by legal discrimination between 'natives' and Europeans. As in the case of the pass law, which was couched in the language of masters and servants, the liquor law (1872) denied servants free access to liquor without permission (a pass) from masters. In practice this came to apply to Africans alone. Although it was difficult to enforce, it was annoying enough to licensed victuallers as it was difficult to distinguish those Africans who were their own masters from those who required liquor passes. The Licensed Victuallers Association petitioned the Legislative Council at the time of the Rebellion for the removal of restrictions on the sale of liquor to 'natives'.[95] They never modified this position and the liquor pass practically remained a dead letter even after 'Bottomley's Bill' raised the issue once more in 1880.[96] The liquor preferences of blacks and whites and the legal discrimination, however, did not enforce segregation in hotels and canteens:

> It is a strange sight to eyes accustomed to regard the white and black races as separate species to see coloured people drinking champagne and jostling the white in bars, paying the same prices as he pays for clothes quite as good as those he wears at the shops, riding beside him and paying as he does in cabs, and generally asserting equality in a most irrepressible manner. This native nuisance is rapidly becoming a serious evil.[97]

Nonetheless, 'Kaffir bars' did emerge adjacent to 'white bars', reflecting different market and social preferences. This became more defined in the 1880s. 'There is a great difference', argued Samuel Mvambo, a Wesleyan clergyman, 'between a European and a native bar'.[98] Europeans continued to drink in 'Kaffir bars', either as a product of social bonds created in the work place, or the strength and cheapness of the liquor.[99]

Canteens and hotels were the social matrices of Kimberley. All paths out of the mines led to these watering holes. When the mineowners tried to prohibit the sale of liquor to 'natives' it was a frontal attack on the central working class leisure activity in Kimberley, based on a peculiarly cohesive colonial industry and merchant and retail trade. J. B. Robinson tried to write a clause into the Liquor Amendment Act of 1883 prohibiting the sale of liquor to Africans within a radius of five miles of Kimberley. It became known as the 'Robinson clause' and he held that it would be one of 'the most humane acts ever done'.[100] Robinson based his case on philanthropy in the service of mine-owners. More subtly, Rhodes invited merchants and wine farmers as fellow travellers up the Road to the North to the interior trade.[101] Rhodes was the better politician, architect of Parliamentary alliances and compromises; for Robinson the 'road to Stellaland' did not 'run through the mine'.[102] But the African liquor market was too important to be traded off against the North.

The value of the Kimberley liquor trade was enormous by all estimates. In March 1883 the Licensed Victuallers assessed themselves at £2,300,000 in Kimberley and Beaconsfield.[103] The figures given in a Parliamentary petition were lower but reflect an enormous proportion of the Cape's liquor market:[104]

Value of properties belonging to wholesale houses	
dealing in liquors	£111,600
Yearly turn over	£685,000
Value of canteens, hotels, etc.	£369,000
Yearly turn over	£814,000

The Robinson clause 'would cause the depreciation of properties, ruin the legitimate trade, and affect the prosperity of the whole colony'.[105] The Licensed Victuallers did not only petition Parliament and speak with their coastal supporters: they elected George Garcia Wolf to the Legislative Assembly as their representative. Wolf was a recent immigrant to Kimberley and was in fact a furniture dealer. Nonetheless, he ably articulated the interests of the Kimberley liquor trade.

Having failed with legislation the mineowners concentrated on controlling the liquor trade locally through the Licensing Board and Court. The substantial drop in licensed houses in 1881 was the first fruit of this closer supervision. Throughout the 1880s, in fact, the number of licensed premises was kept constant, new applications being refused and new victuallers taking the place of bankrupt ones. The discrimination of 'Bottomley's Bill' was relocated by the 1883 Liquor Act, which allowed free trade to black and white but prohibited the sale of liquor in the mining areas and 'native locations'. Crucially the Act removed the right of appeal from the Licensing Board's decisions to the High Court.[106]

The Board was granted almost total control of licensing. It was composed of the Mayors of Kimberley and Beaconsfield, one Divisional Councillor, the Resident Magistrate and two Justices of the Peace.[107] The mineowners did not need a majority on the Board to control it. Often as not the Justices were mineowners – Anthony Goldschmidt and Joseph Robinson – but Good Templars had a fair representation and acted to restrict the expansion of liquor outlets. Licences or privileges were refused on a number of grounds: sales to Africans, convictions against a house, proximity to a company's floors, too many houses in one area or disorderly conduct. The Chief of the Detective Department and the Inspector of the Constabulary reviewed the pedigree of each canteen, hotel or bottle store at the annual courts and made recommendations to the Board. These occasions left the victuallers at the mercy of the police and although represented by legal counsel – Mr Percy and Mr Howard, most often, who also specialised in IDB defense – the 'Board acted arbitrarily in refusing licences to old retail dealers.'[108]

Licences were lost as a result of convictions or suspicion of IDB. In 1882, J. L. Truter claimed that 81 of the 184 Kimberley licence applicants had been involved in IDB and the same applied to 32 of the 46 applicants in Dutoitspan. Not many canteen-keepers were convicted of IDB – they lost their licences instead.[109] In 1883, the German Club in Victoria Road, run by Timm, was refused a licence. 'It might be described as a German Diamond Market', said Detective Burgess, 'and as a well-known resort of German illicits, ex-convicts and others of the lowest class on the Fields.'[110] Others escaped with a caution. Such was the case with the canteen of G. Shilling, 'the Commissioner of Police, having stated that such characters as Mays, "Big Mick" and C. went to the place a good deal'.[111]

The most celebrated IDB den that came under review by the Licensing Court was the Red Light.[112] In 1881 it was run by Charles Hughes and William Holsworth, who had about £2,000 in the business. It was a lucrative hotel taking £1,350 each month from its bar sales.[113] Charles Hughes, an ex-Bank of England clerk, was the sole owner in 1886 when his licence was challenged by the Court. Hughes was charged with being 'of bad fame and character' and the Red Light was said to be 'conducted in an improper manner and drunkenness allowed on the premises'. The main complaint came from C. Mangin Bult, the Registrar of Natives, whose office was next door to the Red Light in Main Street. He gave evidence that on Mondays 'the row in the Kaffir bar was so great' that he could not do his work. The establishment was under constant police surveillance and Detective Trimble reported it was frequented by 'thieves and burglars – Dick Carne, Percival, John Stewart, Black Abrahams, Hicks, William Bell, Charles Stewart, Jim Kelley, Stemmat ... Frank Tamlin ... and Souser'. Senior Detectives Chadwick and Izdebski reported that it was a well known resort of IDBs, but did not consider Hughes a man 'of bad fame and character'. The convenience of having IDBs and thieves in one spot 'for the purposes of arrest', and the 'good character' born by Hughes seems to have convinced the court to grant the licence once again.[114]

Struggle over land was another point of tension between mine and town. The ownership or secure possession of landed property was of crucial importance to merchants and the commercial petty-bourgeoisie. The value of property was enhanced by adequate roads, lighting, sanitation and water facilities. In 1879 the Kimberley Muncipality had been established to provide precisely these services. The Municipality, however, was enclosed by three encroaching bodies: the state, the Mining Boards and the London and South African Exploration Company. 'Government parcelled out the Municipal Corporation from the limits of two separate estates', said George Wolf, 'without according one inch of Crown land, one rood of grazing ground, or the control of wells'.[115] Even though it had been standholders, who had paid for the purchase of Vooruitzicht estate after 1875 through the capitalisation of their plots, the estate remained in the hands of the government. The other estate, called Newton, was owned by the London and South African Exploration Company and covered nearly half the Kimberley Municipality. Consequently, the Muncipality relied on rates levied on households and business premises.

Property in the Mining Areas was excluded from municipal taxation, even though these areas contained property used for non-mining purposes. Roads and water flowed through the Mining Areas but they were 'sacred precincts that only Gods ought to enter'.[116] Where the provisions of adequate services was blocked on the part of the Mining Boards 'that frightful bugbear the Exploration Company'[117] obstructed municipal operations on their property. The land company wished to be exempt from municipal taxation and in fact, being the *de facto* owners of the minerals in

191

the soil, fell under the protection of the consistent 'policy of the Government . . . to protect the mining industry from the imposition of municipal taxation'.[118]

The private ownership of the land on which the old town of Dutoitspan had been founded created the specific conditions for a standholders movement, which mirrored the revolutionary situation created by the private ownership of the Vooruitzicht farm ten years earlier. Times, of course, had changed. The London Company appointed J. B. Currey as their Manager in 1884, and he had to protect the landed interests which he had attempted to curtail as Secretary to Government in 1874. The irony of the situation was not lost on the standholders, and Samuel Austen, Mayor of Beaconsfield, was quick to warn government that 'disturbances' would follow if the standholders grievances against the Company were not attended to. Standholders complained that the Company 'allowed diggers to wash out people with their tailings'.[119] This was a most insidious form of dispossession and many poor standholders had little or no form of redress. In 1885 Parliament established that the London Company had 'by arbitrary acts . . . disturbed and interfered with their . . . tenants . . . causing them loss and damage'.[120]

The number of cases where diggers or mining companies abused the prior occupancy of standholders in Dutoitspan were legion. The most celebrated case was that of Hermanus Prins vs Le Jeune and Company. In the early 1870s, Prins became established as a produce dealer in Dutoitspan. In his line of business the position of his stand was all important, as the produce waggons passed his store to get to market. When the tailings of the Le Jeune and Company blocked up the road his business collapsed. In 1878 he had made £4,522 but in the first five months of 1880 his receipts dwindled to £341. Storbeck, a baker and general dealer, faced a similar situation. Another road ran passed his property, but this road was obstructed by Le Jeune and Company. In February 1880 Storbeck and Prins were both 'caught like rats in a trap'. Storbeck took the Le Jeune Company to court, but he was not satisfied with the 40s damages he was awarded. Prins with £25 and no restitution was little better off. Storbeck, it seems, was incensed enough to assault John Dalton, the Manager of Le Jeune and Company, and served 18 months for the pleasure.[121]

Other companies 'washed out' businesses they disapproved of, taking land they did not necessarily require for mining purposes. This was the case with W. P. Lippiatt, 53 year-old hotel-keeper of Dutoitspan and wealthy standholder. Not only was he 'washed out' but he lost his liquor licence as well.[122] Lippiatt tried to argue his case with George Kilgour, Manager of the London Company before Currey, but 'it took more ceremony to approach him than it does the Queen'.[123] Standholders were entitled to compensation, but the encroachment of mining operations on standholders property depreciated its value and settlements were partial to the mineowners. To go to arbitration 'would be like putting our heads into the jaws of a lion'.[124]

The London Company made little secret of the fact that the mineowners were 'the more important class of their tenants'.[125] In August 1880 the bitter dispute over rent and depositing floors between the diggers and the Company had been resolved.[126] The claim rent had been fixed at 30s a month and it included an acre of depositing floor. Floors had been laid out on a radiating principle and mining operations were privileged over that of standholders' dwelling or mercantile activities:

> ... Main Street of Dutoitspan is not required for mining purposes, but arbitrarily it has been declared mining area ... The Mining Area is declared over 500 houses, and the effect of that area being declared is that although the diggers declare they do not want it, every one of the people there is liable to be moved at 30 days notice ... when these poor unfortunate wretches come to the Company for redress they are told 'you are IDBs'. It is the most shameless thing I have ever heard.[127]

The pact with the mineowners was reinforced by the reservation to the Company of the right to veto the establishment of any bar, canteen, public house, 'Kafir eating-house', 'Kafir store', or bottle store. The Company evicted tenants for the non-payment of rent, for the preferent claim of mining purposes, if bad houses were kept and when neighbours complained. IDB convicts were also evicted.[128] Generally, the company applied a grasping policy of rent extraction which was only tempered by the discrimination imposed by its 'respectable' tenants.

In 1883 the London Company had around 7,000 tenants on its rent roll. It was estimated that there were 1,100 houses in Newton valued at £143,000, and 800 to 900 houses in Dutoitspan valued at £230,000.[129] The new township of Beaconsfield had only just been laid out and it was largely in Belgravia that the 143, 21-year leases had been taken out and the 44, 50-year leases.[130] The London Company was the most profitable enterprise on the Fields and even during the depression in the 1880s never failed to declare 100 per cent in dividends each year. Even though it owned the poorer mines and had fewer tenants than the Vooruitzicht estate it demanded higher rents under less secure tenure. However, more independent black people lived on its property than on Vooruitzicht as the Company refused to allow locations to be proclaimed on its land.

The standholders saw their landlords as a foreign company, which extracted £50,000 a year in rent for overseas shareholders.[131] In 1883 a Standholders League was formed to oppose new conditions written into the stand licences. The immediate effect of these new conditions was that the banks, and more importantly loan companies and building societies, refused to take landed property as security for advances.[132] The League made three demands of their landlords: fixity of tenure; a fair rent and freedom of contract to sub-let. They accepted that licences should be subject to revocation if the land was required for mining purposes but they wanted fair compensation. They were 'frightened by the manner in which the company' proceeded to law, as the company had an endless purse and most standholders were poor men.[133] Consequently, unable to meet the company equally in the law courts, the League wrote a Landlords and Tenants Bill, as they preferred 'an Act of Parliament to a revolution'.[134]

George Goch, a jeweller, who had become a director of the Griqualand West Loan, Trust and Agency Company and Chairman of the Mutual Building Society, was well placed to understand the frustration of the commercial petty-bourgeoisie at their inability to borrow money. The Bill he presented to Parliament was a tenant's manifesto. It was opposed by the London Company and the mineowners who would have had to pay higher compensation.[135] If the Bill had become law the London Company would have taken their proprietorial rights to the Privy Council and would have won. Instead, the Chairman of the London Company, Charles Posno, on the advice of John Merriman, offered stands for sale and the Chief Justice drafted a monthly licence which gave tenants the security of knowing they could not be removed until two years arrear in rent.[136]

In short, the political and ideological struggle over the issue of IDB took place in relation to new circumstances in the 1880s: the concentration of capital in joint stock companies and the clamour for closed compounds. The discourse in which this struggle was conducted contained the same elements as in the 1870s but what was striking was the adoption of different positions by different classes. The main elements of the discourse were free trade, monopoly and economic nationalism or colonial capital accumulation. The mantle of free trade, which the progressive claimholders had worn during the Black Flag Revolt, was refashioned by merchants to use against the mineowners. The tradition of anti-monopoly, which the small diggers had upheld in the 1870s, was transferred to the mercantile community who did not 'get their fair share of profit from the soil'.[137] The emphasis on colonial capital accumulation, or against foreign capital, which colonial merchants had expressed in the 1870s, was taken up by the commercial petty-bourgeoisie. Often these elements were combined as in the following:

> Day by day, the concentration of the mines into fewer hands becomes apparent. Day by day local shareholders are displaced by foreign ones. The industry, and profits of the industry, are slipping from our hands, under the active energies of syndicates in London and Paris; and while the Government are kept alive to the illicit trade in diamonds and to the necessity of more 'traps' and detectives, the consummation of their plans is quietly proceeded with.[138]

The discourse emerged and was formed in relation to particular issues: trapping, closed compounds, liquor law and fixed property. Class conflict over these issues culminated in a substantial challenge by the mercantile community to the mineowners' control over political and economic life in Kimberley.

BARNATO BROTHERS AND ILLICIT DIAMOND BUYING

There was, at the time, overwhelming evidence that Barnato Brothers was the largest illicit capitalist on the Diamond Fields. Armed with this knowledge the mineowners had strong grounds for regarding any opposition to the Diamond Trade Act and the Detective Department as a movement funded by IDBs to lessen the dangers of the illicit trade. This, in turn, left the mineowners with severe doubts about the legitimacy of the grievances of the commercial petty bourgeoisie.

The involvement of the Barnato brothers in IDB began in the early 1870s. Harry Barnato ran the London Hotel, which was a notorious IDB den. He was also in partnership with Aaron Van Praagh, a well-known IDB at the time. In May 1878 he sold the London Hotel and concentrated his business activities on his new partnership with his brother Barney Barnato. 'He has either been depicted as a devil', wrote Louis Cohen, who was Barney Barnato's partner in 1873 and 1874, 'or a spectacled angel on stilts.'[139] Most of the Diamond Fields literature refers either obliquely or quaintly to Barnato's 'lack of a reputation'. Brian Roberts, alone, has systematically exposed Barnato's involvement in IDB.[140] His account is reliable, but to clinch the case additional evidence from court and bank records illuminates the illicit milieu in which Barnato Brothers operated.

The case that proved the IDB suspicions harboured about Barnato Brothers involved Isaac Joel, aged 21 years, who worked for his uncles, Harry and Barney Barnato. It was the first prosecution of a diamond dealer under section 34 of the Diamond Trade Act. The facts seem to have been quite clear. In March 1884 Isaac Joel's record of his purchases and sales corresponded within the normal degree of error: 5,379 carats bought and 5,382¼ carats sold. Chief Detective Fry noticed that a 16½ carat stone had been sold to another dealer, Leopold Herz, for £214 and that it did not appear on the purchase side of Joel's register. By law, stones of over £100 in value or 10 carats in size had to be itemised and accounted for singly. Joel's defence was that he had bought the diamond for under £100, and that it had been sold in a mixed parcel, and therefore need not have been itemised in his register. Diamond dealer after diamond dealer gave evidence at his trial that a diamond of this quality was unlikely to have been of so little value or sold in a mixed parcel by any dealer. Alfred Beit, who bought between 30,000 and 40,000 carats a month, estimated its value at between £10 and £12 a carat. He said it was 'a remarkable stone' and it was 'a very white Cape white . . . a perfect octahedron'.[141] As Isaac Joel was unable to explain how he had obtained the stone, the Detective Department believed he had thrown away bort from his legitimate purchases amounting to 16½ carats and replaced it with the 'exceptionally fine stone' illicitly obtained. Isaac Joel was discharged from this trial, however, owing to a technical error in the indictment. He was immediately re-arrested and allowed bail at £4,000.[142]

Barney and Harry Barnato were in London when Isaac Joel was arrested. They returned to the Diamond Fields with great speed. Barney did his utmost to get the case dropped and this involved special pleading for the intervention of J. B. Robinson, as Chairman of the Protection Board, and an attempt to bribe John Fry, the Chief of the Detective Department. The details of these offers became public knowledge when Dormer, editor of the *Cape Argus* in Cape Town, which was owned by Rhodes,[143] took up the case in December 1884. Unfortunately, Dormer mistook Isaac Joel for his brother, Woolf Joel, and both Woolf Joel and Barney Barnato sued the paper for libel.[144] What had produced this litigation and cast a flood of curious light on the affairs of Barnato Brothers was the flight of Isaac Joel from Kimberley before his second trial. He assumed the name of Jack Joel in London and managed the firm's affairs from the safe sanctuary of Hatton Garden. The Joel parents, who petitioned to have the warrant for his arrest lifted in 1886, claimed that he had left the Colony out of 'sheer fright' in the belief that 'he would not get a fair trial' and that he was in a 'state of mental and nervous prostration from the effects of the prostrated suspense and anxiety of the former trial'.[145]

Over a number of years the Managers of the Standard Bank in Kimberley reported on the 'character' of Barnato Brothers. In 1879 they were 'a respectable firm of diamond buyers and claimholders' worth about £20,000, and in early 1880 the Manager had little to add. After the 'share mania' he noted that they had made a lot of money and were worth £100,000. In 1882 their 'character' took a turn for the worse. 'Men of considerable wealth', noted the Manager, 'but their antecedents are doubtful, if not "shady".' For emphasis he added they 'are supposed to have been mixed up in the illicit trade'. In 1884 he was a little more open in his criticism:

> The firm is not regarded as a respectable one as the partners are considered to be unscrupulous and are suspected to be illicits, but we have never had any trouble with them. Their transactions with us have been numerous and extensive, and their engagements have always been promptly met. I have asked them for their balance sheet, but they refused to give it . . . I consider they have a capital of at least £50,000 in all . . .

The Standard learnt from the Union Bank in London that its opinion of the London firm of Barnato Brothers was 'very different' to its good view of Jules Porges and Company. The Bank concluded that Barnato Brothers 'made money some time back, but it would be hard to say what their means are now'. In 1885 both Harry and Barney Barnato were in London and their Kimberley representatives were A. B. Randall and D. Harris of whom the Bank did not 'entertain a favourable opinion'. In 1887 the firm was simply of 'indifferent reputation'. In 1888 Woolf Joel became a partner and they remained 'somewhat doubtful characters'; the Bank feared that in the event of a crisis 'it would probably be found that they had placed as much of their property as possible beyond the reach of their creditors'. In 1888 they were worth £1,000,000 and by 1890 this figure had been doubled. By this time Barney Barnato had become a 'man of paramount influence' in Kimberley and the Standard Bank feared to either lose his account or cross him politically as 'his opposition would in that case not end locally'.[146]

Bank managers had privileged access to financial information which came not only from their command of bank ledgers, but also from the gossip of the Kimberley Club. Moreover, the gossip of the Club was well-informed as the Protection Board had a close relationship with the Detective Department. The Barnatos were social pariahs and were excluded from the Kimberley Club. Consequently it is interesting to trace with whom their business dealings most commonly lay.

In late 1884, after the Isaac Joel case, the Standard Manager had written: 'Woolf Joel is closely allied with the IDB fraternity and might therefore come within the reach of the law at any time'.[147] The Barnatos were well acquainted with diamond dealers who were hauled before the Special Court. Some managed to escape through bribing or intimidating witnesses, while others got off on appeal to the Supreme Court. In 1881 Johnny Swaebe, broker to Barnato Brothers and David Symons, was sent to the breakwater.[148] Mark Leo, accredited agent of the French and D'Esterre DMC, consistently sold diamonds to Hyam Abahams and Woolf Joel. He was arraigned for not keeping a proper register in a follow up to the Isaac Joel indictment, but he escaped.[149] Simon Blumenthal, another confederate, escaped conviction on appeal and continued to operate from the Orange Free State.[150] He had dealings with another convicted IDB, Myer Myers.[151] Michael Emmanuel, Aaron Schwaab and Elias Jacobs lived together and dealt with Simon Blumenthal and the convicted IDB, Gordon Taylor.[152] These dealers were under constant suspicion and the Barnatos continued to deal with them when they remained free men.

The sequel to the Isaac Joel case was the dismissal of John Fry, the Chief of the Detective Department. He was informed on by a clerk in the Department who plucked up 'a vast amount of moral courage' and exposed some inconsistencies in detective accounts. An investigation was ordered and Basil Roper, Resident Magistrate of Herbert, reported Fry was 'tyrannical and capricious' and had allowed the Department to fall into 'indescribable confusion'.[153] John Fry was suspended in September 1884 and dismissed in February 1885. Roper took over his job at £2,000 a year. John Merriman, who had known John Fry since the early 1870s, wrote that he was 'absolutely penniless with a large family' and had 'been sacrificed to gratify some of the lowest wretches in the colony'.[154]

It was clear that Merriman was referring to Barney Barnato. Moreover, a new newspaper, *The Diamond Field Times* had just been published, which was launched specifically on a campaign against the Detective Department. It was nominally owned by George Garcia Wolf but financed by Barnato.[155] 'There is no doubt in Fry's case,' wrote R. W. H. Giddy to Merriman, 'that Wolf and Barnato moved the Ministry to displace Fry'.[156]

The connection between Wolf, the Licensed Victuallers Parliamentary candidate, and Barney Barnato was suspicious to many mineowners. Wolf came to the Fields in mid-1880 and began as a furniture dealer with £1,500 capital and support from his brother-in-law, N. Hoffnung of N. Hoffnung and Company in London. By 1883 he owned £5,000 worth of fixed property in Kimberley. His sales amounted to £10,697 in this year and his business ran at a loss. In 1884 his premises in Dutoitspan Road were destroyed by fire and with it £8,000 worth of stock. In 1885 he was charged with fraud but acquitted. At this time the Standard Bank manager referred to his character as 'indifferent' whereas earlier it had been 'respectable'. He was elected a Member of the Legislative Assembly in 1883 and remained a representative until 1886 as the champion of commercial and white working class interests. It was clear, however, that he was an unsuccessful businessman.[157]

There is little evidence of financial support from Barnato besides the newspaper enterprise, *The Diamond Fields Times*, which folded in June 1885. Dr Matthews suggested elliptically that Wolf was supported by IDBs when he wrote that on Wolf's election to his vacant seat 'the grave gave up its dead, the Cape Town breakwater its convicts, and the natives "polled early and often" for the successful candidate'.[158] But Wolf was never linked to IDB personally and, given his parlous financial situation, the £2,000 a year needed to support him during the legislative sessions in Cape Town was supplied by the Licensed Victuallers.

THE REVOLT OF THE 'CAMP FOLLOWERS'

The opposition of the commercial bourgeoisie and petty bourgeoisie to the mineowners, patched together out of a fear of compounds, declining prosperity and insecurity of landed tenure, set in motion an extraordinary episode in Cape history. It consisted in a frontal assault on the Detective Department, and in the words of John Merriman, Kimberley was 'surrounded with as many plots and counter-plots as a "shilling dreadful" '.[159]

By 1883 the depression had begun to take its toll of the commercial community. Two of the largest wholesalers, Herman Willigerod and James Ferguson, went bankrupt and swept away large numbers of store and canteen-keepers who were dependent on them.[160] In this economic climate, fundamentally determined by the state of the mines, they sought to protect their futures by an incisive intervention in politics. In 1884, when Kimberley's representation was increased to four, commercial men swept the polls. George Wolf, the Licensed Victuallers candidate, became the senior member, followed by G. Goch, Moses Cornwall and Charles Rudd. Although Charles Rudd was a director of the De Beers DMC and was sent to parliament 'to carry the compound system',[161] he had not speculated widely in the 'share mania' and his major interest remained in the merchant firm of E. W. Tarry and Company. Rhodes, mineowner and landowner, was returned for Barkly West on the 'blanket vote',[162] – that is, the African vote – together with Alfred Hill, partner in the merchant firm of Hill and Paddon.

In stark contrast to the black versus white confrontation during the Black Flag Revolt, the alignment of social and political forces in the 1880s cut sharply across colour lines. George Goch, in particular, drew support from the Afrikaner and black population of Dutoitspan. Goch had been established in Dutoitspan Road since 1872 as a watchmaker, jeweller, optician and dealer in musical instruments. In 1877 he added a circulating library and a well to his interests. In 1881 his stock, which was largely made up of 'fancy goods', was worth £5,000 and the Standard Bank thought he was 'good for' up to £1,000. In 1883 his jewellery stock was worth £20,000, his premises £3,000 and his supporter was the wealthy Cape Town merchant, Maxwell Earp.[163] He first stood for Parliament in 1883 and lost to Wolf. In the following year he was elected with major support from Dutoitspan.

An Africander League had been formed, 'principally of Coloured men', who chose and supported commercial candidates together with the Griqualand West and South African Political Association, composed of white Afrikaners.[164] Afrikaners were defined as those born in the Colony. The point was put with great force by the High Court Interpreter, Joseph Moss, who was an Mfengu:

> We are Africans . . . we are not like Englishmen, who return to their own land. You are not here for a certain period to make money alone and then return to England to make yourselves great men. You are born here, your interest is here, Africa is of very great materiality to you.[165]

The commercial petty-bourgeoisie went to the Cape Parliament as the true inheritors of the colony and demanded their birth-right.

The Kimberley representatives elicited the support of the new Upington-Hofmeyr Ministry (May 1884 – November 1886), which was suspicious of the diamond laws of the mineowners. For Hofmeyr the 'brandy interest' was always paramount, while it was rumoured that IDBs were Upington's best clients.[166] Upington, however, lived off his ministerial salary of £1,750 a year and neglected 'his private interests for politics'.[167] He certainly remitted more IDB sentences in his term of office than Scanlen, his predecessor.[168]

Upington's dismissal of Leigh Hoskyns, the Crown Prosecutor in Kimberley, for having 'been guilty of a breach of trust and discipline, in giving information out of the strict course of duty' to 'active political opponents of the Government of the day' was seen by the mineowners as a vindictive and partial manoeuvre.[169] Upington had asked Hoskyns not to act against the sureties for the diamond dealer, Michael Emmanuel, who had been arrested but had jumped bail. The sureties were Aaron Schwaab and Moses Cornwall, MLA. It was the information that Upington had intervened to spare Cornwall the financial embarrassment of paying the surety, that Hoskyns had passed on to Merriman, Rhodes, Rudd, Goldschmidt, Robinson and Davis. This was the only connection between Moses Cornwall and IDB. He had run a successful clothing establishment in the 1870s but sold his business in 1881 when he became Mayor of Kimberley. In 1882 he became Deputy Sheriff for the Kimberley Division at a salary of £2,000 a year. Unlike Goch, whose business was profitable, and Wolf, whose constituency was secure even if his business was not, Cornwall gave up commercial life for the security of a state salary and a Parliamentary seat (1884–88).[170]

The man, who was to be most closely associated with the attack on the Detective Department, was elected to the Legislative Council in 1884 and he remained a representative until 1910. He was William Ross and his 'antecedents' gave the mineowners cause for grave concern. From 1874 to 1879 he had been the manager of the Oriental Bank in Kimberley. His colleague James Dell, Manager of the Standard Bank, believed Ross was an 'unscrupulous character' and Dell's successor, Henry Crawford, formed the same opinion.[171] From 1881 Ross was the senior partner in the firm of accountants, Ross, Priest and Page (Page was his father-in-law) and through successful speculation in the 'share mania' he made £20,000.[172] Ross was a well-known usurer and he lent money at high interest to IDBs.[173] He also, however, borrowed money from Judge Laurence.[174] The combination of accountancy and usury placed Ross in a similar position to other 'honest' professional men whose services were used by IDBs. It also gave him access to information on the weakest link in the Detective Department, the private detectives.

Private detectives were employed by the Department 'to worm themselves into the confidence' of IDBs to gather information regarding 'their habits, haunts and *modus operandi*'.[175] They were paid between 10s and £1 a day and in 1886 the reward of 25 per cent of the captured diamonds was increased to 50 per cent. Successful private detectives had to be of 'bad character' in order to be trusted by IDBs. They also had to be allowed to deal in diamonds or it became 'impossible to arrive at the details of the illicit trade'.[176] Illicit dealing was abused by private detectives. Douglas Forster, an advocate, conducted a confidential investigation for the Law Department into the Detective Department in August 1886 and concluded that private detectives 'sometimes if not frequently abuse their position and engage on their own account in illicit dealing far beyond the extent permitted by and reported to the Department'.[177] Roper admitted in 1888 that four or five private detectives had been dismissed for unauthorised dealing and also that it was 'impossible to keep an absolute check on their dealings'.[178] It was over the issue of dealing by one private detective in particular, Wassilio Rojesky, that the attack on the Detective Department was commenced.

Wassilio Rojesky was a Pole, who had been born in Austria in 1847. In 1870 he went to Vienna and worked as a produce merchant before beginning a colonial round-the-world tour. He visited Constantinople,

Palestine, Egypt, India, Singapore, China, Sumatra and the Straits Settlement working as railway storekeeper, detective, shop-broker and ivory merchant. In March 1882 he arrived at Cape Town from where he worked his way up the railway line to Kimberley, which he reached in December 1884. He was 'conversant with' 14 languages: English, Dutch, German, Italian, French, Rumanian, Polish, Russian, Slav, Turkish, Greek, Arabic, Hindustani and Malay. He was also 'acquainted with' Serbian and Bulgarian dialects and had a thorough knowledge of Hebrew and Chaldaic. As a result of his reputation as a linguist he was employed by the Detective Department as a private detective. He ran the Slavonian Arms in Dutoitspan and the Prince Rudolph Club in De Beers, which catered for Italian and Austrian mineworkers. He provided more information on IDBs than any other private detective, but dealt on his own account. His private dealing provided the political capital that Ross required, but it was his part in a plot hatched in Kimberley's underworld that was to make him notorious.[179]

Rojesky played the role of *agent provocateur* in an attempt to blow up Roper, Chief of the Detective Department, with dynamite in January 1886. The 'hired assassins' were three Austrians named Antonio Cassalano, 25 years old, whom Rojesky had first met on the railway at De Aar, Paulo Rosich, 26 years old, and Elia Anteglevitch, 25 years old, who had been involved in IDB. Incited by Rojesky they attempted to murder Roper in his house in Lanyon Terrace, which faced the Cricket Ground.[180] Roper was kept informed of the plot by Rojesky and on the night of the 9 January 'Roper and a chosen band of detectives stood waiting' for the attackers 'with guns in their hands loaded with buckshot'. Mrs Roper played the piano and sang 'till 12 to set them off their guard'. Roper watched while 'one villain deposited his packet of dynamite on the stoep' and another lit it, before he gave the signal to fire. 'They made very bad shooting' and eventually Rosich, Anteglevitch and Cassalano were taken in the Austrian quarter of Newton.[181]

The motive of this attempted murder was never successfully explained. Rojesky referred to a 'secret society' while the 'dynamitards' believed they were to be paid by Captain Christian, former Commissioner of Police, Joseph Mylchreest, the last of the wealthy individual diggers (both from the Isle of Man) and some IDBs. There had been a conflict between Christian and Roper over private dealing by private detectives. When Christian trespassed on Roper's preserve and tried to trap one offender, Roper had him removed and took over his post.[182] Roper, it seemed, 'lived in an atmosphere of plots' and Rojesky inserted Christian's name into the 'dynamite conspiracy' for his own ends. Merriman, who was in Kimberley at the time, believed Rojesky was a 'villain of the deepest dye', who started the plot himself, and finding Roper ready to believe all kinds of duplicity 'made it up as he went along with a view of being rewarded for his services'.[183]

In May 1886 Ross moved in the Legislative Council for a commission to investigate the Detective Department. To force the issue he called Rojesky 'an unmitigated scoundrel' at a political meeting in Kimberley Town Hall in July.[184] The Department and Rojesky stood or fell together and Roper tenaciously defended private detectives in general and Rojesky in particular. Consequently, Rojesky sued Ross for defamation of character and the trial took place in September 1886.[185] All three judges condemned Rojesky in one way or another and gave judgement for Ross with costs. Judge Buchanan believed that the action was 'clearly for the public benefit' and that Ross 'would have failed in his duty had he acted otherwise'. Judge Jones concurred with Buchanan and added that the dynamite outrage 'would never have stained the catalogue of crime had it not been for the machinations of the private detective Rojesky'. Judge Laurence, previous antagonist to the diamond laws when he had been editor of the *Diamond News* in 1881, developed an elaborate justification for Rojesky based on his assumption of a criminal *persona*. He also understood Ross' position and the difficulties of the case for whenever Ross tried to validate a charge he was 'confronted with the explanation of the mask'. Laurence thought the whole suit 'ill advised' and had done the Department more harm than good.[186]

The exposure of Rojesky was a powerful weapon with which to strike at the Department. It crowned the general dislike of trapping and was part of a programme to have the Diamond Trade Act abolished altogether. The mineowners, it appeared, were prepared to forgo the Diamond Trade Act in favour of the compound system. Without waiting for legislation, however, they pressed on with the introduction of closed compounds and while Ross agitated in the upper chamber, O'Leary, newly-elected Licensed Victuallers candidate, tried to pass a bill in the Lower House to prevent compounds destroying the trade of Kimberley.

It became known as the 'truck bill' and its major clause prohibited the sale of goods in compounds and if passed, would have outlawed closed compounds. Consequently, in June 1886, when the bill came before Parliament 'the Kimberley detachment ... headed by Rhodes displayed the most remarkable political agility in coming to a compromise.'[187] The main points of the compromise were: 1. all wages were to be paid in current coin and no truck tickets allowed; 2. no Europeans were to be compounded; 3. no mining companies were to import goods for compounds, but had to buy from local dealers and sell only to 'natives'; 4. prices in compounds were not to be lower than prices in Kimberley; 5. all profits in compounds were to be donated to the Municipality; and 6. these transactions were to be safeguarded by the Civil Commissioner and Mayors of Kimberley and Beaconsfield.

This compromise was rejected by a meeting on the Fields dominated by tradesmen from Beaconsfield and they suggested 'that the interests of the Mining Community would be fully protected if only food were supplied to the natives in the compounds'.[188] The Parliamentary representatives put the situation succinctly in a telegram:

> Bill without the compromise has no chance of passing this session, in face of the united and vigorous opposition offered against it by the Mining Interest and the want of unanimity amongst the mercantile community in supporting the Bill.[189]

The session drew to a close and the Bill failed to get a hearing in time. Before the 1887 session, however, the mineowners had succeeded in widening the 'want of unanimity amongst the mercantile community'.

In the struggle for closed compounds the mineowners managed to separate the commercial bourgeoisie from the commercial petty-bourgeoisie. The wholesalers who dominated the Chamber of Commerce were branch houses of coastal merchants. By the late 1880s even their interests were changing. For example, Harry Mosenthal, whom Merriman hailed as a 'commercial Ulysses', also had a substantial stake in diamond mining and land.[190] In addition, influential members of the Chamber were E. W. Tarry and Company and Paul Henwood and Company of Durban, who were the largest ironmongers on the Fields. Henry Robinow, speaking for E. W. Tarry and Company, argued that without compounds and the 'so-called truck system' the mineowners would be driven to 'unification, which is far worse'.[191] More importantly for general wholesalers, compounds presented the opportunity for a captive market which would not damage their turnover.[192] Besides they were large enough to take advantage of the expansion of the interior trade and the opening up of the Gold Fields. With these new sales peaks well in view from their Olympian heights, the commercial bourgeoisie left the storekeepers to fight a lost battle. O'Leary best expressed the fears of small business men 'that the object of the mining community would be not only to do away with white labour . . . but that they would be able to reduce the value of the native labour, giving them smaller wages'.[193] In this belief, O'Leary went to Parliament in 1887 to move his 'truck bill' which was renamed the Labourers' Wages Regulation Bill.

The mineowners attacked the bill, as was expected, as the work of IDBs. The commercial members supported it because compounds interfered with colonial trade. The farmers wanted a compromise. Individual members made outrageous remarks from either end of the political spectrum. Rothman (Graaff-Reinet) said that the 'natives being locked up for six months in these compounds was actually slavery'; Merriman (Aliwal North) remarked that drunken scenes in Bultfontein Road on Saturday night were a 'disgrace to civilisation'. But the key note address came from De Waal (Tulbagh), who was not unacquainted with the truck system on the Cape railways:[194]

> Small shopkeepers also complained against (the compound system) for through the system the trade had been transferred to the large merchant houses. He wished to know what benefit the Colony derived from the

Kimberley mines (Hear, hear). It was true that the diamond export was larger than that of wool and feathers, but the thing is that money did not come back again to the Colony, but went into the pockets of the shareholders who lived in Europe. The only profit the Cape Colonists derived from the mines were the small earnings of the natives. If the natives were not allowed to drink intoxicating drinks, then a large portion of the farmers would derive no benefit whatever from them. The diamond industry was better protected than any other industry in the Colony, and still the Companies were not satisfied; they wished now the monopoly of the Kafir trade. For every native killed by brandy a dozen were killed through accidents in the mines. It was true that the natives did not complain, but the fact was that they knew no better; but it was the small shopkeepers who did . . . Those who were so strongly in favour of the compound system were that not for the sake of the natives, but for the sake of their own pockets.[195]

The Bill became an Act and mining companies were only empowered to sell 'merchandise . . . necessary for the use and well being of artificers and labourers' during their period of detention. Also all such 'necessaries' had to be bought in the electoral division of Kimberley and the companies were to make no profit out of these sales.[196] They were all clauses through which, in later practice, the mineowners were able to drive 'a horse and four'. But they supported Ross' demand for a commission into the diamond trade laws, the Detective Department and closed compounds. The report left the system very much as it had been.[197]

In short, compounds had a devastating effect on the commercial community in Kimberley. What was in the process of happening and what many feared would happen in the future was summed up by an Inspector of the Standard Bank:

Everything points to the conclusion that Kimberley as a commercial centre has seen its best days, and when once the railway is extended across the Vaal it is difficult to see what outlets the merchants will have for their wares beyond the town itself. Even this will be a diminishing source of demand, for not only will the population decrease, but its purchasing power will be much curtailed as the 'Compound' system is developed. Three large compounds have already been started, containing, between them, about 3,000 Kafirs, and others are in contemplation. For the present the companies purchase all supplies from local storekeepers, but this is merely done to allay opposition, and when once the system is firmly established they will buy in the cheapest markets. No intoxicants are allowed in the Compounds, and the fact that Savings Banks have been opened inside and are successful beyond all expectation, is proof that the Canteen keepers, and the storekeepers who supply them, are suffering. The scheme of amalgamation, too, is slowly making headway, and every absorption of small holdings means cheaper working and the employment of fewer hands.[198]

CONCLUSION

In the late nineteenth century few people in Kimberley denied that diamond theft was a crime. They did, however, argue over the culpability of the thief. Judges' addresses at the Criminal Sessions and in the Special Court were filled with the stereotype of the honest African labourer corrupted by his contact with unscrupulous whites who introduced him to theft. Here, the honest African labourer was the 'noble savage' whose entry into civilisation was traumatic and destructive. His actions were determined by the environment into which he entered as a foreigner; he succumbed to temptation and had to be protected from himself. 'Do we as a community', asked Judge Laurence, 'do all that we might do for the Natives whom we attract here in such large numbers and for whose moral as well as material well-being I think we ought to hold ourselves in some measure responsible.'[199]

In contrast to this legal and conventional ideology, there was overwhelming evidence that IDB was the 'custom of the country'. It was jokingly referred to as the 'prevailing industry' in both canteen and court room.[200] The 'raw' African recruit rapidly became acquainted with the moral precepts of colonial diamond law, and like the majority of Kimberley's citizens ignored them. The proof of this disrespect for the diamond law lay in the abolition of the jury system in IDB cases, for the mineowners knew that a jury of Kimberley burghers could not be relied on to convict.

Since IDB was the 'custom of the country' it is suggestive to label it a 'social crime' as distinct from 'anti-social crime' like common theft, forgery, arson or murder. The distinction is between good criminals, who have the support of the community against the property laws of the rich, and the deviant habitual criminals who live by crime often exploiting the working class. E. P. Thompson has warned against such a neat distinction:

> We may feel more sympathy for the food rioter than for the horse stealer, but the records don't authorize us to see one rather than the other as more typical of the labouring people. There is not 'nice' social crime here and 'nasty' anti-social crime there. Crime – in the sense of being on the wrong side of the law – was, for vast numbers of undifferentiated working people, normal.[201]

And yet there is a fine distinction to be made in industrial Kimberley between 'social and anti-social crime' within the structure of the illicit trade, a distinction between diamond workers, both black and white, supplementing wages by theft, and those whose regular occupation was the receipt and sale of stolen diamonds. Both were moved by economic incentives but the rewards were as unequal in the illicit trade as they were in legitimate mining. IDB was very profitable for receivers, but less so for the thieves. Sadly, there is little evidence to quantify the numbers of labourers who became independent craftsmen or traders in the locations through IDB accumulation. There are only the sparse figures for protection passes and the inconclusive evidence of swelling numbers of Africans re-contracting to remain in Kimberley. But in a society predicated on the unequal right to accumulate property and permeated by the opulence of *nouveau riche* wealth, the desire to earn fast, legally or illegally, was all pervasive.

10

Amalgamation

The struggle over the amalgamation of the diamond mines has been personalised by historians into a titanic battle between Rhodes in De Beers Mine and Barnato in Kimberley Mine. The story they tell has become a legend and is basically as follows. Between 1880 and 1887 Rhodes amalgamated all the diamond companies in De Beers Mine with the De Beers DMC. The process of amalgamation in Kimberley Mine was slower, but by 1887 Barnato held a controlling interest in the Kimberley Central, which owned the whole of the mine with the exception of the 90 rich claims belonging to the Compagnie Française. Rhodes, in pursuit of his dream of total unification on his own terms, bought the Compagnie Française for De Beers. In a brilliant manoevre he then sold the Compagnie to the Kimberley Central and placed a Trojan Horse in the enemy camp. It gave De Beers a one-fifth share stake in the Kimberley Mine. Then, after a battle of attrition in production, which provoked a collapse in the price of diamonds, Barnato and Rhodes fought each other in the share markets for a controlling interest in Kimberley Mine. The battle for share control, so the story goes, began in earnest in October 1887 and Rhodes emerged as triumphant victor in March 1888. In the struggle Barnato's supporters deserted him for quick profits, while Rhodes' allies remained firm in the share markets for De Beers. Rhodes frequently attempted to buy off Barnato during the struggle, but it was only when Rhodes and his friends controlled three-fifths of the Kimberley Central stock in March 1888 that Barnato capitulated to Rhodes' terms for the amalgamation of the De Beers and Kimberley Mines, and pledged his support for the formation of De Beers Consolidated Mines Limited.[1]

This story of the amalgamation struggle is pure mythology. It has become almost a biblical parable with Rhodes representing the forces of light, productive industry and triumphant capitalist progress overcoming Barnato representing the forces of evil, criminal commercialism and self-interested greed. Not only has the legend constructed a struggle between the wrong antagonists, but the struggle itself has been misplaced and misunderstood. It is only through a structural analysis and a depersonalisation of the different positions of the De Beers and Central companies, that the process of concentration and final centralisation of diamond production can be understood.

206

AMALGAMATION SCHEMES, 1882–86

In the 1880s numerous schemes for amalgamation of some or all of the diamond mines were hatched. Prior to the final amalgamation the most important were the Erlanger scheme for De Beers Mine (1882), the Rothschild scheme for Dutoitspan Mine (1883), the Standard Bank schemes for Dutoitspan Mine and the liquidation of the Kimberley Mining Board debt (1885), and the Comptoir d'Escompte de Paris project for total unification (1886). Each scheme was planned for a particular purpose and they all failed for different reasons.

The first major scheme, which became identified with Baron Erlanger, a City merchant banker, was not so much a rescue operation of fraudulent and over-capitalised companies as the method by which the major De Beers companies hoped to increase their profits by taking advantage of the slump. The initiative came from Rhodes and the De Beers DMC and it was the first detailed proposal to link closed compounds and underground mining to a greater yield and profitability. A combined mine capitalised at £3 million would, it was projected, produce a net return of 87 per cent on capital within two and a half years of formation. The scheme contained an impressive summary of the current 1882 costs of production by grade of claim, and a prediction of savings and expanded yield under a unified company in which mining would be conducted over 300 days a year instead of only half that under the current regime.[2]

While the principle of amalgamation and the supporting figures were admirable, Baron Erlanger found a lot to quibble with in the valuation of the Victoria company. Erlanger and partners in his merchant bank were the major shareholders in the Victoria owning one-sixth of the £300,600 capital. Rhodes and his fellow De Beers directors assessed the Victoria as a third class company and offered it a 9.3 per cent increase on its capital (22.9 per cent on its Mining Board valuation) in the new unified company. The De Beers directors valued their own company the highest in the mine and proposed to sell it to the new company for one-third of the £2.5 million to be allocated for the purchase of claims, a modest 24 per cent increase on its old capital of £665,550 (53.4 per cent increase on its Mining Board valuation). Despite this moderation, Baron Erlanger wanted more for the Victoria in a unified company if his bank was going to promote it in the London market. His proposal was for a 52 per cent increase on the Victoria capital (70.9 per cent on its Mining Board valuation), but the De Beers directors found this unacceptable and the scheme fell through.[3]

The Rothschild plan for the amalgamation of Dutoitspan Mine was aimed at recovering their speculation in the Anglo–African DMC. While their correspondent, Albert Gansl, was reviewing the situation of the company on the Diamond Fields in late 1882, he reached the conclusion that amalgamation would solve the problems of overproduction, the cost of labour and the great expense of mining supplies.[4] On Gansl's advice the

Rothschilds formed a syndicate, which included J. H. Schröder and Company, to promote an amalgamated company with a capital of £3.25 million in Dutoitspan Mine. The syndicate was to take a very reasonable 2.5 per cent commission (£78,000) in preference shares for its services. The suggested sum for mine debts and working capital was to be £1 million of which £100,000 was allotted for working capital, £400,000 for mine debt and £500,000 for machinery plant. This capital was to be raised by the issue of ordinary shares bearing 8 per cent non-cumulative interest. Problems arose over the distribution of debt relief and a rift developed between European and Cape companies over their respective shares. Cape companies claimed £280,000 to cover their debts, while European companies and the syndicate refused to offer more than £180,000. This debt squabble eventually scuppered a scheme with a lot to recommend it, not least the modest commission charges and the fixed rate of return it offered investors.[5]

The Standard Bank looked to amalgamation to recover their local advances to mining companies. In 1885 all the local banks together held one-fifth (300 claims) of Dutoitspan Mine as a result of the cession of mine property for bad debts. John Merriman acted for the Standard Bank in an attempt to amalgamate the mine, but all the problems of the Rothschild scheme re-emerged. Companies wanted cash to pay their debts and to provide working capital, while the banks were trying to liquidate rather than to extend advances. Moreover, the few viable companies were reluctant to take over the notoriously bad properties that had fallen into the hands of the Standard Bank.[6]

The inflated values of European companies promoted during the 'share mania' also created obstacles to amalgamation. The great over-valuation of the Anglo–African and Phoenix DMCs (both promoted by Lewis and Marks and Jules Porges) was difficult to reconcile with the more realistic capitalisation of Cape companies. The most important of the local concerns was the Griqualand West DMC which had been promoted by J. B. Robinson. As Robinson's affairs drifted towards bankruptcy in 1885, some of his shares were bought up by Frederic Stow, who became the largest shareholder, and N. M. Rothschild and Sons. While Stow encouraged the bank scheme, other shareholders who had bought in at high prices resisted the amalgamation proposal. Other companies like the Orion DMC, controlled by the Mosenthals, would also have nothing to do with the scheme. Smaller local companies, like the prosperous European DMC and Joseph Mylchreest's patchwork of scrap companies, preferred to continue working on their own. In the end, the major companies knew that the bank negotiations were a scuttle operation and they believed they could absorb their lame neighbours more effectively one by one. So in July 1885 the Compagnie Generale, controlled by Charles Roulina, bought the best of the Standard Bank's claim property, getting in ahead of the De Beers DMC probing outside its mine of origin for strategic investments for the first time. Thus, Merriman's first amalgamation venture came to nought.[7]

Soon after this failure Merriman set about amalgamating Kimberley Mine in order to settle the Kimberley Mining Board debt of over £400,000. At the time of Merriman's negotiations Kimberley Mine was in the hands of four major holders: the Kimberley Central (capital £1,346,968); the Compagnie Française (capital £676,861); the Standard (capital £343,585); and the Cape of Good Hope bank (capital £191,372).[8] For the remaining eight holdings (capital £223,988) absorption was only a matter of time. The Kimberley Central had recently embarked on its underground development and was content to wait for its position to improve. The Compagnie Française was in a similar position having stopped production so as to develop its underground works. The Standard was working in the eye of a reef hurricane which threatened to destroy the company. The Cape of Good Hope Bank had supported W. A. Hall in an underground mining venture and by the beginning of 1886 it had locked up £170,000 in the West End of the mine, which 'if it was put up for sale . . . would not fetch £10,000'.[9] Such was the state of the mine when Merriman began amalgamation negotiations on behalf of the Standard Bank.

In early 1884 J. B. Robinson had first suggested that the banks could settle the Kimberley Mining Board debt. When the Standard Bank eventually acted on this suggestion two years later, Merriman hoped he could rely on Robinson's support. He was distressed to discover that Robinson was heavily in debt to the Cape of Good Hope Bank and was acting as their agent against the interests of the Standard Bank. The Cape Bank was a Mining Board debtor and was not keen to pay off the debt, while the other Banks, together with the large mining companies, were Mining Board creditors. The situation was further complicated by interested parties outside the mine. Stow was the solicitor for the Bank of Africa and the Compagnie Française, and he obstructed negotiations for a debenture loan, the General Manager of the Standard Bank believed, because he was the holder of:

> De Beers mining scrip to the extent of £100,000 and the price of which cannot fail to be unfavourably affected directly the Kimberley mine is again in full operation.[10]

When Merriman failed to arrange an amalgamation or to negotiate a loan, the Standard Bank was driven to the conclusion that the Board had no intention of paying its debt. Consequently, the banks went to law and Parliament and in 1886 a debenture loan was floated to pay off the debt.[11]

The most ambitious scheme for amalgamation, the Unified Diamond Mines Limited, was planned to control over-production. It was initiated by Charles Roulina who had built a substantial base in the Dutoitspan Mine with the Compagnie Generale. In 1885 he formed a syndicate – led by the Comptoir d'Escompte de Paris and the Banque de Paris et de Pays-Bas, and including the Mosenthals, Porges and Posno – to promote a monster company with a capital of £10 million. Existing companies were to be paid in scrip for their property; £2 million to cover debts and to provide working capital was to be raised by the issue of debentures. The syndicate guaranteed £600,000 of these debentures and in return for this finance proposed to take 8 per cent of the capital (£800,000) in shares as commission.[12]

Once again Merriman, seasoned diamond amalgamator, was pressed into service and he was supported by Roulina's agent, A. Moulle, the Manager of the Compagnie Generale. In January 1886 they began negotiations in Kimberley. They worked the local companies privately and separately in the hope that the major powers in the mines, the De Beers, Kimberley Central, Standard and Griqualand West, would accept the scheme and draw in the remaining mineowners. The De Beers directors divided in their attitudes to Unified Mines: Rudd opposed total amalgamation on account of his large commercial interests in Kimberley mining machinery and Stow was enthusiastically for the proposal in principle. But all De Beers directors objected to the high valuation in the monopoly company of the United DMC (De Beers Mine), owned by Mosenthals, who were able to exact such a price as a member of the syndicate. The other companies took little interest in the Unified. The control of the Standard and the Griqualand West had passed into the hands of men who eagerly took advantage of the Unified's uplifting effect on the share market. Robinson's controlling interest in these two companies had been ceded to the Cape of Good Hope Bank, which had sold off his shares in small parcels.[13] When the Kimberley Central, whose policy was then in the hands of Richard Atkins, would have nothing to do with the scheme, there was little chance of success for Merriman and Moulle.

The Unified failed to amalgamate the mineowners for a new rash of reasons. First, dividend-paying companies were called on to help regenerate failing companies and the former refused to accept this booster role. Secondly, while Merriman could write that the Unified would bring 'millions of foreign capital' into the Cape and be 'the salvation of the whole country',[14] Kimberley's commercial bourgeoisie, petty bourgeoisie and local mining functionaries were convinced that the wealth of the diamond mines would be taken abroad. On the basis of this feeling, the Upington ministry opposed unification and threatened to put a 33 per cent duty on diamonds.[15] Thirdly, the syndicate's enormous commission was a sore point. Although the De Beers directors appreciated the financial advantages of the syndicate, De Beers did not require any working capital, as there was £200,000 worth of blue ground on their floors which was regarded as their working capital. Rhodes and his colleagues felt that if they joined the scheme they would pay the commission for nothing. Merriman discovered that if De Beers was allowed in 'on the ground floor', that is, allowed to participate in the 'plunder' of the syndicate on the basis of its accumulated blue, the Unified scheme stood a good chance of going through.[16] But the syndicate refused to accept any additional members without the contribution of liquid capital. Fourthly, the timing of the

Unified negotiations was inopportune. The railway reached Kimberley in November 1885 and the mining companies had just begun to experience the first cannonade of cheaper commodity prices from a recovered British economy. Moreover, the consoling effects of rising share prices had begun to encourage share speculation. And finally, when it became clear that De Beers would not be accepted into the Syndicate, the Unified was sabotaged by the publication of a rival scheme of amalgamation championed by Rhodes.[17]

The failure of the Unified made it clear that the major companies had resolved on a process of partial amalgamation, rather than unification in one fell swoop. In addition, amalgamation would have to be seen to be colonial, if only in registration and promotion. The Kimberley Central and the De Beers DMC's, worth only a third of their nominal values in late 1885, had already emerged as the two most likely nuclei for a diamond mining monopoly. They set about crushing smaller companies by 'swamping them with production'.[18]

DE BEERS VS. KIMBERLEY CENTRAL

The De Beers DMC had four major advantages over the Kimberley Central in the struggle for monopoly control of the diamond mines. Most importantly De Beers had perfected an efficient system of labour control through the use of convict labour and the establishment of closed compounds; the company was more effective in the exploitation of labour than the Kimberley Central. Then, as De Beers did not suffer from major reef problems until 1885, the company did not have to cope with the financial burdens of a Mining Board debt. This contributed towards the fact that De Beers never failed to pay an annual dividend even if they were initially modest. Their third advantage lay in the skill and expertise with which the directors ran the company. Despite sharp personal antagonisms, the directors acted as a cohesive unit until wide policy differences emerged in 1886, differences which were only contained by the dominance and personal power of Rhodes. And the last advantage De Beers possessed was the stock of blue on its floors which gave the company a strong bargaining position in the amalgamation stakes.

The Kimberley Central was severely hampered by conflicts in its directorate. In marked contrast to De Beers the original Kimberley Central directors mismanaged their affairs, were inexperienced in finance and split apart during the depression under the weight of reef problems and a proposal to re-register as a British company. Once the inexperienced colonial directors (George Bottomley, Fred English, Percival Tracey) had been purged, the company was more able to cope with the transition to underground mining under the better direction of Francis Baring Gould, Charles Atkinson, Richard Atkins and Reginald Fenton. In fact, the only advantages that the Kimberley Central had over De Beers were its greater productive potentiality and its earlier development of underground mining.

The purpose of amalgamation was the pursuit of monopoly profits and the reduction of the output of diamonds, but in the amalgamation struggle the desired goal was reached on the basis of fierce competition for expanded production through a rapid development of underground mining. The competition in underground caverns determined the positions companies took up in board rooms in Kimberley, London and Paris. In late 1885 the Kimberley Central came 'on stream' with a hauling capacity of 3,000 loads per 24 hour day. At this time De Beers was hauling only 1,200 loads, each of which yielded fewer carats than a Kimberley Central load. In 1886 De Beers began to expand its output by 'picking the eyes' out of their ground. In early 1887 Inspector Rees of the Standard Bank commented:

> The De Beers Company is said to be burrowing regardless of ultimate consequences into rich veins wherever they can be found. Already there are rumours of government interference on account of the reckless disregard of human life which is displayed, and sooner or later it is said the company will have to pay dearly for its present hand to mouth policy.[19]

A similar view was expressed by Edmund de Crano, Managing Director of the Rothschilds' Exploration Company. In November 1887 he reported that the De Beers main shaft was 'not in good condition' and that its capacity was 'being much strained'.[20] The result of pushing production to the limit was the De Beers fire disaster of July 1888.[21] This was the terminal outcome of trying to increase output to keep pace, not simply with the Kimberley Central, but with Kimberley Mine as a whole.

There were differences amongst the De Beers directors over this pursuit of quantity and an open split erupted in late 1886. One group led by Frederic Stow supported a policy of firm foundations, solid investment and rapid debt liquidation, while the other group led by Cecil Rhodes pushed an adventurous policy of company take-overs by share purchases. Rhodes allied himself with Alfred Beit, whose close links with Jules Porges and Company provided Rhodes with the financial influence he required for his policy. Although Stow recognised that Beit and Porges could provide 'better financial arrangements', he felt they possessed less compelling attributes. 'They are pure speculators', he wrote, '[and] I believe it could be made worth their while to dispose of the interests to opponents if it suited.'[22] Both groups of directors aimed at the amalgamation of De Beers Mine and the ultimate fusion of all four mines, but differed over which path to take to their goal.

Alfred Beit has so often been identified with Jules Porges and Company that it is worth noting that he was an independent diamond merchant until he became a partner in the firm in December 1888. Beit first went to the Diamond Fields in 1875 as a clerk to Max Gammius, the diamond representative of the Hamburg house of David Lippert and Company. Beit soon broke free of Lipperts and established himself as an independent local diamond buyer; he also invested in diamond offices and speculated on a

Plate 8 W. P. Taylor's Share and Claim Agency in the late 1880s with brokers and notebooks to the fore. Courtesy De Beers, London.

small scale in diamond shares and claims. In 1883 he began to represent Jules Porges and Company in Kimberley and took a third share of the profits from the diamonds he shipped to London. In late 1884 he reported to his bankers that his capital was £35,000 of which £5,000 was invested in fixed property and the remainder in diamonds and diamond shares. In late 1886 he increased his capital substantially in the speculative boom in both Barberton gold mining and Kimberley diamond shares. By June 1887 he was reputed to be worth £100,000 and he had moved into the top rank of Kimberley share dealers.[23]

The influence of Beit in the Kimberley share market was largely a result of the importance of Jules Porges and Company in the European diamond share and capital markets. Not only was the firm the leading importer of Cape diamonds, but among numerous financial associates in Paris was Jules Porges' former partner, Charles Mege, who had joined the serried ranks of Parisian private bankers, and his brother who was a partner in Ephrussi and Porges, another important private bank. Jules Porges had developed from a diamond merchant into a financier constructing share syndicates, floating debentures and issuing loans.[24] Porges was first approached by Rhodes in late 1886 when De Beers wanted to complete the amalgamation of De Beers Mine. The Victoria, managed by Francis Oats and financed by J. H. Schröder and Company, refused to come to terms with De Beers and as a

213

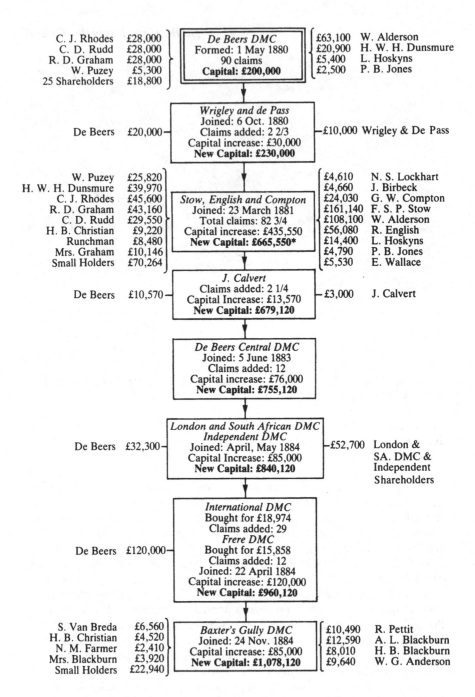

C. J. Rhodes	£28,000	*De Beers DMC*	£63,100	W. Alderson
C. D. Rudd	£28,000	Formed: 1 May 1880	£20,900	H. W. H. Dunsmure
R. D. Graham	£28,000	90 claims	£5,400	L. Hoskyns
W. Puzey	£5,300	**Capital: £200,000**	£2,500	P. B. Jones
25 Shareholders	£18,800			

De Beers	£20,000	*Wrigley and de Pass* Joined: 6 Oct. 1880 Claims added: 2 2/3 Capital increase: £30,000 **New Capital: £230,000**	£10,000	Wrigley & De Pass

W. Puzey	£25,820		£4,610	N. S. Lockhart
H. W. H. Dunsmure	£39,970		£4,660	J. Birbeck
C. J. Rhodes	£45,600	*Stow, English and Compton*	£24,030	G. W. Compton
R. D. Graham	£43,160	Joined: 23 March 1881	£161,140	F. S. P. Stow
C. D. Rudd	£29,550	Total claims: 82 3/4	£108,100	W. Alderson
H. B. Christian	£9,220	Capital increase: £435,550	£56,080	R. English
Runchman	£8,480	**New Capital: £665,550***	£14,400	L. Hoskyns
Mrs. Graham	£10,146		£4,790	P. B. Jones
Small Holders	£70,264		£5,530	E. Wallace

De Beers	£10,570	*J. Calvert* Claims added: 2 1/4 Capital Increase: £13,570 **New Capital: £679,120**	£3,000	J. Calvert

	De Beers Central DMC Joined: 5 June 1883 Claims added: 12 Capital increase: £76,000 **New Capital: £755,120**

De Beers	£32,300	*London and South African DMC* *Independent DMC* Joined: April, May 1884 Capital Increase: £85,000 **New Capital: £840,120**	£52,700	London & SA. DMC & Independent Shareholders

De Beers	£120,000	*International DMC* Bought for £18,974 Claims added: 29 *Frere DMC* Bought for £15,858 Claims added: 12 Joined: 22 April 1884 Capital increase: £120,000 **New Capital: £960,120**

S. Van Breda	£6,560	*Baxter's Gully DMC*	£10,490	R. Pettit
H. B. Christian	£4,520	Joined: 24 Nov. 1884	£12,590	A. L. Blackburn
N. M. Farmer	£2,410	Capital increase: £85,000	£8,010	H. B. Blackburn
Mrs. Blackburn	£3,920	**New Capital: £1,078,120**	£9,640	W. G. Anderson
Small Holders	£22,940			

*This was a reconstruction of the company and ownership is shown of all the new capital

Fig. 7 Capital and shareholders: De Beers DMC, March 1880 – March 1888. (Source: CAD, DOK 3/2; De Beers Company Reports; AAA, Gregory papers). Note: Shareholders are shown for capital increase alone unless otherwise stated.

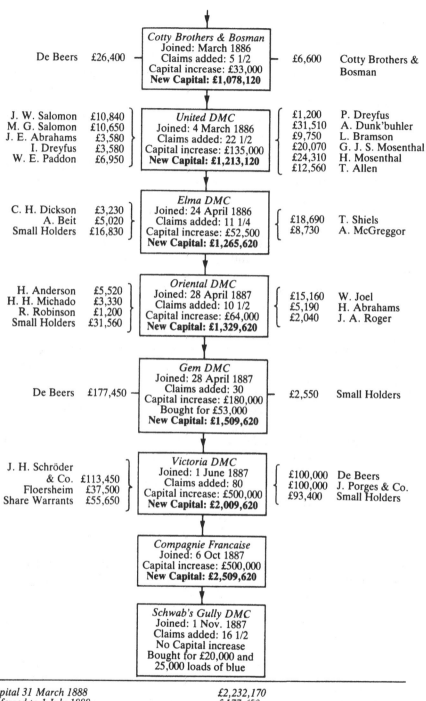

Cotty Brothers & Bosman
Joined: March 1886
Claims added: 5 1/2
Capital increase: £33,000
New Capital: £1,078,120

De Beers — £26,400 — £6,600 — Cotty Brothers & Bosman

United DMC
Joined: 4 March 1886
Claims added: 22 1/2
Capital increase: £135,000
New Capital: £1,213,120

J. W. Salomon £10,840
M. G. Salomon £10,650
J. E. Abrahams £3,580
I. Dreyfus £3,580
W. E. Paddon £6,950

£1,200 P. Dreyfus
£31,510 A. Dunk'buhler
£9,750 L. Bramson
£20,070 G. J. S. Mosenthal
£24,310 H. Mosenthal
£12,560 T. Allen

Elma DMC
Joined: 24 April 1886
Claims added: 11 1/4
Capital increase: £52,500
New Capital: £1,265,620

C. H. Dickson £3,230
A. Beit £5,020
Small Holders £16,830

£18,690 T. Shiels
£8,730 A. McGreggor

Oriental DMC
Joined: 28 April 1887
Claims added: 10 1/2
Capital increase: £64,000
New Capital: £1,329,620

H. Anderson £5,520
H. H. Michado £3,330
R. Robinson £1,200
Small Holders £31,560

£15,160 W. Joel
£5,190 H. Abrahams
£2,040 J. A. Roger

Gem DMC
Joined: 28 April 1887
Claims added: 30
Capital increase: £180,000
Bought for £53,000
New Capital: £1,509,620

De Beers £177,450 — £2,550 Small Holders

Victoria DMC
Joined: 1 June 1887
Claims added: 80
Capital increase: £500,000
New Capital: £2,009,620

J. H. Schröder & Co. £113,450
Floersheim £37,500
Share Warrants £55,650

£100,000 De Beers
£100,000 J. Porges & Co.
£93,400 Small Holders

Compagnie Francaise
Joined: 6 Oct 1887
Capital increase: £500,000
New Capital: £2,509,620

Schwab's Gully DMC
Joined: 1 Nov. 1887
Claims added: 16 1/2
No Capital increase
Bought for £20,000 and
25,000 loads of blue

Capital 31 March 1888 £2,232,170
Deferred to 1 July 1888 £177,450
£2,509,620

Investments:
10,424 £10 Griqualand West DMC shares valued at £62,688
87,744 £1 Bultfontein Consolidated shares valued at £89,444
23,470 £10 Kimberley Central shares valued at £967,856

result Rhodes decided to buy a 6,000 share stake in the 15,000 share Victoria through and on joint account with Jules Porges and Company. Once the shares had been bought and amalgamation completed in June 1887, Rhodes and his colleagues were free to turn their attention to Kimberley Mine.[25]

The greatest threat to the De Beers DMC's projected control of the industry was a unification of Kimberley Mine, followed by its flotation on the London Stock Exchange as a separate company. By August 1887 the only major competitor to the Kimberley Central in the mine was the Compagnie Française, the leading foreign company on the Diamond Fields. It had originally been promoted by Jules Porges and Company and the firm had continued to shape the policy of its board. But the Compagnie's productive performance had been particularly dismal, and unlike the other major companies, which set about increasing profits through the concentration and centralisation of capital, the Compagnie made half its profits through selling its claims.[26]

For the purpose of buying a voice in the future of Kimberley Mine, De Beers contracted to purchase the Compagnie Française in August 1887. Rhodes secured the financial backing of the Rothschilds for this take-over on the advice of Hamilton Smith and Edmund de Crano of their Exploration Company. In April 1887 on Smith's recommendation Gardner Williams had been appointed General Manager of De Beers, and he was appointed precisely because of the influence he exercised through the Exploration Company on the Rothschilds. It was Williams' assessment of the prospects of the De Beers Company that encouraged Smith and de Crano to advance De Beers against its potentially more powerful competitor. At the time the Rothschilds were heavily involved in City speculation in copper and tin, both in the commodities and in mining shares, but they approached the Compagnie Française purchase as a specific package of mining finance involving the issue and underwriting of shares.[27]

When Rhodes arrived in London in late July 1887 to negotiate the finance for and the details of the Compagnie Française contract, Stow was at first unimpressed with Rhodes' talk of amalgamation. He wanted to resign his directorship so as to be free to speculate in the market, and feeling that nothing fresh was in the wind, expressed his lack of enthusiasm for an active part in the pursuit of amalgamation.[28] But within a week he had changed his mind and was generous in his admiration of Rhodes' policy:

> Rhodes has turned up looking as fit as ever. He has just returned from Paris after his *coup d'etat*. The French Company that was is now practically in our hands and the Rothschilds have at last arranged to finance for us. We have a stay or sheet anchor to our stock ... the 'deal', as the Yankees say, has taken the Central and Hatton Garden contingents by such surprise that they go about gasping. It is such crumbs to have the almighty Kimberley crowd by the throat. My own opinion is that before you read this, a cable will announce the amalgamation of the two mines as the Central is now bound to come to us.[29]

With the Rothschilds committed to their shares, and the ownership of the Compagnie preventing the unification of Kimberley Mine, amalgamation on terms dictated by the De Beers company seemed a distinct possibility.

The financial services of the Rothschilds did not come cheap. For a £100,000 commission they guaranteed the Compagnie Française purchase price of £750,000 in cash and £200,000 in debentures. There were also additional prizes for the bankers to collect. As part of a syndicate the Rothschilds bought 50,000 £10 shares from De Beers for £15 each – this provided the £750,000 cash to pay the Compagnie Française shareholders – and arranged for the 28,000 shares of the Compagnie Française to be opted for the 50,000 new De Beers shares. The exercise of the option right was to be at the London market price on the 5 October 1887, provided that the price was not below £16 and not higher than the £20 per share. The profits between these two figures were to be divided between the syndicate and the De Beers DMC. In the end De Beers earned £100,000 from the share option, the Rothschilds took £100,000 as commission and the syndicate £150,000 for underwriting the issue of 50,000 new De Beers shares.[30]

Since 1882 the Kimberley Central had been trying to buy the Compagnie but had failed in the face of their demand to be paid in cash. The Kimberley Central could find no bank to finance such a large purchase for them. In August 1887, when De Beers contracted to buy the Compagnie, the Kimberley Central outbid De Beers with a straight £1.3 million offer in cash. Unknown to De Beers at the time, the Kimberley Central would not have been able to raise this money, as the Standard Bank had refused them a loan of £1.5 million and a £.5 million guarantee similar to that given by the Rothschilds to De Beers.

Both Stow and Rhodes, the two De Beers directors most closely involved in the Compagnie Française purchase, feared that their contract would not be ratified at the crucial shareholders' meeting in Paris on the 6 October 1887, but they differed over how to hedge their risks in the take-over bid. Under pressure from Lord Rothschild, Stow implored Rhodes to settle the ultimate amalgamation with the Central before the Compagnie Française meeting. 'My dear Stow', wrote Rhodes on ship travelling back to Cape Town in September 1887:

> you must perceive that it is entirely to Rothschild's interest to at all hasards (sic) secure the French contract and obtain immediate settlement with Central, as without any risk his shares would go to £25 and he would make half a million without having risked a penny ... he does not care to wait for our gaining our intrinsic value as he no doubt intends to realise on a profit he has already. It is the difference between a speculator's view and an investor's.[31]

Instead, Rhodes wanted Stow to set up a syndicate to buy 9,000 Compagnie Française shares, but the Rothschilds were unwilling to buy shares at their current high prices and Jules Porges had already formed a syndicate with his cousin, Rudolph Kann, the private Parisian banker, and they were making the best of the competition between De Beers and the Kimberley Central

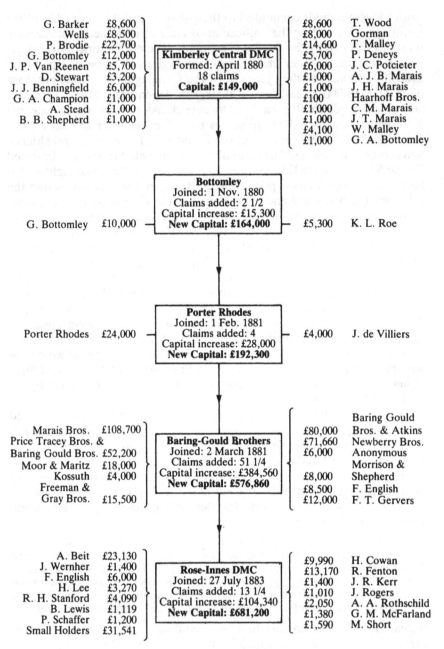

Fig. 8 Capital and shareholders: Kimberley Central DMC, April 1880 – March 1888. (Source: CAD, DOK 3/5 Trust Deeds, AAA, Gregory papers). Note: Shareholders are shown for capital increase alone unless otherwise stated.

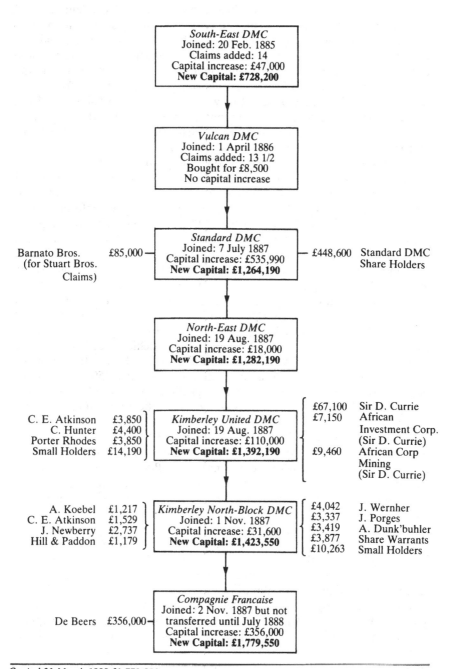

South-East DMC
Joined: 20 Feb. 1885
Claims added: 14
Capital increase: £47,000
New Capital: £728,200

Vulcan DMC
Joined: 1 April 1886
Claims added: 13 1/2
Bought for £8,500
No capital increase

Barnato Bros.
(for Stuart Bros.
Claims)   £85,000 —

Standard DMC
Joined: 7 July 1887
Capital increase: £535,990
New Capital: £1,264,190

— £448,600   Standard DMC
Share Holders

North-East DMC
Joined: 19 Aug. 1887
Capital increase: £18,000
New Capital: £1,282,190

C. E. Atkinson   £3,850
C. Hunter   £4,400
Porter Rhodes   £3,850
Small Holders   £14,190

Kimberley United DMC
Joined: 19 Aug. 1887
Capital increase: £110,000
New Capital: £1,392,190

£67,100   Sir D. Currie
£7,150   African
Investment Corp.
(Sir D. Currie)
£9,460   African Corp
Mining
(Sir D. Currie)

A. Koebel   £1,217
C. E. Atkinson   £1,529
J. Newberry   £2,737
Hill & Paddon   £1,179

Kimberley North-Block DMC
Joined: 1 Nov. 1887
Capital increase: £31,600
New Capital: £1,423,550

£4,042   J. Wernher
£3,337   J. Porges
£3,419   A. Dunk'buhler
£3,877   Share Warrants
£10,263   Small Holders

De Beers   £356,000 —

Compagnie Francaise
Joined: 2 Nov. 1887 but not
transferred until July 1888
Capital increase: £356,000
New Capital: £1,779,550

Capital 31 March 1888 £1,779,550

for Compagnie shares. While Ludwig Lippert, of the Norddeutsche and Commerz und Diskonto banks of Hamburg, was buying shares and proxies for De Beers on the continent – the Rothschilds were collecting proxies in London for the Paris meeting – Charles Schwabacher, Barney Barnato and Otto Staib, a director of the Compagnie were doing the same for the Kimberley Central.[32] So fierce was this competition that £20 Compagnie shares went as high as £53 and Stow was forced to buy 3,500 shares from Porges at this price to gain his influence in favour of De Beers. 'Porges aimed his grimaces against you', Stow wrote to Rhodes, 'and afterwards in a patronizing way said he did not wish to quarrel with you as you might be of use to him in the Colony . . . What sublime impertinence'.[33]

Despite Rhodes' misgivings about the move, a week before the crucial meeting in Paris he was forced to conclude the resale of the Compagnie to the Kimberley Central. The deal was struck just as Lippert informed Stow that they controlled 16,000 out of the 28,000 Compagnie shares. Even this majority was not an adequate safeguard to the complex financial guarantee that the Rothschilds had arranged for the take-over. So, De Beers bought off Central opposition in Paris before the ratification meeting by contracting to re-sell the Compagnie to the Central for £300,000 in cash and 35,600 £10 shares in the Kimberley company. Rather than the myth of the Trojan Horse, this was the price De Beers had to pay to avoid running the risk of losing Rothschilds financial support over the impending option of shares and in the future amalgamation struggle, as Rothschild sales in the market could at any time depress the value of De Beers shares. In return for Rhodes' capitulation the Rothschilds agreed to finance a £500,000 loan for the Kimberley Central, which both signalled their belief in eventual amalgamation and provided some influence over the affairs of the Kimberley company.[34]

With the Kimberley Mine under one command it was the general opinion that the Central would soon acquire the De Beers DMC. The reasons for this view were spelt out by Barney Barnato, an influential shareholder in the Central, at a Special Meeting of the company. He pointed out that the purchase of the Compagnie from De Beers had cost the Central £1.068 million (35,600 Centrals at £300) whereas they had offered £2.1 million, (70,000 Centrals at £300). While he omitted the £300,000 cash they had to pay De Beers, he did go on to make the crucial point that a united Kimberley Mine would produce diamonds worth £1.5 million a year. This output would mean an annual profit of £.9 million which was a 50 per cent return on the company's capital of just under £1.8 million.[35]

It was this prospect that frightened De Beers and led to extended negotiations with Central directors over the terms of fusion. Barney Barnato was one of the most influential of the men who controlled the policy of the Central. In 1887 his firm, Barnato Brothers, had become the largest single holder of diamond scrip in Kimberley after the Barnato DMC and their rich Stuart claims were absorbed by the Standard, which in July

1887 was in turn absorbed by the Kimberley Central.[36] The firm then devoted its substantial resources – with the exception of £200,000 invested in Consols and £40,000 in property in London's East End – to the purchase of both Central and De Beers shares.[37] In October 1887 the commanding position the firm had built up was acknowledged by Rhodes in a letter to Stow written soon after the re-sale of the Compagnie:

> The great comfort I feel now is that the goal is reached. Barnato who has 8,000 De Beers and 1,500 one hundred Centrals or roughly £600,000 of parent stock [3.5 million] is working in everything with me and has given his pledge to go to the end with me and B. Gould though a weak man has made up his mind to go with the tide. Whatever Porges may be I feel for self interest alone Beit has burnt his boats and would sooner quarrel with his home firm than sell me and he is working heartily for the same object. It rests with you now at home to do everything with Mosenthal to amalgamate the balance of home companies on Griqualand West in Dutoitspan and French and d'Esterre in Bultfontein . . . We must have the four mines and I will allow no foreign vulture to step in at the end and form a separate mine on the Stock Exchange apart from us to get a flotation on our name and again sell the English public.[38]

The rough plan that Rhodes outlined in this letter changed in some details over the following nine months – the amount of time he gave himself to see it through – but it was an accurate general forecast. Barnato did throw in his lot well before the legendary struggle and Beit continued to meet opposition from Jules Porges and Company, while it was Baring Gould who changed his position and resolved to oppose Rhodes' scheme for amalgamation.

Throughout October Rhodes and Beit met frequently with Barnato and Baring Gould to discuss the amalgamation of the mines. They reached an agreement that Central and De Beers would be the only final stock and that the 'keys of Dutoitspan and Bultfontein must be gained' before the final fusion.[39] There was agreement on little else and Rhodes and Beit made a contingency plan to buy another one-fifth of Central stock. Rhodes explained the options to Stow:

> The final position of mines will be parent stock, if we do not buy further Centrals, £4,500,000 with two leases of Dutoitspan and Bultfontein . . . [minus the Bultfontein Mining Company] costing about £250,000 per annum. I believe the mines will pay 10 per cent on twenty millions. If we buy out another 356,000 Centrals there will be a debenture debt of £1,000,000 for this and £400,000 for Kimberley and say £400,000 for De Beers old loans. But the capital stock will be reduced by the first amount and the present 1/5 we hold in K. mine which we might cancel leaving, as I said before, about 3,500,000. Now the public will never think about the debenture debt and I believe the parent stock of £3,500,000 would be worth 5 times or thereabouts making a De Beers worth £50 . . . Our mine output is capitalized at 2,009,620 and theirs at 1,785,000 and I believe prices will approximate to near these figures or at any rate to mine for mine . . . I propose to call new title the 'De Beers and South African Diamond Mines Ltd.' and only alter two clauses (one) business of company to include right to purchase scrip of other companies; 2nd increased borrowing powers. However, it may all come to nought as within a

221

fortnight I might settle with Central without going in for this plan of buying their shares.[40]

Sometime in early November, Baring Gould finally refused to accept the equal value of both mines as a basis for amalgamation, believing in the greater intrinsic value of Kimberley Mine.[41] Consequently after lengthy deliberations Rhodes and Beit finally decided on 22 November that De Beers should buy another fifth of the Central,[42] but a week later Rhodes wanted to buy De Beers shares as well. He wanted this kept secret 'as he might change his mind as to which shares it would be best to purchase'.[43] It was at this time that Rhodes induced Barnato to desert the Central, leaving Baring Gould to defend the interests of the great majority of small shareholders. In January 1888 the Standard Bank Inspector reported that 'thanks to the "squaring" of B. I. Barnato' the Kimberley Central was 'on the point of being absorbed against their will by the De Beers Company'.[44]

The 'squaring' of Barnato was secret and expensive. The legend of the struggle between Rhodes and Barnato gives great prominence to Barnato's election to Parliament and to the Kimberley Club in 1888 as the price that Rhodes paid for Barnato's capitulation. Election to Parliament and Club were seals of respectability and essential window-dressing for the formation of the monopoly company, De Beers Consolidated Mines, in March 1888. But the 'squaring' of Barnato lay elsewhere. De Crano of the Rothschilds' Exploration Company was told that 'those directors who furnish money to promote consolidation shall ultimately have the handling of the diamonds',[45] and this was an important factor weighing in favour of the co-operation of both Beit and Barnato with the De Beers DMC. In addition, when De Beers decided to buy Central stock in November 1887, they used the excellent services of both diamond merchants in London, Paris and Kimberley. Barnato and Beit bought from whomever was in the market, notably Sir Donald Currie and Edward Tarry. There was no share struggle between Rhodes and Barnato: Barnato was buying shares for De Beers.[46]

The 'squaring' of Barnato went even further than this. Barnato did not only buy for De Beers; he sold to De Beers as well and at prices well above the going market rate. In January 1888 he sold 11,333 £10 Centrals for £750,000, each share realising the price of £66.[47] In the market at Kimberley prices never went that high (see Table 11). Exactly how much money Barnato made out of this pre-amalgamation speculation is impossible to know. He made the claim to the Manager of the Standard Bank in Kimberley that he had realised £750 for each of his £100 Centrals, but even so, when De Beers Consolidated Mines was formed in March 1888, he owned nearly one-fifth of both Central and De Beers stock.[48]

Barnato not only made a lot of money prior to amalgamation, but he was tempted with the offer of a perpetual fortune after monopoly had been

Table 11 *Share prices, Kimberley Central and De Beers DMCs, Kimberley, Jan.–June 1888*[49]

1888	Central	De Beers
1 January	£38	£27
1 February	£46	£35
1 March	£48	£36
1 April	£42	£47
1 May	£40	£38 1/2
1 June	£34	£32 1/2
30 June	£31 1/2	£26 3/4

established as one of the five Life Governors of De Beers Consolidated. The Life Governors were one of the most controversial aspects of the new company. Originally it was proposed that the Life Governors were to take all the profit after a 30 per cent dividend had been distributed to share-holders. These terms were haggled over and under the influence of Lord Rothschild the distribution was raised to 36 per cent before the Governors took the remainder. There were some who believed that the system of Governors was open to abuse. The *Economist* wrote that 'the principle of paying directors by results' was 'impolitic and objectionable' at all times, for the interests of the directors would be 'so as to manipulate matters as to be able to pay a dividend which will entitle them to take their fees'.[50] But Rhodes disagreed. In his view the object of the Governors was to have men with a large stake in the company to conserve and advance its interests.[51] Barnato certainly came to believe this and emphasised that he was an investor and not a speculator in De Beers. He considered it the 'finest property in the world' and intended to keep 'the major portion' of his fortune in De Beers stock. He wrote to Lord Rothschild:

> If I had been but a temporary speculator I should long ago have agreed to the very suggestive plan for the flotation of Kimberley Mine on the London Stock Exchange and I feel sure that for an immediate profit it would have been a much more remunerative operation.[52]

The rich rewards of the office of Life Governor were intended to entice Barnato away from such a 'suggestive plan'.

In March 1888, when De Beers Consolidated Mines was formed to absorb both the Central and De Beers DMCs, it controlled over 100,000 Central shares. De Beers directly owned only 59,000 of these Centrals; they included the 35,600 shares from the Compagnie purchase and 23,470 bought during the amalgamation struggle. De Beers spent £967,856 on these shares and had to rely on a number of different sources for finance. Rhodes asked N. M. Rothschild and Sons for £300,000 to buy diamond shares on joint account, but when they declined Rhodes went elsewhere.

Table 12 *Market value, Kimberley Mines, London, March 1888*

Company	Paid-up Capital	Market Value
De Beers	£2,510,000	£10,250,000
Kimberley Central	£1,422,950	£ 5,834,095
Griqualand West	£1,075,000	£ 1,182,500
Anglo-African	£1,010,160	£ 475,000
New Consolidated	£ 605,000	£ 755,000
South African	£ 136,000	£ 136,000
New Jagersfontein	£ 129,000	£ 322,500
Bultfontein	£ 200,000	£ 700,000
Dortsfontein	£ 175,000	£ 200,000
Britannia	£ 105,000	£ 90,000
United	£ 55,000	£ 200,000
Small mines	£ 250,000	£ 500,000
London and South African Exploration	£ 50,000	£ 1,800,000
Total	£7,723,110	£22,445,095

[*The Statist*, 10 March 1888, 275]

He borrowed £635,728 from the local banks and over £300,000 from Jules Porges and Company. Rhodes also encouraged other concerns in whose financial policies he had a say to invest in diamond shares. Gold Fields of South Africa put £141,907 into both Centrals and De Beers; the New Jagersfontein DMC spent £216,000 on Central shares.[53]

In early 1888 the De Beers attempt to take-over the Central by share purchases dominated the mining markets in Kimberley and London. In Kimberley the largest share-broker, Tallerman and Ansell, had a monthly turnover of £1 million and £100 was a poor day's profit for them.[54] In London the 'bulls' ruled in that part of the Stock Exchange called the 'diamond diggings'. Stock jobbers were attracted from other markets, but for the most part a group of 40 or 50 men controlled the speculation. 'They are buckram Titans, wrote the *Statist*, 'carrying on their shoulders a fool's paradise'.[55] In March 1888 the market value of the mines soared to nearly £23 million (see Table 12). While the asking price of the Exploration Company at 36 times its nominal capitalisation was exceptional in any boom, the overall market value of the mines was remarkable when it is remembered that the share in most demand, the £10 De Beers, which reached £47, had been worth only £3 10s in January 1885.

The colossal inflation in share prices was dangerous and no more so than to the Colonial banks, which had lent vast sums of money against the security scrip. They feared a deliberate attempt to bear shares:

It was only last week [first week of February] that Beit and Barnato, assisted by their London firms, attempted to bear De Beers' shares, but Van Beek[56] had previously made arrangements with a German syndicate and on his cable to them every share thrown on the market was bought up and the bear was defeated. Powerful French syndicates would also step in if a serious fall were anticipated.[57]

In April the bears were successful and a panic set in. Rhodes publicly blamed the banks for withdrawing credit and privately pointed his finger at the diamond merchant, Harry Mosenthal. The banks denied any instrumental role and privately explained the collapse through the detrimental impact of Rhodes' speech to the De Beers Mining Company on 31 March 1888, in which he threatened to subdue his opponents by collapsing the price of diamonds to 14s a carat.[58] 'I had no idea it was so bad', wrote Herman Eckstein, 'Porges and others have come forward so well and this must break the back of the bear movement'.[59] But shares continued to plummet and Mosenthals, Porges, Barnato and Rothschilds mopped up shares at low prices in the slump after the boom.[60]

After March 1888 De Beers stopped buying Central shares and negotiated for the option of the substantial minority of Central shares that they did not control into the De Beers Consolidated. Baring Gould opposed the terms of option – equal value of the two mines – and the offer of a Life Governorship to him was intended to overcome his opposition, but he refused to betray his shareholders in the way Barnato had done. Baring Gould held out until October 1888, when he won a better deal for Central shareholders in the fusion of the two mines.[61] As a result of his commitment to his company and his obstruction of De Beers, he was denied the profits of the fifth Life Governorship by Rhodes, Beit and Barnato.[62] Even after Baring Gould agreed to settle a small minority of Central shareholders managed to obstruct unification by going to law. Consequently, the Central was forbidden to merge with De Beers Consolidated – which was not a similar diamond mining company because of the powers it assumed in its Trust Deed – and in February 1889 the Central was put into liquidation. In any case the vast majority of shareholders had opted their shares into De Beers Consolidated. On the 28 September 1889 the Central liquidators deposited a cheque for their credit on De Beers Consolidated for £5,338,650 and on the same day drew in favour of De Beers for £5,326,260 representing the largest financial transaction in the history of the Cape. The share capital of De Beers stood at £3.95 million with an additional £4.5 million in debentures. A practical monopoly of the four mines was only achieved in 1891 at a total cost of £14.5 million. De Beers Consolidated, the company that Rhodes predicted would be worth 'the balance of Africa', had asserted its control of the commanding heights of the Cape economy.[63]

THE EFFECTS OF MONOPOLY

The most immediate effect of monopoly was unemployment both in the Amsterdam cutting industry and in Kimberley. Between 1888 and 1889 the producers increased the price of diamonds by 50 per cent, but the price the manufacturers paid for rough stones was doubled. The consequence was that thousands of Dutch diamond workers in the Amsterdam cutting industry were the casualties of a price war between rough and cut merchants in London and Paris. In Kimberley the position was similar. It was exacerbated by the virtual closure of Dutoitspan and Bultfontein Mines. Between 1887 and 1890 the number of Europeans, including contractors, employed in the mines fell by 25 per cent and the number of Africans by 50 per cent. By 1890 this contraction in the work force represented a wage saving of £623,648 to De Beers Consolidated.[64]

Unemployment and poverty on the Diamond Fields amongst Europeans became so embarassing to Cecil Rhodes, who became Cape Prime Minister in 1890, that he established a Parliamentary Select Committee to investigate and defuse the situation. As Merriman and Barnato were leading members of the Committee, it was not surprising that a majority report concluded that 'distress and poverty have arisen from natural causes, so they must be left to natural remedies'.[65] They also produced figures to show that the diamond industry employed more men in 1890 than in 1887 (the figures included the river diggings) and argued that even though closed compounds were bad for small retailers, this disadvantage was far outweighed by the benefits to Africans from a 'moral and economic point of view'.[66] There was, however, a minority report made by Sir Thomas Upington and Gordon Sprigg which contradicted the majority report on almost every finding. The minority report did not take the view that poverty was the result of natural causes and argued for state intervention to remedy the effects of monopoly: 'the state is fairly entitled to interfere when the action of that corporation [De Beers Consolidated] is calculated to be detrimental to the common weal'.[67] The report put forward a number of specific measures to alleviate the distress, such as the freedom to wash debris and the compulsory working of the poorer mines of Bultfontein and Dutoitspan.

Some of these measures were being demanded by a new organisation on the Diamond Fields called the Knights of Labour. They were prominent in the public agitation to have the newly-discovered mine at Wesselton thrown open to the public. While Rhodes' government stalled over the issue, the mine was bought by De Beers. The Knights 'impeached' Barnato and Rhodes for 'abuse of their public power and place to further and promote their private interest'.[68] In turn they were labelled 'socialists' by the mineowners for they organised skilled and unskilled Europeans against the 'forces of Capital and Monopoly, or the insidious attack of cheap labour competition'.[69] The Knights were one among a number of groups, which included the Dutch Reformed Church, working to find a solution to or to alleviate unemployment.

Kimberley became a company town under the monopoly control of De Beers Consolidated Mines. But there was one powerful force they did not control. It could not be compounded and neither could it be driven away to the Rand. The London and South African Exploration Company, the owner of the Dutoitspan and Bultfontein mine estate, was undoubtedly the most prosperous company in Kimberley. But the De Beers monopoly had a disastrous effect on landed property. Between 1890 and 1892 land fell 200 to 300 per cent in market value.[70] The company fought a rear-guard action against De Beers, trying to keep open the mines and a rump of a local economy. The London Company had little to thank Rhodes for:

> Mr Rhodes remember Kimberley in gratitude. Remember your struggles at De Beers. Remember what the diamond fields have done for you, and your greater and wider projects. Do not forget the town which has made you Prime Minister: the town which, even for the wealth that has created, primarily, your pre-eminence, is proud of your Napoleonic enterprise, yet would prefer that you had confined your ambitions to, let us say, Paris rather than Moscow.[71]

CONCLUSION

There was, indeed, a struggle between Rhodes and Barnato and the burning of midnight oil in a corrugated iron cottage, but the struggle was not over the control of the mines but over the powers to be given to De Beers Consolidated. Rhodes wanted the monopoly to be the basis for a colonial exploration and investment company with a wide range of political powers; Barnato had to be persuaded that this grand scheme could be built on the profits of diamond mining. The proposal for Life Governors appealed to him and he made it a touchstone of his co-operation in the new venture. So why then has the legend persisted so long? The answer lies in the appeal of the story of the share struggle between Barnato and Rhodes; De Beers directors could hardly tell their shareholders that the company was heavily in debt to bankers and debenture holders because they had been forced to bribe Barnato to join them. And this underlines the key point: the Central came out of the amalgamation struggle with a much better deal than De Beers. In the end the greater productive potentiality of the Kimberley Mine forced a compromise on Rhodes that he had tried to avoid when he bought the Compagnie Française. This fact has been forgotten in the subsequent visible success of De Beers. But as they paid heavily for their 'sheet anchor' in Rothschilds they also paid heavily for the honour of monopolising the mines. So, it is fundamentally inaccurate to say, as Professor Lewsen has recently, that Barnato 'lost his famous duel with Rhodes for control of the diamond industry'.[72] If anybody laughed all the way to the bank at the time it was Barnato Brothers and thereafter the firm made handsome profits as a major shareholder and leading member of the Diamond Syndicate.

Appendix Table 1 The average daily number of diamond mine workers, white and black, with average weekly wages, 1881–99

		Kimberley	De Beers	Dutoitspan	Bultfontein	Total
1881	w.	800 £5–7.5	300 n.d.	1000 £5–8	1000 £5–8	3100
	b.	3000 £1 15s	2000 n.d.	8000 £1 5s	4000 £1 5s	17000
1882	w.	700 £5–7.5	300 £4.6–8	n.d. £5–8	n.d. £5–8	–
	b.	4000 £1 10s	2000 £1 5s	n.d. £1 10s	n.d. £1 10s	–
1883	w.	400 £5–8	200 £4.5–8	320 £4.5–6.5	220 £4.5–6.5	1140
	b.	2000 £1 10s	1260 £1 10s	2800 £1 5s	2300 £1 5s	8360
1884	w.	300 £4.5–7	250 £4.5–6	400 £4–6	260 £4–6	1210
	b.	1500 £1 5s	1700 £1 5s	3300 £1 5s	2500 £1 5s	9000
1885	w.	450 £4.25–6.5	320 £3.75–6	770 £4–6	360 £4–6	1900
	b.	1500 £1	1730 £1	4500 15s	3600 15s	11330
1886	w.	430 £5.8–6.25	200 £5.6–6.5	590 £4.3–5	290 £3–6.25	1510
	b.	2000 £1 5s	2400 £1	4030 18s	2530 19s	10960
1887	w.	740 £4–6.25	500 £4.75–6.5	420 £4.25–6.25	260 £4–6	1920
	b.	2500 £1 10s	3000 £1 5s	3200 £1	2600 £1	11300
1888	w.	560 £5–6.5	480 £5–7	380 £4–6.25	260 £4–6.25	1680
	b.	2000 £1 10s	2500 £1	2500 18s	2600 18s	9600
1889	w.	337 £4.5–6.25	550 £5–6.25	297 £4.25–6	88 £4.5–7	1272
	b.	2300 £1 10s	2160 £1 10s	1852 18s 2d	518 18s	6830
1890	w.	398 £4–7	672 £3.5–7	271 £2.75–6	68 £2.75–6	1409
	b.	1402 32s	2474 29s 6d	1498 18s–25s	466 18s–25s	5840
1891	w.	483 £4–6.5	791 £4–6.5	193 £3.5–6	125 £3.5–6	1592
	b.	1648 24s	3073 24s	1153 16s–25s	898 19s	6772
1892	w.	505 £4–6.5	922 £4–6.5	96 £3.25–6	186 £3.5–5	1709
	b.	1804 21s	3910 21s	654 16s	933 16s.5	7301
1893	w.	439 £3.5–6	1042 £3.5–6	45 £3.5–6	217 £3.5–5	1743
	b.	2456 21s	4115 21s	82 20s	1074 17s	7727
1894	w.	418 do.	1000† do.	72 £3–6	63 £3–6	1553
	b.	1883 do.	3360† do.	290 17s	259 18s	5792
1895	w.	368 do.	971 do.	87 £4–6	167 £3.5–6	1593
	b.	1878 do.	3573 do.	482 19s 6d	839 17s 6d	6772
1896	w.	391 do.	1003 do.	65 £3.5–6	281 do.	1740
	b.	1791 do.	3537 do.	387 20s	1044 20s	6759
1897	w.	378 do.	1119 do.	14 do.	135 do.	1646
	b.	1908 do.	4078 do.	46 do.	910 18s	6942
1898	w.	384 do.	1154 do.	14 do.	101 £4–6	1653
	b.	2116 do.	5058 do.	43 do.	717 20s	7934
1899	w.	369 do.	1123 do.	29 do.	89 do.	1610
	b.	2022 do.	5222 do.	108 do.	670 do.	8022

Source: Cape Statistical Registers.

NOTE: The wage for black workers includes lodging; the lowest wage for white workers was for overseers and the highest for mechanics.

† One third of De Beers workers from 1894–1899 were employed at workshops jointly for Kimberley, De Beers and Premier Mines.

n.d. no data

228

Appendix Table 2 Non-colonial DMCs formed in 1881, in all mines, showing vendors' and invested capital, the number of claims and their average value, and the fixed and circulating portions of capital

	Capital			Claims		Capital	
	Total £	Vendors' £	Invested £	Number	Av. val. £	Fixed £	Circulating £
1. Compagnie Francaise	560,000	522,320	37,680	94	5,000	522,320	37,680
2. North Block	110,900	30,900	80,000	5.7	16,060	90,900	20,000
Kimberley Total	*670,900*	*553,220*	*117,680*	*99.7*	*10,530*	*613,220*	*57,680*
3. London & S. African	194,000	144,000	50,000	96	1,500	144,000	50,000
4. Victoria	300,600	175,600	125,000	96.4	2,292	220,000	80,600
De Beers Total	*494,600*	*319,600*	*175,000*	*192.4*	*1,896*	*364,000*	*130,600*
5. African	100,000	100,000	–	34	1,000	34,250	65,750
6. Anglo-African	650,000	216,110	433,890	111	5,010	556,110	93,890
7. Cape of Good Hope	136,350	45,350	91,000	49	2,333	114,350	22,000
8. Kimberley	200,000	200,000	–	46	1,372	63,120	136,880
9. Orion	250,000	249,930	70	45	5,000	225,000	25,000
10. Central Mining	100,000	n.d.	n.d.	128	n.d.	n.d.	n.d.
11. Anglo-French	326,000	n.d.	n.d.	80	n.d.	n.d.	n.d.
12. Gordon	100,000	77,500	22,500	42	n.d.	n.d.	n.d.
Du'pan Total	*1,862,350*	*888,890*	*547,460*	*535*	*2,943*	*992,830*	*343,520*

Appendix Table 2 (*cont.*)

	Capital			Claims		Capital	
	Total £	Vendors' £	Invested £	Number	Av. val. £	Fixed £	Circulating £
13. Adamant	80,000	66,000	14,000	36	1,833	66,000	14,000
14. Bultfontein Homestead	35,000	–	35,000	44	409	18,000	17,000
15. Bultfontein Mining	110,000	80,000	30,000	89.5	793	71,000	39,000
Bultfontein Total	*225,000*	*146,000*	*79,000*	*169.5*	*1,011*	*155,000*	*70,000*
Total	3,252,850	1,907,710*	919,140*	996.5	3,550	2,125,050†	601,800†
%	100	67*	33*			78†	22†

Sources: PRO, BT 31; SBA; Company Reports.
Note: Fixed capital is the amount a company paid for its claims; circulating capital is the sum set aside for plant, machinery, working expenses and reserve (called or uncalled)
*Total or % for 13 out of 15 companies. †Total or % for 12 out of 15 companies.
n.d. no data

Appendix Table 3 Colonial DMCs formed in 1881, in Kimberley Mine, showing vendors' and invested capital, the number of claims and their average value, and the fixed and circulating portions of capital

	Capital			Claims		Capital	
	Total £	Vendors' £	Invested £	Number	Av. val. £	Fixed £	Circulating £
1. Barnato	115,000	92,500	22,500	4	25,000	100,000	15,000
2. Beaconsfield	135,000	101,880	33,120	12	10,000	120,000	15,000
3. British	106,300	68,800	37,500	11	9,000	99,000	7,300
4. Cape	330,000	271,630	58,370	42.75	6,310	269,784	60,216
5. Gem	140,000	120,000	20,000	6.75	19,703	133,000	7,000
6. Central	576,680	576,680	–	75.75	7,612	576,860	56,290
7. North East	90,000	77,500	12,500	7	11,142	78,000	12,000
8. Octahedron	66,500	48,830	17,670	19	2,775	52,766	13,734
9. Rose-Innes	207,750	169,850	37,900	19	10,466	198,858	8,892
10. South East	120,000	77,500	42,500	13	8,284	107,700	12,300
11. Standard	343,600	268,000	75,000	35	9,086	318,000	25,600
12. Vulcan	82,400	72,400	10,000	13	5,530	71,900	10,500
Total	2,313,230	1,946,170	367,060	258.25	10,409	2,125,868	187,542*
%	100	84	16			92	8

Sources: Prospectuses of Diamond Mining and Other Companies, Kimberley 1881; SBA; Company Reports.
Note: Fixed Capital is the amount a company paid for its claims; circulating capital is the sum set aside for plant, machinery, working expenses and reserve (called or uncalled).
*Total excludes Kimberley Central's £56,290 for plant, which was not included in capital.

Appendix Table 4 Colonial DMCs formed in 1881, in De Beers Mine, showing vendors' and invested capital, the number of claims and their average value, and the fixed and circulating portions of capital

	Capital			Claims		Capital	
	Total £	Vendors' £	Invested £	Number	Av. val. £	Fixed £	Circulating £
1. Baxter's Gully	80,000	62,000	18,000	14	n.d.	n.d.	n.d.
2. Birbeck	88,000	70,000	18,000	21	n.d.	n.d.	n.d.
3. De Beers	665,000	665,000	10,000	97.5	6,621	645,550	20,000
4. De Beers Central	76,000	64,000	12,000	13	5,076	66,000	10,000
5. Elma	105,000	90,000	15,000	11.25	8,888	100,000	5,000
6. Eagle	80,000	52,500	27,500	14.5	4,827	70,000	10,000
7. Frere	109,000	49,000	60,000	16.75	5,701	95,500	13,500
8. Independent	40,000	33,000	7,000	5.5	6,000	33,000	7,000
9. International	131,700	84,200	45,500	29.25	3,700	111,650	20,050
10. Oriental	98,680	78,680	20,000	16	5,500	84,680	14,000
11. Perseverence	50,000	33,340	16,660	17	2,000	34,000	16,000
12. Petree	91,000	78,500	12,500	26	3,019	78,500	12,500
13. Pleiades	80,000	80,000	–	25	2,000	50,133	29,867
14. Schwab's Gully	94,000	94,000	–	10.5	8,428	88,500	5,500
Total	1,788,380	1,524,220	264,160	317.25	5,147	1,457,513*	163,417*
%	100	85	15			90*	10*

Sources: Prospectuses of Diamond Mining and Other Companies, Kimberley, 1881; SBA; Company Reports.
Note: Fixed capital is the amount a company paid for its claims; circulating capital is the sum set aside for plant, machinery, working expenses and reserve (called or uncalled).
*Total or % for 12 out of 14 companies.
n.d. no data

Appendix Table 5 Colonial DMCs formed in 1881, in Dutoitspan Mine, showing vendors' and invested capital, the number of claims and their average value, and the fixed and circulating portions of capital

	Capital			Claims		Capital		
	Total £	Vendors' £	Invested £	Number	Av. val. £	Fixed £	Circulating £	
1. Adamanta	58,500	25,500	33,000	15	3,000	45,000	13,500	
2. Britannia	155,000	130,000	25,000	45	3,088	139,000	16,000	
3. British	58,500	29,250	29,250	15	3,000	45,000	12,500	
4. Caledonian	20,000	10,000	10,000	10	1,500	15,000	5,000	
5. Consolidated	60,000	45,700	14,300	54	8,000	43,200	16,800	
6. Dutoitspan	106,000	70,670	35,330	86	1,000	86,000	20,000	
7. Eldorado	62,900	35,400	27,500	50	928	46,400	16,500	
8. European	105,000	60,000	45,000	31	3,000	93,000	12,000	
9. Fry's Gully	125,000	117,000	8,000	62	1,650	102,300	22,700	
10. Globe	68,000	40,000	28,000	38	1,500	57,000	11,000	
11. Griqualand West	283,000	188,680	94,320	131	2,000	262,000	15,000	
12. Hercules	93,000	48,000	45,000	26	3,000	78,000	15,000	
13. Ne Plus Ultra	85,000	51,450	33,550	25.25	3,059	77,250	7,750	
14. Royal	45,000	30,000	15,000	33	1,000	33,000	12,000	
15. Standard	65,000	30,000	35,000	29	1,750	50,750	14,250	
16. Victoria	60,000	40,000	20,000	31	1,600	49,600	10,400	
Total	1,449,900	951,650	498,250	681.25	2,442	1,222,500	227,400	
%	100	66	34			84	16	

Sources: Prospectuses of Diamond Mining and Other Companies, Kimberley, 1881; SBA; Company Reports.
Note: Fixed Capital is the amount a company paid for its claims; circulating capital is the sum set aside for plant, machinery, working expenses and reserve (called or uncalled).

Appendix Table 6 Colonial DMCs formed in 1881, in Bultfontein Mine, showing vendors' and invested capital, the number of claims and their average value, and the fixed and circulating portions of capital

	Capital			Claims		Capital	
	Total £	Vendors' £	Invested £	Number	Av. val. £	Fixed £	Circulating £
1. Aegis	45,000	30,000	15,000	27.5	1,200	33,000	12,000
2. Alliance	50,000	35,000	15,000	42	1,000	42,000	8,000
3. Atlas	45,000	15,000	30,000	33	910	30,000	15,000
4. Bultfontein Central	72,500	n.d.	n.d.	n.d.	n.d.	n.d.	n.d.
5. Bultfontein Colonial	70,000	35,000	35,000	51	1,000	51,000	19,000
6. Cosmopolitan	30,000	15,000	15,000	26.5	754	20,000	10,000
7. Crown	50,000	25,000	25,000	30	1,250	37,500	12,500
8. Eclipse	55,000	27,500	27,500	36	1,250	45,000	10,000
9. Equitable	20,000	15,000	5,000	12	1,250	15,000	5,000
10. Excelsior	53,000	53,000	–	35	1,100	38,500	14,500
11. French & d'Esterre	115,600	52,900	62,700	88	1,075	94,600	21,000
12. Lilienstein	28,000	13,000	15,000	18	1,200	21,600	6,400
13. Pullinger	130,500	87,500	43,000	79	1,433	113,250	17,250
14. Union	40,000	40,000	–	36	1,000	36,000	4,000
Total	804,600	443,900	288,200	514	1,149	577,450	154,650
%	100	61	39			79	21

Sources: Prospectuses of Diamond Mining and Other Companies, Kimberley, 1881; SBA; Company Reports.
Note: Fixed Capital is the amount a company paid for its claims; circulating capital is the sum set aside for plant, machinery, working expenses and reserve (called or uncalled).
*Total or % for 13 out of 14 companies.
n.d. no data.

Appendix Table 7 DMCs, with capital, operating on and liquidated before 1 Jan. 1886

Operating on 1 Jan. 1886		Liquidated before 1 Jan. 1886	
Kimberley		*Kimberley*	
Kimberley Central	(£728,000)	Octahedron	(£ 66,500)
Compagnie Française	(£560,000)	North West	(£167,680)
Standard	(£343,000)	South West	(£182,320)
Barnato Central	(£115,000)	Vulcan	(£ 82,400)
Beaconsfield	(£132,000)		
North East	(£ 90,000)		
North Block	(£129,970)		
Total	(2,097,970)	Total	(£498,900)
De Beers		*De Beers*	
De Beers	(£1,045,120)	Birbeck	(£ 88,000)
Elma	(£105,000)	Eagle	(£ 80,000)
Oriental	(£ 98,680)	Frere	(£109,000)
Schwab's	(£122,000)	International	(£131,700)
Victoria	(£300,000)	Perseverance	(£ 50,000)
Gem	(£140,250)	Pleiades	(£ 80,000)
United	(£ 45,000)	Petree	(£ 91,000)
Total	(£1,856,050)	Total	(£629,700)
Dutoitspan		*Dutoitspan*	
Anglo-African	(£660,000)	Caledonian	(£ 20,000)
Phoenix	(£300,000)	Kimberley	(£250,000)
Compagnie Generale	(£326,000)	Dutoitspan	(£106,000)
Griqualand West	(£285,740)	Eldorado	(£ 65,000)
Britannia	(£155,000)	Fry's Gully	(£125,000)
Cape of Good Hope	(£ 95,000)	Globe	(£ 68,000)
Central	(£100,000)	Standard	(£ 65,000)
West End	(£170,000)	Victoria	(£ 60,000)
Hercules	(£ 93,000)	Royal	(£ 45,000)
Orion	(£250,000)		
African	(£100,000)		
British	(£ 60,000)		
Ne Plus Ultra	(£ 84,230)		
Adamanta	(£ 58,560)		
European	(£105,000)		
Gordon	(£100,000)		
Gordon Claims	(£ 30,000)		
Total	(£2,972,530)	Total	(£804,000)

Appendix Table 7 (*cont.*)

Operating on 1 Jan. 1886			Liquidated before 1 Jan. 1886		
Bultfontein			*Bultfontein*		
Bultfontein Homestead	(£ 49,000)		Aegis	(£ 45,000)	
Adamant	(£ 80,000)		Alliance	(£ 50,000)	
French & d'Esterre	(£115,600)		Atlas	(£ 45,000)	
Bultfontein Colonial	(£ 70,000)		Lilienstein	(£ 28,000)	
Pullinger	(£130,000)		Union	(£ 40,000)	
Compagnie Diamant	(£120,000)		Excelsior	(£ 53,000)	
Bultfontein Central	(£ 72,000)		Spes Bona	(£115,000)	
Hatton	(£ 15,000)		Crown	(£ 50,000)	
Franco-Africaine	(£100,000)		Cosmopolitan	(£ 30,000)	
Bultfontein Mining	(£140,000)				
Total	(£891,600)		Total	(£456,500)	
Grand Total			*Grand Total*		
Kimberley	[7]	£2,097,970	Kimberley	[4]	£498,900
De Beers	[7]	£1,856,050	De Beers	[7]	£629,700
Dutoitspan	[7]	£2,097,970	Dutoitspan	[9]	£804,000
Bultfontein	[10]	£ 892,670	Bultfontain	[9]	£456,500
Total	[41]	£7,819,150*	Total	[29]	£2,389,100

Sources: Prospectuses of Diamond Mining and Other Companies, Kimberley, 1881; SBA; company reports.

* In addition there were 56 private companies or partnerships with minimal capital, except W. A. Hall, assessed at £80,864, and W. and B. Stuart, assessed at £32,562, in Kimberley Mine.

Appendix Table 8 Production Statistics of the De Beers DMC since its formation in 1880

Year ended 31st March	No. of Loads of Blue Hauled	No. of Loads of Dead Ground Hauled	No. of Loads of Blue Washed	No. of Carats of Diamonds Found	Amount received by Sale of Diamonds £	No. of Carats per Load of Blue	Amount realised per Carat Sold s. d.	Amount realised per Load s. d.	Balance of Blue on floors	Dividends paid during the Year £ / % s. d.	Cost of Production per Load s. d.	Capital of Company during the Year £
1881	73,642	50,000	73,642	51,682	62,367	.7	24 1	16 11	Nil.	11,600 = 5½		200,000
1882	99,439	96,731	96,439	76,859	104,552	.79	27 3	21 8	3,080	19,966 = 3	13 2	665,550
1883	179,785	143,369	166,136	149,396	158,675	.89	21 3	19 1¼	16,649	37,714 = 5⅔	11 9½	665,550
1884	220,046	204,977	173,666	177,246	198,268	1.02	22 5	22 10	63,029	52,148 = 7	10 0	755,120
1885	398,614	427,215	323,325	278,018	287,470	.85	20 8	17 9	138,318	62,666 = 7½	8 1	841,550
1886	391,749	569,551	299,407	395,001	323,499	1.31	16 4½	21 7	230,660	121,814 = 12	8 3½	1,045,120
1887	589,317	404,387	487,296	560,254	517,104	1.15	18 5½	21 2⅔	288,133	199,349 = 16	8 2⅛	1,265,620
1888	890,508	6,714	857,906	979,732	984,086	1.14	20 1¾	22 11¼	303,405	508,042 = 25	9 6½	†2,332,170
Total	2,843,100	1,902,944	2,477,817	2,668,188	2,636,023	1.07	19 9	21 33	303,495	*1,013,299 = 71⅔	9 6½	

*In addition to above dividends, 41 per cent. has been distributed in bonus shares. † Exclusive of £177,450 out of capital.

Source: *The Statist*, 9 June, p. 651.

237

Appendix Table 9 Production Statistics of the Kimberley Central DMC since its formation in 1880

Year ended 30th April	No. of loads of blue hauled	No. of loads of dead ground hauled	No. of loads of blue washed	No. of carats of diamonds sold	Amount received by sale of diamonds	Amount realised per carat sold	Amount realised per load	Balance of blue on floors	Cost of production per load	Dividends paid during the year		Capital of company during the year
					£	s. d.	s. d.		s. d.	£	%	£
1881	53,434	n.d.	43,867	89,814¾	138,933	n.d.	n.d.	9,567	n.d.	90,402	= 38*	576,860
1882	167,476	251,967	157,303	210,554½	353,316	33 6	44 11	19,740	27 10	78,664	= 13½	576,860
1883	344,205	285,468	314,385	434,890	482,314	n.d.	40	49,560	21 10	100,951	= 17½	576,860
1884	n.d.	n.d.	n.d.	n.d.	n.d.	n.d.	n.d.	2,150	n.d.	–	–	691,200
1885	156,797	n.d.	156,000	195,058	200,687	20 7	25 7	25,402½	n.d.	–	–	728,200
1886	234,265	n.d.	171,645**	174,569	159,288	n.d.	26	103,202	10 6	–	–	728,200
1887	402,266	n.d.	333,900	407,623½	408,691	18 11	***	172,568	n.d.	72,820	= 10[1]	728,200
1888	966,936	733,210	915,481	1,037,993½	1,078,221	n.d.	n.d.	262,480	n.d.	601,121[3]	= 47[2]	1,779,550

* 10% on £164,300; 23% on £192,300; 12¾ bonus on £192,300; 5% on £576,860.

** Includes lumps/tailing loads.

*** Blue removed with up to 50 per cent of shale per load. In contrast, De Beers DMC only removed 'clean' blue.

Source: Annual Reports and AGMs

n.d. = no data

[1] £20,000 to reserve fund.   [2] £30,000 to reserve fund.   [3] £91,467 on £815,590 (11%), £125,297 on £1,392,190 (9%), £384,357 on £1,423,550 (27%)

Appendix Table 10 Production Statistics of the De Beers Consolidated Mines Ltd. 1889–1903 for Kimberley and De Beers Mines

Year ending	Number of loads of blue hoisted	Number of loads of blue washed	Number of carats of diamonds found	Value of diamonds produced £	Average number of carats per load	Average value per carat s.	d.	Average value per load s.	d.	Cost of production per load s.	d.	Number of loads of blue on floors at close of year, exclusive of lumps	Dividends paid. Amount £	s.	d.
March 31, 1889 prior to Consolidation	944,706	712,263	914,121	901,818	1.28	19	8.75	25	3.75	9	10.5	***243,960 / 476,403	188,329	10	0
March 31, 1890	2,192,226	1,251,245	1,450,605	2,330,179	1.15	32	6.75	37	2.75	8	10.5	***159,437 / 1,576,821	789,682	0	0
March 31, 1891	1,978,153	2,029,588	2,020,515	2,974,670	.99	29	6	29	3.75	8	8	1,525,386	789,791	0	0
*June 30, 1892	3,338,553	3,239,134	3,035,481	3,931,542	.92	25	6	23	5	7	4.3	1,624,805	1,382,134	5	0
June 30, 1893	3,090,183	2,108,626	2,229,805	3,239,389	1.05	29	0.6	30	6.75	6	11.6	2,606,362	987,238	15	0
June 30, 1894	2,999,431	2,577,460	2,308,463½	2,820,172	.89	24	5.2	21	10.6	6	6.8	3,028,333	987,238	15	0
June 30, 1895	2,525,717	2,854,817	2,435,541½	3,105,957	.85	25	6	21	8	6	10.8	2,699,233	987,238	15	0
June 30, 1896	2,698,109	2,597,026	2,363,437½	3,165,382	.91	26	9.4	24	4.5	7	0.1	2,800,316	1,579,582	0	0
June 30, 1897	2,515,889	3,011,288	2,769,422½	3,722,099	.92	26	10.6	24	8.6	7	4.3	2,304,917	1,579,582	0	0
June 30, 1898	3,332,688	3,259,692	2,603,250	3,451,214	.80	26	6.2	21	2.1	6	7.4	2,377,913	1,579,582	0	0
June 30, 1899	3,504,899	3,311,733	2,345,466	3,471,060	.71	29	7.2	20	11.5	6	7.7	2,937,784	1,579,582	0	0
June 30, 1900	1,673,664	1,522,108	1,000,964	1,794,222	.67	35	10.2	23	6.9	7	6.2	2,722,595			
June 30, 1901	2,120,397	2,616,873	2,000,495½	3,959,383	.76	39	7	30	3.1	8	5	2,226,119	1,579,582	0	0
June 30, 1902	2,062,459	1,961,858	1,499,299½	3,484,247	.76	46	5.7	35	6.2	8	5.6	2,326,720	†2,445,000	0	0
June 30, 1903	2,370,503	2,561,940	1,574,189½	3,819,653	.61	48	6.3	29	9.8	7	3.1	2,135,283	†2,175,000	0	0
Total	37,347,577	35,615,691	30,551,057	46,170,993	.8578	30	2.7	25	11.1				18,629,563	0	0

*These figures are for a period of fifteen months. **Taken over from De Beers Mining Company. ***Taken over from Central Company.
†Includes £520,000 bonus dividends. ‡In addition to this the Life Governors received £858,020.
Source: G. Williams, The Diamond Mines of South Africa, Vol. II, p. 320

Notes

PREFACE

1 C. van Onselen, *Chibaro. African Mine Labour in Southern Rhodesia 1900–1933*, London, 1976.
2 C. Perrings, *Black Mineworkers in Central Africa. Industrial Strategies and the Evolution of an African Proletariat in the Copperbelt 1911–1941*, London, 1979.
3 L. Vail and L. White, 'Forms of Resistance: Songs and Perceptions of Power in Colonial Mozambique' in D. Crummey (ed.), *Banditry, Rebellion and Social Protest in Africa*, London, 1986, 195.
4 Bill Freund, *Capital and Labour in the Nigerian Tin Mines*, London, 1981; *The Making of Contemporary Africa. The Development of African Society Since 1800*, London, 1984.

I DIAMOND MINING: AN OVERVIEW

1 K. Shillington, *The Colonisation of the Southern Tswana 1870–1900*, Johannesburg, 1985, 44–55.
2 For the literature, see for example, J. A. I. Agar-Hamilton, *Road to the North*, London, 1937; C. W. de Kiewiet, *British Colonial Policy and the South African Republics 1848–72*, London, 1929.
3 PRO, BT 31, 1577/5168.
4 SAL, *Merriman Diaries*, 9 March 1875.
5 G. Lenzen, *The History of Diamond Production and the Diamond Trade*, London, 1970, 5–21.
6 A carat was the standard diamond weight measure and roughly equalled 200 grams.
7 E. Streeter, *Precious Stones and Gems*, London, 1877, 30; M. Bauer, *Precious Stones*, London, 1904, 210, 255.
8 G. F. Williams, *The Diamond Mines of South Africa*, New York, 1905, Vol. II, 168–87.
9 T. C. Kitto, *Report on the Diamond Mines of Griqualand West*, Kimberley, 1879, 69 in Smalberger Papers in UCT Jagger Library; P. M. Laurence, 'Diamonds' in C. Cowen (ed.), *The South African Exhibition*, Cape Town, 1886, 266.
10 H. Emmanuel, *Diamonds and Precious Stones: Their History, Value and Distinguishing Characteristics*, London, 1867, 90.
11 A load of blue weighed 1,600 lbs (720,400 kg). A solid cubic yard of blue was equal to three loads and a solid cubic yard of reef was equal to two and three quarter loads. A load of 16 cubic feet was equal to nine cubic feet of solid blue or ten feet of solid reef. (T. Reunert, *Diamond Mines of South Africa*, Cape Town, 1892, 27).
12 CPP, G34–'83, *RIDM*, 24, 28.
13 W. P. Taylor, *African Treasures: Sixty Years Among Diamonds and Gold*, London, 1932, 44; M. Bauer, *Precious Stones*, 212; G. F. Williams, *The Diamond Mines of South Africa*, Vol. II, 153.
14 A claim was 30 square feet.

15 T. C. Kitto, *Report on the Diamond Mines*, 49, 97, in Smalberger Papers in UCT Jagger Library.

16 *Diamond News*, 24 April 1877, De Beers Special Commissioner; CPP, G27–'82, *RIDM*, 24; CPP, G28–'88, *RIDM* 11.

17 *Diamond Field*, 13 Oct. 1876, 'Dutoitspan'; T. C. Kitto, *Report on the Diamond Mines*, 77; CPP, G34–'83, *RIDM*, 27, 28; CPP, G26–'87, *RIDM*, 7, 8.

18 L. Phillips, *Some Reminiscences*, London, 1924, 28.

19 CPP, G101–'83, *Report by T. P. Watson upon the Excavations at the Diamond Mines of Kimberley and De Beers*, 9; CPP G107–'83, *Report upon the Financial Position of the Kimberley Mining Board*, passim.

20 G. F. Williams, *The Diamond Mines of South Africa*, Vol. I, 248–53.

21 Th. van Tijn, 'Geschiedenis van de Amsterdamse diamanthandel en Nijverheid, 1845–97', *Tijdschrift Voor Geskiedenis*, 87 (1) 1974, 19.

22 CAD, GLW 24, *From Inspector of Claims 1871–74*, Walter Ward to J. B. Currey, 3 March 1873.

23 CAD, GLW 39, *Diamond Fields Commission* (26 Feb. 1873), W. A. Hall, Answers to Questionnaire; CAD, GLW 24, *From Inspector of Claims 1871–74*, Walter Ward to J. B. Currey, 5 May 1873.

24 J. W. Matthews, *Incwadi Yami*, New York, 1887, 178.

25 *Diamond News*, 30 May 1874, Local and General.

26 CAD, GLW 24, *From Inspector of Claims 1871–74*, Petition of W. A. Hall, 10 March 1873; *Diamond News*, 11 July 1874, Letter from Leopold Burkner, and 19 June 1877, 'The Mines'; M. Chaper, *Note Sur la Region Diamantifere de l'Afrique Australe*, Paris, 1880, 81; J. N. Paxman, 'The Diamond Fields and Mines of Kimberley', *Minutes and Proceedings of the Institute of Civil Engineers*, 74, IV, 1882–83, 8.

27 CPP, G34–'83, *RIM*, 41.

28 T. C. Kitto, *Report on the Diamond Mines*, 79.

29 *Diamond News*, 24 April 1877, 'Oats' Report for the Diamond Fields Association' and 26 April 1877, Letter, Colonel Crossman to the Diamond Fields Association; CPP, G34–'83, *RIM*, 68; G28–'88, *RIM*, 16; G22–'89, *RIM*, 17, 20. From 1872 to 1876 an average of 150,000 loads of reef were removed each year, while in 1882 alone three million loads of reef were extracted.

30 *Daily Independent*, 10 June 1887, Annual General Meeting, Kimberley Central DMC, Baring Gould's speech.

31 CPP, G34–'83, *RIM*, 44; G28–'88, *RIDM*, 4.

32 A. Moulle, *Geologie General et Mines de Diamants de l'Afrique du Sud*, Paris, 1886, 140; CPP, G28–'88, *RIM*, 18.

33 W. J. Morton, *South African Diamond Fields*, New York, 1877, 24.

34 J. W. Matthews, *Incwadi Yami*, 179–81; G. F. Williams, *The Diamond Mines of South Africa*, Vol. I, 255.

35 P. Richardson and J. J. Van-Helten, 'Labour in the South African Gold Mining Industry, 1886–14' in S. Marks and R. Rathbone (eds.), *Industrialisation and Social Change in South Africa: African Class Formation, Culture and Consciousness 1870–1930*, London, 1982.

36 CPP, G34–'83, *RIM*, 54.

37 A. Moulle, *Geologie Generale*, 119.

38 J. W. Matthews, *Incwadi Yami*, 184.

39 A. R. Sawyer, *Mining at Kimberley*, Newcastle, 1889, 31–3; G. F. Williams, *The Diamond Mines of South Africa*, Vol. II, 65–6.

40 CPP, G34–'83, *RIM*, 55; A. Moulle, *Geologie Generale*, 119.

41 Standard Bank Archive (SBA), 700:24, W. W. Kenrick to J. & P. Higson, Manchester, 25 Aug. 1884.

42 CPP, G22–'89, *RIDM*, 4; A. R. Sawyer, *Mining at Kimberley*, 21–7; G. F. Williams, *The Diamond Mines of South Africa*, Vol. I, 308.
43 G. F. Williams, *The Diamond Mines of South Africa*, Vol. I. 315.

2 AFRICAN LABOUR IN THE EARLY DAYS

1 BPP, 732, *Further Correspondence respecting the affairs of the Cape of Good Hope*, No. 54, Sir Henry Barkly to Lord Kimberley, 29 Oct. 1872, 130. At the times of the two censuses the number of Females to every 100 Males in Kimberley was:

	Europeans	All Others	Mixed and Others	Mean
1877	60.08	17.01	no data	32.73
1891	80.44	38.03	92.60	53.84

2 BPP, C 1401, *Further Correspondence relating to the Colonies and States of South Africa*, Enclosure in No. 1, Richard Southey to Sir Henry Barkly, 30 June 1875, 2; E. von Weber *Vier Jahre in Afrika 1871–75*, Leipzig, 1878, 443.
3 CAD, GLW 55, *From Inspector of Claims*, Howse to J. B. Currey, 18 Nov. 1874.
4 CAD, GLW 71, *From Servants Registrar's Office*, W. J. Coleman to J. B. Currey, 18 Nov. 1873; C. Payton, *The Diamond Diggings*, 137, 139. For the absence of Zulu from Zululand, see J. Guy, 'The Destruction and Reconstruction of Zulu Society' in S. Marks and R. Rathbone (eds.), *Industrialisation and Social Change in South Africa*, 176–9.
5 CAD, GLW 71, *From Servants Registrar's Office*, W. J. Coleman to J. B. Currey, 6 June 1873; L. Phillips, *Some Reminiscences*, 19. See K. Shillington, 'The Impact of the Diamond Discoveries on the Kimberley Hinterland: Class Formation, Colonialism and Resistance among the Tlhaping of Griqualand West in the 1870s' in S. Marks and R. Rathbone (eds.), *Industrialisation and Social Change in South Africa*.
6 See for example S. T. van der Horst, *Native Labour in South Africa*, Cape Town, 1942, and T. R. Davenport, *South Africa: a Modern History*, London, 1977.
7 F. Boyle, *The Savage Life*, London, 1876.
8 'Migrant Labour and the Pedi, 1840–80' in S. Marks and A. Atmore (eds.), *Economy and Society in Pre-Industrial South Africa*, London, 1980, and *The Land Belongs To Us: The Pedi Polity, the Boers and the British in the Nineteenth-century Transvaal*, Johannesburg, 1984.
9 'Kinship, Ideology and the Nature of Pre-colonial Labour Migration: Labour Migration from the Delagoa Bay Hinterland to South Africa up to 1895' in S. Marks and R. Rathbone (eds.), *Industrialisation and Social Change in South Africa*; and thesis.
10 'Labour Migration in Basutoland 1870–80' in S. Marks and R. Rathbone (eds.), *Industrialisation and Social Change in South Africa*.
11 P. Delius, 'Migrant Labour and the Pedi', 296, in Marks and Rathbone (eds.), *Industrialisation and Social Change in South Africa*.
12 W. Beinart, *The Political Economy of Pondoland 1860–1930*, Cambridge, 1982, 55.
13 CPP, G16–'76, *BBNA*, 12.
14 P. Harries, 'Slavery, Social Incorporation and Surplus Extraction: the Nature of Free and Unfree Labour in South East Africa', *Journal of African History*, 22, 1981, 319.
15 CAD, GLW 71, *From Servants Registrar's Office*, W. J. Coleman to J. B. Currey, 19 Aug. 1874.
16 CAD, GLW 17, *Memo of an Arrangement made by Mr John Edwards with Sekukune, Paramount Chief of Sequati's People on the 13 August 1873*.
17 Ibid. Southey refused to sanction this arrangement because he believed one or two gun dealers might be able to control the headmen, through whatever means, and consequently 'interfere with the flow of labour'. (PRO, CO 879/6, Confidential African Print, No. 59, *Sale of Arms in Griqualand West; Despatch from Governor*, 24 Aug. 1874, 10.)
18 For the government's attitude to recruitment, see R. Sieborger, 'The Recruitment and

Organisation of African Labour for the Kimberley Diamond Mines 1871–88', unpub. M.A., Rhodes University, Grahamstown, 1976, 50–98; J. A. I. Agar-Hamilton, *The Road to the North 1852–86*, London, 1937, 142.

19 *Diamond Field*, 4 Aug. 1876, Editorial; CAD, GLW 118, *Records*, No. 944, 'Report on Labour Generally for the Year 1876' (UCT, Smalberger Papers).

20 P. Harries, 'Kinship, Ideology and the Nature of Pre-Colonial Labour Migration', 150–4.

21 Introduction to S. Marks and R. Rathbone (eds.), *Industrialisation and Social Change in South Africa*, 19.

22 CAD, GLW 182, *Semi-Official Letters*, Richard Southey to Sir Henry Barkly, 3 Aug. 1873 (UCT, Smalberger Papers).

23 J. M. Smalberger, 'Alfred Aylward, the Continuing Rebel: Early Days on the Diamond Fields', *South African Historical Journal*, 7, 1975, 36–37.

24 E. Von Weber, *Vier Jahre in Afrika 1871–75*, 124–125.

25 CAD, GLW 71, *From Servants Registrar's Office*, W. J. Coleman to J. B. Currey, 26 Sept. 1872.

26 Ibid., 30 Jan., 5 April 1873; CAD, GLW 54, *From Inspector of Claims, Dutoitspan*, W. B. Smith to J. B. Currey, 30 Jan. 1873.

27 BPP, C 732, *Further Correspondence . . . Cape of Good Hope*, Sir Henry Barkly to Lord Kimberley, 29 Oct. 1872, 131.

28 C. Payton, *The Diamond Diggings*, 157.

29 CAD, GLW 71, *From Servants Registrar's Office*, W. J. Coleman to J. B. Currey, 6 Aug. 1874.

30 *The Statute Law of Griqualand West*, Cape Town, 1882, 27. See also J. M. Smalberger, 'The Role of the Diamond Mining Industry in the Development of the Pass-Law System in South Africa', *The International Journal of African Historical Studies*, 9 (3) 1976.

31 Ibid. See also Figure 2, Number of Labour Contracts Registered (1873–1898).

32 CAD, GLW 80, *Records*, No. 38, Lanyon Memo, 6 Jan. 1876. A 'native' was defined as a subject of a principal chief living outside the province of Griqualand West.

33 CAD, GLW 55, *From Inspector of Claims*, Howse to J. B. Currey, 18 April 1874; GLW 64, *Letters Miscellaneous*, James Hall to J. B. Currey, 29 Sept. 1874; GLW 103, *Records*, No. 1103, Memo from Gilbert Percy, 5 May 1877, Report from Lord, 31 May 1877.

34 CAD, GLW 8, *Despatches from the Administrator*, Major Lanyon to Sir Henry Barkly, 13 March 1877, containing the Attorney-General's report on Ordinance 10 of 1876.

35 J. M. Smalberger, 'Alfred Aylward, the Continuing Rebel: Early Days on the Diamond Fields', 39.

36 CAD, NA 450, E. A. Judge to Under Secretary for Native Affairs, 18 June 1884.

37 PRO, CO 879/9, Confidential African Print, No. 96, *Report of Lieutenant-Colonel Crossman on the Affairs of Griqualand West*, 1 May 1876, 18.

38 *Griqualand West Government Gazette*, 23 May 1876, 'Annexure setting forth the Laws at present in force relating to Native Labour' attached to *Report of the Commission upon the Griqualand Labour Question*. The Registrar issued two other passes: a 'return pass' to Africans leaving the Fields for home; and a 'free pass' to Africans in search of work, usually for seven days, when they first arrived in Kimberley.

39 C. Payton, *The Diamond Diggings*, 160.

40 *Mission Field*, No. 16, April 1872, 'Some Sketches of the Bishop's Visit to the Diamond Fields', 16.

41 CA, GLW 62, *Miscellaneous*, 'List of Native Claimholders whose Licences were Suspended', 25 July 1872.

42 CAD, GLW 39, *Diamond Fields Commission*, Report, (June 1873) f. 8.

43 L. Michell, *The Life of the Rt Honourable Cecil John Rhodes 1853–1902*, London, 1910, Vol. I, 37, quoting Cecil Rhodes to Dr Sutherland, 17 Dec. 1871.

44 Natal Archives Depot, Hathorn Papers 1/103, J. Richardson to Ken Hathorn, 17 Dec. 1871.

45 Ibid., 2/20, Ken Hathorn to Mrs Hathorn, 8 July 1871.
46 *The Diamond Diggings*, 190.
47 Ibid., 106.
48 Ibid., 209.
49 CAD, GLW 24, *Petitions*, Report of Walter Ward of Petition of W. A. Hall, March 1873.
50 J. W. Matthews, *Incwadi Yami*, 100.

3 THE NEW COLONIAL STATE, 1873–75

1 SBA, Inspection Report (Kimberley) 20 Dec. 1873, Report; *Diamond Field*, 8 Oct. 1873, Notice and Letter from John Anderson.
2 *Diamond Field*, 4 June 1873, 'Public Meeting on Mining Grievances'.
3 *Diamond Field*, 26 Nov. 1873. The members of the Association's Committee were: William Ling, G. W. Willis, G. R. Blanch, James Gifford, James Armstrong, S. G. Jones, John Cundill, G. T. Reed, John Stanton, H. J. Vickers, C. F. Fall, J. J. O'Leary, D. Burns, I. Harper, John Anderson, Tom Peel, S. J. Rhodes, M. Kelly, George McKay, T. Brooks, F. C. Alexander, J. Hagia, W. B. Sampson, G. McFarland, J. E. Stuart.
4 SBA, Inspection Reports (Kimberley) 7 Aug. 1872, ff 8, 9; 20 Dec. 1873, f 54.
5 *Diamond Field*, 23 Nov. 1873, 'Tucker's Manifesto'.
6 *Diamond Field*, 30 Aug. 1873, 'Graham's Manifesto'.
7 *Diamond Field*, 6 Aug. 1873, Letter from Dr Blanco; 22 Nov. 1873, 'Green's Manifesto'; KPL, Paton Papers, Note Book III; SBA, Inspection Report (Kimberley) 23 June 1875, ff 92, 108.
8 *Diamond Field*, 26 Nov. 1873. The results of the Kimberley Division election were:

	Kimberley	Dutoitspan	*Total*	
Graham	401	448	849 ⎫	
Green	597	214	811 ⎬	2,312
Tucker	616	36	652 ⎭	

9 J. B. Currey, *Half a Century in South Africa*, Typescript in South African Library, chapter 12, 15.
10 CAD, GLW 52, *Petitions*, 2 April 1873. The petition was signed by 675 people but only 108 were claimholders and only 28 had 'jumped' their claims.
11 CAD, GLW 39, *Diamond Fields Commission*, June 1873, Report.
12 Ibid.
13 CAD, GLW 54, *From Inspector of Claims*, Opinion of Shippard, 13 Aug. 1874.
14 CAD, GLW 39, *Diamond Fields Commission*, Stafford Parker's answer to Commission Question 12.
15 Ibid., Hall's answer to Commission Question 12.
16 J. B. Currey, *Half a Century in South Africa*, chapter 12, 16.
17 First Kimberley Mining Board: J. W. Matthews (Chairman), G. T. Lee, W. Ling, J. J. O'Leary, W. M. Frames, Kidger Tucker, D. Francis, Dr Wilson, J. H. W. Rausch. Not elected: Gillfillan, William Knight, F. Baring Gould, Henry Green, J. J. Stanford, J. J. Reid, E. F. Gray. (*Diamond News*, 23 June 1874).
Second Kimberley Mining Board: J. H. W. Rausch (Chairman), D. Francis, J. Gifford, P. J. Odendaal, Kidger Tucker, J. B. Turner, G. Tearnan, G. McFarland. Six candidates of eight sponsored by 'capitalists' failed to get elected: G. T. Lee, J. Mountford, T. D. Barry, W. W. Paddon, W. H. Craven, C. Stransky. After the rebellion William Ling, a rebel leader, beat Anthony Goldschmidt, a 'capitalist', for a seat on the Board. (*Diamond News*, 5 Jan. 1875, 6 July 1875).
18 First De Beers Mining Board: R. Baxter (Chairman), Captain S. Lowe, J. Birbeck, G. Hall, S. Cotty, W. R. Mayne, J. Cundill, W. H. Dunsmure, T. Shiels (*Diamond News*, 25 June 1874).

Second De Beers Mining Board: J. Cundill (Chairman), R. Baxter, Captain S. Lowe, S. Cotty, Swift, Wright, Bennett, C. J. Rhodes [resigned 6 Feb. 1875] E. F. Gray. (*Diamond News*, 5 Jan. 1875).

First Dutoitspan Mining Board: J. Fry (Chairman), J. W. Wardle, S. Yonge, M. Commaille, J. J. Wilson, J. J. Rothman, F. Lehmkuhl, J. W. Perzenthal, P. G. Roos. (*Diamond News*, 25 June 1874).

Second Dutoitspan Mining Board: J. Fry (Chairman), E. Solz, M. M. de Kok, A. Foster, R. M. Connolly, L. Hond, F. Lehmkuhl, J. J. Wilson, J. J. Rothman. (*Diamond News*, 9 Jan. 1875).

No Mining Boards were elected for Bultfontein at this time.

19 CAD, GLW 24, *Petitions*, G. R. Blanch to J. B. Currey, 10 Dec. 1873, 12 March 1874.
20 CAD, GLW 67, *Letters from Mining Board, Kimberley*, Gray report, 9 March 1874. An additional reason for its collapse was the dismissal of P. L. Buyskes, the Kimberley Resident Magistrate. Buyskes was dismissed for 'throwing himself into the arms of the disaffected' and because of his bias against servants in his court. He had supported the Vigilance Committee in his rulings and awards of fines. (CAD, GLW 184, *Semi-Official Letters*, R. Southey to Sir Henry Barkly, 20 Aug. 1874, f 19.)
21 *Diamond News*, 18 Aug. 1874, 'Mass Meeting'.
22 CAD, GLW 184, *Semi-Official Letters*, R. Southey to Sir Henry Barkly, 20 Aug. 1874, f 21.
23 Ibid.
24 Ibid.
25 CAD, GLW 19, *Miscellaneous*, M. Spurgin to G. Percy, 29, 31 Aug. 1874; Percy to J. B. Currey, 12, 17 Sept. 1874; BPP, C 1342 (1875) *Correspondence Relating to the Colonies and States of South Africa, Part I: Cape of Good Hope and Griqualand West*, Enclosure 1 in No. 1, 26 Nov. 1874.
26 P. M. Laurence, 'Diamonds', in C. Cowen (ed.), *The South African Exhibition, Port Elizabeth 1885*, Cape Town, 1886, 271.
27 CAD, GLW 19, *Miscellaneous*, Percy to J. B. Currey, 2 Nov. 1874.
28 Ibid.
29 CAD, GLW 19, *Miscellaneous*, G. Percy to J. B. Currey, 17, 22 Sept., 5 Oct. 1874.
30 For Aylward's early career on the Diamond Fields see J. M. Smalberger, 'Alfred Aylward, the Continuing Rebel: Early Days on the Diamond Fields', *South African Historical Journal*, 7, 1975.
31 CAD, GLW 19, *Miscellaneous*, Percy to J. B. Currey, 24 Sept. 1874. The OFS still claimed the Diamond Fields; this issue was only settled in 1876 by the British payment of £90,000 as compensation.
32 Ibid., 20 Nov. 1874.
33 Ibid.
34 BPP, C 1342 (1875) *Correspondence Relating*, Enclosure 5 in No. 1, from *Diamond Field*, 11 Nov. 1874.
35 *Diamond Field*, 15 Oct. 1873, Resident Magistrate Court, Kimberley *Diamond News*, 14 Feb. 1874, Editorial; *Diamond Field*, 12 Feb. 1875, 'The Artful Dodger'.
36 BPP, C 1342 (1875) *Correspondence Relating*, Enclosure in No. 9, Southey's opening address to the Legislative Council, 5 March 1875, 4.
37 *Diamond Field*, 5 March 1875, 'Mass Meeting'.
38 *Diamond Field*, 17 March 1875, 'Mass Meeting'; CAD, GLW 19, *Miscellaneous*, Thomas to Percy, 25, 28 April 1875.
39 CAD, GLW 184, *Semi-Official Letters*, R. Southey to Sir Henry Barkly, 18 March 1875, f 335.
40 Ibid.
41 *Diamond Field*, 21 March 1875, 'The Manifesto'.
42 BPP, C 1342 (1875), *Correspondence Relating*, Enclosure 1 in No. 10, R. Southey to Sir

Henry Barkly, 20 March 1875, 87; Enclosure 7 in No. 10, Sir Henry Barkly to R. Southey, 30 March 1875, 101.

43 Ibid., Enclosure 3 in No. 22, Currey's Minute, 24 March 1875, 121.
44 CAD, GLW 185, *Semi-Official Letters*, R. Southey to Sir Henry Barkly, 25 March 1875.
45 *Diamond News*, 8 April 1875, Resident Magistrate Court (7 April).
46 *Diamond Field*, 21 April 1875, 'Notes'; L. Cohen, *Reminiscences of Kimberley*, 201.
47 CAD, GH 12/5, Enclosure 3 in Despatch 40, R. Southey to Sir Henry Barkly, 22 April 1875.
48 Ibid., Enclosure 4.
49 *Diamond News*, 3 Sept. 1874, Editorial.
50 CAD, GLW 19, *Miscellaneous*, Thomas to Percy, 24 April 1875.
51 *Diamond Field*, 17 April 1875, Resident Magistrate Court (12 April).
52 *Diamond Field*, 10 Feb. 1875, Report of the Licensed Victuallers Meeting.
53 CAD, GLW 185, *Semi-Official Letters*, 25 March.
54 BPP, C 1342 (1875), Enclosure 2 in No. 16, D'Arcy to Southey, 13 April 1875, 75.
55 Ibid.
56 Ibid.
57 *Diamond News*, 13 April 1875, Proclamation No. 10 of 1875.
58 *Diamond News*, 30 Sept. 1875, 'The State Trials'.
59 *Diamond News*, 17 April 1875, 'Deputation Meeting'.
60 CAD, GLW 185, *Semi-Official Letters*, R. Southey to Sir Henry Barkly, 17 April 1875.
61 Ibid.
62 Ibid.
63 CAD, GLW 19, *Miscellaneous*, Enclosure in G. Percy to J. B. Currey, 15 May 1876.
64 CAD, GLW 185, *Semi-Official Letters*, R. Southey to Sir Henry Barkly, 12 June 1875.
65 *Diamond News*, Extra, 1 July 1875.
66 *Diamond News*, 25, 28, 30 Sept. 1875, 'The State Trials'.
67 *Diamond Field*, 24 July 1875, 'Lecture on Rebellion'.
68 Ibid.
69 Ibid.
70 De Kiewiet, *The Imperial Factor in South Africa*, 49. Most reminiscences of pioneers also belittle Aylward. For example, see L. Cohen, *Reminiscences of Kimberley*, 217–21.
71 *Diamond News*, 30 Sept. 1875, 'The State Trials'.
72 *Diamond Field*, 24 July 1875, 'Lecture on Rebellion'.
73 SBA, Inspection Report (Kimberley), 1 Sept. 1876, f 189; 20 March 1877, ff 120, 186, 198.
74 *Diamond News*, 30 Sept. 1876, J. B. Robinson vs. William Ling, High Court. For Aylward's subsequent career in South Africa see, D. McCracken, 'Alfred Aylward: Fenian Editor of the Natal Witness', *Journal of Natal and Zulu History*, 4 1981.

4 THE BLACK FLAG REVOLT: AN ANALYSIS

1 An earlier version of this chapter appeared as 'The 1875 Black Flag Revolt on the Kimberley Diamond Fields', *Journal of Southern African Studies*, 7 (2) 1981.
2 De Kiewiet, *The Imperial Factor in South Africa*, London, 1937, 49–59. For other accounts, see I. B. Sutton, 'The Diggers Revolt in Griqualand West 1875', *International Journal of African Historical Studies*, 12 (1) 1979; B. Roberts, *Kimberley: Turbulent City*, Cape Town, 1976, 30–40.
3 Ibid.
4 Ibid.
5 Ibid. In *A History of South Africa: Social and Economic* Oxford, 1941, 53, he wrote that 'Kimberley was the cradle and testing ground of social and economic policy'.
6 See S. Trapido, ' "The Friends of the Natives": merchants, peasants and the political and

ideological structure of liberalism in the Cape, 1854–1910' in S. Marks and A. Atmore (eds.), *Economy and Society in Pre-Industrial South Africa*, London, 1980, 247–74 for a convincing analysis of Cape Liberalism.

7 Natal Archives Depot, Hathorn Papers 2/27, Ken Hathorn to Chris Hathorn, 6 Aug. 1871.
8 *Diamond News*, 28 April 1874, Legislative Council Debate, Dr Graham (24 April); 13 April 1875, 'Local and General'; T. Reunert, *Diamond Mines of South Africa*, 20; A. Moulle, *Geologie Generale*, 103.
9 CAD, GLW 55, *From Inspector of Claims, Dutoitspan*, J. Wright to J. B. Currey, 1 Oct. 1874; PRO, CO 879/9, Confidential African Print, No. 89, *Preliminary Report by Lieutenant-Colonel Crossman on the Financial Condition of Griqualand West*, 5 Feb. 1876, 10.
10 *Berliner Missions Berichte*, 1876, 112.
11 See chapter 2, 29–30.
12 *Diamond News*, 18 June 1874, Letter from Aylward, 'Three Important Questions'.
13 *Incwadi Yami*, 209.
14 *Diamond Field*, 11 Feb. 1874, Letter from Peter.
15 BPP, C 1342 (1875), *Cape of Good Hope and Griqualand West* Enclosure 1 in No. 1, R. Southey to Sir Henry Barkly, 26 Nov. 1874, 2. A total of 2,265 Europeans signed a petition for a Royal Commission of investigation into the affairs of Griqualand West and 1,000 were of Dutch or foreign descent. See also BPP, C 1401 (1876), *Further Correspondence . . . Colonies and States of South Africa*, Enclosures 4, 5, 6 in No. 20, Sir Henry Barkly to Lord Carnarvon, 7 Aug. 1875, 23, 24, for lists of rebels, their origins and occupations.
16 *Diamond Field*, 31 July 1875, 'Affidavit of Barend Van Buuren, 19 June 1875'. This affidavit was used by the prosecution in the preliminaries of the state trial of the rebel leaders.
17 *Diamond News*, 18 June 1874, Letter from Aylward, 'Three Important Questions'.
18 *Diamond News*, 11 Aug. 1874, Supplement, Letter from Aylward.
19 CAD, GLW 55, *From Inspector of Claims, Dutoitspan*, Howse to J. B. Currey, 13 June 1874; GLW 184, *Semi-Official Letters*, R. Southey to Sir Henry Barkly, 28 Aug. 1874, f 42.
20 CAD, GLW 51, *From Inspector of Roads, Kimberley*, W. Ward to J. B. Currey, 13 Dec. 1873; Standard Bank Archive, GM/LO, Letter Book IV, 18 Feb. 1874; *Diamond Field*, 4 Feb. 1874, 'Local and General'; *Diamond News*, 4 June 1874, Letter from Goodliffe; *Diamond News*, 28 July 1874, Report of Kimberley Mining Board 20 July, Dr Matthews; *Diamond News*, 21 November 1874, Editorial; Kimberley Public Library, Paton Papers, *Provincial Engineer's Report*, 9 March 1875, 4.
21 *Diamond News*, 11 July 1874, Letter from L. Burkner; *Diamond Field*, 13 Jan. 1875, 'Notes'; *Diamond Field*, 19 Dec. 1874, 'Local and General'; E. von Weber, *Vier Jahre in Afrika 1871–75*, 443; A. Moulle, *Geologie Generale*, 106; G. Williams, *The Diamond Mines of South Africa*, Vol. I, 229, 231.
22 See figure 2, Number of Labour Contracts Registered (1873–1879).
23 *Diamond Field*, 7 Oct. 1874, 13 Jan. 1875, 'Local and General'; E. von Weber, *Vier Jahre in Afrika*, 224.
24 BPP, C 1342 (1875), *Cape of Good Hope and Griqualand West*, Enclosure 1 in No. 32, R. Southey to Sir Henry Barkly, 25 Feb. 1875, 181.
25 BPP, C 1342, Encl. 5 in No. 1, Sir H. Barkly to Lord Carnarvon, 7 Dec. 1874, 13.
26 CAD, GLW 83, *Records*, No. 762, Coleman Report, 2 March 1876.
27 CAD, GLW 80, *Records*, No. 440, Resolution passed at a Meeting of Liquor Licensing Court, 23 Dec. 1875.
28 *Berliner Missions Berichte*, Report of Rev. Meyer, April–November 1875, 111.
29 CAD, GLW 19, *Miscellaneous*, Draft of Native Regulations; *Diamond News*, 22 Jan. 1874, De Beers Diggers Committee to R. W. H. Giddy; 8 April 1875, 'Proprietors Notice'; *Report of Colonel Crossman*, Enclosure No. 3, Report of Committee of Diggers, November 1875.
30 CAD, GLW 71, *From Servants Registrar's Office*, Coleman to J. B. Currey, 18 Dec. 1874;

BPP, C 1342 (1875), *Cape of Good Hope and Griqualand West*, Enclosure 1 and 2 in No. 20, Tucker and Ling to Sir Henry Barkly, 9 April 1875, R. Southey to Sir Henry Barkly, 14 April 1875, 105–11.

31 *Diamond Field*, 21 March 1875, 'Manifesto'.

32 *Diamond News*, 16 May 1874, Queen vs. Attwell Brothers, Circuit Court (12 May). The Attwell Brothers were accused of beating one Stuurman, a 'Kaffir', to death. Their defence rested on the belief that he had stolen a diamond. They were convicted of culpable homicide and sentenced to five years hard labour.

33 For example, *Diamond News*, 28 Nov. 1874, Queen vs. John Durack, Resident Magistrate Court, Dutoitspan (26 Nov.).

34 *Diamond Field*, 19 Aug. 1874, 'Mass Meeting' (15 Aug.), O'Leary.

35 *Diamond News*, 30 Jan. 1875, Unnamed case, Resident Magistrate Court, Kimberley; CAD, GLW 64, *Letters Miscellaneous*, Memorial from Licensed Claimholders in Bultfontein, 6 July 1874; CAD, GH 12/5 Enclosure in No. 42, R. Southey to Sir Henry Barkly, 22 April 1875.

36 *Diamond Field*, 16 Sept. 1874, Letter from 'Scrutator', 'The Future'. See also 7 Oct. 1874, Editorial, for a similar view of the world. This was the second number of the newspaper after it was taken over by the Committee of Public Safety.

37 Ibid.

38 Ibid.

39 SBA, Inspection Report (Kimberley), 7 Aug. 1872, ff 8, 9; 20 Dec. 1873, f 54; 23 June 1875, f 118; CAD, GLW 82, *Records*, No. 467, H. Tucker to Major O. Lanyon, 2 Feb. 1876. *Diamond News*, 28 May, 28 July 1874, Hendrik Jones vs. George Blakemore and Kidger Tucker, Circuit Court. This case revealed an extremely complicated hierarchy within share-working. Hendrik Jones, a 'person of colour', who was the servant cum sub-contractor of the European share-worker, eventually won £297 of a 136 carat diamond sold for £850.

40 *Diamond Field*, 28 Oct. 1874, Letter from William Ling, 'Economy vs. Monopoly'; *Diamond Field*, 13 Feb. 1875, Ebden vs. Ling, Circuit Court (10 Feb.), evidence of Ling; CAD, GLW 185, *Semi-Official Letters*, R. Southey to Sir Henry Barkly, 10 April 1875; SBA, Inspection Report (Kimberley) 23 June 1875, f 102; South African Library, Merriman Papers, No. 47, George Paton and John Merriman, 20 Sept. 1874, f 5.

41 BPP, C 1342 (1875), *Cape of Good Hope and Griqualand West*, Enclosure 3 in No. 1, 5.

42 *Diamond Field*, 4 Nov. 1874, Editorial, 'The Liquor Trade'; *Diamond News*, 23 June, 3 Dec. 1874, Editorial.

43 CAD, GLW 52, *Petitions 1873–4*, Memorial of A. Aylward, n.d.; *Diamond News*, 11 Aug. 1874, Editorial, 'The Liquor Trade'; *Diamond News*, 11 Aug. 1874, Supplement, Letter from A. Aylward; J. Smalberger, 'Alfred Aylward, the continuing Rebel', 35.

44 *Diamond Field*, 1 May 1875, Editorial and Extra.

45 Ibid.

46 *Diamond Field*, 24 July 1875, 'Lecture on Rebellion'.

47 *Diamond News*, 25 June 1874, Editorial.

48 CAD, GLW 185, *Semi-Official Letters*, R. Southey to Sir Henry Barkly, 17 April 1875.

49 *Diamond News*, 8 Dec. 1874, Editorial.

50 SBA, Inspection Report (Dutoitspan) 17 Nov. 1873; Inspection Report (Kimberley) 23 June 1875, f 86; Inspection Report (Port Elizabeth) 31 July 1876, f 613.

51 *Diamond News*, 13 Aug. 1874, Advertisement; SBA, Kimberley Branch P/O Book, Manager to General Manager, 17 Dec. 1874; Inspection Report (Kimberley) 23 June 1875, f 90; 1 Sept. 1876, ff 165–7, 230–9.

52 CAD, GLW 185, *Semi-Official Letters*, R. Southey to Sir Henry Barkly, 10 April 1875. Tucker was supported by Jones, Rudd and Company of Port Elizabeth, in which Thomas Rudd, elder brother of Charles Rudd, was the senior partner.

53 BPP, C 1342 (1875), *Cape of Good Hope and Griqualand West* Enclosure 2 in No. 4, Petition from Bankers, Professional Men, Merchants, Claimholders, Dealers, Diggers and others of Griqualand West, 34.

54 CAD, GLW 1888, *Drafts of Letters Despatched*, R. Southey to Sir Henry Barkly, 4 Aug. 1874, f 9.

55 BPP, C 1401 (1876), *Further Correspondence ... Colonies and States of South Africa*, Enclosure in No. 1, R. Southey to Sir Henry Barkly, 30 June 1875, 2–3. Von Weber, *Vier Jahre*, 443, estimated 20,000 Africans on the Fields at any one time and 80,000 working in Kimberley each year. At 10s per week he estimated £450,000 paid in wages each year. Geo Manning (*Crossman Report*, 34) estimated 8,500 Africans on the Fields in 1875, paid 25s per week, or £60 a year, totalling £510,000. The Registrar of Natives, Coleman, estimated that there were 9,000 registered servants in Kimberley in 1875, besides 1,000 domestics, cooks, and hotel and restaurant servants. (CAD, GLW 80, *Records*, No. 38, Coleman to Chief Clerk, 5 Jan. 1876).

56 J. B. Taylor, *A Pioneer Looks Back*, London, 1939, 42.

57 J. B. Currey, 'The Diamond Fields of Griqualand West and their Probable Influence on the Native Races of South Africa', *Journal of the Society of Arts*, XXIV, 1876, 379; *Diamond News*, 15, 25 Aug. 1874, Editorial, 'Legislative Council debate on Gun tax' (12, 18 Aug.); CAD, GLW 71, *From Servants Registrar's Office*, Coleman to J. B. Currey, 19 Aug. 1874.

58 BPP, C 1401 (1876), *Further Correspondence ... Colonies and States of South Africa*, Enclosure in No. 1, R. Southey to Sir Henry Barkly, 30 June 1875, 2.

59 Ibid.

60 CAD, GLW 185, *Semi-Official Letters*, R. Southey to Sir Henry Barkly, 17 April 1875.

61 Ibid., 10 April 1875.

62 SAL, Merriman Papers, R. Southey to J. X. Merriman, 8 Sept. 1874.

63 For Southey's involvement in land speculation on the eastern frontier see T. Kirk, 'The Cape Economy and the Expropriation of the Kat River Settlement, 1846–53' in S. Marks and A. Atmore (eds.) *Economy and Society in Pre-Industrial South Africa*, 240–1.

64 *Griqualand West Government Gazette*, 7 Jan. 1876, 'Report of the Surveyor-General for 1873–1875'; SAL, Merriman Papers, No. 47, George Paton to J. X. Merriman, 20 Sept. 1874.

65 *Diamond News*, 11 April 1874, 'Legislative Council Debate on the Mining Bill'.

66 In late 1873 Finlasons Company and the Mount Ararat Company were floated in Dutoitspan mine. Both were wound up by June 1874. Henry Green and Alphonse Levy were directors of Finlasons.

67 *Diamond News*, 3 Jan. 1874, 'Advertisement'; SBA, Kimberley Branch P/O Book, Manager to General Manager, 22 Jan. 1874. For Rudd's early commercial ventures, see R. V. Turrell, 'Rhodes, De Beers and Monopoly', *Journal of Imperial and Commonwealth History*, X, 3, 1982, 313–16.

68 CAD, GLW 183, *Semi-Official Letters*, R. Southey to Sir Henry Barkly, 30 July 1874. A detailed description of other influences at work in the passage of the Mining Ordinance can be found in Merriman Papers, George Paton to J. X. Merriman, 20 Sept. 1874.

69 CAD, GLW 188, *Drafts of Letters Despatched*, R. Southey to Sir Henry Barkly, 4 Aug. 1874, f 9.

70 *Report of Colonel Crossman*, Enclosure No. 6, 62.

71 SAL, Merriman Papers, George Paton to J. X. Merriman, 20 Sept. 1874; CAD, GLW 185, *Semi-Official Letters*, R. Southey to Sir Henry Barkly, 10 April 1875.

72 23 June 1874, Editorial. In 1875 there were 185 licensed diamond dealers, but only a handful of these were shippers, although all tried direct exporting at one time or another.

73 *Diamond Field*, 24 Oct. 1874, Editorial.

74 The Posno family dominated the Amsterdam Diamantslijperij-Maatschappij, which was a combination of jewellers who owned the majority of cutting factories in the industry. See

Th. van Tijn, 'Geskiedenis van de Amsterdamse Diamanthandel en Nijverheid 1845–1897', *Tijdschrift vor Geskiedenis*, 87 (1) 1974, 28.

75 Mosenthals were also a major shareholder in the London and South African Exploration Company.

76 London diamond merchants: 1865 – 57; 1870 – 77; 1875 – 153. (*Kelly's Post Office Directories*, London Trades).

77 SBA, Inspection Report (Kimberley) 20 Dec. 1873, f 49; 23 June 1875, f 102; 1 Sept. 1876, f 197.

78 CAD, GLW 185, *Semi-Official Letters*, R. Southey to Sir Henry Barkly, 10 April 1875.

79 SBA, Letter Book V, GM/LO, 12 Aug. 1874; Inspection Report (Kimberley) 31 Dec. 1877, f 188.

80 *Diamond News*, 6 May 1875, Editorial; *Diamond Field*, 22 May 1875, Letter from the Committee of the Moderate Party.

81 *Diamond Field & Diamond News*, 24 July 1875, 'Lecture on Rebellion'.

82 *Diamond News*, 18 May 1875, Editorial.

83 *The Imperial Factor in South Africa*, 49.

84 For a debate in the newspapers on the subject of usury, see *Diamond Field*, 7 Jan. 1874, Editorial; *Diamond News*, 8, 26 Jan. 1874, Editorial.

85 CAD, GLW 184, *Semi-Official Letters*, R. Southey to Sir Henry Barkly, 27 Aug. 1874, f 29.

86 SBA, Letter Book V, GM/LO, 7 Jan. 1875.

87 SBA, Inspection Report (New Rush), 7 Aug. 1872, f 9; CAD, GLW 185, *Semi-Official Letters*, R. Southey to Sir Henry Barkly, 17 April 1875; SAL, Merriman Letter Book I, J. X. Merriman to King, Son and Company, 16 Feb. 1875, f 200; *Diamond News*, 4 May 1876, H. G. Eliot vs. W. A. Hall, High Court.

88 SBA, Inspection Report (Kimberley), 23 June 1875, ff 78, 88, 96.

89 *Diamond Field*, 4 Jan. 1873, 'Meeting on Mining Grievances'.

90 *Diamond News*, 17 Nov. 1881, J. B. Robinson vs. Richardson, High Court (16 Nov.), Letter from G. R. Blanch.

91 SBA, Inspection Report (Kimberley), 23 June 1875, f 78.

92 BPP, C 1401 (1876), *Further Correspondence ... Colonies and States of South Africa*, Enclosure in No. 1, R. Southey to Sir Henry Barkly, 30 June 1875, 4; CAD, GH 27/1, Sir Henry Barkly to Lord Carnarvon, 5 May 1875, f 63.

93 *Diamond Field*, 15 Oct. 1873, Resident Magistrate Court, Kimberley.

94 *Diamond News*, 14 Feb. 1874, Editorial.

95 CAD, GLW 184, *Semi-Official Letters*, R. Southey to Sir Henry Barkly, 1 Sept. 1874, f 57.

96 *Diamond Field*, 18 Feb. 1874, Letter from J. X. Merriman.

97 CAD, GLW 183, *Semi-Official Letters*, R. Southey to F. G. Goodliffe, 4 May 1874, f 170.

98 CAD, GLW 184, *Semi-Official Letters*, R. Southey to Sir Henry Barkly, 1 Sept. 1874, f 57.

99 SBA, Inspection Report (Kimberley) 23 June 1875, ff 121, 122. The London Company had an income of £10,000 a year.

100 CAD, GLW 184, *Semi-Official Letters*, R. Southey to Sir Henry Barkly, 1 Sept. 1874, f 51.

101 *Diamond Field*, 12 Feb. 1875, 'Mass Meeting'.

102 SAL, Merriman Papers, No. 25, H. B. Christian to J. X. Merriman, 1874; No. 32, Paterson to J. X. Merriman, 13 Feb. 1874: 'You must get us out of the Diamond Estate speculation before you come down to Parliament, or I shall go into opposition to you there'.

103 SAL, Merriman Letter Book I, J. X. Merriman to King, Son and Company, 15 Sept. 1874, f 121.

104 SAL, Merriman Diaries, 9 March 1875; Merriman Papers, No. 12, Paterson to J. X. Merriman, 17 March 1875. Merriman and Manuel, his then partner, bought into the land syndicate at the rate of £50,000 for the whole farm. They took a one-sixteenth share for £3,200.

105 *Diamond News*, 4 Dec. 1877, R. W. Murray vs. J. Ferguson, High Court.

106 Kimberley Public Library, Paton Papers, 109H.
The subscribers were:

Green and Paton	£15,000	A. Goldschmidt	£	2,000
Paddon Brothers	£15,000	J. Levy	£	2,000
J. Ferguson	£10,000	M. Tamulz	£	3,000
C. Sonnenberg	£10,000	J. Myres	£	5,000
T. Crowder	£ 5,000	C. North	£	5,000
Lewis and Marks	£ 5,000	J. Heall	£	2,500
H. Feltham	£ 5,000	A. G. Biden	£	2,500
M. M. Steytler	£ 5,000	D. Curwen	£	1,000
Lublina and Bonas	£ 4,000	Dr Cumming	£	1,000
J. J. Ball	£ 1,000	C. Cairncross	£	1,000
				£100,000

107 CAD, GLW 185, *Semi-Official Letters*, R. Southey to Sir Henry Barkly, 5 May 1875.

108 *Diamond News*, 4 Dec. 1877, R. W. Murray vs. J. Ferguson, High Court.

5 COMPANY MINING

1 BPP, C 1342 (1875), *Correspondence Relating to . . . Griqualand West*, Enclosure 17 in No. 22, Sir Henry Barkly to R. Southey, 1 May 1875, 135.

2 Ibid., Enclosure 3 in No. 22, J. B. Currey's Minute, 24 March 1875, 122.

3 PRO, CO 879/9, Confidential African Print, No. 89, *Preliminary Report by Lieutenant-Colonel Crossman on the Financial Condition of Griqualand West*, 5 Feb. 1876; Confidential African Print, No. 96, *Report of Lieutenant-Colonel Crossman, R. E., on the affairs of Griqualand West*, 1 May 1976.

4 *Diamond News*, 8 July 1879, 'The Bank Statements'. Between June 1878 and June 1879 the estimated value of machinery purchased was £100,000. By 1881 J. W. Matthews estimated that £650,000 had been devoted to machinery in the formation of companies (*Incwadi Yami*, 251) and R. W. Murray estimated a figure of £750,000 (*Mining Journal*, 4 June 1881, Letter); SBA, Inspection Report (Kimberley), 15 March 1879, 'Report'; SBA, GM/LO 15 Aug. 1879 (Henry Files). See also Appendix Table 2

5 PRO, CO 879/17, Confidential African Print No. 215, Enclosure 2 in No. 3, C. Warren to B. Frere, 14 July 1879, 19.

6 SBA, Inspection Reports (Kimberley), 23 June 1875, f 102, 20 March 1877, f 202.

7 *Diamond News*, 23 May 1874, Editorial.

8 *Diamond News*, 30 June 1874, Legislative Council debate on Diamond Trade Ordinance, speech of J. B. Currey.

9 P. M. Laurence, 'Diamonds', in C. Cowen (ed.), *The South African Exhibition, Port Elizabeth 1885, Capt Town, 1886, 271*.

10 L. Cohen, *Reminiscences of Kimberley*, 78.

11 SBA, GM/LO, 14 April 1883 (Henry Files); SBA, Inspection Report (Kimberley), 12 Feb. 1887, ff 148, 149.

12 G. Yogev, *Diamonds and Coral: Anglo-Dutch Jews and Eighteenth-Century Trade*, Leicester, 1978, 154. In the 1870s A. Mosenthal and Company was mainly a partnership between the Mosenthal and Salamons families. In 1876 the partners were Adolph Mosenthal, J. W. Salamons, M. G. Salamons, Louis Bramson, W. E. Paddon. In 1879 Louis Bramson retired and Harry and George Mosenthal became partners. In 1882 W. E. Paddon retired and Adolph Mosenthal died leaving a personal estate of £350,000. He left

his capital in the firm. In 1888 William Mosenthal and Emil Goldschmidt were admitted as partners. See also chapter 4, p. 60. (SBA, Inspection Reports (Port Elizabeth), 31 July 1876, f 613, 25 Jan. 1879, f 765, 29 Sep. 1888, f 164).

13 CPP, G3–'88, *Commission ... into the Diamond Trade Acts*, ev. of E. W. Heckrath, Q.2476, 2481; SBA, GM/LO, 21 May 1890 (Henry Files).

14 *Diamond News*, 13 Oct. 1877, Pickler vs. Martin, High Court (10 Oct.).

15 R. V. Turrell (ed.) *The Philipson Stow Papers*, Document, 3, F.S.P. Stow to R. English, 3 March 1885.

16 SBA, Inspection Reports (Kimberley), 12 Nov. 1881, f 291, 2 Nov. 1882, f 373, 29 Nov. 1884, f 89, 7 Nov. 1885, f 73, 12 Feb. 1887, f 51; McGregor Museum (Kimberley), Philipson Stow Papers, memo of F. T. Gervers, 2 Feb. 1891 and circa 1892.

17 Ibid.; SBA Inspection Report (Kimberley), 4 Oct. 1890, f 26. For the Diamond Syndicate (Wernher, Beit & Co.; Barnato Bros.; A. Mosenthal & Sons; A. Dunkelsbuhler & Co.; Joseph Bros.) in the 1890s, see R. V. Turrell, 'Sir Frederic Philipson Stow: the Unknown Diamond Magnate', *Business History*, 28 (1) 1986, 69–71.

18 SBA, GM/LO, 14 April 1883 (Henry Files); SBA, Inspection Reports (Kimberley), 1 Sep. 1876, f 244, 15 March 1879, 'Securities'.

19 SBA, Inspection Report (Kimberley), 12 Feb. 1887, f 159.

20 Th. van Tijn, 'Geskiedenis van de Amsterdamse Diamanthandel en Nijverheid, 1845–97', *Tijdschrift Voor Geskiedenis*, 87 (1) 1974, 19–30, 34–7, 39–41.

21 *The Statist*, 29 Oct. 1887, 'London vs. Amsterdam', 488.

22 Ibid.

23 Th. van Tijn, 'Geskiedenis', 43; *Daily Independent*, 19 Feb. 1876, 'Diamond Market'; SBA, XL, 22 Dec. 1875, 3 May 1877 (Henry Files).

24 CAD, GLW 138, *Records*, Colonial Secretary to Kimberley Mining Board, 8 July 1879.

25 SBA, Inspection Report (Kimberley), 12 Nov. 1881, f 407.

26 *Daily Independent*, 21 March 1876, 'Value of Claims'; SBA, Inspection Report (Kimberley), 31 Dec. 1877, f 188; SBA, GM/LO 17 July, 5 Aug. 1876 (Henry Files).

27 Thomas Lynch, a Chevalier of the Papal Order of St. Gregory, was worth £15,000, owned claims with H. B. Webb in Kimberley Mine valued at £9,000 and was to receive five per cent commission for floating the Company. (SBA, Inspection Report (Kimberley), 1 Sept. 1876, f 193).

28 A London merchant house formed in 1876 with a capital of £200,000 mostly held by D. P. Blaine, the senior partner. The firm's colonial house was Blaine and Company of Port Elizabeth. (SBA, Inspection Report (Port Elizabeth), 31 July 1876, ff 371, 381, 467).

29 *Diamond News*, 6 Sept. 1877, T. Lynch vs. J. B. Robinson, High Court, Judgement (4 Sept.) In June 1876 Lynch lost £6,000 to Godfrey Davis in a game of poker and, after he sold Phoenix Buildings to pay what he owed, he was still worth £10,000.

30 SBA, GM/LO, 12 Oct. 1876 (Henry Files).

31 SBA, GM/10, 1 Dec. 1876, 20 April 1877; SBA, Inspection Report (Kimberley), 31 Dec. 1877, ff 48, 70.

32 Methodist Missionary Society, SA XVIII, Bechuanaland File, 1872–74, Calvert to Boyce, 13 Oct. 1873; SBA, Inspection Reports (Kimberley), 1 Sept. 1876, f 203, 20 March 1877, f 198, enclosure in 20 March 1877, Statement by Paddon Brothers, 19 Sept. 1876, 31 Dec. 1877, f 68.

33 SBA, Inspection Report (Kimberley), 15 March 1879, f 57.

34 In 1875 Martin Lilienfeld established himself in London as a diamond merchant with £50,000 he took out of his Hopetown firm. In 1878 he went into partnership with Emil Castens. In the same year Neumann and Michaelis set up their own firm in Kimberley which was dissolved in 1880. In 1882, when Lilienfeld's capital was £100,000, Castens retired and Neumann became a partner resident in Kimberley. In 1885 the firm went bankrupt. By this time Michaelis had become associated with Alfred Beit. Neumann moved to the de Kaap

Valley and then to the Rand speculating with Carl Hanau and Carl von Beek. He eventually went into partnership with H. J. King in 1890. SBA, Inspection Reports (Kimberley), 23 June 1875, f 100, 29 Nov. 1884, f 137, 7 Nov. 1885, f 103, 21 Jan. 1888, f 106, 3 Oct. 1891, f 109; Inspection Reports (Port Elizabeth), 25 March 1879, f 759, 13 Feb. 1883, f 642; Inspection Reports (Johannesburg), 25 Oct. 1887, f 91, 19 Jan. 1889, f 96; GM/LO, 6 Dec. 1878 (Henry Files).

35 The partnership of John Lewis, Leo Marks and Joseph Marks owned 15 claims worth £60,000 in 1879. (Ibid.)

36 SBA, Inspection Report (Kimberley), 3 Feb. 1880, f 177.

37 CAD, GDM 2/2, Cape DMC Letter Book, Ramsay Denny to Lilienfeld, 24 June 1880, f 10, 13 Aug. 1880, f 57.

38 RHL, Ms. Africa, S 115, C. J. Rhodes to Mother, 17 March 1871, 63; *Diamond Field*, 26 Aug. 1874, Thomas Rudd and others vs. Thomas Grant and others (Court of Queen's Bench); CAD, GLW 41, R. E. Wallace and Co. to J. B. Currey, 20 June 1873; *Diamond Field*, 12 July 1873, Report of Diggers Association Meeting; *Diamond News*, 5 Sep. 1874, advert. for sale of wire tramway; SAL, Merriman Letter-Book I, J. X. Merriman to C. North, 20 April 1874, f 14, 30 July 1874, f 93, 16 Jan. 1875, f 187; *Diamond News*, 7 Nov. 1874, Supplement, advert, for sale of Craven Club; *Diamond News*, 19 Dec. 1874, notice re. bottling business; *Diamond News*, 2 April 1874, advert for sale of ice.

39 L. Cohen, *Reminiscences of Kimberley*, London, 1911, 46.

40 Thomas Rudd was the senior partner in the Port Elizabeth firm, Jones, Rudd and Company, capital £44,000. *Diamond News*, 3 Jan. 1874, Prospectus; SBA, GM/LO, 22 Jan. 1874; *Diamond News*, 29 Aug. 1874, 'Old De Beers'; *Diamond News*, 2 Sept. 1875, 'Local & General'.

41 SBA, Inspection Reports (Cape Town), 11 May 1871, f 69, 12 Aug. 1874, ff 121, 133, 221; Inspection Report (Kimberley), 23 June 1875, f 104; Kimberley Branch P/O Book, Manager to GM, 19 Dec. 1874; N. Rouillard (ed.), *Matabele Thompson: His Autobiography and Story of Rhodesia*, Johannesburg, 1957, 107.

42 *Diamond Field*, 24 Oct. 1874, Report of Kimberley Mining Board; *Diamond Field*, 28 Oct. 1874, Letter from William Ling; CAD, GLW 52 *Petitions*, Petition against Walsh and Company water contract from John Dick-Lauder (Rhodes' agent), E. W. Tarry and others, 27 Oct. 1874; *Diamond Field*, 28 Nov. 1874, 'Water Contract'; *Diamond News*, 24 Aug. 1878, Baring Gould and Atkins vs. Kimberley Mining Board, High Court (23 Aug.); *Diamond News*, 15 March 1879, Report of Kimberley Mining Board (13 March).

43 *Diamond Field*, 28 Nov. 1874, 'Local & General'; CAD, GLW 51, From Mining Board, Dutoitspan, J. Fry to J. B. Currey, 28 Nov. 1874; *Diamond News*, 1 Dec. 1874, Report of Dutoitspan Mining Board (25 Nov.), 8 Dec. 1874, Letter from James Hall, 15 Dec. 1874, Letter from James Hall, 17 Dec. 1874, Letter from John Fry; *Diamond Field* 9 Dec. 1874, Letter from C. D. Rudd.

44 RHL, Ms. Africa S 134, Note Book VI, C. J. Rhodes to C. D. Rudd, 7, 8 Dec. 1874; SAL, Merriman Letter-Book, I, J. X. Merriman to C. North, 23 July 1874, f 86; *Diamond News*, 29 Aug. 1874, Reports of De Beers Mining Board (22, 24 Aug.); SBA, Inspection Report (Kimberley), 20 March 1877, ff. 59–60.

45 *Diamond News*, Reports of the De Beers Mining Board, 30 July 1874, (21, 23 July), 5 Sept. 1874 (1 Sept.), 2 Feb. 1875 (28 Jan.) 9 Feb. 1875 (4 Feb.), 25 May 1875 (21 May); CAD, GLW 64, *Letters Miscellaneous*, C. D. Rudd and others to J. B. Currey, 6 Aug. 1874; *Diamond News*, 1 Aug. 1874, 'Occasional Notes', 27 Oct. 1874, 'Local & General', 6 April 1875, 'Local & General'; RHL, Ms. Africa, t 14, C. J. Rhodes to Frank Rhodes, 19 Aug. 1875, f 243.

46 *Diamond News*, 8 July 1875, advert, for Engineer; *Diamond News*, Reports of the De Beers Mining Board, 26 June 1875 (23 June), 16 Dec. 1875 (8 Dec.), 11 Jan. 1876 (27, 28 Dec. 1875), 27 Jan. 1876 (6 Jan.); *Diamond News*, 15 Jan. 1876, 'Resident Magistrates

Court'; *Crossman Report* (May 1876), 46–47; UCT, Barry Papers, BC 127, 3 & 20 Jan. 1876.
47 *The Diamond Magnates*, 58.
48 RHL, Ms. Africa S 134, Note Book IV, C. J. Rhodes to either E. W. Tarry or W. Alderson, c. Oct. 1876, ff 14–15.
49 *Diamond News*, 10 Feb. 1876, Resolutions of Public Meeting (3 Feb.); *Diamond News*, Reports of De Beers Mining Board, 7 March 1876 (23 Feb.), 20 April 1878 (10 April); *Diamond News*, 2 Oct. 1877, 'By Our Special', 9 April 1878, 'De Beers', 5 Nov. 1878, C. J. Rhodes vs. De Beers Mining Board, High Court (31 Oct.); N. Rouillard (ed.) *Matabele Thompson: His Autobiography and Story of Rhodesia*, Johannesburg, 1957, [First published 1936], 107.
50 *Diamond News*, 24 April 1877, 'By Our Special'.
51 RHL, Ms. Africa, t 14, C. J. Rhodes to C. D. Rudd, 9 Oct. 1875; *Diamond News*, 15 April 1876, 'Abandoned Claims for sale', 22 Sept. & 6 Oct. 1877, 'By Our Special', 24 April 1877, 'Diamond Fields Association', Report by F. Oats; SBA, Inspection Reports (Kimberley), 1 Sept. 1876, f 211, 31 Dec. 1877, ff 76, 134, 138, 183; SBA, GM/LO, 3 Feb. 1880; CAD, GLW 153, Records, No. 730, Petition for Fixity of Claim Tenure, March 1880. See also chapter 10, figure 7, De Beers DMC shareholders.
52 RHL, Ms. Africa, t 14, C. J. Rhodes to C. D. Rudd, 11 April 1876.
53 *Diamond News*, 7 Nov. 1878, Queen vs. J. B. Finlason, Magistrate Court (4 Nov.).
54 *Diamond Fields Advertiser*, 14 July 1880, Petition from 104 Claimholders, 40 Managing Overseers and 313 Overseers.
55 *Diamond Fields Advertiser*, 30 July 1880, Legislative Council Debate on Searching Ordinance (29 July).
56 Ibid.
57 *Diamond Fields Advertiser*, 14 July 1880, Petition from 104 Claimholders, 40 Managing Overseers and 313 Overseers.
58 *Diamond Fields Advertiser*, 20 July 1880, Editorial.
59 *Diamond Fields Advertiser*, 30 July 1880, Legislative Council Debate on Searching Ordinance, speech of H. Green (29 July).
60 RHL, MS. Africa, S 228, C2A, No. 40, J. H. Lange to C. J. Rhodes, 22 Dec. 1891.
61 CAD, GLW 118, *Records*, No. 944, W. Coleman to Colonial Secretary, 18 April 1878; SBA, GM/LO, 13 Feb. 1880, Half Yearly Report (Henry Files).
62 Ibid.; CAD, LND 1/222, Schute to Captain Yonge, 7 May 1883.
63 See C. C. Ballard, 'Migrant Labour in Natal 1860–79: with Special Reference to Zululand and the Delagoa Bay Hinterland', *Journal of Natal and Zulu History*, I, 1978, 25–40.
64 *Griqualand West Government Gazette*, 23 May 1876, 'Report of the Commission upon the Griqualand Labour Question', paragraph 10.
65 'Report', paragraph 11.
66 'Report', paragraph 12.
67 'Report', paragraph 24.
68 'Report', paragraph 26.
69 'Report', paragraph 19
70 R. Sieborger, 'The Recruitment and Organisation of African Labour', M. A. thesis, Rhodes University (Grahamstown), 1976, 68–77, 101–5.
71 CAD, CO 3344, No. 129, Minute for the Colonial Secretary, 21 Dec. 1880.
72 'Report', paragraph 3.
73 CAD, GLW 120, No. 1451, Minutes for the Executive Council, 18 May 1878.
74 PRO, CO 879/9, Confidential African Print No. 84, 'Memorandum on South African Affairs', by Fairfield, Jan. 1876, 8. See also N. Etherington, 'Labour Supply and the Genesis of South African Confederation in the 1870s', *Journal of African History*, 20, 1979.
75 CAD, GLW 17, No. 4, W. O. Lanyon to J. Rose-Innes, 22 Feb. 1880.

76 CAD, CO 3344, No. 129, W. Coleman to Colonial Secretary, 11 Dec. 1880.
77 CPP, G16–'76, *BBNA*, 13.
78 *Diamond Fields Advertiser*, 18 Aug. 1880, Editorial.
79 See for example, UCT, Smalberger Papers, Kimberley Central DMC, Directors Minute Book I, 5 July 1881, f 112, 28 Feb. 1882, f 236.
80 CPP, G33–'82, *BBNA*, 181.
81 CAD, GLW 17, *Transvaal Despatches*, W. J. Coleman's minute on the Labour Question, 14 Feb. 1880.
82 *Diamond Fields Advertiser*, 18 Aug. 1880, 'The Labour Market'.
83 CAD, CO 3344, No. 129, W. J. Coleman to Colonial Secretary, 11 Dec. 1880.
84 *Daily Independent*, 12 Oct. 1880, Editorial.
85 R. F. Sieborger, 'Recruitment and Organisation of African Labour', 108–10.
86 E. von Weber, *Vier Jahre in Afrika 1871–75*, Leipzig, 1878, letter of 1 May 1872.
87 *Diamond News*, 4 April 1876, R. W. Murray's Auction Sales, 'The Sale of the Belgravia Residence and Landed Property of R. Southey'.
88 British Museum, Insurance Plan of Kimberley, October 1895.
89 CPP, G15–'85, Report of the Manager of Vooruitzicht Estate, 2.
90 *Diamond News*, 11 Jan. 1876.
91 CAD, GLW 108, No. 2120, 27 August 1877.
92 *Griqualand West Government Gazette*, 1 Sept. 1877, 'Report by Medical Inspector, Dutoitspan, for Year Ending 30 June 1877'.
93 *Daily Independent*, 11 Aug. 1883, Report of the Kimberley Town Council.
94 CAD, GLW 80, *Records*, No. 440, Shippard comment on Resolution passed at Meeting of Licensing Court, Kimberley, 23 Dec. 1875.
95 UCT, Smallberger Papers, T. Kitto, *Report on the Diamond Mines of Griqualand West*, 1979, 59.
96 Ibid., 104.
97 CAD, GLW 152, *Records*, No. 625, Government Notice No. 151 of 1879; UCT, Smalberger Papers, Report of the Joint Committee Representing the Mines . . . and Draft of Searching Rules and Regulations, 12 May 1882.
98 *Diamond News*, 8 April 1875, Proprietor's Notice; *Berliner Missions Berichte*, 1876, Report of Rev. Meyer, April–Nov. 1875, 111.
99 CAD, GLW 153, No. 835, W. Coleman to Colonial Secretary, 14 April 1880; CPP, A 14–'77, *Results of the Census in Griqualand West*.
100 *Diamond News*, 29 March 1879, 'Report on the Sanitary Condition of Kimberley', (Dr. J. W. Matthews and Dr. Shillito).
101 Ibid.
102 Ibid.
103 For the system of 'native locations' in Griqualand West, see K. Shillington *The Colonisation of the Southern Tswana 1870–1900*, Johannesburg, 1985, 61–83.
104 PRO, CO 108/2, Minutes of the Executive Council, Griqualand West, August 1873– October 1880, Minutes of 15 July 1879.
105 USPG, Reports, 30 Sept. 1878.
106 CAD, GLW 131, *Records*, No. 301, H. B. Webb to Scholtz, 27 Jan. 1879.
107 Government Notice No. 152 of 1880 (7 Sept.). Act 6 of 1876 and Act 8 of 1878 of the Cape Colony were made applicable to Griqualand West by Act 11 of 1879 (13 June). See *The Statute Law of Griqualand West*, 289 and Appendix I, 466.
108 *Diamond News*, 30 April 1881, Report of the Kimberley Town Council.
109 USPG, Reports, Mitchell, 30 Sept. 1881.
110 CPP, G26–'83, *Report of the Manager of Vooruitzicht*, 6.
111 *Daily Independent*, 24 Feb. 1883, Jim Squire vs. Denis Doyle, Magistrates Court.
112 CPP, G2–'88, *Commission on Convicts and Gaols*, ev. of Bradshaw, Resident Magistrate

of Beaconsfield, Q.1495. (Beaconsfield was the new township laid out near Dutoitspan in 1883.)

113 *Diamond News*, 29 March 1879, 'Report on the Sanitary Condition of Kimberley'.

114 See chapter 2, p. 29–30.

115 SBA, Inspection Reports (Kimberley), 15 March 1879, f 23, 3 Feb. 1880, f 103, 12 Nov. 1881, f 219, 29 Sept. 1883, f 133.

116 USPG, Reports, April 1886.

117 *Daily Independent*, 13 April 1883, Report of the Kimberley Town Council, 1 Dec. 1883, Report of the Kimberley Mining Board.

118 CAD, GLW 153, *Records*, No. 835, W. Coleman to Colonial Secretary, 14 April 1880; CAD, NA 186, No. 13, D. Heming to Under Secretary of Native Affairs, 26 Feb. 1881.

119 *Diamond News*, 24 Dec. 1881, Report of the Kimberley Town Council.

120 Ibid., 15 Dec. 1883.

121 CCP, G2–'85, *BBNA*, 209.

122 See chapter 2, note 32, and for the pass system, pp. 27–29.

123 *Griqualand Government Gazette*, 8 June 1878, Government Notice No. 108, An Act to Amend the Law Relating to Passes.

124 From February 1879 to July 1881 individual protection passes were published in the Government Gazette.

125 Methodist Missionary Society, SA XXVIII, Bloemfontein File 1880–81, J. Calvert to Secretary, 14 July 1880; CAD, HA 790, No. 334 (1883), Petition of . . . Native Residents and Labourers on the Diamond Fields [in favour of the restriction of the sale of liquor to Africans in Kimberley, the so-called Robinson liquor clause]; USPG, Reports, Mitchell, 31 Dec. 1885 & 31 Dec. 1886.

126 SBA, Inspection Reports (Kimberley), 15 March 1879, f 23, 12 Nov. 1881, ff 37–42, 3 Oct. 1891, f 90; Inspection Report (Port Elizabeth), 17 June 1885, f 173.

127 In 1878 James Poote owned 13 claims in Dutoitspan and in 1881 he put them into the Ne Plus Ultra DMC. In 1883 his shares were worthless and he sold them, together with shares in the European DMC, at a loss. In 1879 Gwayi Tyamzashe owned three claims in Dutoitspan Mine. In 1885 he was the last black claimowner in Kimberley. (CAD, DOK 2/3, Share Transfers.)

128 *Daily Independent*, 4 Dec. 1882, Affidavit of J. Moss, 22 Dec. 1882, 'Horse Theft', 12 July 1883, advert. for the Malay Camp, 13 Dec. 1883, 'Formation of an Africander League'; CAD, AG 126, J. Moss to Registrar of the High Court, 25 Feb. 1886; P. M. Laurence, Reports of Cases in the High Court of Griqualand West, Johannesburg, 1973, Vol. III, Rojesky vs. Ross, Judgement, 143.

129 *Transvaal Advocate and Commercial Advertiser*, 10 Jan. 1876, 'Diamond Fields – Native Advancement'. Thanks to D. Copland for this reference.

130 Methodist Missionary Society, SA XVIII, Bechuanaland File 1872–74, Slade to Perks, 25 Sept. 1874, Bloemfontein File 1880–81, Culshaw to Secretary, 4 April 1880; USPG, Reports, Canon Gaul, 2 Nov. 1881, 21 March 1883, 9 Jan. 1884 & Michaelmas 1884, Sister Catherine, April 1886; USPG, Letters and Papers, Canon Gaul, 3 Jan. 1885 & 30 Sept. 1885.

131 CAD, HA 796, No. 88 (1885), Petition of the Coloured Population of Kimberley.

132 *Daily Independent*, 10 Oct. 1882, Editorial.

133 See M. W. Swanson, 'The Sanitation Syndrome; Bubonic Plague and Urban Native Policy in the Cape Colony, 1900–09', *Journal of African History*, 28 (3) 1977.

134 CAD, GLW 84, *Records*, No. 917, Petition of C. J. Rhodes and others, 4 March 1876; *Diamond Fields Advertiser*, 22 Jan. 1885, Report of Kimberley Mining Board.

135 CAD, LND 1/227, H. Hutton to Assistant Commissioner, 13 Sept. 1886 & 23 Sept. 1887, Marquard to Haarhoff, 27 Oct. 1888.

136 SAL, Merriman papers, C. J. Rhodes to J. X. Merriman, 16 May 1880.

6 THE 'SHARE MANIA'

1 PRO, CO 107/7/19807, Comments on Warren Despatch, 13 Dec. 1879. The imperial war debt was £245,410 and the Province owed £90,000 to the Bank of England; £62,500 to the London and South African Exploration Company; £63,904 to the banks for overdrafts; and £15,651 to the Crown Agents.

2 SBA, GM/LO, 29 April, 15 Dec. 1881 (Henry Files). These figures for capitalisation in 1881 are correct, whereas the figures in Rob Turrell, '*Kimberley: Labour and Compounds*' (1982) 72, are, as a result of a printing error, incorrect.

3 See Appendix 2–6, for a detailed breakdown of this table.

4 H. Frankel, *Capital Investment in Africa: Its Course and Effects*, London, 1938, 63–64.

5 SBA, GM/LO, 12 Nov. 1881 (Henry Files).

6 SBA, GM/LO, 16 April 1880 (Henry Files).

7 SBA, GM/LO, 6 Aug. 1880, 11 Feb. 1881 (Henry Files). The total assessment of the mine was £1,588,710.

8 Ibid. The two exceptions were the Compagnie Française (£5,000) and the Cape (£4,500).

9 CAD, GDM 2/6, Kimberley Share Exchange Company, Letter Book, f 265, Thomson to Fairbridge and Petit, 18 Nov. 1880.

10 SBA, GM/LO, 11 Feb. 1881.

11 *Diamond News*, 7 April 1881. Committee members were: Dr Murphy (Chairman), T. G. Slater, B. Barnato, J. G. Poole,. E. M. Litkie, P. J. Richter, R. Granichstadten, H. Abraham, H. L. Lyon.

12 SBA, Inspection Report (Kimberley), 12 Nov. 1881, f 478.

13 *Griqualand West Investors' Guardian and Commercial Record*, 12 May 1881, 'Time Bargains'.

14 SBA, GM/LO, 8 April 1881 (Henry Files).

15 SBA, GM/LO, 1 April 1881 (Henry Files). In January the discounts and overdrafts of the Standard Bank totalled £399,000; in September they were £786,000, three quarters of the paid-up capital of the Bank. (SBA, XL, 24 Nov. 1881, [Henry Files])

16 *Diamond News*, 31 March 1881, Editorial.

17 *Griqualand West Investors' Guide and Commercial Record*, 5 May 1881.

18 *Lantern*, 2 April 1881, 6.

19 *Diamond News*, 31 March 1881, Editorial.

20 SBA, Inspection Report (Kimberley), 12 Nov. 1881, f 481.

21 See p. 113.

22 SBA, Inspection Report (Kimberley), 29 Nov. 1884, f 93.

23 Ibid., 15 March 1879, f 63; 3 Feb. 1880, f 153; 12 Nov. 1881, ff 293, 155–65; 29 Nov. 1884, f 93.

24 Ibid., 12 Nov. 1881, f 297; 29 Sept. 1883, f 85.

25 Ibid., 12 Nov. 1881, f 489.

26 Ibid., 29 Nov. 1884, f 175.

27 Ibid., 21 Jan. 1888, f 125.

28 In 1862 McKenzie began as a contractor for the Cape Town Council with little or no capital. Some years later he started a landing, shipping and forwarding agency at the docks. He bought unoccupied waste land on which he built houses from bricks made on the soil, employing his dock labourers when his dock business was slack. On 31 December 1880 his assets amounted to £151,545 of which his landed property was valued at £80,000.

29 CAD, MOIB, 2/1596, No. 351, First Report of Trustees, 29 March 1882.

30 Ibid.

31 CAD, MOIB, 2/1583, Trustees Report, 5 Oct. 1882.

32 SBA, Inspection Report (Port Elizabeth), 30 Jan. 1882, f 497.

33 Ibid., f 541; 29 Sept. 1888, f 79. In 1881 he owned £8,000 worth of fixed property and borrowed £28,000 from the Standard Bank.

34 SBA, Inspection Report (Port Elizabeth) 30 Jan. 1882, f 595; 26 May 1884, f 511. He bought £35,000 worth of diamond scrip which was worth £7,000 in 1882.

35 SBA, Inspection Report (Kimberley), 30 Jan. 1882, f 595; 13 Feb. 1883, f 588.

36 CAD, GDM 2/6, Kimberley Share Exchange Company, Letter Book, Thomson to Fairbridge & Petit, 13 Jan. 1881, f 479.

37 However, dealing in shares of unquoted companies was a common practice on the Exchange. See BPP, 1888, *Select Committee on East India (Hyderabad Deccan Mining Company)*, ev. of F. Levien, Q. 1–41.

38 SBA, GM/LO, 25 March 1881 (Henry Files).

39 *Investors' Guardian and Commercial Record*, 5 May 1881, 3.

40 SBA, GM/LO, 12 Nov. 1881 (Henry Files).

41 CPP, A9–'82, *Select Committee on Illicit Diamond Buying*, ev. of S. Marks, Q.260–63; GDM 2/3, Dutoitspan DMC, Letter Book, Birkenstock to Knights & Hearle, 16 Sept. 1881, f 338.

42 SBA, Inspection Report (Kimberley), 12 Nov. 1881, f 331. In 1880 Knight's claims were worth £12,000.

43 SBA, Inspection Report (Kimberley), 7 Nov. 1885, f 106; CPP, A7–'91, *Select Committee on Griqualand West Trade and Business* ev. of P. J. Marais, Q.2074–2082.

44 SBA, Inspection Report (Kimberley), 12 Nov. 1881, f 333. On the 30 June 1883 the partners' capital was £220,249: Isaac Lewis, £59,031; Barnett Lewis, £74,168; Sammy Marks, £87,050. The major items in their assets were mining scrip (£102,954) and the Hatherley Transvaal Distillery (£60,000). [GM/LO, 25 August 1883, (Henry Files)]

45 See pp. 3, 74, 77.

46 CAD, GDM 2/6, Kimberley Share Exchange Company, Letter Book, O. Skill to P. Rothwell, 25 Nov. 1880, f 288.

47 'The Anglo–French is now almost entirely in the hands of Charles Roulina and Mr Charles Herz of Paris. The former holds 3/4 of the claims for which he paid £130,000 and the latter 1/8 which cost him £28,000'. [SBA, GM/LO, 12 Nov. 1881 (Henry Files).]

48 PRO, BT 31, 15606/2838, Anglo–African Diamond Mining Company, Memorandum of Association. The vendors were: Joseph Lewis, Elia Marks, Joseph Marks, Montagu Davis, Isaac Lewis, Barnet Lewis, Samuel Marks, Samuel Paddon, Anthony Goldschmidt, Charles Sonnenberg and Julius Wernher.

49 SBA, GM/LO, 10 Feb. 1882 (Henry Files); N. M. Rothschild and Sons Archive, London, 4/47, A. Gansl to N. M. Rothschild and Sons, 21, 29 March 1882.

50 Ibid., 30 Aug. 1882.

51 Ibid., 28 Sept. 1882.

52 Ibid., 16 Nov. 1882.

53 The Victoria Company (1881), capital £300,000, was a reflotation of the Hamburg registered *Diamant Commandit Gesellschaft* (1880), capital £80,000. J. H. Schröder and Company took over the £80,000 mortgage of the Hamburg Company. Major shareholders of the Victoria Company were: J. H. Schröder and Sons, Erlanger and Company, David Lippert, James Ferguson and Louis Floersheim. [SBA, GM/LO 2 June 1881 (Henry Files); PRO, BT 31, 15498/2825, Memorandum of Association, Victoria Company]

54 CAD, DOK 2/1, Standard DMC, Share Transfers. In March 1881 Standards were selling at £280.

55 *Prospectuses of Diamond Mining and Other Companies*, Kimberley, 1881.

56 *Dutoitspan Herald*, 29 Sept. 1880, 'Mining Companies'.

57 *Diamond News*, 5 Oct. 1880, Editorial.

58 *Diamond News*, 17 Nov. 1881, High Court, Robinson vs. Richardson.

59 *Diamond News*, 6 Dec. 1881, Editorial.

60 CAD, DOK 2/1, Cape DMC, Share Transfers. The Company was formed on 30 June 1879 in Port Elizabeth with a capital of £100,00 in £10 shares. Its directors were H. B. Christian, R. Petit, J. A. Holland, and Emil Castens. The Lilienfelds, Castens, Christians and John Dixon were the largest original holders in the company. On 25 August 1880 John Dixon, a Leeds merchant, sold his shares to Barnet Lewis (1,307), R. M. Roberts (1107), and Wernher [for Porges] (600).

61 CAD, GDM 2/2, Cape DMC, Letter Book, Ramsay Denny to Grellert, 2 July 1880, f 20; Holland telegram to J. B. Robinson, 20 July 1880, f 39; Ramsay Denny to J. B. Robinson, 8 Sept. 1880, f 93; Ramsay Denny to M. Lilienfeld, 29 Sept. 1880, f 113; Ramsay Denny to Dyason and Carlisle, 20 Dec. 1880, f 196; Ramsay Denny to J. B. Robinson, 13 Jan. 1881, f 250. The capital of the company was increased to £330,000; Robinson and Marcus held 8,424 and 6,173 shares respectively.

62 *Diamond News*, 17 Nov. 1881, High Court, Robinson vs. Richardson (editor of the *Diamond News*). Judge Buchanan found that the defendants had proved no fraud in the promotion of the Crystal. Robinson, at this time a Member of the Cape Legislature, sued for £10,000 but was awarded 50s and costs. He failed even to win an apology.

63 CAD, DOK 3/2, Cape DMC Trust Deed, 28 Dec. 1881.

64 CAD, GDM 5/2, South West DMC Liquidation. The Cape of Good Hope Bank held both these companies from 1884 until 1886 when they were sold to Sir Donald Currie.

65 *Investors' Guardian and Commercial Record*, 21 July 1881.

66 CAD, GDM 2/2, Cape DMC, Letter Book, J. A. Holland to Grellert, 9 March 1881, f 378.

67 KPL, Fry's Gully DMC, Journal; SBA, Inspection Report (Kimberley), 12 Nov. 1881, f 229.

68 The British DMC paid dividends out of advances so as to hold diamonds for a rise in the market, but the Standard Bank regarded this as a fraud on the shareholders. (SBA, GM/LO, 5 Aug. 1881, 28 Oct. 1882).

69 SBA, Inspection Report (Kimberley), 12 Nov. 1881, f 229.

70 See R. V. Turrell, 'Rhodes, De Beers and Monopoly', 313–19.

71 RHL, Ms. Africa, S 1647, Hildersham Hall Papers, Cecil Rhodes to Aunt Sophy, 29 June 1880.

72 CAD, DOK 3/2, De Beers DMC, Trust Deed, Annexure C.

73 See chapter 10: figure 7, De Beers DMC shareholders, p. 214.

74 RHL, Ms. Africa t 14, Cecil Rhodes to Charles Rudd, 1 Feb. 1881. The De Beers share transfers for April 1880 to March 1881 are missing from the Cape Archives and it is unknown what he paid to buy back into the company. Rhodes sold shares in Cape Town through Bolus Brothers. (GDM, 2/6, Kimberley Share Exchange Company, Letter Book, O. Skill to Bolus Brothers, f 189)

75 CAD, DOK 3/2, De Beers DMC, Trust Deed, 23 March 1881, Annexure C; DOK 2/1–2/4, Share Transfers; SBA, Inspection Report (Kimberley) 29 Sept. 1883, ff 103, 225.

76 See *Prospectuses of Diamond Mining and Other Companies*, Kimberley, 1881.

77 RHL, Ms. Africa t 14, Cecil Rhodes to Charles Rudd, 1 June 1881.

78 Capital £20,000: directors – T. Lynch, E. W. Tarry, H. B. Wallis, O. J. Skill, C. J. Rhodes, R. D. Graham; major shareholders – O. J. Skill.

79 The assessed value of the Beaconsfield claims was only £40,395. It is not known how much the Compagnie Française sold them for, but they made £200,000 from selling claims in 1881. The Kimberley North Block DMC paid £90,000 for five claims and Robinson bought another block, for an unspecified sum, and put them into the Standard DMC. (SBA, Inspection Report (Kimberley), 12 Nov. 1881, f 326).

80 SBA, Inspection Report (Kimberley), 12 Nov. 1881, f 482.

81 CAD, DOK 3/1, Beaconsfield DMC, Trust Deed, 4 May 1881.

82 See chapter 5, p. 84.

83 CAD, DOK 3/4, International DMC, Trust Deed; KPL, International DMC, Volume 1;

Prospectuses of Diamond Mining and Other Companies, Kimberley, 1881, 62; SBA, Inspection Report (Kimberley), 29 Sept. 1883, ff 243, 244, 623; RHL, Ms. Africa t 14, Cecil Rhodes to Charles Rudd, 1 Feb. 1881; CAD, LND 105, W. Ward to Secretary of Land Dept., 1 Aug. 1881; *Notulen der Commissie op 24 Juin 1884 aangestel tot onderzoek van zaken betrekkelijk Jagersfontein*, Bloemfontein, ev. of Richard Fryer Jones, 19.

84 H. Raymond, *B. I. Barnato: A Memoir*, London, 1897; S. Jackson, *The Great Barnato*, London, 1970.

7 THE DEPRESSION AND STRIKES OF 1883 AND 1884

1 SAL, 'The President and Members of the Board of the Compagnie Française', 3. The calculation of capital and company liquidations have been collated from company and bank records. The capital does not include the 56 private holdings, most of which were insignificant with the exception of W. A. Hall, assessed at £80,864, and W. & B. Stuart, assessed at £32,562. See Appendix table 7. See also Table 1, exports and imports of the Cape Colony, 1869–88.

2 The four per cent return is calculated on a capital of £10 million and the figures for net profit are taken from A. Moulle, *Geologie Generale et Mines de Diamants de L'Afrique du Sud*, Paris, 1886, 120 and 'To the President and Members of the Board of Directors of the Compagnie Française', 5.

3 CPP, G30–'84, *RIDM*. Production costs changed from year to year, but these figures make clear the relative average richness of each mine.

4 CAD, NA 186, Coleman to Secretary of Native Affairs, 8 & 32, 19 Jan. and 2 May 1881.

5 *The Griqualand West Investors' Guardian and Commercial Record*, 21 July 1881, British DMC First Annual Report, 5.

6 RHL, Ms Africa t 14, Rhodes to Rudd, 1 Feb. 1881, 2, 3; *The Statist*, 9 June 1888, 651.

7 For the debate see *Griqualand West Investors' Guardian and Commercial Record*, 'The Labour Question', 24 Nov. 1881, 1, 8, 29 Dec. 1881; *Diamond News*, 22 Dec. 1881, 7 Feb. 1882. For 'civilised labour' on the Rand see R. Davies, 'Mining Capital, the State and Unskilled White Workers in South Africa', *JSAS*, 3 (1) 1976.

8 *Diamond News*, 22 Dec. 1881, Editorial.

9 Ibid.

10 CPP, G28–'85, *RIDM*, 12.

11 CPP, A9–'82, *Select Committee on IDB*, Q.218.

12 Ibid., Q.217.

13 It is interesting to note a shift in official racial terminology in 1885. Up to this date Indians, Malays and 'persons of colour' had been included under the heading 'Europeans' by government officials, while only 'Kaffirs and Hottentots' were classed as 'natives'. But in 1885 the Registrar of Deaths announced that this practice was 'undoubtedly misleading' and 'persons of Asiatic descent' and 'other coloured people' were classified separately for official purposes from then onwards. (*Diamond Fields Advertiser*, 13 Jan. 1885) In mine labour statistics 'Coloureds' were only enumerated separately in 1883 and 1884 and thereafter lumped with 'natives and others'.

14 A. Moulle, *Geologie Generale*, 116; CPP, G 11–'90, *Reports of the Inspectors of Mines*, 38. These figures are averages for employment and wages and take little account of seasonality and discontinuities in production.

15 Ibid.; G34–'83, G30–'84, *RIDM*, 19, 21.

16 CPP, A9–'82, *Select Committee on IDB*, ev. of Sammy Marks, Q.351.

17 *Diamond Fields Advertiser*, 15 Aug. 1885, 'Bultfontein Mining Company'.

18 Elsa Smithers, *March Hare*, Oxford, 1935, 134; CAD, GDM, 6/1, Birkbeck, DMC Pay-sheets.

19 CPP, G3–'88, *Commission on the Diamond Trade Acts, the Detective or Searching*

Department, the Compound System and other matters connected with the Diamond Mining Industry of Griqualand West, ev. of A. W. Davis, Q.2600, Q.2607.

20 CPP, G34–'83, *RIM*, 34.

21 Ibid., 31, 60.

22 Ibid., 35, 47; *Diamond Fields Advertiser*, 23 Dec. 1882, 'Report of Meeting of Representatives of Diamond Interests' (London); CPP, G91–'83, *Reports of Resident Magistrates*, encl. by Inspector of Mines.

23 AAA, Gregory Papers, DMP B–6, 'Statement Respecting De Beers Mine', May 1882.

24 *Diamond News*, 1 June 1882, Annual Report; *Daily Independent*, 31 May 1883, Annual Report. Later annual reports did not break down the work-force in such detail. The rising costs of the Kimberley Central's wage bill was crucial in the sequence of strikes. The inability of the company to keep its complement of workers and to keep African wages down, despite recruitment from Inhambane in Mozambique can be traced in the Directors Minutes. See University of Cape Town, Smalberger Papers, Directors Minute Book I, 5 July 1881, f 112; 30 Dec 1881, f 178; 28 Feb. 1882, f 236; 24 Aug. 1882, f 302; 20 Nov. 1882, f 346; Directors Minute Book II, 8 May 1883, f 37; 28 Jan. 1884, f 255; 29 Feb. 1884, f 278.

25 CAD, GDM 5/2, *Insolvency Papers*, Crown Prosecutor to Kimberley Mining Board, 29 April 1885.

26 N. M. Rothschild and Sons Archive (RAL), A. Gansl to N. M. Rothschild and Sons, 7 Sept. 1882; *Daily Independent*, 10 May 1884, De Beers DMC Annual Report; *Daily Independent*, 19 Jan. 1885, French and d'Esterre Half Yearly Report.

27 *Diamond Fields Advertiser*, 31 Jan. 1885, 'Another Coloured Contractor'.

28 Rhodes (De Beers), Robinson (Standard), Baring Gould (Central), D'Esterre (French and D'Esterre), Ward (Anglo–African), Goldschmidt (MLA and sharebroker), Kilgour (London and South African Exploration), Hoskyns (advocate).

29 SAL, Merriman Papers, C. J. Rhodes to J. X. Merriman, 16 May 1880. See also A. Purkis, 'The Politics, Capital and Labour of Railway Building in the Cape Colony 1870–85, unpub. D.Phil., Oxford 1978.

30 RHL, Ms. Africa S 134, VI, C. D. Rudd to C. J. Rhodes, n.d., 55.

31 'The Imperial Factor in South Africa in the Nineteenth Century', *Journal of Imperial and Commonwealth History*, 3 (1) 1974, 125.

32 'Labour Supply and the Genesis of South African Confederation in the 1870s', *Journal of African History*, 20, 1979.

33 *Diamond News*, 24 Feb. 1881.

34 RHL, Ms. Africa s 229, C. J. Rhodes to J. Scanlen, 3 Sept. 1882, f 5(b).

35 See the most recent example, J. Flint, *Cecil Rhodes*, London, 1974, 61.

36 K. Shillington, *The Colonisation on the Southern Tswana, 1870–1900*, 142, 155–61.

37 CPP, A9–'82, *Select Committee on Illicit Diamond Buying*, iii–iv.

38 Ibid., iii.

39 *Griqualand West Investors Guardian and Commercial Record*, 24 Nov, 1 Dec. 1881.

40 *Daily Independent*, 18 Nov. 1882, 'Report of Working Men's Association Meeting', Prince Imperial Hall.

41 CPP, G62–'83, *Report of Manager of the Vooruitzicht Estate*.

42 CPP, G28–'85, *Report of the Inspector of Machinery*. In 1884 he estimated that the cost of living of an artisan was between £2 15s and £3 10s a week.

43 CPP, G50–'85, *Correspondence Regarding the Dismissal of J. L. Fry*, Report, 18. The system cost £30,836 per annum in salaries alone.

44 Ibid., Annexure D, Letter from Tinling, 1 Oct. 1884, 78.

45 Ibid., 77.

46 *Daily Independent*, 2 March 1883, Kimberley Mining Board Meeting.

47 *Daily Independent*, 13 oct. 1883, 'Amended Regulations'.

48 *Daily Independent*, 10 May 1884, De Beers DMC Annual General Meeting, speech of Frederic Stow. The Kimberley Central proposed to resolve the strike by excluding the engine-houses and work-shops from the searching area. (UCT Smalberger Papers, Kimberley Central DMC, Directors Minute Book I, 16 Oct. 1883, f 157.)

49 *Daily Independent*, 29 April 1884, 'The Test Case'.

50 Ibid. Advocate Lord's defence of four workers who refused to strip in March 1884 provides a lucid account of the October 1883 compromise.

51 UCT, Judge Papers, B 46, *Medical Commission Report*, 1883. The best account of the epidemic is in Hans Sauer, *Ex-Africa*, London, 1937, 72–9 and the case for the opposition can be found in J. W. Matthews, *Incwadi Yami*, London, 1887, 108–11, 424–5. At this time Matthews was crippled by gambling debts and forced to give up his seat in Parliament to concentrate on his profession and an offer of the compounds 'which meant another £600 per annum' was enough to sway his medical judgement. In this connection there is an interesting account of the affair by the daughter of Dr Smith, Rhodes House Library, Ms. Africa t 11, *Reminiscences of Mrs Tony Hickman.*

52 *British Medical Journal*, 12 Jan. 1884, 83; 2 Feb. 1884, 245.

53 UCT, Judge Papers, B 76, E. A. Judge *An Autobiographical Account of his Life in South Africa*, Ms., f 405.

54 Ibid., f 412.

55 Ibid., f 407; H. Sauer, *Ex Africa*, 78; *Daily Independent*, 27 March 1884, 20 May 1884, *Queen vs. H. A. Wolff.*

56 *Daily Independent*, 13 Dec. 1883, 'Basutoland Quarantined'.

57 J. Angove, *In the Early Days*, Kimberley, 1910, 158.

58 E. A. Judge, *An Autobiographical Account*, f 412; Standard Bank Archive (Johannesburg), General Manager to London Office, 15 Dec. 1883.

59 *Daily Independent*, 29 April 1884, 'The Test Case'. For the new policy, Anglo–American Archive (Johannesburg), Gregory Papers, Kimberley Central DMC, Directors Minute Book II, 16 Feb. 1884 and 9 April 1884. This contrasted with their earlier conciliatory policy.

60 *Daily Independent*, 5 April 1884, 'Artisans' Association Meeting', 12 April 1884, 'Overseers Meeting'.

61 *Daily Independent*, 26 April 1884, 'Combined Working Mens' Committee Meeting'.

62 *Daily Independent*, 24 April 1884, 'Combined Working Mens' Committee Meeting'.

63 *Daily Independent*, 26 April 1884, 'Combined Working Mens' Committee Meeting'; UCT, Smalberger Papers, Kimberley Central DMC, Directors Minute Book II, 9 April 1884, f 318; 19 April 1884, f 328; 21 April 1884, f 332.

64 *Daily Independent*, 26 April 1884,'Combined Working Mens' Committee Meeting'.

65 Ibid.

66 *Daily Independent*, 3 May 1884, Editorial.

67 *Daily Independent*, 29 April 1884, 'The Race Course Meeting'.

68 *Daily Independent*, 1 May 1884, 'Kimberley Mining Board Meeting'.

69 In 1884, when Kimberley's representation was increased to four, commercial men swept the polls. G. G. Wolf, the Licensed Victuallers candidate, became the senior member, followed by George Goch, Moses Cornwall and Charles Rudd, who was a large mining machinery merchant besides being a director of De Beers DMC. William Ross, who was to champion merchant causes in the Legislative Council, was also elected in 1884. Alfred Hill, partner in the merchant firm of Hill and Paddon, and Cecil Rhodes, mine and landowner, were elected for Barkly West. Rhodes' brief spell in the government came to an end in the middle of May when the Uppington-Hofmeyr ministry assumed office and formed a loose alliance with Kimberley's commercial members.

70 *Daily Independent*, 3 May 1884, Editorial.

71 *Daily Independent*, 26 April 1884, 'Combined Working Mens' Committee Meeting'. The Kimberley Central Directors recognised that if the water gear was closed down they would

be forced to capitulate. (Smalberger Papers, Kimberley Central DMC, Directors Minute Book II, 28 April, 1884, f 349.)

72 *Daily Independent*, 3 May 1884, Editorial.

73 Ibid.

74 UCT, Smalberger Papers, Kimberley Central DMC, Directors Minute Book II, 1 May 1884, f 350; CAD, 1/KIM, 3/1/11, Inquest 29 April 1884.

75 *Daily Independent*, 3 May 1884, Editorial.

76 Ibid.

77 CAD, 1/KIM, 3/1/11, Inquest 29 April 1884.

78 *Daily Independent*, 3 May 1884, Editorial.

79 CAD, CO, 3453, No. 16, E. A. Judge to Under Colonial Secretary, 30 April 1884; *Daily Independent*, 8 May 1884, 'Cape Infantry'; *Daily Independent*, 20 May 1884, Editorial.

80 *Cape Hansard*, 1884, 36.

81 *Daily Independent*, 26 April 1884, 'Combined Working Mens' Commitee Meeting', speech of James Brown, one of the three Committee leaders.

82 *Daily Independent*, 29 Aug. 1882, 'Wages and the Kimberley Mining Board'.

83 *Daily Independent*, 16 and 18 Oct. 1883, 'Employers' Meeting'.

84 UCT, Smalberger Papers, Kimberley Central DMC, Directors Minute Book I, 28 Feb. 1883, f 421.

85 UCT, Smalberger Papers, Kimberley Central DMC, Directors Minute Book II, 26 April 1884, f 347; 3 May 1884, f 350; 7 May 1884, f 354.

86 Ibid., 26 April 1884, f 346.

87 *Cape Hansard*, 1884, 39.

88 *Daily Independent*, 18 Oct. 1883, 'Employers' Meeting'.

8 THE CLOSED COMPOUND SYSTEM

1 *Diamond Fields Advertiser*, 19 Jan. 1885; *Daily Independent*, 12 June 1885, 'Inauguration of the Compound System' and 8 May 1886, De Beers DMC, Annual General Meeting, comments by C. D. Rudd; G3–'88, *Commission . . . into the Diamond Trade Acts*, ev. of F. R. Thompson, Q. 108; N. Rouillard (ed.) *Matabele Thompson: His Autobiography and Story of Rhodesia*, Johannesburg, 1957, 42–3.

2 *Daily Independent*, 12 June 1885, 'Inauguration of the Compound System'.

3 G. F. Williams, *Diamond Mines*, Vol. II, 53. F. R. Thompson's autobiography *Matabele Thompson* was reminisced long after the events described in the 1880s and 1890s and is unreliable on facts and figures.

4 The clearest statement of this view is to be found in CPP, A9–'82, *Select Committee on IDB*, Report. For historians subscribing to this view, see S. van der Horst, *Native Labour in South Africa*, 79, 82; G. V. Doxey, *The Industrial Colour Bar in South Africa*, 34; J. Smalberger, 'IDB and the Mining Compound System in the 1880', 398–414; C. van Onselen, *Chibaro*, 128–30.

5 CPP, A9–'82, *Select Committee on IDB*, ev. of S. Marks, Q.260–3.

6 RAL, 4/47, A. Gansl to N. M. Rothschild and Sons, 7 Sept. 1982.

7 CPP, A9–'82, *Select Committee on IDB*, ev. of S. Marks, Q.199–200, 324–5; G2–'88, *Commission on Convicts and Gaols*, ev. of J. Gouldie, Q.812–24.

8 J. W. Matthews, *Incwadi Yami*, 192. The company referred to was owned by Joseph Mylchreest.

9 Ibid., 193.

10 *Daily Independent*, 15 Dec. 1884, Kimberley Central DMC, Half-Yearly Report, 31 Oct. 1884.

11 AAA, Gregory Papers, DMP B–6, 'Statement Respecting De Beers Amalgamation', May 1882.

12 CPP, G101–'83, *Report by T. P. Watson on Diamond Mines*, 9.
13 SBA, 700:24, W. Kenrick to J. & P. Higson, 25 August 1884; SBA, GM/LO, 15 Sept. 1884 (Henry Files).
14 *Daily Independent*, 2 May 1885. Shafts in mine: Kimberley Central, claims 197, 348; Compagnie Française, claim 258; Stuart Brothers, claims 171, 172; Standard, claims 139, 140; W. A. Hall, claim 616.
15 SBA, Inspection Report (Kimberley), 7 Nov. 1885, f 95.
16 MM, Philipson Stow Papers, Report of Kimberley Central GM, Year ending 30 June 1888; Report of GM and Chief Engineer, 28 Feb. 1888.
17 MM, Philipson Stow Papers, Stow Letter-Book IV, F. S. P. Stow to Messrs. J. Taylor and Sons, 15 Jan. 1885, ff 8–9.
18 Ibid., Stow Letter-Book V, F. S. P. Stow to Scott, 2 March 1887; *Daily Independent*, May 1887, De Beers AGM.
19 AAA, Gregory Papers, De Beers DMC, Directors Minutes, 29 April, 9 May 1887.
20 G. F. Williams, *The Diamond Mines of South Africa*, Vol. I, 315.
21 *Diamond Fields Advertiser*, 19 June 1886; *Daily Independent*, 11 June 1887; MM, Philipson Stow Papers, Annual Report 30 June 1888.
22 *Reports of Cases in the High Court of Griqualand West*, Vol. III, Pt. IV, W. Kenrick vs. Kimberley Central DMC, 428; G. F. Williams, *Diamond Mines*, Vol. II, 47.
23 CPP, G13–'88, *Report of District Surgeon*, 23.
24 *Quarterly Bulletin of the Bloemfontein Mission*, No. 81, July 1881, 101.
25 SAL, Kimberley Central DMC, General Regulations, 'Special Rules for Regulating Blasting Operations in the Kimberley Mine', 27 Feb. 1886, 26; and 'Rules and Regulations for the Working of Diamond Mines, Promulgated under Act 19 of 1883', Rule 38, 45.
26 Ibid., General Regulations, 20.
27 CAD, LND 1/285, 'General Rules and Regulations for the Working of Diamond Mines', 1 July 1889, f 1563.
28 SBA, Inspection Report (Kimberley) 12 Nov. 1881, f 65; SAL, Merriman Papers, 1885, G. Smith to J. X. Merriman.
29 CPP, G3–'88, *Commission . . . into the Diamond Trade Acts*, Q.849.
30 See pp. 134, 141, 144, 198–204.
31 See Appendix table 1.
32 *Mining Journal*, 9 Dec. 1882, 'South African Diamond Mines'.
33 CPP, G3–'88, *Commission . . . into the Diamond Trade Acts*, Q.2131.
34 CPP, A7–'91, *Select Committee on Trade and Business in Griqualand West*, ev. of G. F. Williams, Q.4245.
35 CPP, G2–'88, *Commission on Convicts and Gaols*, Second Report, xliii.
36 CAD, CO 3454, no. 244, F. S. P. Stow telegram to Graham, 4 Oct. 1884, Wright telegram to Graham, 11 Oct. 1884, Colonial Under-Secretary to E. A. Judge, 12 Jan. 1886; CO 3556, no. 51, E. A. Judge to Colonial Under-Secretary, 4 Oct. 1887; CPP, G2–'88, *Commission on Convicts and Gaols*, First Report, iv.
37 R. F. Sieborger, 'Recruitment', 129–31.
38 CPP, G40–'86, *RIDM*, 12.
39 CPP, G22–'89, *RIDM*, 9, quoting Gardner Williams in De Beers report for year ending 31 March 1888.
40 Between July 1884 and June 1887 over 8,000 people were convicted each year in Kimberley and sent to gaol; of these over 3,000 were convicted under the pass laws while double that number had been arrested for the same offences (CPP, G2–'88, *Commission on Convicts and Gaols*, First Report, ii).
41 In 1887 there was a daily average of 2,238 convicts in the Cape Colony of whom 870, or over one-third, were imprisoned in Kimberley (*Cape Hansard*, 1888, 58–9).
42 CAD, CO 3556, no. 28, E. A. Judge to Colonial Under-Secretary, 19 July 1887; CO 6410,

no. 23, R. G. Scott (Convict Station Superintendent) to High Sheriff, Cape Town, 18 April 1889; CPP, G3–'94, *Labour Commission*, ev. of R. G. Scott, Q.17446.

43 CAD, CO 6427, no. 51, R. G. Scott to Law Department, 22 April 1890.

44 Ibid.

45 *Cape Hansard*, 1892, 10.

46 *Daily Independent*, 8 May 1886, De Beers DMC, Annual General Meeting; CPP, G2–'88, *Commission on Convicts and Gaols*, Second Report, xliii; CAD, CO 6427, no. 46a, Enclosure in R. G. Scott to Law Department, 18 March 1890; CPP, A7–'91, *Select Committee on Trade and Business in Griqualand West*, ev. of G. F. Williams, Q.4245; CPP, G3–'94, *Labour Commission*, ev. of R. G. Scott, Q.17318, 17322.

47 CAD, CO 6427, no. 49, R. G. Scott to Law Department, 18 April 1890.

48 *Statistical Registers of the Colony of the Cape of Good Hope, 1890–99.*

49 CAD, CO 3526, no. 166, E. A. Judge to Colonial Under-Secretary, 14 April 1886; CPP, G2–'88, *Commission on Convicts and Gaols*, ev. of S. Dallas (dismissed Convict Station Superintendent), Q.1037; CAD, CO 6396, no. 58, R. G. Scott to Visiting Magistrate, 14 May 1888.

50 *Daily Independent*, 9 Aug. 1884, 'Convict Strike'; CAD, CO 3454, no. 227, Colonial Under Secretary telegram to E. A. Judge, 18 Nov. 1884; CO 3556, no. 70, F. R. Bradshaw (Resident Magistrate) to E. A. Judge, 6 Dec. 1887.

51 CAD, CO 6396, no. 115, Macleod Robinson (Visiting Magistrate) to Colonial Under-Secretary, 13 Aug. 1888.

52 *Daily Independent*, 12 June 1886, 'Miners Union Meeting', speeches by Baring Gould and Davis; CPP, G3–'88, *Commission . . . into the Diamond Trade Acts*, ev. of J. Gifford, Q.2205.

53 CPP, A7–'91, *Select Committee on Trade and Business in Griqualand West*, ev. of J. P. Kriel (Dutch Reformed Minister) Q. 1804–05; CAD, NA 411, W. Craven to Secretary of Native Affairs, 23 June 1896.

54 CAD, NA 455, J. G. Leary to Under Secretary for Native Affairs, 9 March 1889.

55 CPP, G22–'89, *RIDM*, 9.

56 A. R. Sawyer, *Mining at Kimberley*, Newcastle-under-Lyme, 39; J. J. Van-Helten, 'British and European Economic Investment in the Transvaal with Specific Reference to the Witwatersrand Gold Fields and District, 1886–1910', unpub. Ph.D., University of London, 1981, app. II, table 18; *Statistical Registers of the Cape Colony*, 1890–99.

57 CAD, LND 1/220, Captain Erskine to Secretary for Lands and Mines, 9 April 1886.

58 *Berliner Missions Berichte*, 1889, 116.

59 UCT, Judge Papers, B 47, Commission of Enquiry into the De Beers Disaster, 4 August 1888; G. F. Williams, *Diamond Mines*, Vol. II, 39.

60 CPP, G2–'88, *Commission on Convicts and Gaols*, First Report, ii.

61 *Diamond News*, 29 March 1879, 'Report on the sanitary condition of Kimberley'. The total population of Kimberley (excluding the smaller township of Dutoitspan) was, according to the 1877 census, 14,169 (6,574 Europeans and 7,595 Others). The European death-rate was 40 per thousand.

62 The 1888 figure is calculated from a Kimberley (excluding Beaconsfield) population of 28,000 (12,000 Europeans and 16,000 Others) (*Statistical Register of the Cape Colony, 1889*).

63 CPP, G3–'89, *BBNA*, 17.

64 *Diamond News*, 29 March 1879, 'Report on the sanitary condition of Kimberley'.

65 CPP, G52–1901, *BBNA*, 74. For the change in causes of death, CPP, *Reports of the District Surgeon*, G3–'86, 22, G19–'87, 18; G1–'90, *Commission on Liquor Laws*, App. I, 1058.

66 CAD, NA 455, J. G. Leary to Under Secretary of Native Affairs, 9 March 1889; NA 411, W. Craven to Secretary of Native Affairs, 23 June 1896.

67 G. F. Williams, *Diamond Mines*, Vol. II, 53–60.

68 CAD, LND 1/369, W. Craven to Commissioner of Crown Lands, 16 Oct. 1891, L550.
69 CPP, G52–1901, *BBNA*, 74.
70 UCT, Judge Papers B 47, *Commission of Enquiry into the De Beers Disaster*, 4 Aug. 1888.
71 CAD, NA 411, G. W. Barnes (Protector of Natives) to Under Secretary for Native Affairs, 13 July 1896.
72 CPP, G2–'88, *Commission on Convicts and Gaols*, First Report, ii.
73 CAD, NA 411, G. W. Barnes to Under Secretary for Native Affairs, 13 July 1896.
74 CPP, G1–'90, *Commission on Liquor Laws*, ev. of Dr J. E. McKenzie, Q.6871, 6886–6887.
75 *The South African Mines, Commerce and Industries*, 25 April 1903, 'Report on "Compound System" ', 145. I am grateful to Professor van Onselen for drawing this to my attention.
76 CPP, G2–'88, *Commission on Convicts and Gaols*, ev. of F. R. Thompson, Q.186.
77 *The South African Mines, Commerce and Industries*, 25 April 1903, 145.
78 F. Wilson and D. Perrot (eds.) *Outlook on a Century: South Africa 1870–1970*, Johannesburg, 1972, 301.
79 South African Parliamentary Papers, U.G. 34–1914, 161. I am grateful to Neil Anderson for this reference.
80 BPP, (1904), *South African Mines (Mortality)*, Enclosure in no. 6 & 9.
81 BPP, Cd. 2025 (1904), *Correspondence Relating to Conditions of Native Labour Employed in the Transvaal Mines*, no. 4, 22 Feb. 1904, 41.
82 See P. Richardson, *Chinese Mine Labour in the Transvaal*, London, 1982, 34.
83 BPP, Cd. 2025 (1904), op. cit., no. 17, Lyttelton telegram to Lord Milner, 9 May 1904, 67; Cd. 1897 (1904), *Minutes of Proceedings and Evidence of the Transvaal Labour Commission*, 'Report on Mortality among Natives Employed on the Mines of the Witwatersrand', 389.
84 BPP, Cd. 2025 (1904), op. cit., enclosure 1 in no. 12, Memorandum from the Native Affairs Department, 31 March 1904, 62.
85 C. van Onselen, *Chibaro*, 131–3.
86 Ibid., 50.
87 Ibid., 57.
88 C. A. Perrings, *Black Mineworkers in Central Africa*, London, 1979, 168.
89 Ibid., 174–7, 202.
90 S. Stichter, *Migrant Laborers*, Cambridge, 1985, 90.
91 C. A. Perrings, *Black Mineworkers*, 240.
92 H. Wolpe, 'Capitalism and Cheap Labour-Power in South Africa: from Segregation to Apartheid', *Economy and Society*, 1 (4) 1972, 425–56.
93 S. Stichter, *Migrant Laborers*, 29–57.
94 K. Shillington, *The Colonisation of the Southern Tswana*, 90–114.
95 *Diamond News*, 2 May 1876, Editorial.
96 CPP, G8–'83, *BBNA*, Appendix, 3.
97 Ibid., 5.
98 R. V. Turrell, 'Kimberley: Labour and Compounds, 1871–1888' in S. Marks and R. Rathbone (eds.) *Industrialisation and Social Change in South Africa*, 57.
99 CPP, G22–'89, *RIDM*, 6.
100 CPP, G3–'88, *Commission . . . into the Diamond Trade Acts*, ev. of A. Davis, Q.2846.
101 G. F. Williams, *Diamond Mines*, Vol. II, 57.
102 CPP, G3–94, *Labour Commission*, ev. of W. H. Powell (Location Superintendent), Q.17188–17183. See also Chapter 5, 'Social Geography'.
103 CPP, G29–1903, *BBNA*, 91.
104 Ibid.
105 See B. Willan, *Sol Plaatje: South African Nationalist 1876–1932*, Heinemann, 1984, 29.

106 In 1891 Shangaan and Pedi were still in a majority in the mine labour force (CPP, G7–'92, *BBNA*, 16); but by 1895 South Sotho and Tswana had taken over (G5–'96, *BBNA*, 34; G19–'97, *BBNA*, 32; G31–'99, *BBNA*, 31; G25–1902, *BBNA*, 80); and in 1897 Tswana flocked to the mines (G42–'98, *BBNA*, 36) after the rebellion and the rinderpest epidemic.

107 CPP, G5–'96, *BBNA*, 34; G31–'99, *BBNA*, 34; C. van Onselen, *Chibaro*, 131.

108 CPP, G24–'91, *RIDM*, 5.

109 CPP, G3–'88, *Commission . . . into the Diamond Trade Acts*, ev. of J. Gifford, Q.2200.

110 CAD, NA (B1475), Stephens to Civil Commissioner, 17 May 1895.

111 CPP, A7–'91, *Select Committee on Trade and Business in Griqualand West*, ev. of T. Griffin (General Manager of Bultfontein Consolidated), Q.1968. For the system of piece-work payment, see G31–99, *BBNA*, 34.

112 CPP, G3–'88, *Commission . . . into the Diamond Trade Acts*, ev. of J. Gifford (Kimberley Central Compound Manager), Q.2222.

113 Ibid., ev. of F. R. Thompson, Q.120.

114 CAD, LND 1/346, Captain Erskine (Mine Inspector) to Chairman of De Beers Consolidated, 29 May 1890.

115 CPP, G24–'91, *RIDM*, 5.

116 CPP, G27–'92, *RIDM*, 11.

117 CAD, NA 455, J. G. Leary (Protector of Natives) to Under Secretary of Native Affairs, 7 Oct. 1889.

118 Ibid., J. Davis Allen (Manager of the Anglo–African DMC) to J. G. Leary, 2 Sept. 1889.

119 CPP, G8–'95, *BBNA*, 20.

120 CAD, NA 411, G. W. Barnes (Protector of Natives) to Secretary of Native Affairs, 13 July 1896.

121 Ibid.

122 Ibid., 163.

9 ILLICIT DIAMOND BUYING AND THE TOWN ECONOMY

1 RHL, Ms Africa S 228, C7A, C. Nind to C. J. Rhodes, 11 Jan. 1892, f 170.

2 CPP, G77–'82, *Reports on the Kimberley Police Force and Detective Department by B. V. Shaw*.

3 CPP, G3–'88, *Commission . . . on the Diamond Trade Acts*, ev. of B. Roper, Q. 1837.

4 SBA, Inspection Report (Kimberley), 12 Nov. 1881, f 484. In 1881 the bank estimated that from £50,000 to £80,000 of diamonds was exported each week.

5 SBA, Private Correspondence, L. Michell to F. J. Dormer, 22 May 1885 (Henry Files).

6 J. W. Matthews, *Incwadi Yami*, 195. For the case of the James Brothers, CPP, A9–'82, *Select Committee on IDB*, ev. of Feltham Q. 23.

7 *Daily Independent*, 26 Oct. 1882. For example, Myer Myers was sentenced to 10 years hard labour for selling 292 carats which did not come from his claim in Dutoitspan.

8 CAD, LND 1/343, Civil Commissioner to Assistant Commissioner, 27 March 1890.

9 J. W. Matthews, *Incwadi Yami*, 227.

10 CPP, G2–'85, *BBNA*, 209.

11 P. M. Laurence, 'Diamonds' in C. Cowen (ed.) *The South African Exhibition*, 280.

12 Ibid.

13 We do not know enough about the reinvestment of migrant earnings in cattle, let alone the impact of IDB on rural wealth. In 1872 one anonymous informant wrote: 'A native returning to his kraal without diamonds was quite an exception and . . . many good stones were exchanged by them with farmers cattle'. (CAD, GLW 30, *From Colonial Office*, Colonial Secretary to R. W. H. Giddy, 7 Oct,. 1872).

14 CAD, CO 3344, No. 98, Captain Harrel's Report on the Detective Department, November 1880.

15 J. W. Matthews, *Incwadi Yami*, 198; CAD, GLW 132, *Records*, No. 566, Statement of Charlie alias Plaatje (a 'native' detective), 5 March 1879.

16 CPP, G3–'88, *Commission . . . on the Diamond Trade Acts*, ev. of Adam Mackintosh, Q. 416; CAD, Ag 1604, Nov. 4509, Vol. 2, Arthur Garcia to Law Department, 8 Jan. 1906.

17 J. W. Matthews, *Incwadi Yami*, 187.

18 SBA, Private Correspondence, L. Michell to GM, 17 April 1882 (Henry Files).

19 L. Cohen, *Reminiscences*, 25.

20 Slang Jewish expression for an illicit or stolen diamond.

21 J. W. Matthews, *Incwadi Yami*, 232; L. Cohen, *Reminiscences*, 205.

22 CPP, G3–'88, *Commission . . . on the Diamond Trade Acts*, ev. of H. Koski, Q. 1326–1363.

23 CPP, A9–'82, *Select Committee on IDB*, ev. of H. S. Caldecott, Q. 912.

24 Ibid., ev. of J. L. Truter, Q. 762–764, P. W. Tracey, Q. 458–460, Feltham Q. 103.

25 CPP, G3–'88, *Commission . . . on the Diamond Trade Acts*, ev. of B. Roper, Q.1832.

26 CPP, G77–'82, *Reports on the Kimberley Police Force*, 24.

27 J. W. Matthews, *Incwadi Yami*, 213.

28 CPP, G3–'88, *Commission . . . on the Diamond Trade Acts*, ev. of B. Roper, Q. 1604.

29 J. W. Matthews, *Incwadi Yami*, 213.

30 Ibid., 212.

31 J. Angove, *In the Early Days: Reminiscences of Pioneer Life on the South African Diamond Fields*, Kimberley, 1910, 71.

32 A lightly written description of 'running the gauntlet' is in *Diamond Fields Advertiser*, 19 Dec. 1887.

33 J. W. Matthews, *Incwadi Yami*, 201.

34 CAD, CO 3454, No. 242, Blignault (OFS Government Secretary) to Civil Commissioner, Kimberley, 4 December 1884.

35 *Daily Independent*, 13 Dec. 1883, 'Shooting Case at Bank's Drift'.

36 *Diamond Fields Advertiser*, 24 March 1885, Boshof Circuit Court. See also J. W. Matthews, *Incwadi Yami*, 203–4 and L. Cohen, *Reminiscences*, 165.

37 SBA, XL, 1 Oct. 1885 (Henry Files).

38 SBA, Inspection Report (Pietermaritzburg) 30 June 1885, f 171: A 'good part of the £22,000 produce now on the water' was made up of stolen diamonds.

39 Ibid.

40 Ibid., ff 170–4. See also J. B. Taylor, *A Pioneer Looks Back*, London, 1939, 91.

41 SBA, GM/LO, 7 Aug. 1889 (Henry Files).

42 CAD, AG 1644, No. 8616, H. Chadwick to T. Upington, 23 March 1886.

43 Ibid., Beaton report, 20 March 1888.

44 CPP, G3–'88, *Commission . . . on the Diamond Trade Acts*, ev. of H. Koski, Q. 1344.

45 Ibid., ev. of H. Cohen, Q. 2402, 2466.

46 Ibid., Q. 2391.

47 R. V. Turrell (ed.) *The Philipson Stow Papers*, Document 78, Enclosure in F. T. Gervers to F. S. P. Stow, March 1892. For the secret reserve, see R. V. Turrell, 'Sir Frederick Philipson Stow: the Unknown Diamond Magnate', *Business History*, 26 (1) 1986.

48 L. Cohen, *Reminiscences*, 185.

49 Washington, US Consular Reports, Vol. 14, No. 38, Report of Siler, 12 June 1889.

50 CAD, GLW 138, *Records*, No.1 570, Petition of 30 European Convicts, 13 June 1879. (UCT, Smalberger Papers.)

51 Ibid., Memo of Charles Warren for Executive Council, 15 June 1879; Ibid., No. 1675, Colonial Secretary to Kimberley Mining Board, 8 July.1879; CAD, GLW 139, *Records*, No. 1850, Kimberley Mining Board to Colonial Secretary, 16 July 1879.

52 *Diamond Fields Advertiser*, 24 Jan. 1884, Queen vs. Junker (23 Jan.)

53 In many cases people were convicted even though the trap diamond was never found. (G3–'88, *Commission . . . on the Diamond Trade Acts*, ev. of B. Roper, Q. 1766–78.)
54 *Cape Blue Book*, 1881–84 and *Cape Statistical Register*, 1885–89.
55 *Cape Hansard*, 1892, 256.
56 CPP, G3–'88, *Commission . . . on the Diamond Trade Acts*, Q. 1974.
57 Ibid.
58 *Cape Hansard*, 1892, 139 (Innes).
59 CPP, G3–'88, *Commission on the Diamond Trade Acts*, ev. of A. Posno, Q.746–762.
60 CAD, Special Court, Vol. 512, Queen vs. David Cohen, 27 March 1884.
61 CPP, A9–'82, *Select Committee on IDB*, Q. 129.
62 J. W. Matthews, *Incwadi Yami*, 188.
63 CAD, GLW 162, *Records*, No. 2509, Statement to Meynenett, 3 Sept. 1880.
64 CAD, CO 1371, No. 120, J. W. Harker to H. Tucker, 17 Feb. 1887.
65 *Diamond Fields Advertiser*, n.d. quoted in J. W. Matthews, *Incwadi Yami*, 194.
66 CPP, A9–'82, *Select Committee on IDB*, Q. 927.
67 CPP, G12–'85, *Police Commissioner's Report*, 27; ibid., G36–'88, 11.
68 *The Friend*, 12 June 1889, Volksraad Debate. 'The President said that he had read in newspapers about Mr. Cecil Rhodes' way of dealing with mining properties and that if the same people who could go to Lobengula for concessions were to get hold of all our mines, it would be prejudicial to the State and the independence of the Free State would be jeopardised.'
69 SAL, *Our Diamond Industry*, 1885, 33.
70 SBA, Inspection Report (Kimberley), 12 Nov. 1881, f. 496.
71 CPP, A100–'82, *Petition of Merchants, Standholders, Storekeepers, and Others owning Real Property and engaged in Trade in Kimberley*.
72 SBA, Inspection Report (Kimberley), 12 Nov. 1881, f 495.
73 CAD, GLW 87, No. 1587, Percy report, 22 May 1876.
74 *Griqualand West Statutes*, 291.
75 CPP, A66–'82, *Petition of Licensed Kaffir Eating-House Keepers*.
76 CPP, A9–'82, *Select Committee on IDB*, Q. 940.
77 Ibid., ev. of P. W. Tracey, Q. 506; *Daily Independent*, 14 Feb. 1885, Criminal Sessions.
78 Ibid., ev. of S. Marks, Q. 183.
79 For example, Hill and Paddon, advertised new lines suitable for the 'Kaffir trade': wool blankets and spoon-knives; assorted moleskin cloth in white, tan and printed; hats and boots. Often the advertisement for the 'Kaffir' and the 'Dutch' trades were combined. (*Daily Independent*, 15 Dec. 1884).
80 Such as, groceries, provisions, oilman's stores and household sundries.
81 SBA, Inspection Report (Kimberley), 2 Nov. 1882, f 562.
82 SBA, GM/LO, 9 Aug. 1884 (Henry Files).
83 CPP, G14–'86, *Report on Vooruitzicht Estate*, 4.
84 CPP, A9–'82, *Select Committee on IDB*, ev. of Baring Gould, Q. 1038.
85 Ibid., Q. 1039.
86 CPP, G34–'83, *RIDM*, 13.
87 *Diamond News*, 15 Sept. 1874, 'Liquor Commission'.
88 CPP, G1–'90, *Liquor Laws Commission*, 875.
89 J. W. Matthews, *Incwadi Yami*, 100.
90 *Daily Independent*, 29 Dec. 1880, Editorial.
91 Excluding 'Kaffir Beer', which did not compete with spirits until the 1890s.
92 CPP, A9–'80, *Select Committee on Adulteration of Spirits*, ev. of P. Hahn, Q. 1605.
93 *Diamond News*, 14 March 1874, 'Liquor Commission'.
94 CPP, G1–'90, *Liquor Laws Commission*, ev. of J. H. Parkin, Q. 6577.

95 *Diamond Field*, 17 March 1875; CPP, A9–'82, *Select Committee on IDB*, ev. of P. W. Tracey, Q. 575, '... definition of "native" is difficult to arrive at'.
96 CPP, A9–'82, *Select Committee on IDB*, ev. of J. Rose-Innes, Q. 1136–1129.
97 *Daily Independent*, 2 Feb. 1882, 'Anon'.
98 CPP, G1–'90, *Liquor Laws Commission*, Q. 7333.
99 Ibid., ev. of G. D. Peiser, Q. 6649.
100 *Daily Independent*, 27 Sept. 1883, Editorial, and Parliamentary report-back speech of J. B. Robinson.
101 RHL, Ms Africa, S 229, Folio 8, C. J. Rhodes to T. Scanlen, 4 June 1883. In 1883 Rhodes estimated the value of manufactured goods bought in Kimberley and sent to Mankoroane's country and the interior at £120,000.
102 *Daily Independent*, 29 Sept. 1883, G. G. Wolf's Parliamentary report-back speech.
103 Ibid., 3 March 1883, Licensed Victuallers Meeting.
104 CAD, HA 790, No. 351 (1883) *Petition ... of Merchants of Kimberley and Dutoitspan*. In 1888, the first year in which there was a systematic survey of consumption in the Cape, the wholesale selling price of liquor amounted to £505,171 (of which imported and colonial spirits equalled £206,742), while the retail selling price was estimated at £900,000. (CPP, G1–'90, *Liquor Laws Commission*, Appendix R, 1069).
105 Ibid.
106 *Daily Independent*, 20 May 1884, Crosby vs. Kimberley Licensing Court.
107 CPP, C1–'85, *Select Committee on Liquor Licensing Act*, ev. of G. G. Wolf, Q. 11.
108 Ibid.
109 CPP, A9–'82, *Select Committee on IDB*, Q. 727.
110 *Daily Independent*, 23 March 1883, Licensing Court.
111 Ibid., 27 Feb. 1886, Licensing Court.
112 For vivid descriptions of the Red Light, see J. R. Couper, *Mixed Humanity*, 22 and L. Cohen, *Reminiscences*, 250–4.
113 SBA, Inspection Report (Port Elizabeth), 30 Jan. 1882, f 625; *Daily Independent*, 10 Jan. 1882, For Sale Advertisement.
114 *Daily Independent*, 13 March 1886, Licensing Court (8 March).
115 Ibid., 20 April 1883, 'The Coming Election'.
116 Ibid., 29 Sept. 1883, G. G. Wolf's Parliamentary report-back speech.
117 Ibid.
118 CAD, LND 1/275, E. A. Judge to Commissioner of Crown Lands, 23 Feb. 1888, f 1299.
119 CPP, A27–'85, *Select Committee on the Dorstfontein and Bultfontein Landlords and Tenants Bill*, ev. of S. Austen, Q. 314.
120 Ibid., Appendix N, Preamble to Landlords and Tenants Bill, which the Select Committee found to be true.
121 *Diamond Fields Advertiser*, 16 July 1880, H. Prins vs. Le Jeune and Company, and Storbeck vs. Le Jeune and Company; CPP, A27–'85, *Select Committee on the ... Tenants Bill*, ev. of H. Prins Q. 451–509. Le Jeune and Company was a partnership of H. B. Webb, H. Le Jeune, C. J. Rhodes, R. Graham, E. Gray and J. Dalton.
122 Ibid., ev. of W. F. Lippiatt, Q. 662–675; CAD, GDM 2/3, Dutoitspan DMC Letter-Book, Turner to Licensing Court, 8 March 1882, f 219.
123 Ibid., ev. of W. F. Lippiatt, Q. 708.
124 Ibid., ev. of G. Goch, Q. 962.
125 Ibid., Appendix B, J. B. Currey petition, 23 June 1885.
126 CAD, AG 111, *Heads of Agreement for the Settlement of Matters in Dispute ... between the Government of Griqualand West, the Proprietors ... the Claimholders ... and the Standholders*, 27 Aug. 1880.
127 CPP, A27–'85, *Select Committee on the ... Tenants Bill*, ev. of G. Goch, Q. 973.
128 Ibid., ev. of J. B. Currey, Q. 1419–1939.

129 Ibid., ev. of S. Austen Q. 130–135; ibid., ev. of G. Goch, Q. 875, 893.

130 Ibid., ev. of J. B. Currey, Q. 1313, 1510.

131 *Daily Independent*, 19 Jan. 1884, Letter from Standholders League to London Exploration Company.

132 Ibid., 13 Dec. 1883, Letter of Committee of Standholders League to Standholders.

133 CPP, A27–'85, *Select Committee on the . . . Tenants Bill*, ev. of G. Goch, Q. 960.

134 Ibid., ev. of S. Austen, Q. 113.

135 Ibid., ev. of C. J. Rhodes, Q. 1240.

136 SAL, Merriman Papers, 89, J. B. Currey to J. X. Merriman, 24 Dec. 1884; ibid., J. X. Merriman to C. J. Posno, 5 Sept. 1884; CPP, A7–'91, *Select Committee on Trade and Business*, ev. of J. B. Currey, Q.2787.

137 SAL, 'Our Estate in the Cape Colony and its Management', 1886, 5.

138 Ibid., 8.

139 *Reminiscences*, 52.

140 *The Diamond Magnates*, 139–52.

141 CAD, Special Court, Vol. 512, Queen vs. Isaac Joel, March/April 1884, f 19.

142 CAD, AG 124, Crown Prosecutor telegram to Attorney General, 5 June 1888.

143 RHL, Ms Africa S 134, Note Book III, interview with F. J. Dormer, 14 July 1919.

144 See B. Roberts, *The Diamond Magnates*, 146–50.

145 CAD, AG 124, Petition of Kate and Joel Joel.

146 SBA, Inspection Reports (Kimberley), 15 March 1879, f 49, 3 Feb. 1880, f 109, 12 Nov. 1881, f 229, 2 Nov. 1882, f 386, 29 Nov. 1884, f 37, 7 Nov. 1885, f 33, 12 Feb. 1887, f 26, 21 Jan. 1888, f 21; SBA, XL, 16 Feb. 1888 (Henry Files); SBA, P/O Kimberley, Smart to GMs, 29 Oct. 1888, f 83; SBA, Inspection Report (Kimberley) 4 Oct. 1890, f 26.

147 SBA, Inspection Report (Kimberley), 29 Nov. 1884, f 115.

148 L. Cohen, *Reminiscences*, 372; CPP, A12–'85, *Remission of IDB Sentences*.

149 CAD, Special Court, Vol. 526, Queen vs. Mark Leo, May/June 1884.

150 *Daily Independent*, 20 April 1883, Queen vs Simon Blumenthal; ibid., 4 Aug. 1883, 'Blumenthal Discharged'.

151 Ibid., 13 Feb. 1883, Queen vs. Myer Myers.

152 Ibid., 6 March 1883, Queen vs. Elias Jacobs; ibid., 15 Sept. 1883, Queen vs Gordon Taylor. In 1883 Elias Jacobs was worth £18,000; in 1886 £29,000; and in 1888 £91,870. (SBA, Inspection Reports (Kimberley), 7 Nov. 1885, f 88, 21 Jan. 1888, ff 79–80)

153 CPP, G50–'85, *Roper Report*, 16, 80.

154 SAL, Merriman Papers, J. X. Merriman to Agnes Merriman, 27 Jan. 1885.

155 George Wolf and not Woolf Joel, as Roberts *The Diamond Magnates*, 148, mistakenly notes, was the nominal proprietor.

156 SAL, Merriman Papers, 84, R. W. H. Giddy to J. X. Merriman, 11 March 1885.

157 SBA, Inspection Reports (Kimberley), 12 Nov. 1881, f 241, 2 Nov. 1882, f 498, 7 Nov. 1885, f 147; *Daily Independent*, 12 Feb. 1884, Inquest (17 Jan.) and report of P. Sim on the financial position of G. G. Wolf and Co.

158 J. W. Matthews, *Incwadi Yami*, 319.

159 SAL, Merriman Papers, J. X. Merriman, to Agnes Merriman, 21 Jan. 1886.

160 SBA, Inspection Report (Kimberley), 29 Sept. 1883, ff 190–211, 342–2.

161 RHL, Ms Africa S 134, vi, C. D. Rudd, to C. J. Rhodes, n.d.

162 N. Rouillard (ed.) *Matabele Thompson*, 109.

163 SBA, Inspection Report (Kimberley), 22 March 1877, f 164; Inspection (Cape Town), 29 Sept. 1883, f 687.

164 The committee of the Afrikander League: Charles Powell (Chairman), Perreira (Secretary), Coverwell, Abrahamse, Sasse, Jim Murphy (an American), Joseph Moss (*Daily Independent*, 26 Jan. 1884). The Committee of the GLW and the South Africa Political

Association: J. B. Marais, C. Y. Griffin, G. Beet, J. J. Coghlan, C. Howard, C. Rothman, J. Wege, Van Wyk, P. de Vos, J. D. Hosman (*Daily Independent*, 22 Dec. 1883).

165 *Daily Independent*, 13 Dec. 1883, 'The formation of an Afrikander League'.

166 *Daily Independent*, 29 April 1884, 'Our Cape Town Letter'.

167 SBA, Inspection Report (Cape Town), 21 Sept. 1889, f 224.

168 CPP, A12–'85, *Remission of IDB Sentences* 1881–85.

169 *Cape Law Journal*, Vol. II, 1885, 'Dismissal of Crown Prosecutor', 190.

170 SBA, Inspection Reports (Cape Town), 12 Aug. 1874, f 128, 13 July 1878, f 416; SBA, Inspection Reports (Kimberley), 12 Nov. 1881, f 247, 2 Nov. 1882, f 328, 29 Nov. 1884, f 63.

171 SBA, Inspection Reports (Kimberley), 12 Nov. 1881, f 389, 29 Nov. 1884, f 173, 7 Nov. 1885, f 126. 'We have not the slightest confidence in the man', wrote the Manager in 1885, 'no belief in his honesty and his word cannot be taken. When we get rid of these bills we shall not let his name reappear'.

172 SBA, Inspection Report (Kimberley), 12 Nov. 1881, f 464.

173 CAD, GLW High Court (civil), Vol. 94, No. 2803 (1884), J. G. Ross vs. W. Ross. J. G. Ross, a usurer, sued William Ross, as his Kimberley executor, for losing £200,000 of his money. The case exposed Ross' financial dealings with numerous IDBs – Simon Blumenthal, David Symons, A. C. Mather, J. Kennedy – and Ross' attempt to amalgamate the two dubious companies, the Caledonian and Globe DMCs. The charge of fraud against William Ross was not proved.

174 SBA, Inspection Report (Kimberley), 29 Nov. 1884, f 173.

175 CAD, AG 1644, No. 7616, Forster Report, August 1886.

176 CPP, G3–'88, *Commission . . . on the Diamond Trade Acts*, ev. of B. Roper, Q. 1553.

177 CAD, AG 1644, No. 8616, Forster Report, August 1886.

178 CPP, G3–'88, *Commission . . . on the Diamond Trade Acts*, ev. of B. Roper, Q. 1553.

179 *Diamond Fields Advertiser*, 8 May 1886, Letter from Rojesky.

180 *Diamond Fields Advertiser*, 24 April 1886, 'The Dynamite Conspiracy'. Cassalano was sentenced to ten years hard labour and the others received nine years.

181 SAL, Merriman Papers, 6, J. X. Merriman to Agnes Merriman, 11 Jan. 1886.

182 CAD, AG 123, Civil Commissioner to Law Department, 9 Sept. 1885; ibid., Hampden Willis to Law Department, 9 Oct. 1885.

183 SAL, Merriman Papers, 28 J. X. Merriman to Agnes Merriman, 24 Jan. 1886.

184 *Diamond Fields Advertiser*, 23 July 1886, 'The Kimberley Members and their Constituents'.

185 The evidence in this case was printed in CPP, G3–'88, *Commission . . . on the Diamond Trade Acts*, Appendix N.

186 The judgment is in P. M. Laurence, *Reports of Cases in High Court of Griqualand West*, Vol. IV, 141–75.

187 For the 'horse trading' see P. Lewsen, *Selections*, 214.

188 *Daily Independent*, 19 June 1886, 'The Truck System'.

189 Ibid., Telegram from G. Goch, W. Ross, M. Cornwall and J. J. O'Leary.

190 SAL, Merriman Letter-Book, J. X. Merriman to H. Mosenthal, 5 April 1886, f 344.

191 *Daily Independent*, 5 June 1886, Chamber of Commerce.

192 N. Rouillard (ed.) *Matabele Thompson*, 43.

193 *The Record and Beaconsfield Advertiser*, 7 Aug. 1886, 'The Coming Election'.

194 De Waal earned a handsome commission from the butchers, D. P. Graaff and Company, by securing for them the contract to supply the 'tommy shops' on the Kimberley railway extension. (SBA, Inspection Report (Cape Town), 14 Sept. 1885, f 99.)

195 *Cape Hansard*, 1887, 130.

196 H. Tennant and E. M. Jackson (eds.), *Statutes of the Cape of Good Hope*, Vol. III, No. 23 of 1887, 2476.

197 CPP, G3–'88, *Commission . . . on the Diamond Trade Acts*. Its members were J. D. de Villiers, T. Upington, W. Rose, J. J. O'Leary, F. Baring Gould, R. Heinrichsen, H. A. Rogers.
198 SBA, Inspection Report (Kimberley), 12 Feb. 1887, f 172.
199 *Daily Independent*, 14 Feb. 1885, Criminal Sessions. For the conventional stereotype, see J. W. Matthews, *Incwadi Yami*, 187–90.
200 L. Cohen, *Reminiscences*, 148.
201 'Eighteenth-Century Crime, Popular Movements and Social Control', *Bulletin of the Study of Labour History*, Vol. 25, 1972, 10.

10 AMALGAMATION

1 Chilvers, *The Story of De Beers*, London, 1939, is the standard history of the De Beers DMC and its successor De Beers Consolidated Mines. The chapter on the formation of De Beers Consolidated is based almost exclusively on the Stow *Memoir*, which Chilvers was the first to use. But he misread the document in crucial sections and ignored Stow's moral condemnation of the inclusion of Barnato as a Life Governor of De Beers. The *Memoir* was written in 1898 and was based on Stow's private and official papers supplemented by research Stow commissioned into newspaper reports covering the period in which the amalgamation negotiations were conducted. The purpose of the *Memoir* was to present a case against Rhodes, whom Stow believed had 'defrauded' Baring Gould of his right to the fifth Life Governorship. The *Memoir* was written soon after Barnato committed suicide in June 1897, in an attempt to force Rhodes to do the right thing by Baring Gould. In Stow's own words:

> My object in preserving and collecting into this form the facts connected with the affairs of the Company is to have a record manifesting the part played by others and myself as Diamond Diggers and subsequently Life Governors in building up a monopoly which has on the one hand been roundly condemned while on the other it has met with approbation if not applause. And further to establish the fact that there were five actors entitled to share the credit though perhaps in different degrees, of having carried to a successful issue a mining achievement which is almost without parallel in the annals of mining enterprises, and to demonstrate that one of these by the action of a colleague has been defrauded of the fruits of his labour; that two of the others apparently view with indifference this nefarious transaction and by their inaction lend weight to the supposition that they intend to retain all the advantages accruing from the *mala fide* conduct referred to. [R. V. Turrell (ed.) *The Philipson Stow Papers*, forthcoming.]

The *Memoir* presents the amalgamation from the point of view of De Beers and has to be compared and contrasted with the *Fenton Memorandum* and Fenton's *The True History of the Amalgamation of the Diamond Mines* (written in 1911 and acquired by the Rhodes House Library in 1956) which gives a concise view of the negotiations as seen by a director of the Kimberley Central. A comparison was made by Sir Theodore Gregory, but was not included in his *Ernest Oppenheimer and the Economic Development of Southern Africa*, Cape Town, 1962 and can be found amongst his research papers (Box 40) deposited in the Anglo–American Corporation Archive. From the annotated comparison it is apparent that Gregory realised that Barnato had thrown in his lot with Rhodes as early as October 1887, but in *Oppenheimer*, 52, 53 he does not deal with the amalgamation in any detail and falls back on the conventional story. Gregory gives no indication of how Rhodes and Barnato 'came to terms' and implies it was through the legendary leviathan struggle in the share markets. Gardner Williams, General Manager of De Beers and author of *The Diamond Mines of South Africa*, New York, 1905, certainly contributed to the story of the share struggle, but he re-told the version Rhodes and Barnato agreed to present to their shareholders in 1888 and 1889. This version gets its first complete treatment in a secondary account in Paul Emden's *Randlords*, London, 1935, 54–6 and has been repeated and embellished over the past 40 years, most recently by Brian Roberts, *The Diamond Magnates*, London, 1972, 202 and John Flint *Cecil Rhodes*, London, 1974, 84–92. The reinterpretation offered here is based on a close reading of the Stow *Memoir* and the Stow Papers supplemented by new material from the Standard Bank Archive.

2 AAA, Gregory Papers, 'Statement Respecting De Beers' Mine', 1882.

3 *Diamond News*, 30 March 1882, 'Amalgamation of the De Beers Mine'; CAD, GDM 6/1, Alderson, Dusmure and Rhodes to Birbeck DMC, 22 May 1882.

4 RAL, 4/47, Albert Gansl to N. M. Rothschild and Sons, 16 Nov. 1882.

5 SBA, XL, 23 Aug. 1883 (Henry Files).

6 SAL, Merriman Papers, L. Michell to J. X. Merriman, 9 Feb. 1885; Thomas to L. Michell, 4 March 1885; R. W. H. Giddy to J. X. Merriman, 11 March 1885; J. X. Merriman to L. Michell and Thomas, 26, 28, 29 March, 2 April 1885; C. J. Posno to Merriman, 8 April 1885.

7 SAL, Merriman Letter-Book II, Merriman to Michell and Thomas 21 April 1885; Merriman Papers, L. Michell to J. X. Merriman, 21 July 1885; MM, Philipson Stow Papers, Stow Letter-Book V, Stow to H. B. Hart, 9 Oct. 1886, f 24 and 8 Dec. 1886, f 130.

8 The Cape of Good Hope Bank controlled the North-West DMC, the South-West DMC and W. A. Hall and Company. The capital stated is the Mining Board valuation in the case of the Cape Bank holding, but the nominal capital in the case of the others. (SAL, Merriman Letter-Book II, J. X. Merriman to Thomas and Michell, 14 Feb. 1885, ff 118–129.)

9 SAL, Merriman Papers, J. X. Merriman to Agnes Merriman, 5 Feb. 1886.

10 SBA, GM/LO, 26 Jan. 1884 (Henry Files).

11 SAL, Merriman Papers, J. B. Robinson to J. X. Merriman, 5 Jan. 1884; Michell to J. X. Merriman, 2 April 1885. See J. Henry *The First Hundred Years of the Standard Bank*, 63–76 for the problem of the Kimberley Mining Board Loan and bank problems in general with diamond advances.

12 SAL, Merriman Papers, C. J. Posno to J. X. Merriman, 30 Sept. 1885, 25 March 1886.

13 SAL, Merriman Letter-Book II, J. X. Merriman to C. J. Posno, 29 Dec. 1885; J. X. Merriman to Reid, 3 Feb. 1886, ff 276, 277. The Cape of Good Hope Bank held £400,000 of diamond shares, which included one-fifth of the Standard's nominal capital and one-twentieth of De Beers' capital.

14 SAL, Merriman Letter-Book II, J. X. Merriman to J. B. Robinson, 11 Jan. 1886, f 243.

15 SAL, Merriman Papers, J. X. Merriman to Agnes Merriman, 29 Jan. 1886.

16 SAL, Merriman Letter-Book II, J. X. Merriman to C. J. Posno, 3 March 1886, f 302; J. X. Merriman to A. Moulle, 4 March 1886, f 306.

17 SAL, Merriman Letter-Book II, J. X. Merriman to C. J. Posno, 27 March 1886, ff 328–42.

18 SAL, Merriman Papers, J. X. Merriman to C. J. Posno, 22 Oct. 1885.

19 SBA, Inspection Report (Kimberley) 12 Feb. 1887, f 174. It should be noted that the Standard Bank held the account of the Kimberley Central but not that of De Beers. Consequently, the bank wanted the Central to monopolise the mines, in which case it would keep the monopoly company's account. However, the Cape of Good Hope Bank, which kept the De Beers account, had been on the verge of bankruptcy for some years and was supported through heavy borrowing from the Standard Bank.

20 RAL, T43/15, E. G. de Crano to N. M. Rothschild and Sons, 28 Nov. 1887.

21 See above, p. 159.

22 MM, Philipson Stow Letter-Book V, F. Stow to C. J. Rhodes, 23 Dec. 1886, f 150.

23 SBA, Inspection Report (Kimberley) 29 Nov. 1884, f 41; 7 Nov. 1885, f 179; Inspection Report (Port Elizabeth) 4 July 1887, f 29; Barlow Rand, HE 49, 31 Dec. 1888, Partnership Deed.

24 At the end of 1889, when Jules Porges retired from his firm, he took out £750,000 in cash, £1

million in shares and left £500,000 in the firm to be paid out in two years. Jules Porges and Company, which was renamed Wernher, Beit and Company, was left with a capital of £1 million in cash, diamonds and non-speculative investments and between £1.5 and £2.5 million in various shares and interests of a speculative nature. (SBA, African Banking Corporation, General Manager, South Africa, to Chief Manager, 31 Dec. 1891, Vol. 1, f 174)

25 RHL, Ms. Africa t 14, C. J. Rhodes to C. D. Rudd, 12 Dec. 1886; R. V. Turrell (ed.) *The Philipson Stow Papers*, Documents 4, 14, 15, F. Stow to De Beers DMC, 29 Nov. 1886, 19 May 1887, 26 May 1887.

26 SAL, 'To the President and Members of the Board of the Compagnie Française', 9, 10.

27 *The Statist*, 11 Feb. 1888, 10; 24 March 1888, 332; 5 May 1888, 506; 12 Oct. 1889, 411–12; C. E. Harvey, *The Rio Tinto Company, an Economic History of a leading International Mining Concern 1873–1954*, Penzance, 1981, 67–74.

28 R. V. Turrell (ed.) *The Philipson Stow Papers*, Document 18, F. Stow to H. S. Caldecott, 28 July 1887.

29 Ibid., Document 19, F. Stow to H. S. Caldecott, 4 Aug. 1887.

30 CAD, DOK 3/2, Provisional Agreement between N. M. Rothschild and Sons and De Beers Mining Company, 11 Aug. 1887; *Diamond Fields Advertiser*, 30 Sept. 1887, Special Meeting, De Beers DMC; R. V. Turrell (ed.) *The Philipson Stow Papers*, Document 33, F. Stow to C. J. Rhodes, 18 Oct. 1887; Document 34, C. J. Rhodes to F. Stow, 22 Oct. 1887. The details of the sale were: £750,000 in cash for claims, machinery, plant and Mining Board paper; £200,000 in debentures bearing six per cent per annum against first hypothecation of Compagnie's claims repayable in five years; Compagnie to receive 35,000 loads of blue ground from De Beers and to continue working for a year, but on 1 March 1888 De Beers could cancel second six months of working for a payment of £15,000 per month; and Compagnie shareholders could subscribe for 50,000 De Beers at maximum price of £20 and minimum of £16 per share. (*Diamond News*, 8 Oct. 1887.)

31 R. V. Turrell (ed.) *The Philipson Stow Papers*, Document 24, C. J. Rhodes to F. Stow, 5–10 Sept. 1887.

32 Ibid., Document 25, F. Stow to C. J. Rhodes, 15 Sept. 1887.

33 Ibid., Document 29, F. Stow to C. J. Rhodes, 27 Sept. 1887.

34 AAA, Gregory Papers, De Beers DMC, Directors Minutes, 15 Nov. 1887; MM, Philipson Stow Papers, C. Meyer to F. Stow, 13 Sept. 1887; RAL, T43/2, C. Meyer to N. M. Rothschild and Sons, 5 Oct. 1887; R. V. Turrell (ed.) *Philipson Stow Papers*, Documents 22, 25, 29, F. Stow to C. J. Rhodes, 8, 15, 27 Sept. 1887; SBA, GM/LO Vol. 21, 14 Sept. 1887, f 777, 28 Sept. 1887, f 836, 2 Nov. 1887, f 945; SBA, XL, Vol. 30, 22 Sept. 1887, f 9, 29 Sept. 1887, ff 2–3, 6 Oct. 1887, f 10; *Daily Independent*, 2 Nov. 1887 and *Diamond Fields Advertiser*, 5 Nov. 1887, Special General Meeting, Kimberley Central DMC; SBA, GM/LO, Vol. 22, 14 March 1888, f 489. The £500,000 loan was arranged by a Rothschild syndicate which included Jules Porges and Company. The loan was for seven years at 5½ per cent: £150,000 to repay a Standard Bank loan; £200,000 to settle the take-over of the Compagnie; £100,000 to pay the De Beers Commission to the Rothschilds in the original Compagnie purchase; and £50,000 to remove reef and revert to the open-cast system of mining.

35 *Diamond Fields Advertiser*, 5 Nov. 1887, Special General Meeting, Kimberley Central DMC.

36 See figure 8, p. 218.

37 SBA, Inspection Report (Kimberley), 21 Jan. 1888, f 21.

38 R. V. Turrell (ed.) *The Philipson Stow Papers*, Document 34, C. J. Rhodes to F. Stow, 22 Oct. 1887.

39 Ibid.

40 Ibid.

41 AAA, Gregory Papers, Box 40, FD–5, Reginald Fenton, *The True History of the Amalgamation of the Diamond Mines*, p. 6.
42 R. V. Turrell (ed.) *The Philipson Stow Papers*, Document 39, F. Stow to C. J. Rhodes, 23 Nov. 1887.
43 RAL, T43/15, Edmund de Crano to N. M. Rothschild and Sons, 28 Nov. 1887.
44 SBA, Inspection Report (Kimberley), 21 Jan. 1888, f 181.
45 RAL, T43/15, Edmund de Crano to N. M. Rothschild and Sons, 28 Nov. 1887.
46 SBA, GM/LO, Vol. 22, 30 Nov. 1887, f 40; R. V. Turrell (ed.) *Philipson Stow Papers*, *The Memoir*, forthcoming.
47 Inspection Report (Kimberley) 21 Jan. 1888, f 21.
48 R. V. Turrell (ed.) *Philipson Stow Papers*, *The Memoir*, forthcoming; SBA, GM/LO, Vol. 22, 14 March 1888, f 492; MM, Philipson Stow Papers, De Beers Directors telegram to London, 14 March 1888. Barnato Brothers owned 27,000 out of 142,295 Central shares (18.97 %) and 48,000 out of 251,000 De Beers shares (19.12 %).
49 SBA, GM/LO, Half Yearly Report, 8 Aug. 1888.
50 2 June 1888, 295.
51 R. V. Turrell (ed.) *Philipson Stow Papers*, Document 41, C. J. Rhodes to F. Stow, 14 April 1888.
52 RAL, T43/25, 14 May 1888. It appears that Lord Rothschild acted for Barnato in settling the terms of the Life Governorship. (RAL T43/23, Lord Rothschild telegram Barnato, n.d.; T43/24 Barnato telegram Lord Rothschild, 14 May 1888).
53 RAL, T43/15, Edmund de Crano to N. M. Rothschild and Sons, 28 Nov. 1887; SBA, GM/LO, Vol. 22, 14 March 1888, f 490, 23 May 1888, f 760; A. P. Cartwright, *Gold Paved the Way*, London, 1967, 45. It is likely that De Beers spent more on their Centrals than they admitted to their shareholders; the cost of their purchases averaged out at £41 per Central share.
54 SBA, Inspection Report (Kimberley), 21 Jan. 1888, f 180.
55 10 March 1888, 'The Diamond Rig', 274.
56 In the early 1880s Van Beek, the diamond representative of the Mosenthals in Kimberley, was worth £80,000. In the mid 1880s he left the firm and went into business for himself. In 1886 he borrowed £10,000 to buy shares on joint account with S. Allkins and he 'rapidly forged to the front' of Kimberley speculators. In early 1888 the Standard Bank Manager assessed his position:

> He is in close touch with all the leading speculators and has his own correspondents in London and Paris, and is probably the best informed speculator on the fields. His transactions are on an enormous scale (his turnover with us for the past 7 weeks being nearly a million) and his current commitments and risks are of a two fold nature. As far as his capital, and overdrafts, will allow he buys and sells scrip for cash, and his risk is in this case confined to a possible fall in prices on the stocks in hand at any one time. But beyond this he both buys and sells 'on time', and when he buys, the scrip remains in the sellers' hands (or perhaps in the hands of others from whom the seller intends buying) until the settling day arrives, so that if the latter fails to deliver (owing to an intermediate rise in prices) Van Beek would have to replace the shares in order to deliver to the persons to whom he had resold them. On the other hand a fall in prices might render the purchaser unable to complete. His risks in this way probably run into hundreds of thousands, but I think he exercises care in the selection of names, and he seems to be getting more careful every day now that prices are ruling so high.

> [SBA, Inspection Report (Kimberley) 21 Jan. 1888, f 143.]
57 SBA, GM/LO, 8 Feb. 1888, enclosure, paragraph 22.
58 R. V. Turrell (ed.) *Philipson Stow Papers*, Document 41, C. J. Rhodes to F. Stow, 14 April 1888. The General Manager of the Standard Bank commented:

> As you will have gathered from our previous remarks, Mr Rhodes is in our opinion very

unscrupulous in his efforts to obtain his desired results. He is pretty generally known to be extreme and uncertain in his views, and it is not we think necessary to take action in the matter beyond instructing Mr Smart to quietly check any glaring attempt to misrepresent the Bank.

[GM/LO, Vol. 22, 16 May 1888.]

Sir Percy Fitzpatrick remembered this meeting and said afterwards that Rhodes told Beit '... tomorrow they will sell like hell'. (*South African Memories*, London, 1932, 32.)

59 Barlow Rand, HE 50, H. Eckstein to J. B. Taylor, 19 April 1888, ff 174–5.
60 SBA, XL, Vol. 31, 7 & 14 June 1888. In March 1888 Lord Rothschild held 17,366 De Beers shares and in July 1888 his holding was up to 36,850. (De Beers Share Register, Open Mine Museum, Kimberley.)
61 In March 1888 Barnato opted his shares into De Beers Consolidated at the rate of 10 £10 Centrals for 14 De Beers £10 shares, a 40 per cent advance on the nominal capital of De Beers. In October the remaining Central shareholders exchanged 10 £10 Centrals for 22 £5 De Beers Consolidated shares plus 51s, an advance of a little over 10 per cent on the nominal capital of De Beers.
62 See 'Sir Frederic Philipson Stow: the Unknown Diamond Magnate', *Business History* 26(1) 1986.
63 R. V. Turrell (ed.) *The Philipson Stow Papers*, Document 41, C. J. Rhodes to F. Stow, 14 April 1888; SBA, GM/LO, Vol. 24, 9 Oct. 1889; Inspection Report (Cape Town) 4 Oct. 1890, f 50; P. Emden, *Randlords*, 265–6; T. Reunert, *Diamonds and Gold in South Africa*, Cape Town, 1893, 40.
64 *The Statist*, 11 Jan. 1890, 'Diamond Production', 49; *Diamond Fields Advertiser*, 20 June 1891, 'Trade and Labour Prospects on the Diamond Fields'; Th. van Tijn, 'Geskiedenis van de Amsterdamse Diamanthandel en Nijverheid, 1845–97', *Tijdschrift Voor Geskiedenis*, 87 (2) 1974, 161. See also Appendix table 1.
65 CPP, A7–'91, *Select Committee on Trade and Business of Griqualand West*, x. Its members were Upington, Theron, Fuller, Merriman, Barnato, Sprigg, Molteno and Wiener and it reported on 12 Aug. 1891.
66 Ibid.
67 Ibid., xiv.
68 SAL, *The Knights of Labour Manifesto*, 30.
69 Ibid., 10.
70 SBA, Inspection Report (Kimberley), 31 Dec. 1892, f 49.
71 *Diamond Fields Advertiser*, 19 May 1894, 'An Outside View of the Compound System'.
72 P. Lewsen, *John X. Merriman: Paradoxical South African Statesman*, Yale University Press, 1982, 134.

Bibliography

ARCHIVAL SOURCES

STATE ARCHIVES

Public Record Office (London) (PRO)
BT 31 Register of Dissolved Companies
CO 107/1–9, Original Correspondence, Griqualand West, 1875–80
CO Confidential African Prints:
  879/6, No. 59, Sale of Arms in Griqualand West; Despatch from Governor and enclosures, 24 Aug. 1874
  879/7, No. 75A, Difficulties at the Diamond Fields; Memorandum by Mr Malcolm, 15 May 1875
  879/8, No. 76, Affairs of Griqualand; Further Correspondence, 2 Aug. 1874 – 27 May 1875
  879/8, No. 78, Affairs of Griqualand West; Further Correspondence, 5–15 June 1875
  879/8, No. 83, Cape and Griqualand West; Papers, 1 Jan. – 15 Dec. 1875
  879/9, No. 86, Native Question in South Africa; Memorandum by Mr Fairfield, 9 Dec. 1875
  879/9, No. 89, Finances of Griqualand West; Lieutenant-Colonel Crossman's Preliminary Report, 5 Feb. 1876
  879/9, No. 96, Griqualand West; Colonel Crossman's Report, 1 May 1876
  879/9, No. 98, Laws Affecting Natives in Orange Free State, Transvaal and Cape; Despatch from Governor, 7 Feb.. 1876
  879/15, No. 174, Financial Affairs of South African Colonies; Correspondence, 24 Aug. 1877–28 May 1879
  879/17, No. 215, Financial Condition of Griqualand and Annexation; Correspondence 27 Aug. 1879–9 Dec. 1880

National Archives (Washington)
Cape Town, US Consular Records, Vols. 11, 12, 20 June 1872 – June 1892

Natal Archives (Pietermaritzburg)
Theophilus Shepstone Collection, Vol. 21, 1877
Hathorn Papers, Letters 1870–72

Cape Archives (Cape Town) (CAD)
Griqualand West Archive (GLW), Vols. 1–190, 1871–October 1880
Gold and Diamond Mining Company Documents (GDM):
  Minute Books of Liquidated Companies, 1/1–1/8, 1881–92
  Letter-Books, 2/1–2/7, 1881–85

278

Share Registers, 3/1–3/10, 1881–85
Insolvency Papers, 5/1–5/3, 1882–84
Miscellaneous Documents, 6/1–6/7, 1880–81
Deeds Office, Kimberley (DOK)
Letters Received, 1/1–1/10, 1881–92
Share Transfers, 2/1–2/27, 1881–90
Trust Deeds, 3/1–3/14, 1876–93
Letters Despatched, 4/1–4/2A, 1877–89
Bonds and Deeds Cancelled, 1872–1922
Government House (GH)
Administrator and Secretary to Government Despatches, 12/7–12/11, 1876–80
Correspondence and Reports on Bailie's Mission, 19/12, 1879
Insolvent Estates (MOIB), 1880–90
Crown Lands and Mines (LND)
Papers Received, 1/73–1/400, 1879–91
Papers Transferred from Public Works Department, 1881–97
Colonial Office (CO)
Report of Enquiry into the Detective Department, 4528
Reports of Resident Magistrates and Civil Commissioners, 4526, 1882/3
Papers Relating to Prison Labour, 4534, 1885/6
Reports of District Surgeons, 4535, 1887/8
Papers of Liquor Laws Commission, 4537, 1890
Letters from Civil Commissioners, 3344–3581, 1880–88
Letters from Resident Magistrates, 3371–3606, 1881–88
Surveyor General, Griqualand West (SGGLW)
Correspondence, 1–9, 1872–80
Letters Received, 16–22, 1875–80
Letters Despatched Regarding Land Claims, 26
Grant and Lease Registers, 46–50
Lewis Michell Collection, A 540
Ms, *Sixty Years In and Out of South Africa*
Tucker, J. E., Collection A 921, Reminiscences of Kidger Tucker
Attorney-General (AG)
Detective Department Papers, 1644
Detective Department Papers, 1604
Native Affairs Department (NA)
Letters Received, 294–312, 1872–92
Miscellaneous Letters Received, 298–406, 1873–86
Protector of Natives, Kimberley, 448, 1881
Charges Against the Registrar, Coleman, 450, 1885
Labour Contracts, 186, 190, 195, 198, 202, 205, 206, 1881–87
From De Beers, 411
House of Assembly (HA) Petitions, 778–806, 1880–88
Special Court, 1883, 1884

OTHER ARCHIVES

Standard Bank Archive (SBA) Johannesburg
General Manager to London Office Correspondence (GM/LO), 27 Letter-Books, January
    1867 – January 1892 (One Henry File covers this Period)
London Office to General Manager Correspondence, 33 Letter Books, 1871–90 (One Henry
    File covers this Period) (XL)

Bibliography

Inspection Reports
  Barberton, 4 Reports, 22.4.1897 – 6.12.1890
  Beaconsfield, 7 Reports, 18.6.1888 – 20.11.1894
  Cape Town, 15 Reports, 11.5.1871 – 28.2.1895
  Dutoitspan, 2 Reports, 17.11.1873 – 29.11.1882
  Kimberley, 20 Reports, 23.1.1872 – 31.12.1894
  Johannesburg, 3 Reports, 25.10.1887 – 28.9.1891
  Durban, 4 Reports, 19.2.1881 – 11.2.1888
  King William's Town, 3 Reports, 15.5.1882 – 6.5.1887
  Pietermaritzburg, 2 Reports, 30.6.1885 – 3.1.1887
  Port Elizabeth, 10 Reports, 31.7.1876 – 5.4.1890
Private/Official Copying Book, 19.6.1873 – 8.4.1875
Private/Official, Kimberley Manager to General Managers, 6.6.1885 – 23.4.1895

Anglo American Archive (AAA) Johannesburg
Gregory Papers

Barlow Rand Archive, Sandton, Transvaal
Herman Eckstein Papers (HE)
  Kimberley Letters, 12–14, 1887–1889
  London Letters, 49–65, 1888–90
  Eckstein Letters, 124–129, 1886–92

McGregor Museum (MM) Kimberley
Stow, F. S. P. *Memoir of the formation of the De Beers Mining Company Limited and its subsequent transformation into the De Beers Consolidated Mines Limited with five life governors*, 1898
Stow Papers
  The Amalgamation Negotiations, 1887–89
  Compilation of the Memoir, 1897–98
  Sale of Diamonds and the Secret Reserve, 1890–94
  Sale of Stow's Life Governorship to Rhodes, 1890–92
  Letter Books, 10 Vols, IV, V, 1885–90

University of Cape Town, (UCT) Jagger Library
Smalberger Papers
J. D. Barry Papers, BC 127, Pocket Diary, 1876
Bolus Papers, BC 234, Letters from Gregorowski and Hartzenberg, 1872
Judge Papers, BC 500, *An Autobiographical Account of his Life in South Africa*
Maynardville Papers, BC 114, Letters from Farmer and Fuller, 1886, 1890

N. M. Rothschild and Sons Archive (RAL) London
Translation File, T 43
Gansl Correspondence, 4/47, 1882

South African Library (SAL) Cape Town
Merriman Papers, 1870–90
Merriman Letter-Books, 1870–90
J. B. Currey Papers, Letters, 1875, 1890
  Ts., J. B. Currey, *Half a Century in South Africa, c.* 1900

280

United Society For the Propagation of the Gospel (USPG) London
Letters and Reports from Bloemfontein and Bechuanaland Missions, 1870–90

Methodist Missionary Society (MMS) London
Letters and Reports, Dutoitspan and Kimberley, 1870–90

Rhodes House Library (RHL) Oxford
Hildersham Hall Collection, Ms Africa, S 1647, c. 1876–80
Basil Williams Papers, Ms Africa, S 134
Rhodes Papers, Ms Africa, S 228, Files C2A, C7A, C7B, C8, C9, C24, C26–C28
Michell Papers, Ms Africa, S 229
Rudd Trust, Ms Africa, t 14, 1874–1901

Kimberley Public Library (KPL)
Paton Papers, Business Books I–III, 1881–96
    Note Books I–X, 1863–94
Beaconsfield Municipal Council, Letters Received, Vols. 1–14, 1883–90
Company Documents, 21 Vols., 1880–85

PUBLISHED AND SECONDARY SOURCES

British parliamentary papers (Irish University Press)
C. 508–'72 *Further Correspondence respecting Affairs of the Cape of Good Hope*
C.732–'73 *Further Correspondence respecting Affairs of the Cape of Good Hope*
C.1348–'75 *Correspondence relating to Griqualand West*
C.1342–'75 *Correspondence relating to the Colonies and States of South Africa, part I. Cape of Good Hope and Griqualand West*
C.1401–'76 *Further Correspondence relating to the Colonies and States of South Africa*
C.2220–'79 *Further Correspondence respecting the Affairs of South Africa*
C.2584–'80 *Further Correspondence respecting the Affairs of South Africa*
C.2755–'81 *Correspondence respecting the Affairs of Basutoland*

Cape Parliamentary Papers (CPP) Selected
Blue books on native affairs, 1880–90
Reports on convicts, 1880–90
Reports by inspectors of diamond mines (RIDM), 1881–92
Reports on hospitals, 1882–69
Police commissioners reports, 1881–89
Reports of district surgeons, 1882–89
Reports of the manager of Vooruitzicht, 1882–89
Reports of the registrar of deeds, 1880–90
A14–'77 Results of the census in Griqualand West
A9–'82 Select Committee on illicit diamond buying in Griqualand West
A66–'82 Petition of Kimberley Kaffir eating-house keepers for alteration of regulations
A73–'82 Petition of the chairman of the mining board representing the claimholders of Kimberley Mine on hospital tax
A100–'82 Petition of Kimberley merchants on the housing of natives
G77–'82 Reports on the Kimberley police force and detective department by Bernard V. Shaw

Bibliography

G86–'82 Report of the commission appointed to inquire and report upon the working and management of the diamond mines of Griqualand West, 1881–82

G107–'93 Report by A. E. Judge upon the financial position of the Kimberley Mining Board

G101–'83 Report by T. P. Watson on the diamond mines

A2–'84 Report by Inspector Schute on the dynamite explosion

A11–'84 Select Committee on the Vooruitzicht estate

A27–'85 Select Committee on the Dorstfontein and Bultfontain landlords and tenants bill

A15–'85 Select Committee on the Beaconsfield municipality bill

C1–'85 Select Committee on the liquor licensing act

G50–'85 Correspondence regarding the dismissal of J. L. Fry

G2–'88 Report of the committee on convicts and gaols

G3–'88 Report of the commission appointed to inquire into and report on the diamond trade acts, the detective or seaching department, the compound system and other matters connected with the diamond mining industry of Griqualand West

G1–'90 Report of the liquor laws commission, 1889–90

A7–'91 Report of the Select Committee on Griqualand West trade and business

G3–'94 Report of the labour commission, Vols. II, III

Other official sources

The Statute Law of Griqualand West: comprising government notices, proclamations and ordinances together with an appendix containing the regulations promulgated and enacted from the date of the annexation of the province as British Territory to the date of its annexation to the Cape Colony. Published by authority, Cape Town, 1882

Statutes of the Cape of Good Hope, 1652–1895, ed. by H. Tennant and E. M. Jackson, Cape Town, 1895

Cape House of Assembly Debates (Hansard) 1885–94

P. M. Laurence (ed.), Reports of Cases in the High Court of Griqualand West, Vols. I–V

Newspapers, periodicals and directories

The Argus Annual and Cape of Good Hope Directory (1888)

The Daily Independent (1875–93)

The Diamond Field (1870–77)

The Diamond Fields Advertiser (1878–90)

The Diamond Fields Times (Oct. 1884 – Aug. 1885)

The Diamond News (1870–83)

The Directory of Directors, London (1870–90) ed. by T. Skinner

The Dutoitspan Herald (1882)

The Economist (1870–90)

The General Directory of South Africa (1888)

The Griqualand West Investors' Guardian and Commercial Record (1880–81)

Kelley's Post Office Directories, London, 1865, 1870, 1875, 1880, 1889

The Mining Journal (1870–90)

The Mission Field, London (1870–90)

Record of the failures in the financial, international, wholesale and manufacturing branches of commerce in the United Kingdom, 1865–84, by Richard Seyd

The Statist (1870–90)

South African Mining Manual for 1888, London, ed. by W. R. Skinner

The Stock Exchange Year-Book (1881–90) ed. by T. Skinner

Turner's Griqualand West Directory and Guide to the Diamond Fields (1878, 1885)

Griqualand West Government Gazette, (1876–80)

BOOKS AND ARTICLES ON KIMBERLEY AND DIAMONDS

Angove, J., *In the Early Days: Reminiscences of Pioneer Life on the South African Diamond Fields*, Kimberley, 1910

Anon., *Our Estate in the Cape Colony and its Management*, Cape Town, 1886

Ashmead, E., *Twenty-five Years of Mining 1870–1894*, London, 1909

Atkinson, C. E. & Scott, A., *A Short History of Diamond Cutting*, London, 1888

Babe, J. L., *The South African Diamond Fields*, New York, 1872; facs. repr. Kimberley, 1976

Bauer, M., *Precious Stones: a Popular Account of their Characters, Occurrences and Applications, with an Introduction to their Determination for Mineralogists, Lapidaries, Jewellers etc.*, London, 1895, repr. 1904

Beit, A., *The Will and the Way*, London, 1957

Blackburn, D. & W. Caddell, *Secret Service in South Africa*, London, 1911

Board for the Protection of Mining Interests, *Our Diamond Industry*, Kimberley, 1885

Boutan, E., *Le Diamant*, Paris, 1886

Boyle, F., *To the Cape for Diamonds*, London, 1873
   The Savage Life, London, 1876

Bryce, J., *Impressions of South Africa*, London, 1897

Burrows, E. H., *A History of Medicine in South Africa*, Cape Town, 1958

Burton, R. F., *Explorations of the Highlands of Brazil with a Full Account of the Gold and Diamond Mines*, 2 Vols., London, 1869

Butler, J., 'Cecil Rhodes', *International Journal of African Historical Studies*, 10, 2, 1977

Chaper, M., *Note sur la Region Diamantifere de l'Afrique Australe*, Paris, 1880

Chapman, S., 'Rhodes and the City of London: Another View of Imperialism', *Historical Journal*, 28, 3, 1985

Chilvers, H. A., *The Story of De Beers*, London, 1939

Churchill, Lord R. S., *Men, Mines and Animals in South Africa*, 3rd edn, London, 1893

Cohen, L., *Reminiscences of Kimberley*, London, 1911

Colvin, I., *The Life of Jameson*, London, 1922

Couper, J. R., *Mixed Humanity*, Cape Town, 1892

Cowen, C. (ed.), *The South African Exhibition, Port Elizabeth 1885*, Cape Town, 1886

Crisp, W., *Some Account of the Diocese of Bloemfontein in the Province of South Africa from 1863 to 1894*, Oxford, 1895

Cunnynghame, A., *My Command in South Africa 1874–1878*, London, 1890

Currey, J. B., 'The Diamond Fields of Griqualand West and their Probable Influence on the Native Races of South Africa', *Journal of Society of Arts*, XXIV, 1876

Curson, H. H., *History of the Kimberley Regiment*, Kimberley, 1963

De Launay, L., *Les Diamants du Cap*, Paris, 1897

Dieulafait, L., *Diamonds and Precious Stones*, London, 1874

Dixie, F., *Land of Misfortune*, London, 1882

Emmanuel, H., *Diamonds and Precious Stones: their History, Value and Distinguishing Characteristics*, London, 1867

Farini, G. A., *Through the Kalahari Desert*, London, 1886; facs. repr. Cape Town, 1973

Fitzpatrick, P., *South African Memories*, London, 1932

Flint, J., *Cecil Rhodes*, London, 1974

Fort, C. S., *Alfred Beit*, London, 1932

Galbraith, J. S., 'Cecil Rhodes and Dreams', *Journal of Imperial and Commonwealth History*, 1, 1, 1973

Griffith, G., *The Memoirs of an Inspector*, London, no date

Harris, D., *Pioneer, Soldier and Politician*, London, 1931

Bibliography

Holub, E., *Seven Years in South Africa: Travels, Researches and Hunting Adventures between the Diamond Fields and the Zambesi, 1872–1879*, London, 1881

Hornsby, A. H., *The South African Diamond Fields*, Chicago, 1874

Jackson, S., *The Great Barnato*, London, 1970

Jacobs, H. & Chatrain, N., *Le Diamant*, Paris, 1884

Knights of Labour, *Manifesto of Knights of Labour of South Africa*, Kimberley, 1892

Lenzen, G., *The History of Diamond Production and the Diamond Trade*, London, 1970

Lewinsohn, R., *Barney Barnato*, London, 1937

Lewsen, P. (ed.), *Selections from the Correspondence of J. X. Merriman 1870–1890*, Vol. 1, Cape Town, 1960

Lady Loch & Mrs. Stockdale (eds.) *Sister Henrietta, 1874–1911*, London, 1914

Lockhardt, J. G. & Woodhouse, C. M., *Rhodes*, London, 1963

M. E., *Life on the Diamond Fields*, London, 1875

McCracken, D., 'Alfred Aylward: Fenian Editor of the *Natal Witness*', *Journal of Natal and Zulu History*, IV, 1981

Macmillan, M., *Sir Henry Barkly: Mediator and Moderator, 1815–1898*, Cape Town, 1970

Matthews, J. W., *Incwadi Yami, or Twenty Years' Personal Experience in South Africa*, London, 1887; facs. repr. Johannesburg, 1976

Matthews, Z. K., *Freedom for my people: the autobiography of Z. K. Matthews – Southern Africa 1901 to 1968*, London, 1981

Mawe, J., *An Old English Book on Diamonds*, London, 1823; repr. 1950

Merriman, J. X., 'Some Comparative Statistics of the Cape Colony' in *Transactions of the South African Philosophical Society*, Vol. II, Pt II, 25 Feb. 1880

'The Commercial Resources and Financial Position of South Africa', *Royal Colonial Institute*, Vol. 16, 1884/5

Michell, L., *The Life of the Rt Honourable Cecil John Rhodes*, 2 Vols., London, 1910

Michielson, A., *De Diamant Economie, Prys en Conjunctuur*, Antwerp, 1955

Millin, S. G., *Rhodes*, London, 1933

Mitchell, H., *Diamonds and Gold*, London, 1889

Morton, W. J., 'South African Diamond Fields and the Journey to the Mines', *American Geographical Society*, New York, 13 March 1877

Moulle, A., *Geologie Generale et Mines de Diamante de l'Afrique du Sud*, Paris, 1886

Murray, R. W., *The Diamond Fields Keepsake for 1873*, Cape Town, 1886

South African Reminiscences, Cape Town, 1894

Newbury, C., 'Out of the Pit: the Capital Accumulation of Cecil Rhodes', *Journal of Imperial and Commonwealth History*, 10, 1, 1981

Noble, J. (ed.), *Official Handbook of the Cape Colony*, Cape Town, 1886

Illustrated Official Handbook of the Cape and South Africa, Cape Town, 1893

Pauling, G., *Chronicles of a Contractor*, London, 1926

Paxman, J. N., 'The Diamond Fields and Mines of Kimberley', *Minutes and Proceedings of the Institute of Civil Engineers*, Vols. 74, Pt. IV, 1882/3

Payton, C. A., *The Diamond Diggings of South Africa*, London, 1872

Phillips, L., *Some Reminiscences*, London, 1924

Phillips, Mrs. L., *Some South African Recollections*, London, 1899

Ransome, S., *The Engineer in South Africa*, Westminster, 1903

Raymond, H. B., *B. I. Barnato*, London, 1897

Reunert, T., *Diamond Mines of South Africa*, Cape Town, 1892

Diamonds and Gold in South Africa, Cape Town, 1893

Roberts, B., *The Diamond Magnates*, London, 1972

Kimberley: Turbulent City, Cape Town, 1976

Robertson, M., *Diamond Fever: South African Diamond History, 1866–1869, from Primary Sources*, Cape Town, 1974

Rouillard, N. (ed.), *Matabele Thompson: His Autobiography and Story of Rhodesia*, London, 1936; facs. repr. Johannesburg, 1957

Sauer, H., *Ex-Africa*, London, 1937

Sawyer, A. R., *Mining at Kimberley*, Newcastle-under-Lyme, 1889

Scully, W. C., *Reminiscences of a South African Pioneer*, London, 1913

Silver, S. W., *Silver's Handbook to South Africa*, London, 1887

Smalberger, J. M., 'IDB and the Mining Compound System in the 1880s', *South African Journal of Economics*, 42, 1974

'Alfred Aylward, the Continuing Rebel: Early Days on the Kimberley Diamond Fields', *South African Historical Journal*, 7, 1975

'The Role of the Diamond Industry in the Development of the Pass-law System in South Africa', *International Journal of African Historical Studies*, 9, 3, 1976

Smith, K., *Alfred Aylward: the Tireless Agitator*, Johannesburg, 1983

Smithers, E., *March Hare*, Oxford, 1935

Streeter, E., *The Great Diamonds of the World*, London, 1882

Precious Stones and Gems, London, 1877

Sutton, I. B., 'The Diggers Revolt in Griqualand West 1875', *International Journal of African Historical Studies*, 12, 1, 1979

Taylor, J. B., *A Pioneer Looks Back*, London, 1939

Taylor, W. P., *African Treasures: Sixty Years Among Diamonds and Gold*, London, 1932

Thomas, H. (Ed.), *Cornish Mining Interviews*, Camborne, 1896

Trollope, A., *South Africa*, 2 vols., London, 1878

Turrell, R. V., 'The 1875 Black Flag Revolt on the Kimberley Diamond Fields', *Journal of Southern African Studies*, 7, 2, 1981

'Rhodes, De Beers and Monopoly', *Journal of Imperial and Commonwealth History*, 10, 3, 1982

'Kimberley: Labour and Compounds, 1871–1888' in S. Marks & R. Rathbone (eds.), *Industrialisation and Social Change in South Africa: African Class Formation, Culture and Consciousness 1870–1930*, London, 1982

'Kimberley's Model Compounds', *Journal of African History*, 25, 1, 1984

'Diamonds and Migrant Labour in South Africa, 1869–1910', *History Today*, Vol. 36, May 1986

'Sir Frederic Philipson Stow: the Unknown Diamond Magnate' in R. P. T. Davenport-Hines (ed.) *Speculators and Patriots*, London, 1986

'The Rothschilds, the Exploration Company and Mining Finance', *Business History*, 28, 2, 1986

'"Finance ... the Governor of the Imperial Engine": Hobson and the Case of Rothschild and Rhodes', *Journal of Southern African Studies*, 13, 3, 1987

[with J. J. Van-Helten] 'The Investment Group – the Missing Link in British Overseas Economic Expansion before 1914', *Economic History Review*, 35, 2, 1987

(ed.) *The Philipson Stow Papers* (forthcoming)

van Tijn, Th., 'De Algemene Nederlandsche Diamantbewerkersbond (ANDB): Een Success en Zijin Verklaring', *Bijdragen en Medelingen Betreffend des Geskiedenis der Nederlanden*, 88, 3, 1973

'Geskiedenis van de Amsterdamse Diamanthandel en Nijverheid, 1845–1897', *Tijdschrift Voor Geskiedenis*, 87, 1, 1974 & 87, 2, 1974

Vescelius-Sheldon, L., *An IDB in South Africa*, London, 1889

Yankee Girls in Zululand, London, 1889

Bibliography

Vickers, H. J., *Griqualand West, its Area, Population, Commerce and General Statistics*, Kimberley, c. 1880

Vindex, *Cecil Rhodes: his Political Life and Speeches, 1881–1900*, London, 1900

von Weber, E., *Vier Jahre in Afrika, 1871–1875*, Leipzig, 1878

Warren, Sir C., *On the Veldt in the Seventies*, London, 1902

W. E. T., *The Adventures of Solomon Davis*, London, 1887

Wienthal, L. (ed.) *Memories, Mines and Millions*, London, 1929

Williams, A. F., *Some Dreams Come True*, Cape Town, 1948

Williams, B., *Cecil Rhodes*, London, 1921

Williams, G. F., *The Diamond Mines of South Africa*, 2 Vols., London, 1902; repr. New York, 1905

Wilmot, A., *The Life and Times of Richard Southey*, London, 1904

Worger, W., 'Workers as Criminals: the Rule of Law in Early Kimberley, 1870–1885' in F. Cooper (ed.), *Struggle for the City*, Beverly Hills, 1985

Wright, H. M. (ed.), *Sir James Rose Innes: Selected Correspondence 1884–1902*, Cape Town, 1972

Yogev, G., *Diamonds and Coral: Anglo-Dutch Jews and Eighteenth-Century Trade*, Leicester, 1978

OTHER BOOKS AND ARTICLES

Agar-Hamilton, J. A. I., *The Road to the North: South Africa, 1852–1886*, London, 1937

Arndt, E. H. D., *Banking and Currency Development in South Africa, 1652–1927*, Cape Town and Johannesburg, 1928

Atmore, A. & Marks, S., 'The Imperial Factor in South Africa: Towards a Reassessment', *Journal of Imperial and Commonwealth History*, 3, 1, 1974

Ballard, C. C., 'Migrant Labour in Natal 1860–1879: with special reference to Zululand and the Delagoa Bay Hinterland', *Journal of Natal and Zulu History*, I, 1978

Bate, W., *Lucky City: the First Generation at Ballarat, 1851–1901*, Melbourne, 1978

Beinart, W., 'Joyini Inkomo: Cattle Advances and the Origins of Migrancy from Pondoland', *Journal of Southern African Studies*, 5, 2, 1979

The Political Economy of Pondoland 1860–1930, Cambridge, 1982

'Chieftaincy and the Concept of Articulation: South Africa c. 1900–1950', in B. Jewsiewicki (ed.), *Mode of Production: the Challenge of Africa*, Quebec, 1985

Blainey, G., 'Lost Causes of the Jameson Raid', *Economic History Review*, 18, 1965

The Rush that Never ended: a History of Australian Mining, Melbourne, 1963

Bundy, C., *The Rise and Fall of the South African Peasantry*, London, 1979

Cain, P. J. & Hopkins, A. G., 'The Political Economy of British Expansion Overseas 1750–1914', *Economic History Review*, second series, 33, 4, 1980

Cain, P. J., 'J. A. Hobson, Financial Capitalism and Imperialism in Late Victorian and Edwardian England', in A. N. Porter & R. F. Holland (eds.) *Money, Finance and Empire 1790–1960*, London, 1985

Cartwright, A. P., *The Corner House*, London, 1965

Gold Paved the Way, London, 1967

Caughey, J. W., *The Californian Gold Rush*, Los Angeles, 1948; repr. 1975

Chapman, S., *The Rise of Merchant Banking*, London, 1984

Clarence-Smith, W. G., *Slaves, Peasants and Capitalists in Southern Angola 1840–1926*, Cambridge, 1979

Cohen, G. A., *Karl Marx's Theory of History: a Defence*, Oxford, 1978

Cohen, R., 'Resistance and Hidden Forms of Consciousness among African Workers', *Review of African Political Economy*, No. 19, Sept./Dec. 1980

Cooper, F., 'Peasants, Capitalists and Historians: Review Article', *Journal of Southern African Studies*, 7, 2, 1981

Crisp, J., *The Story of an African Working Class: Ghanaian Miners' Struggles 1870–1980*, London, 1984

Curthoys, A. & Markus, A. (eds.) *Who are Our Enemies? Racism and the Australian Working Class*, Canberra, 1978

Davenport, T. R. *The Afrikaner Bond 1880–1911*, London, 1966

South Africa: a Modern History, London, 1977

Davies, R. H., 'Mining Capital, the State and Unskilled White Workers in South Africa 1901–1913', *Journal of Southern African Studies*, 3, 1, 1976

Capital, State and White Labour in South Africa, 1900–1960, Brighton, 1979

De Kiewiet, C. W., *British Colonial Policy and the South African Republics, 1848–1872*, London, 1929

The Imperial Factor in South Africa, London, 1937

A History of South Africa: Social and Economic, Oxford, 1941

Delius, P., *The Land Belongs to Us: the Pedi Polity, the Boers and the British in the Nineteenth-Century Transvaal*, first pub. 1983, London, 1984

Doxey, G. V., *The Industrial Colour Bar in South Africa*, Oxford, 1961

Emden, P., *Randlords*, London, 1935

Etherington, N. A., 'Labour Supply and the Genesis of South African Confederation in the 1870s', *Journal of African History*, 20, 2, 1979

'Theories of Imperialiam in Southern Africa Revisited', *African Affairs*, 81, 324, 1982

Theories of Imperialism: War, Conquest and Capital, Beckenham, 1984

First, R. & Scott, A., *Olive Schreiner*, London, 1980

Foster, J., *Class Struggle and the Industrial Revolution: Early Industrial Capitalism in Three English Towns*, London, 1974

'Imperialism and the Labour Aristocracy', in J. Skelly (ed.), *The General Strike 1926*, London, 1976

Frankel, S. H., *Capital Investment in Africa: its Course and Effects*, London, 1938

Freund, W., *Capital and Labour in the Nigerian Tin Mines*, London, 1981

The Making of Contemporary Africa: the Development of African Society, London, 1984

'Labor and Labor History in Africa: a Review of the Literature', *African Studies Review*, 27, 2, 1984

Galbraith, J. S., *Crown and Charter: The Early Years of the British South Africa Company*, Los Angeles, 1974

Goldberg, M., 'Formulating Worker Consciousness', *Social Dynamics*, 7, 1981

Gordon, R., *Mines, Masters and Migrants*, Johannesburg, 1977

Greenhalg, P., *West African Diamonds 1919–1983*, Manchester, 1985

Gregory, T., *Ernest Oppenheimer and the Economic Development of Southern Africa*, Cape Town, 1962

Guy, J. J., *The Destruction of the Zulu Kingdom: the Civil War in Zululand 1879–1884*, London, 1979

Hammond-Tooke, W. D., *The Bantu-Speaking People of Southern Africa*, London, 1974

Harries, P., 'Slavery, Social Incorporation and Surplus Extraction: the Nature of Free and Unfree Labour in South East Africa', *Journal of African History*, 22, 1981

'Kinship, Ideology and the Nature of Pre-Colonial Labour Migration: Labour Migration from the Delagoa Bay Hinterland to South Africa', in S. Marks & R. Rathbone (eds.), *Industrialisation and Social Change in South Africa 1870–1930*, London, 1982

Harrison, R. (ed.), *Independent Collier: the Coal Miner as Archetypal Proletarian Reconsidered*, New York, 1978

Hay, D. and others (eds.), *Albion's Fatal Tree: Crime and Society in Eighteenth-Century England*, Harmondsworth, 1975

Henry, J. A., *The First Hundred Years of the Standard Bank*, Oxford, 1963

Herman, L., *A History of the Jews of South Africa*, Cape Town, 1935

287

Bibliography

Hobsbawm, E. J., *Labouring Men: Studies in the History of Labour*, London, 1964

Hopkins, A. G., 'The Victorians and Africa: a Reconsideration of the Occupation of Egypt, 1881', *Journal of African History*, 27, 1986

Innes, D., *Anglo-American and the Rise of Modern South Africa*, London, 1984

Jeeves, A., *Migrant Labour in South Africa's Mining Economy: the Struggle for the Gold Mines' Labour Supply, 1890–1920*, Johannesburg and Kingston, 1985 (ed.)

Jewsiewicki, B. (ed.), *Mode of Production: the Challenge of Africa*, Quebec, 1985

Johnstone, F., *Class, Race and Gold a Study at Class Relations and Racial Discrimination in South Africa*, London, 1976

'"Most Painful to our Hearts": South Africa Through the Eyes of the New School', *Canadian Journal of African Studies*, 16, 1, 1982

Kay, G., *Development and Underdevelopment: a Marxist Analysis*, London, 1975

Keegan, T., 'The Restructuring of Agrarian Class Relations in a Colonial Economy: The Orange River Colony, 1902–1910', *Journal of Southern African Studies*, 5, 2, 1979

'Trade, Accumulation and Impoverishment: Mercantile Capital and the Economic Transformation of Lesotho and Conquered Territory', *Journal of Southern African Studies*, 12, 2, 1986

Rural Transformations in Industrializing South Africa, London, 1987

Keppel-Jones, A., *Rhodes and Rhodesia: the White Conquest of Zimbabwe 1884–1902*, Kingston and Montreal, 1983

Kimble, J., 'Labour Migration in Basutoland, c. 1870–1885', in S. Marks and R. Rathbone (eds.) *Industrialisation and Social Change in South Africa 1870–1930*, London, 1982

Kubicek, R. V., *Economic Imperialism in Theory and Practice: the Case of South African Gold Mining Finance, 1886–1914*, Durham, N. C., 1979

Lacey, M., *Working for Boroko: the Origins of a Coercive Labour System in South Africa*, Johannesburg, 1981

Levy, N., *The Foundations of the South African Cheap Labour System*, London, 1982

Lewis, J., 'The Rise and Fall of the South African Peasantry: a Critique and Reassessment', *Journal of Southern African Studies*, 11, 1, 1984

Lewsen, P., *John X. Merriman: Paradoxical South African Statesman*, Newhaven, 1982

Lipton, M., 'Men of Two Worlds: Migrant Labour in South Africa', *Optima*, special issue, 1980

Mandel, E., *Late Capitalism*, first pub. 1975, London, 1978

The Second Slump, London, 1978

Marks, S. & Trapido, S., 'Lord Milner and the South African State', *History Workshop Journal*, 8, 1979

Marks, S. & Atmore, A. (eds.), *Economy and Society in Pre-Industrial South Africa*, London, 1980

Marks, S. & Rathbone, R. (eds.), *Industrialisation and Social Change in South Africa: African Class Formation, Culture and Consciousness 1870–1930*, London, 1982

Marks, S. & Richardson, P. (eds.), *International Labour Migration*: Historical Perspectives, London, 1984

Marks, S., 'Scrambling for South Africa: Review Article', *Journal of African History*, 23, 1982

The Ambiguities of Dependence in South Africa: Class, Nationalism and State in Twentieth Century Natal, Baltimore and Johannesburg, 1986

Mendelsohn, R., 'Blainey and the Jameson Raid: the Debate Renewed', *Journal of Southern African Studies*, 6, 2, 1980

Morris, M., 'The Development of Capitalism in South Africa', *Journal of Development Studies*, 12, 3, 1976

'The Development of Capitalism in South African Agriculture: Class Struggle in the Countryside', *Economy and Society*, 5, 1976

288

Murray, C., *Families Divided: the Impact of Migrant Labour in Lesotho*, Cambridge, 1981

O'Meara, D., *Volkskapitalisme: Class, Capital and Ideology in the Development of Afrikaner Nationalism 1934–1948*, Cambridge, 1983

Palmer, R. & Parsons, N., *The Roots of Rural Poverty in Central and Southern Africa*, London, 1977

Peires, J., *The House of Phalo: a History of the Xhosa People in the Days of their Independence*, Los Angeles, 1982

Perrings, C., 'The Production Process, Industrial Labour Strategies and Worker Responses in the Southern African Gold Mining Industry: Review Article', *Journal of African History*, 18, 1, 1977

    Black Mineworkers in Central Africa: Industrial Strategies and the Evolution of an African Proletariat in the Copperbelt 1911–1941, London, 1979

Phimister, I., 'Rhodes, Rhodesia and the Rand', *Journal of Southern African Studies*, 1, 1, 1974

Phimister, I. & van Onselen, C., *Studies in the History of African Mine Labour in Colonial Zimbabwe*, Gwelo, 1978

Ranger, T., 'Growing from the Roots: Reflections on Peasant Research in Central and Southern Africa', *Journal of Southern African Studies*, 5, 1, 1978

Rex, J., 'The Compound, the Reserves and the Urban Location', *South African Labour Bulletin*, 1/2, 1974

Richardson, P., *Chinese Mine Labour in the Transvaal*, London, 1982

Rubinstein, W. E., 'The Victorian Middle Classes: Wealth, Occupation and Geography', *Economic History Review*, 30, 4, 1977

    'Wealth, Elites, and the Class Structure of Modern Britain', *Past and Present*, No. 76, Aug. 1977

    Men of Property, London, 1981

Samuel, R. (ed.), *Miners, Quarrymen and Saltworkers*, London, 1977

Sandbrook, R. & Cohen, R. (eds.), *The Development of an African Working Class*, London, 1975

Shillington, K., *The Colonisation of the Southern Tswana 1870–1900*, Johannesburg, 1985

Simons, H. J. & Simons, R. E., *Class and Colour in South Africa, 1850–1950*, Harmondsworth, 1969; repr. London, 1983

Stedman Jones, G., 'Class Expressionism Versus Social Control', *History Workshop Journal*, No. 4, 1977

Stichter S., *Migrant Labour in Kenya: Capitalism and African Response, 1895–1975*, London, 1982

    Migrant Labourers, Cambridge, 1985

Swanson, M. W., 'The Sanitation Syndrome: Bubonic Plague and Urban Native Policy in the Cape Colony, 1900–1909', *Journal of African History*, 18, 3, 1977

Taylor, I., Walton, P., & Young, J., *Critical Criminology*, London, 1975

Therborn, G., *The Ideology of Power and the Power of Ideology*, London, 1980

Thompson, E. P., 'Time, Work-Discipline and Industrial Capitalism', *Past and Present*, No. 38, 1968

    'Eighteenth Century Crime, Popular Movements and Social Control', *Bulletin of the Study of Labour History*, Vol. 25, 1972

    Whigs and Hunters, London, 1975

    The Poverty of Theory and Other Essays, London, 1978

    'Eighteenth-Century English Society: Class Struggle Without Class', *Social History*, 3, 2, 1978

Trapido, S., 'South Africa in a Comparative Study of Industrialisation', *Journal of Development Studies*, 7, 1970

    'Landlord and Tenant in a Colonial Economy: the Transvaal 1880–1910', *Journal of Southern African Studies*, 5, 1, 1978

Bibliography

'" The Friends of the Natives": Merchants, Peasants and the Political and Ideological Structure of Liberalism in the Cape, 1854–1910', in S. Marks and A. Atmore (eds.) *Economy and Society in Pre-Industrial South Africa*, London, 1980

Vail, L. & White, L., *Capitalism and Colonialism in Mozambique. A Study of Quelimane District*, London, 1980

'Forms of Resistance: Songs and Perceptions of Power in Colonial Mozambique', in D. Crummey (ed.), *Banditry, Rebellion and Social Protest in Africa*, London, 1986

van der Horst, S., *Native Labour in South Africa*, London, 1942; repr. London, 1971

van Onselen, C., 'Black Workers in Central African Industry: a Critical Essay on the Historiography and Sociology of Rhodesia', *Journal of Southern African Studies*, 1, 2, 1975

Chibaro: African Mine Labour in Southern Rhodesia 1900–1933, London, 1976

Studies in the Social and Economic History of the Witwatersrand, 1886–1914, Vol. 1, New Babylon; Vol. 2, New Nineveh, London, 1982

Warren, B., *Imperialism: Pioneer of Capitalism*, London, 1980

Warrick, P. (ed.), *The South African War: the Anglo-Boer War, 1899–1902*, London, 1980

Webster, E. (ed.), *Essays in South African Labour History*, Johannesburg, 1978

Willan, B., *Sol Plaatje: South African Nationalist 1876–1932*, London, 1984

Wilson, F., *Labour in the South African Gold Mines 1911–1969*, Cambridge, 1972

Wilson, F. & Perrot, D., *Outlook on a Century: South Africa 1870–1970*, Lovedale and Johannesburg, 1972

Wolpe, H., 'Capitalism and Cheap Labour in South Africa: from Segregation to Apartheid', *Economy and Society*, 1, 4, 1972

'The Theory of Internal Colonialism: the South African Case', in I. Oxaal et al. (eds.) *Beyond the Sociology of Development*, London, 1975

UNPUBLISHED THESES AND PAPERS

Faro, C. D., 'People of Colour on the Kimberley Diamond Fields, c. 1875–1885', M.A., School of Oriental and African Studies, University of London, 1985

Kallaway, P., 'Black Responses to an Industrialising Economy: "Labour Shortage" and "Native Policy" in Griqualand West, 1870–1890', University of Witwatersrand, *Conference on Southern African Labour History*, April 1976

Purkis, A. J., 'The Politics, Capital and Labour of Railway Building in the Cape Colony, 1870–1885', D.Phil., University of Oxford, 1978

Sieborger, R. F., 'The Recruitment and Organisation of African Labour for the Kimberley Diamond Mines, 1871–1888', M. A., Rhodes University, Grahamstown, 1976

Trapido, S., 'Poachers, Proletarians and Gentry in the Early Twentieth-Century Transvaal', ICS, *Comparative Commonwealth Social History Seminar*, 1, 1983

Van-Helten, J. J., 'British and European Economic Investment in the Transvaal with Specific Reference to the Witwatersrand Gold Fields and District, 1886–1910', Ph.D., University of London, 1981

White, A. N., 'The Stockenstrom Judgement, the Warren Report, and the Griqualand West Rebellion, 1876–1878', M.A., Rhodes University, Grahamstown, 1977

Worger, W., 'The Making of a Monopoly: Kimberley and the South African Diamond Industry, 1870–1895', Ph.D., Yale University, 1982

Index

Index